The Airships Akron & Macon

*Flying the XF9C-1, Lieutenant Howard L. Young
approaches the Akron's trapeze, 3 May 1932. This was the first day
that planes were operated on the Akron's trapeze.*

*While the plane wobbles on the single hold of its skyhook, the
yoke of the trapeze is cranked up to engage the lock in the "third pole";
at the same time, stabilizing arms move down to engage the jaws of steadying
points on the plane's wings. Note that Young is reaching to guide one of
these arms into the jaw on the left wing.*

The yoke is up and locked in the claw
of the "third pole" and the stabilizing arms are finally engaged
in the steadying points on the wings. The XF9C
is ready to be swung in.

*Young and his XF9C are swung up and
into the Akron's airplane compartment. It was
customary to leave the plane's engine idling until it was
at the point of passing through the door; similarly,
upon launching, the plane's engine was not started until
it was clearing the door.*

*As the plane is hoisted through the door,
Young cuts his engine. Raised all the way in, the
plane will be transferred from the yoke of the trapeze to one of the
trolleys of the hangar's overhead monorail system, and
shunted off to one of the four corners.*

THE AIRSHIPS AKRON & MACON

FLYING AIRCRAFT CARRIERS OF THE UNITED STATES NAVY

BY

RICHARD K. SMITH

NAVAL INSTITUTE PRESS

ANNAPOLIS, MARYLAND

Preface

In researching and writing this book it was not feasible to follow the conventional academic fads and formulae for treating military subjects, which in recent decades have tended toward abstract studies of policy, civil-military relations, or so-called "strategy." This created something of a problem in methodology, and decision was finally made for an old-fashioned narrative approach to the subject, improvising along the way.

The subject of the book is "hardware"; its materials are technological. So this is a chronicle of men and machines; of two machines and their auxiliaries, the men who made them go, and the promise which inspired their research and development; the problems of their operations, the performance they labored to achieve, and the pressures they worked against.

Superficially, this is the story of a failure; but I believe that examinations of our failures should be as instructive as those of our successes—and certainly less delusive. Essentially, however, it is a chronicle of a novel weapons system which was nearing its technological end point, and was finally overwhelmed by competing systems which offered more attractive trade-offs. Most significant, historically, is that it describes the first multimillion-dollar weapons system born of twentieth-century technology which was terminated without being tested in combat, and allowed to pass completely out of existence.

An effort has been made to assume a point of view which corresponds to the realities of aeronautics during the interwar years. In the climate of Mach 3-plus, the rigid airship may seem baroque; but the airmen of 1919–1939 were not clairvoyants, and we should not do them the injustice of criticizing them with hindsight. Toward this end I have felt obliged to resist the notion that the rigid airship was predestined to oblivion by the airplane's ascendency; to insist upon attention to the airship's unique capabilities; and to call for some sympathetic understanding of the problems which afflicted the experiment.

As this is the history of a formidable might-have-been, it must of necessity include some *if*'s, *but*'s, and *maybe*'s. I trust the reader will make the same effort to bear with such speculations as I have made to hold them to a minimum.

Chicago, Illinois
12 February 1965

Acknowledgments

The research and writing of this book has incurred many obligations, especially to Elbert L. Huber, Archivist in Charge of the Navy Branch of the National Archives; to Rear Admiral Ernest M. Eller, U.S. Navy (Retired), Director of Naval History; and to Lee M. Pearson, Bureau of Naval Weapons historian, who provided invaluable assistance during the summer of 1959.

Captain Garland Fulton, U.S. Navy (Retired), and Dr. Karl Arnstein made available a wealth of material. Thanks to Mr. Thomas A. Knowles, president of the Goodyear Aerospace Corporation, materials formerly the property of Goodyear-Zeppelin were made available; on this count I am especially grateful to the labors of Mr. James P. Banks, GAC's former public relations manager.

Captain Donald M. Mackey, U.S. Navy (Retired), Rear Admiral D. Ward Harrigan, U.S. Navy (Retired), Rear Admiral Scott E. Peck, U.S. Navy (Retired), Rear Admiral Harold B. Miller, U.S. Navy (Retired), and Vice Admiral T. G. W. Settle, U.S. Navy (Retired), provided materials and submitted to extensive correspondence.

Frank Rogers, of the University of Illinois Library's Reference Department; Mrs. Curtice Meyers, of the Akron Public Library; Miss Elizabeth Drewry, director of the Franklin D. Roosevelt Library; and Miss Esther Mueller, of the Air Force Museum, extended themselves on my behalf on several occasions. The *Akron Beacon-Journal* allowed access to their clipping and photo files; the Sperry Gyroscope Company provided unpublished materials on Lawrence Sperry's trapeze experiments; Dr. Gerhard R. Fisher provided materials on the *Macon*'s radio device; Carl B. Fritsche provided materials on the Metalclad airship; and Dr. Ronald Wynne provided vital assistance and counsel during my summer in Washington, D.C.

With respect to the book's extensive illustrations, the patience of the staffs at the Naval Photographic Center, Anacostia, and the public information office at Moffett Field must be acknowledged. Only through the assistance of Rear Admiral Daniel F. Smith, U.S. Navy, and the courtesy of Fox-Movietone News were the rare views of the spy basket and the F9C's without their undercarriage obtained. After the Navy's pre-1940 negative files were transferred to the National Archives, the staff of its Still Picture Branch provided timely assistance on many occasions.

Others who provided useful data were Chief Aviation Machinist's Mate Loren A. Alford, U.S. Navy (Retired), Mr. Kurt Bauch, Captain Ralph S. Barnaby, U.S. Navy (Retired), Rear Admiral Calvin M. Bolster, U.S. Navy (Retired), the late Ray E. Brown, Mrs. Charles P. Burgess, Lieutenant Commander William C. Cody, U.S. Navy (Retired), Captain Howard N. Coulter, U.S. Navy (Retired), the late Colonel Clyde V. Finter, U.S. Air Force (Retired), Mr. M. L. Flickinger, Captain A. W. Gorton, U.S. Naval Reserve (Retired), Lieutenant Commander Leo E. Gentile, U.S. Navy (Retired), Dr. Jerome C. Hunsaker, Vice Admiral Frederick N. Kivette, U.S. Navy (Retired), Commander Richard Harwood Knight, U.S. Navy (Retired), Commander Roland G. Mayer, U.S. Navy (Retired), Rear Admiral Charles A. Nicholson, U.S. Navy (Retired), Lieutenant Commander John J. O'Brien, U.S. Navy (Retired), Dr. F. W. Reichelderfer, Rear Admiral Thomas H. Robbins, Jr., U.S. Navy (Retired), Captain Harry E. Shoemaker, U.S. Navy (Retired), Rear Admiral Leroy C. Simpler, U.S. Navy (Retired), Mrs. John H. Towers, Vice Admiral Frederick M. Trapnell, U.S. Navy (Retired), Mr. Ralph Upson, Mrs. Harry Vissering, Captain P. V. H. Weems, U.S. Navy (Retired), Captain George V. Whittle, U.S. Navy (Retired), Mr. Gordon S. Wiley, Mr. David C. Wiley, and Mr. William C. Young.

Special mention is due the members of the American Aviation Historical Society and the Wingfoot Lighter-Than-Air Society for their assistance, especially to Dr. Douglas H. Robinson, Dr. A. D. Topping, Charles L. Keller, William T. Larkins, John C. Mitchell, and to Willis L. Nye, whose drawings appear in the text. All photographs, charts, and drawings, unless otherwise indicated, are official U.S. Navy material. And many thanks are due Rear Admiral John D. Hayes, U.S. Navy (Retired), and his wife.

I am very grateful to Dr. William H. McNeill and Dr. Walter Johnson, of the University of Chicago's Department of History, for their constant encouragement; and finally, to Dr. J. Leonard Bates, of the University of Illinois Department of History, whose several suggestions served to make this book much better than it would have been otherwise.

Table of Contents

The Promise

In the twilight of 12 February 1935, the USS *Macon* was lost off Point Sur, California; she was the Navy's last operational rigid airship, and her loss marked the end of an era. The rigid airship's military career was short. It was controversial, ever dramatic, awesome in its technological achievements, and charged with portent. It nevertheless ended within the life-span of a generation, the first twentieth-century weapons system to pass into oblivion.

In the history of aeronautics the forty-year epic of the rigid airship is unique. The last rigid airship vanished from the face of the earth in 1940, and it represents one of the few aspects of aeronautics which has come to an end.

Development of the rigid airship as an instrument of warfare was initiated by the Germans, whose embryonic airships of World War I were a qualified success as long-range bombers, naval scouts, and in one spectacular instance as a long-range, heavy payload cargo carrier. The Allied powers had airship programs of their own, but of modest scope, and usually focused upon the smaller, nonrigid blimp. The wartime performances of the German Zeppelins[1] accelerated airship development in England, France, Italy, and the United States; but none of these efforts approximated the Germans' systems of design, engineering, and production of rigid airships, nor their scope of military airship organization, training, and operations.

By the end of the war, however, the airship's military utility in Europe had been severely compromised. With the exception of the United States, the relatively little rigid airship experimentation conducted during the postwar years was directed toward developing its commercial possibilities; and, with the exception of the Germans, these commercial efforts were rather spasmodic and confused. For a variety of political, eco-nomic, and emotional reasons, interest in the rigid airship flickered and died. In France, all official interest vanished with the loss of the *Dixmude* in 1923; in Italy, airship experimentation trailed off to nothing after the loss of the *Italia* in 1928; and in England the airship staggered through a maze of politics until 1930, when its future was snuffed out by the R101 disaster. When the Germans were permitted to resume airship construction by the Locarno Treaties, the direction of their work was commercial; but it fell victim to the Byzantine politics of the Third Reich, the American helium policy, and, finally, World War II.

The outstanding exception to this commercial orientation was the United States, where the U.S. Navy maintained an active interest in the rigid airship's military utility until the end of the 1930's. This perseverance can be attributed to two factors: (1) America's geographic position relative to the world balance of power between the world wars; and (2) the possession of vast reserves of nonflammable helium for use as a lifting gas.

European nations had no helium resources and had to fly their airships with highly flammable hydrogen, and wartime experience had proved that an airship inflated with hydrogen was a grotesque instrument of aerial warfare. But the American "monopoly" of helium permitted the United States a rational basis for continuing the airship's military development.

Properly, the rigid airship was as instrument of very-long-range reconnaissance over ocean areas. Because distances within Europe were relatively short and the operating ranges of airplanes increased rapidly, even by 1918 it was clear that Europe had grown too small for the employment of a military airship. Only England might have had strategic use for the type, to patrol her Western Approaches; but there was no political necessity for this. The United States, however, looked outward upon two great oceans in which an enemy fleet could "disappear"—as the Spanish Fleet had in 1898—to suddenly turn up off the American coast, at the vital Panama Canal, or—at Pearl Harbor.

The Atlantic Ocean was secured by the implicit alliance between American and British sea power; but in the Pacific, where the United States looked askance upon the imperial designs of Japan, an increasingly uneasy political situation prevailed. In a great desert sea like the Pacific, a squadron of swift, far-ranging airships could perform vital scouting service. Scouting work was ordinarily performed by cruisers; but at the conclusion of the Washington Conference on the limitation of naval armaments in 1922, the U.S. Navy did not possess a single modern cruiser. The Navy's 4:6:6 Program of 1916[2] had provided more than adequately for capital ships; but it failed to balance its prospective force of capital ships with an adequate number of cruisers. The ten *Omaha*-class cruisers which it authorized, and which came off the ways during the 1920's, could not begin to support the Fleet's Pacific commitments.

In the Nine-Power Treaty, which developed out of the Washington Conference, the United States had insisted upon rendering lip service to the so-called "Open Door" in China. This ill-considered habit of United States foreign policy framed a formidable commitment 5,000 miles west of Pearl Harbor. And this was aside from the United States' obligation to protect its possessions of Guam and the Philippines. From the Treaty of Portsmouth in 1905 to the attack on Pearl Harbor in 1941, there was only one serious menace to the "Open Door" in China, and this was Japan. The Anglo-Japanese Alliance of 1902 which facilitated the concentration of British naval power in Europe, the destruction of the Russian Fleet at Port Arthur and Tsushima, and subsequent Japanese naval construction, made Japan the paramount naval power in the Orient. With the removal of the German Fleet from the political scene in 1919, the Japanese Navy became the third most powerful naval force in the world.

If the United States Fleet was committed to action against the Japanese it would be at a distinct disadvantage by virtue of the great distances in the Pacific, and a base situation which left much to be desired. In order to obtain Japanese acceptance of the short end of the Washington Conference's 5:5:3 ratio, the United States agreed to "freeze" its inadequate fortifications and naval facilities on Guam and in the Philippines. This left the U.S. Fleet without advanced bases necessary for maintaining a battle fleet west of Pearl Harbor. The Pacific situation was further complicated by Japan holding the Marshall, Caroline, and Mariana Islands, which sat astride communications between Pearl Harbor and the Philippines. Besides providing the Japanese with a defense in depth, these islands also gave them bases from which the southern flank of an American naval movement from Pearl Harbor toward the Japanese home islands could be threatened.

In the event of war with Japan and the necessity of moving the U.S. Fleet across the Pacific, an extraordinarily large force of scout cruisers would be necessary to scout ahead of the battle force, determine the strength and disposition of enemy forces, and prevent his cruisers from finding the American forces. Aside from employment in the van of the battle force, the U.S. Navy had need of a second force of cruisers to cover a serious threat on its flank.

The ten *Omaha* ships could not possibly fulfill these needs. By 1932 the Navy's cruiser strength had been supplemented by nine heavy cruisers,[3] and nine more were on the ways;[4] but the problem of base facilities and the great distances in the Pacific remained the same. And relative to accelerated Japanese naval construction this was an inadequate cruiser force even in prospect. Here the rigid airship came in: it would supplement the scout cruiser.

Immediately before World War I, Commander Jerome C. Hunsaker made a visit to Europe to obtain estimates of its progress in military aeronautics. When he returned he remarked that airships would not revolutionize naval warfare, but they would serve as an important auxiliary to a fleet. Hunsaker observed that "the principal function of the dirigible in naval warfare is to supplement the work of scout cruisers, and its offensive powers would be rarely called upon."[5] And as the Navy studied an expansion of its tiny aeronautical organization, the United States' geographic position was remarked upon and it was noted that "our scouting in both [the Atlantic and Pacific] must cover long distances and [thus] demands the airship."[6] This, in sum, was the basic assumption behind the U.S. Navy's experiment with the rigid airship. And after the Navy's General Board—a board of senior flag officers who until 1947 advised the Secretary of the Navy on naval policy —had studied German airship operations, it observed that the performances of the German Zeppelins were "so remarkable that it is most necessary for the Navy of the United States to develop dirigibles of this type as soon as possible."[7] This recommendation was signed by Admiral George Dewey.

The World War ended before the Navy—starting from nothing—could produce a rigid airship. But when the future policy of naval aviation was examined after the war, the rigid airship enjoyed a prominent place in the discussions. Admiral Henry T. Mayo, Commander in Chief, Atlantic Fleet, informed the General Board:

> For reconnaissance and scouting purposes they would be self-sustaining for long periods. I think you will get to the point where the rigid dirigible will be self-protecting. It will be large enough to carry fighting machines [i.e., airplanes] for protection, which with the use of helium gas will make it pretty reliable. It can go long distances, can cover large areas; it will be in the air what large and fast scout cruisers would be on the sea.[8]

And Captain Ernest J. King, recently returned from European duties, told the Board:

> I don't see how the long distance reconnaissance is going to be carried on without using dirigibles, and the rigid appears to be a better type for that than the non-rigid. . . . There certainly does not seem to be any very great promise in airplanes for long-distance scouting. It would appear that you would have to go into the dirigibles for that purpose—a very long radius.[9]

This behind-closed-doors testimony by Mayo, King, and others was complemented by Admiral William S. Sims' public judgment that:

> I am thoroughly convinced from my observance of the naval lessons of this war that in the future rigid airships will be part of the fleet of every first-rate naval power.
> Delay of one year now in the development of this art will serve to keep the United States in an unfavorable position in comparison with those of the other great powers for some years.[10]

After the General Board completed its study of the rigid airship's naval prospects, it reported in the spring of 1919, by way of a recommended policy:

> Rigid airships are a necessity for supplementing long distance scouting for the Fleet.
> A fleet without rigid airships is at a most serious disadvantage as compared to one with rigid airships.
> Rigid airships should be established [in the United States] as an industry. . . . The government should undertake the construction and development of rigid airships.[11]

The rigid airship had three important aspects of performance which recommended its use in naval warfare. It had (1) three times the speed of the fastest surface vessels; (2) several times the load-carrying ability of the largest airplanes built during the interwar years; and (3) in the 1920's at least ten times the out-and-back range of military airplanes. At the end of the 1930's it still retained a three-to-one edge in this aspect of performance. In the late 1920's a fourth and vital aspect of the airship's performance was developed: this was its ability to serve as an airplane carrier.

The airship was an instrument of very-long-range reconnaissance over ocean areas, where it could be attacked only by gunfire from surface ships or by airplanes. Even the relatively slow Zeppelins of World War I were able to steer clear of naval gunfire and shadow units of the Royal Navy from beyond gun range. As for airplanes, they were severely restricted by their limited performance and simple logistics: airplanes had to operate from a shore base or an aircraft carrier, and from these they could not range very far. The combat-loaded fighter and dive bomber of the interwar years rarely enjoyed a radius of action of more than 250 miles. So it was not unreasonable in the 1920's, at least, to assume that the airship should enjoy a monopoly of the air anywhere 500 miles away from land.

One valid criticism continually directed against the airship was its "vulnerability." But this criticism should be balanced by consideration of the question: "Vulnerable to what, and under what circumstances?" "Vulnerability" is a relative matter, especially in war. Everything is vulnerable if hit hard enough or often enough. Few vessels proved to be as vulnerable as the aircraft carrier of World War II; and few vessels proved to be as useful. The primary consideration in weaponry is if the weapon in question can perform a useful function before it falls victim to whatever vulnerability it possesses. Criticism of the airship came to be so exaggerated and pressed so vigorously that it hardened into prejudice, which assumed that a single man with a rifle could destroy an airship. This prejudice was usually based upon recollections of the flaming hulls of the hydrogen-inflated German Zeppelins falling out of the sky over London. But during the 1920's, at least, it was felt that the airship's vulnerability was countered by the promise of its utility.

For example, in the event of war with Japan during the 1920's, the general terms of War Plan ORANGE called for the U.S. Fleet to secure communications to the Philippines by neutralizing the Japanese mandated islands. The Fleet could advance behind a screen of rigid airships operating hundreds of miles in its van, while a second airship screen could be thrown out to the northwest as pickets to watch for a Japanese flanking movement from the home islands or from Formosa. Airship screens would relieve the Navy's pathetically small number of cruisers of this distant scouting duty and permit them to reinforce the battle line. And it must be borne in mind that in the decade following 1918 the Navy's strategy and tactics centered upon the battle line; the task force concept was a creation which waited upon the late 1930's.

This, in theory, was the function of the rigid airship and the purpose of its development by the U.S. Navy. It carried the rigid airship to the highest state of its military development, which was realized in the airships ZRS4&5,[12] better known as the USS *Akron* and the USS *Macon*.

Although the *Akron* and the *Macon* were conceived in terms of the same general mission as the German naval airships of 1914–1918, a single novelty of design made them wholly different. This was their ability to carry airplanes which could be launched and retrieved while they were in flight. The airships' airplanes introduced a fundamental military difference from all previous scouting airships by providing a remarkable measure of flexibility in scouting operations.

With weather permitting visibility of 30 miles, a Zeppelin of the first World War could sweep a path 60 miles wide and, operating at a speed of 45 mph, during 12 hours of daylight could search approximately 32,000 square miles of ocean. But the *Akron* and *Macon* and their airplanes could search almost four times this area in the same period of time. Flying at a cruising speed of 60 mph, with one of its hook-on airplanes stationed 60 miles out on each beam, the airship increased its sweep of vision from 60 miles to 180 miles, and during the same 12 hours could cover approximately 129,000 square miles.

Ten airplane-carrying airships, operating out of Pearl Harbor in two relays of five airships, could advance a scouting line almost 1,200 miles wide, and within six days have it almost in sight of the Bonin Islands.[13] This was more than three times as fast as a force of cruisers could cover this distance; a scouting line of this width would require at least 40 cruisers; and as late as 1940 there was not a military airplane in the world which could, combat-loaded, fly from Pearl Harbor to the Bonins—and back.

This was the great promise of the *Akron* and the *Macon*. Here were instruments of relatively high speed and phenomenal endurance which, in the environment of the interwar years, could not be equalled by any other means. But however great was the promise, it remained only a promise.

The discrepancy between the airships' promise and performance was in no small part the cause of much of the controversy surrounding them. Its career as an airplane carrier terminated on a tangent of confusion, contradictions, and frustrations during the last half of the 1930's. But when this concept was conceived as a bright promise in the 1920's, it was in terms of a progressive and farsighted development.

The Airships Akron & Macon

CHAPTER ONE

Toward a Farsighted Development

The period 1919–1928 holds the germinal years of the Navy's rigid airship operations. In these years the Navy obtained its first three rigid airships and established the Lakehurst Naval Air Station as its center of lighter-than-air aeronautics; the Bureau of Aeronautics initiated design work on a high-performance, fleet-type airship; and the rigid airship flew through a political crisis which catalyzed the procurement of the *Akron* and the *Macon*.

In 1919 the Navy received authorization for the airships ZR1, ZR2,[1] and the Lakehurst Air Station. The ZR1, better known as the *Shenandoah,* had to be designed and wait upon completion of the Lakehurst hangar before she could be erected; as a result she did not fly until 1923. ZR2, however (which never had a name), came sooner by purchase in England; this was the British R38, which was not destined to see America. On 24 August 1922, the R38 crashed in England during her trial flights. Among the 44 killed were Lieutenant Commander Lewis H. Maxfield and 15 other U.S. Navy personnel. In view of what subsequently became known of the R38, she was no loss; but the deaths of Maxfield and his crew deprived the Navy's tiny airship organization of one of its few senior officers with wartime airship experience, and too great a percentage of its most experienced personnel.

In the meantime a third airship, built by the Luftschiffbau Zeppelin Company, was acquired in Germany. This was the LZ-126, designated ZR3 by the Navy, and commissioned as the USS *Los Angeles.* She was obtained by way of compensation for two wartime Zeppelins the United States was supposed to have received as the spoils of war, but which the German crews had destroyed in order to prevent their passing into Allied hands. Considerable petty jealousy was displayed by the Allies over the United States receiving this brand new Zeppelin. The Americans wanted an airship of about 3,500,000 cubic feet, but had to settle for 2,470,000 cubic feet, and with the stipulation that it should be restricted to "civil purposes," i.e., not be given overt military employment. This did not prevent the Navy from operating her, because it had accepted responsibility for aiding the development of commercial airship transportation in America.

The *Shenandoah* made her first flight on 4 September 1923; the *Los Angeles* was delivered to the United States on 15 October 1924. Neither represented a fleet-type airship. The *Shenandoah's* design was derived from data abstracted from German Zeppelins forced down in Allied territory during the war, and by 1923 her essentials were at least five years old. The *Los Angeles* represented the very latest by way of the Zeppelin Company's technology, but she was a nonmilitary aircraft. Both were too small in cubic volume, and hence in useful lift and endurance, to permit extended operations with the Fleet; both were training ships and flying laboratories to serve the needs of research and development, and these functions they served well.

During 1924–1925, under the command of Lieutenant Commander Zachary Lansdowne, the *Shenandoah* participated in one exercise with the Scouting Fleet and two minor operations with the battleship *Texas.* With the Scouting Fleet she succeeded in finding the "enemy," but suffered the embarrassment of having to withdraw from the exercise prematurely because of mechanical difficulties. Admiral Newton A. McCully, ComScoFor (Commander, Scouting Force), remarked that although her performance did not demonstrate an extraordinary ability for scouting, "her possibilities should not be measured by this experience; with further experience she will undoubtedly improve her performance and will be a valuable adjunct to the Scouting Fleet."[2]

The U. S. Navy's ZR2 (British R38) on the field at Cardington, England. She never had a name, was never formally accepted, and never saw the United States. Unknown to the Navy, she was a faulty design, and broke in half during her fourth trial flight, 23 August 1921, after only 56.5 hours in the air.

Rear Admiral William A. Moffett, Chief of the Bureau of Aeronautics, converses with friends during the Shenandoah's visit to San Diego's North Island in October 1924. Never an "armchair admiral," Moffett made the 19-day transcontinental round trip aboard the airship. Flag quarters—a hammock!

A few years later the State Department obtained permission from the former Allied Powers for the Navy to use the *Los Angeles* in military operations, and she participated in 1931's Fleet Problem XII held off the west coast of Panama. Operating from a mooring mast built over the after deckhouse of the tanker USS *Patoka,* the *Los Angeles* scouted for the BLUE Fleet, which was defending the Canal's Pacific approaches. At this time she was under the command of Lieutenant Commander Vincent A. Clarke, Jr. Early on the morning of 19 February she discovered the enemy BLACK Fleet, and by careful use of cloud cover kept the enemy units under surveillance for several hours without being detected. But in the afternoon planes from BLACK'S carriers finally found her; and after one plane made a dive-bombing run on her, the umpire on board, Commander Alger Dresel, ruled the airship "destroyed."[3]

Admiral William V. Pratt, Chief of Naval Operations, remarked that he thought one of the outstanding points of the Fleet Problem was "the justification, under favorable circumstances, of the lighter-than-aircraft, as shown by the use of the *Los Angeles.*"[4] But Pratt's judgment—or McCully's estimate of the *Shenandoah*—by no means reflected a consensus within the Navy Department.

During 1923–1931, the Navy's two rigid airships made more than a few flights to appear in the air over holiday parades, county fairs, conventions, and on other occasions of public ballyhoo; operations which the more fleet-minded airship officers criticized as "hand-waving flights." But only upon four occasions were they exercised with units of the Fleet. It was this experience in military operations that the airship sorely needed. By the end of the 1920's a few outstanding problems in this area had yet to be faced, many others remained to be discovered, and these could not be solved by barnstorming flights. The early operations of the *Akron* and the *Macon* would reflect this lack of experience and the pernicious effects of too much barnstorming.

In the meantime the Bureau of Aeronautics was assembling data for an airship which would be everything the *Shenandoah* and the *Los Angeles* could not be. In March 1924, Starr Truscott, an engineer in the Bureau's Lighter-Than-Air Design Section, synthesized prevailing thought on this "next airship" in a memorandum which has a peculiar significance at this early date. In its pages the dim outlines of the ZRS4&5 make their first appearance.

Truscott proposed that the Bureau immediately undertake preliminary studies for a scouting airship of a "highly advanced design."[5] The Lakehurst hangar dictated an airship less than 800 feet long; but this would still allow an airship of five or six million cubic feet. On one point the memorandum was emphatic: if a rigid airship was to expect any success as a fleet scout, it must carry airplanes—as a means of protection and an extension of the airship's ability to obtain information. The ambidextrous mission of the planes should be noted, for it held a dualism in concept which would confuse the ZRS4&5's military operations until 1934.

If the proposed airship were to launch and retrieve planes while in flight, its speed would have to be high— a cruising speed of 60, a full speed of about 80 knots. No method had been worked out for operating airplanes from airships, but it was "believed to be feasible to carry planes . . . and to pick them up from below by means of a loop suspended from the ship, and engaged by a hook on top of the plane." Not less than three and no more than six planes should be carried, and these would be fighter types, either TS-1's, UF-1's,[6] or maybe even some later design weighing in the range of 2,500 to 3,000 pounds. This feature, among others, could not be fulfilled without an airship of "unusual size," five- or six-million cubic feet; but it was felt that every effort should be made to hold it as close as possible to the five million figure.

Preliminary design calculations were begun in the spring of 1924. In the meantime the British initiated construction on two airships of 5,000,000 cubic feet which were to be inflated with hydrogen. In order to obtain a helium-inflated airship of approximately the same performance, the Bureau's engineers were forced to discard the favored five-million figure and settle upon a design of 6,000,000 cubic feet, 780 feet long, with a maximum diameter of 122 feet.[7]

By April 1924, preliminary calculations had been prepared, and the hitherto nameless proposal was given the designation "Design No. 60." There was nothing startling about Design No. 60, and during 1924–1925 it remained what is sometimes considered a "conventional"[8] design, and to the eye appeared as little more than an enlargement of the *Los Angeles.* But it was not so much a design *per se* as it was a very flexible idea, a general concept within which the Bureau's engineers could work out a variety of design problems. Within its framework many major aspects of structure and several novel auxiliary features were examined; some were retained, many were thrown out. Thus De-

On 27 January 1928, off Newport, Rhode Island, the Los Angeles *landed on the after flight deck of the carrier USS* Saratoga (CV-3), *the only time a rigid airship ever landed on a conventional aircraft carrier.*

The Shenandoah *moored to the mast on the Fleet oiler USS* Patoka (AO-9) *in Narragansett Bay during the summer of 1924. The* Patoka *is the only ship in the Navy which served this mission. The airship had to be "flown" while at the mast.*

sign No. 60 assumed different "appearances" at different times; but in its military essence it never differed much from its ZRS4&5 realization.

In 1926, Design No. 60 experienced its last radical change. The *Shenandoah*'s startling break-up in 1925, occurring at a time when airships of unusually large cross sections were under study, indicated a need for much greater hull strength to meet American storm conditions. Criticism was focused on the "conventional" wire-braced type of main ring, or main frame, and new attention was given the relatively heavy but rugged and inherently stiff deep ring. Thus Design No. 60 had its maximum diameter increased to 135 feet to accommodate the employment of deep rings, and concomitantly had its volume increased to 6,500,000 cubic feet.

Coincident to the Navy's efforts with the rigid airship was the partnership arranged between the Goodyear Tire and Rubber Company and Luftschiffbau Zeppelin which, in the fall of 1923, created the ancillary Goodyear-Zeppelin Corporation. The Luftschiffbau was driven into this partnership by the effects of the Treaty of Versailles, which had wiped out the large airship's future in Germany, and by the chaotic political and economic conditions of Germany in 1919–1923. No one could foresee that the Dawes Plan and the Locarno Treaties of 1925 would serve to remove these disabilities. So the men of the Luftschiffbau had little choice in their future as of 1923; they had to stake their all and their best on their American alliance.

This German-American agreement transferred the North American rights to the Zeppelin patents to the Goodyear-Zeppelin Corporation, and the Luftschiffbau's key engineering personnel,[9] headed by Dr. Karl Arnstein, were made available to the new company. Two-thirds of the company was controlled by Goodyear, the remainder by Zeppelin, and the arrangement went into effect upon the Luftschiffbau's delivery of its LZ-126—the *Los Angeles*—to the Navy.

The transatlantic delivery flight of the LZ-126—the second nonstop east-to-west crossing of the Atlantic by air—was attended by world-wide excitement. Less noticed, but of greater significance for the future, was the transatlantic crossing of the SS *George Washington* a month later, which returned Commander Garland Fulton to the United States. Also on board were Dr. Arnstein and his assistants, on their way to Akron, Ohio. Fulton had been in charge of the Navy's inspection staff during the construction of the LZ-126, and was now en route to new duties in Washington. Once back in the

Bureau of Aeronautics, he was appointed head of the Lighter-Than-Air Design Section, where he became the guiding hand of the Navy's endeavors in lighter-than-air aeronautics for the next 15 years.

Garland Fulton graduated from the Naval Academy second in the class of 1912, which proved to contain an extraordinary constellation of naval figures. Also among the class of 1912 were Richard E. Byrd, P. V. H. Weems, Ellis M. Zacharias, Louis E. Denfeld, Daniel E. Barbey, and Dewitt C. Ramsey. For the first two years of his career Fulton served as a line officer, but in 1914 obtained a transfer to the Navy's Construction Corps,[10] and was sent to the Massachusetts Institute of Technology for postgraduate work in engineering. At M.I.T. he took an elective in general aeronautics taught by Jerome Hunsaker, whom the Navy loaned to the Institute in 1913 to organize its aeronautic curriculum. After his graduation in 1916, Fulton went to the Brooklyn Navy Yard to supervise the installation of guns on merchant ships, but was released from this duty when the Bureau of Construction and Repair's Aircraft Division called for engineers. The Division was headed by Hunsaker, since recalled from his academic duties in Cambridge. Fulton remained in the Aircraft Division, and later in the Bureau of Aeronautics after its creation in 1921, as general assistant to Hunsaker, until he received his orders to Germany relative to the construction of the LZ-126.

From 1925 to his retirement in 1940, Fulton exerted a greater influence on the direction of the Navy's lighter-than-air aeronautics than any other individual not in a policy-making position. During 1925–1933, Rear Admiral William A. Moffett, Chief of the Bureau, never attended hearings before congressional committees or the Navy's General Board where vital airship matters would be discussed, without having Fulton with him. And when the Admiral could not be present, Fulton represented him.

Fulton's stature is further underscored by his several expressions on airship matters, submitted to Admiral Moffett by way of reports and memoranda, which were subsequently echoed in the Admiral's speeches and writings, and in his formulation of policy on lighter-than-air aeronautics.[11] And Moffett's successor, Rear Admiral Ernest J. King, who regarded Fulton as "the Navy's top lighter-than-air man,"[12] relied equally as much upon him.

Fulton never made any headlines, and his press clippings were very few; but while others took the limelight

Luftschiffbau Zeppelin engineers en route to their new employment with Good-year-Zeppelin in Akron. Front, l. to r.: Eugene Schoettel, Benjamin Schnitzer, Dr. Karl Arnstein, chief engineer, Eugene Brunner, Dr. Wolfgang Klemperer. Middle: Walter G. E. Mosebach, Lorens Rieger, Herman Liebert. Rear: Kurt Bauch, Hans Keck, Erich Hilligardt, Paul K. Helma, William Fischer.

Commander Garland Fulton, 1925.

Except for the Metalclad ZMC-2, the Los Angeles and the blimps J-3 and J-4 were the Navy's whole inventory of airships in October 1929. The J-3 was a TC type procured from the Army in 1926; it was lost on 4 April 1933 while searching for Akron survivors. The J-4 was a lash-up of an Army TC-type envelope and a Navy-designed control car; it survived until 1940, when it was judged obsolete and was dismantled.

and came and went from serving at their primary duties, he continually headed the effort to establish lighter-than-air aeronautics and the rigid airship in the Navy. If it was not clear at that time, it is certainly clear in retrospect that Garland Fulton can be considered the "Mr. Rigid Airship" of naval aviation.

Only a few months after returning to the Bureau, Fulton submitted a significant memorandum to Admiral Moffett. Observing that the rigid airship's development as of 1925 was at about the same stage in which the airplane had been during 1915–1919, and that it could not hope to enjoy a similarly intensive development involving billions of dollars, he remarked that "the best airships can hope for is a steady, farsighted, progressive development."[13] Toward this end he suggested that, as a matter of policy, the Bureau include in its estimates for fiscal 1927 a request for two airships of 6,000,000 cubic feet and an airship base on the West Coast. The proposal was not unique; similar and even more comprehensive schemes had been discussed in the Bureau since 1919. But Fulton's outline of development was to be accepted and realized in the *Akron* and *Macon* and the airship base at Sunnyvale, California, known today as Moffett Field.

Fulton pointed out that Navy war plans called for nine to eleven rigid airships; he was discussing airships which could not fly before 1929, and if authorization was delayed a year it would mean 1930, and if the situation was permitted to remain static there would be no airships by either time. But little could be done in the spring of 1925. It was going to take the violent events of fall to shatter the status quo in the airship question.

When the *Shenandoah* was torn to pieces by a thunderstorm over Ohio on the night of 2–3 September 1925, killing fourteen of her crew, including Lansdowne, there was precipitated what might well be called the "LTA crisis of 1925–1926." In the subsequent uproar the entire Navy airship effort was hurriedly put on trial, and with a prepared verdict of condemnation. An economy-minded Congress clamored to close the Lakehurst Air Station and terminate airship experimentation, and an hysteric press shrilled for an end to spending the taxpayers' money on "murderous airships." But Admiral Moffett battened down all hatches against the foul weather and succeeded in navigating the airship's case through a maze of congressional hearings and legislative tangles, to the fair weather of the Five Year Aircraft Program.

While the furor was at its height, Admiral Moffett insisted to Secretary of the Navy Curtiss D. Wilbur that airship development should continue; and he proposed a program of two 6,000,000-cubic-foot, fleet-type airships, one 1,250,000-cubic-foot training airship, and an airship base on the West Coast. Secretary Wilbur referred the proposal to Admiral Edward W. Eberle, CNO, which led to a hearing before the General Board. At this hearing the airship was not considered in a vacuum; to the contrary, it was a case of the airship versus the cruiser.

The Navy's general estimate of the airship had undergone something of a change since the first World War. In 1919, the most eminent figures in the Navy had considered it a vital necessity; but only six years later a special board appointed by the Secretary of the Navy to study aviation policy—the so-called Eberle Board—concluded that "the airship has some valuable characteristics, but due to great vulnerability is of doubtful value in war."[14] This tempering of judgment was due to the effects of the Washington Conference combined with the Harding-Coolidge "normalcy."

When the hopeful estimates of the airship were advanced in 1919, the war had been over less than a year and the postwar period held every indication that the nation would be generous with its upkeep of the peacetime Navy. In such circumstances a few million dollars could easily be spared for a six-year program of a dozen airships of the type discussed in 1919. But the Neo-Hamiltonian politics of the 1920's, pursued behind the shelter of the Washington Conference's treaties, smashed the expectations of 1919. Secretary of the Treasury Andrew Mellon applied the fiscal axe to Navy estimates with a vengeance, and the purse strings remained tightly drawn until the 1930's. In this climate of peace and penury ships had to come first, aircraft second. But on the second count, the airplane was a better investment by way of progress realized relative to unit cost, than was a rigid airship.

In 1926 the Navy had drawn up a building program of about 200,000 tons of cruisers to match accelerated construction in England and Japan. Since the World War, the rigid airship's proponents had been wont to elaborate upon Admiral Sir John Jellicoe's remark that a rigid airship could perform the scouting work of two cruisers. But however well an airship might surpass a single cruiser by its ability to range swiftly over great distances in search of an enemy, the airship could supply no substitute for a cruiser's gun power.

Admiral Hilary Jones, president of the General

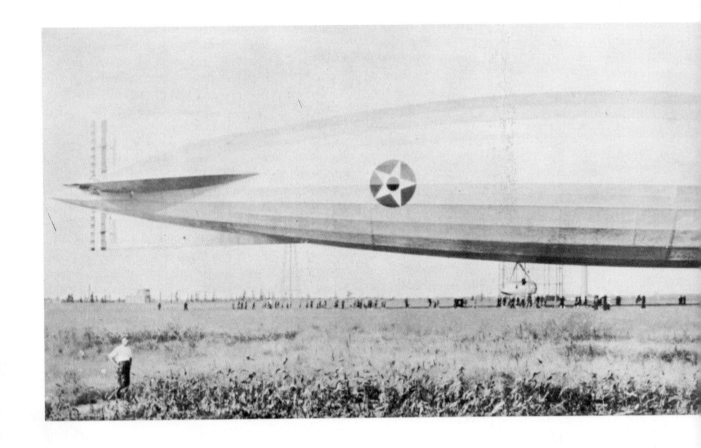

The Shenandoah *leaving the hangar at U.S. Naval Air Station, Lakehurst, New Jersey. The first American-built rigid airship, she originally flew on 4 September 1923.*

Last flight! While en route to St. Paul from Lakehurst, the Shenandoah *failed structurally in a storm over southern Ohio on 3 September 1925, and broke in two, with a loss of 14 of her crew of 43. At right, the after section of the wrecked* Shenandoah *lies in an Ohio cornfield. Lieutenant Commander Charles E. Rosendahl, senior officer in the forward section of the ship after it snapped in two, free-ballooned the nose for two hours, finally landing it fourteen miles away from the wreck of the after section. The* Shenandoah *was a modified design of the German 1916 model L-49, and consequently was essentially an obsolete design even before being flown. Her destruction, following so closely upon the tragic loss of ZR-2, resulted in considerable criticism of the airship program.*

The Los Angeles weighs-off, preparatory to making a "flying moor" to Lakehurst's high mast. The disadvantage of the high mast was that the airship had to be "flown" at the mast by a skeleton crew. Shortly after development of the low "stub" mast, this mooring tower was demolished.

Right: While moored at the high mast in the summer of 1926, the Los Angeles was caught in a sudden but gentle wind shift; her tail went up until she stood on her nose atop the mast, where she pirouetted 180 degrees, and brought her tail down to a normal attitude, parallel to the wind. Damage was negligible, but it was a disconcerting experience, providing a dramatic illustration of the high mast's shortcomings, and served to hasten development of the low mooring mast.

Board, was afraid that this distinction might go unnoticed,[15] and that the money for the proposed airships would be subtracted from cruiser funds. This did not upset Admiral Moffett. When Admiral Henry A. Wiley asked Moffett, "Do you consider this type of aircraft of sufficient importance to risk the loss of a cruiser to secure the appropriation?" Moffett shot back "yes," and reaffirmed his belief that rigid airships were part of a balanced Fleet.[16] And Moffett described the formulation of his judgment of the airship:

When I first came in contact with rigid airships I couldn't see anything to them. I couldn't see that they were any good as a means of scouting or transportation; you couldn't get it going when you wanted it; you couldn't get it out of the hangar [in high winds]. Lansdowne came to me. I listened to him very carefully. At first, I refused to have anything to do with it. I listened to Lansdowne's arguments and he persuaded me . . . that was my experience. It is a noteworthy thing that every officer who has anything to do with these ships . . . is in favor of them and thinks they will be of great value to the Navy.[17]

At this same hearing Captain William H. Standley, Director of War Plans, remarked that he thought the airship's military value was doubtful, but called attention to the question's "political feature." In 1920 the Army-Navy Joint Board had reaffirmed the exclusive responsibility given the Navy during wartime for the rigid airship's development. This mandate called for the Navy to make its data available to the Army's lighter-than-air branch, and also to assist private groups interested in developing the rigid airship for commercial uses.

The Army's Air Service had become very dissatisfied with this arrangement, and since 1922 had been clamoring to have it revised. If the Navy abandoned the rigid airship, the Army was standing by to grab it up, and Standley added, "I don't think we want to be placed in this position." Nine years later, when the Navy's last rigid airship went down off Point Sur, when the Army's airship organization was breathing its last, and the "political feature" no longer existed, Standley would not be as solicitous over the airship question. Captain Emory S. Land emphasized the same political angle, and the Navy's stewardship toward commercial airship development. Admiral William W. Phelps wondered if letting the rigid airship slip to the Army would give the Army the political leverage to dislodge naval aviation from its coastal bases; Land thought so, and Captain Arthur B. Cook observed that on this count the Joint Board mandate was a two-edged sword.[18]

In other words, if the Navy refused its responsibilities toward the rigid airship, the Army would take them over. Not only would this be a loss of face, but it would give the Army's "airpower" clique an instrument by which they could fly thousands of miles out to sea. Ipso facto, the airpower clique, which wanted a separate air force desperately and resented the Navy maintaining extensive air bases ashore, could argue that with the Army being able to patrol the seas with rigid airships the facilities which served the Navy's relatively short-ranged flying boats were an expensive redundancy. And with their always exaggerated line of argument, they might even succeed in compromising naval aviation in the public mind before the aircraft carrier's promise could be developed. So the Navy, and especially the naval aviators, could not afford to treat the airship lightly, and for more reasons than one.

The General Board made a token recommendation: One fleet-type airship capable of carrying airplanes should be built. The funds for this airship had to be obtained by an appropriation entirely separate from the regular appropriation. In other words, if Congress chose to make the Navy a "gift" of an airship, that was fine; but Congress would not be given an opportunity to mix cruisers with airships, of dividing expensive cruisers by relatively cheap airships, and going home satisfied that it had provided adequately for the Fleet.

But Admiral Moffett wanted more than a single airship; he wanted a program which would make the airship a vital part of the Fleet. Determined to blow the case wide open, he prevailed upon Representative Thomas S. Butler (Republican, Pennsylvania), a "Big Navy" congressman and chairman of the House Committee on Naval Affairs, to introduce H.R. 7375, which was designed to give the airship question a thorough airing. It called for replacing the *Shenandoah* with an airship of not more than 7,000,000 cubic feet at a cost of $5,000,000; but it insisted—in contradiction of the General Board's stipulation—that the funds had to be provided from the regular Navy appropriation. This was Moffett's way of forcing a showdown.

This piece of legislation, with its exhaustive hearings, cleared the decks for H.R. 9690, the enabling legislation of the Navy's so-called Five Year Aircraft Program which, among other things, authorized the construction of the ZRS4&5.

A maze of hearings before the House and Senate committees on appropriations and naval affairs continued into the spring of 1926. Here Secretary Wilbur and

U. S. Naval Air Station, Lakehurst, New
Jersey, in 1929. At right is Hangar No. 1
with the old-fashioned docking rails
leading from its doors. Tracks for the
stern beam have yet to be laid, and the
railroad-tracked, mooring-out circles
have yet to be graded.

Known as the "tin balloon" or the "tin
blimp," the Metalclad ZMC-2 represented
the prototype of a unique and very promising airship design. The development of
the Metalclad was frustrated by the chronic
shortage of airship funds, and the feeling
that the first commitment had to be for
the more proven Zeppelin-type airship.

Admirals Eberle and Jones conceded the authorization of two airships instead of one, but remained obdurate in their insistence that airship money must not be taken from regular Navy funds. Admiral Moffett was equally insistent that lighter-than-air aeronautics must be considered a legitimate part of the Navy. It is significant that although Moffett thought the sacrifice of one cruiser was a fair exchange for two fleet-type airships, when asked if he would sacrifice some of his airplane funds and transfer them to the airship's cause, he replied with an unequivocal "no."[19]

At these hearings many figures, Army, Navy, and civilian, testified. A great deal of attention was attracted by Lieutenant Commander Charles E. Rosendahl, senior surviving officer of the *Shenandoah* disaster. Rosendahl graduated from the Naval Academy with the class of 1914, and after nine years of sea duty entered lighter-than-air aeronautics in April, 1923, and was later ordered to the *Shenandoah* as one of her initial complement. On her last flight Rosendahl was on board as navigator, and after she had broken in half, he and Lieutenant Roland G. Mayer free-ballooned the bow section to a safe landing. Catapulted into prominence overnight by virtue of the *Shenandoah* disaster, he would remain a very prominent figure in the ZRS4 and ZRS5 period and thereafter. As a result of his commands of the *Los Angeles* and the *Akron,* two books and many periodical articles which he wrote on behalf of the rigid airship, and his crusader's zeal, he became the most widely known personality of lighter-than-air aeronautics in the United States.

The decisions which grew out of these hearings resulted in saving the Lakehurst Air Station, which Congress had earlier recommended closing, and in the Five Year Program. But the program held only an authorization, not an appropriation, and this was a problem. Admiral Moffett finally managed to convince the Department to include airship money in the regular estimates for fiscal 1927; but it was later axed by the Bureau of the Budget.

The Five Year Program also authorized a small Metalclad airship, an experimental proposition of 200,000 cubic feet. Its unique design was due to the genius of Ralph Upson, a pioneer in American lighter-than-air aeronautics who, while a Goodyear engineer, had taught many of the Navy's wartime blimp pilots how to fly. In 1929 his Metalclad flew as the successful ZMC-2; but in 1926 it only served to muddle the issue of the larger, conventional rigid airships. Aside from the idea of a "metal airship" exercising a magic of its own, it also provided an excuse for not spending eight million dollars on the larger ones. When President Coolidge sent the budget to Congress in December he remarked that it might be the "better part of wisdom" to see how the Metalclad worked out before going ahead with the more expensive airships. So the airship funds were lost, and the ZRS4&5 program was retarded by one year.

Also during this period the airship question was afflicted by a helium shortage. This had its roots in politics and economics, not geology. The quest for a nonflammable lifting gas had taken the Navy into helium production during World War I, and extraction plants were built in the vicinity of Fort Worth and Petrolia, Texas. By the mid-1920's these gas fields were approaching exhaustion, which created the syllogism: no helium, no airships. The Cliffside gas structure which reached from the Texas panhandle into Colorado and environs was rich in helium, but this source was three hundred miles away from existing extraction plants. The problem was either to obtain funds from Congress for a pipeline to the new sources, or to build a new plant in the Cliffside fields. This was not resolved until 1929, when a new plant was built at Amarillo. In the meantime, the "helium shortage" was a weapon in the hands of the economy-minded in their effort to eliminate "expensive" airship operations.

Time was running out. Someone, somehow, had to find a way to get some airship money. William C. Young, Goodyear-Zeppelin's sales manager, appealed to Representative James Begg (Republican, Ohio), who during the House debates on the Navy appropriation for fiscal 1928 managed to slip in an amendment which provided $200,000 toward the construction of one of the two airships. This paltry sum would not buy the fabric to cover a 6,000,000-cubic-foot airship; but it was enough to permit the Bureau of Aeronautics to seek out a contractor. Directly, it facilitated the airship design competition of 1927.

On 16 January 1927, the Navy publicly invited designs and bids on one rigid airship. The competition closed at midnight, 16 May, and for the next few weeks a board of judges[20] examined the thirty-seven designs submitted. Most of these were of a crackpot species. Goodyear-Zeppelin not only submitted the incomparably best designs, but was the only party that bid on construction, and thus won the competition hands down. Again money difficulties arose.

James Begg's rhetoric was deficient in the phrasing of

Dr. Hugo Eckener, of Luftschiffbau Zeppelin, and airship operator par excellence, *shows drawings of the Luftschiffbau's new LZ-127 to Navy airship men at Lakehurst in the spring of 1927. At that date the LZ-127 was still under construction; it would take to the air in 1928 as the famous* Graf Zeppelin. *Standing, l. to r.: Lieutenant Commander Herbert V. Wiley, Lieutenant Roland G. Mayer (C.C.), and Commander Garland Fulton (C.C.). Seated: Captain Edward S. Jackson, commanding officer of Lakehurst Air Station, Eckener, and Lieutenant Commander Charles E. Rosendahl, commanding officer of the* Los Angeles. *Besides the airship's military utility, the Navy had accepted the responsibility for furthering its technological development for commercial purposes. The liaison between American and German airship men was very close.*

his amendment; it mentioned only one airship, and at a limit in cost of $4,500,000. Goodyear-Zeppelin did not believe it could build one airship within this cost. This was not extraordinary; there were no criteria in America for estimating costs of rigid-airship construction with accuracy. Admiral Moffett and Fulton thought a form of cost-plus might be the only way out, but the Department would not hear of it. Goodyear did believe, however, that it could build two airships for $8,000,000, as the second production is always cheaper. But because of the legislation tangle the airship question was still adrift when 1927 came to an end.

At this point William C. Young went to work again. Having been informed that although President Coolidge seemed to be dead set against airships, he in fact held no convictions on the subject, Young set out to sell the President on the merits of large rigid airships. Coolidge probably could not have cared less. Six months previously he had announced that he did not choose to run in 1928; and who could say that the "better part of wisdom" as articulated in 1926 might not be just the opposite two years later? Thus on 19 March 1928, the House Committee on Naval Affairs received a communication from the President which urged that funds be provided for, not just one, but two rigid airships.[21]

But while Bill Young was outflanking the prejudices of Congress through the White House, a newcomer was outflanking Goodyear-Zeppelin by appealing to the prejudices of Congress. This was Lawrence Wilder of the American Brown-Boveri Electric Corporation, whose group controlled the New York Shipbuilding Corporation of Camden, New Jersey, a number of concerns in electrical manufacture, and which had a nominal connection with Brown-Boveri, Ltd., of Switzerland. An economic buccaneer who roved the financial seas of the 1920's, Wilder was attracted by the prospect of expanding his already badly pyramided empire with the plunder available in the Navy's airship program.

Through Congressmen Robert L. Bacon (Republican, New York) and Burton L. French (Republican, Idaho), Wilder was granted a special hearing before the House Subcommittee on Appropriations, at which he assured its members that he could build airships cheaper than Goodyear-Zeppelin. He did not have a staff of engineers familiar with airship design and construction just at that moment, but he thought he could round up one easily. Building airships would be simple for his New York Shipbuilding Corporation; after all, airships were ships, they weren't balloons.[22] As a result of this

hearing Representative French suggested to Secretary Wilbur that the Navy ought to call for new designs and bids. Thus was determined the design competition of 1928. And realization of the airships was delayed yet another year.

The design competition of 1928 closed on 28 July, and for the next ten days a board of judges studied the designs.[23] In this they were assisted by C. P. Burgess and Ray E. Brown. Charles P. Burgess was BuAer's authority on airship design, and probably one of the outstanding authorities in the world on the subject. The younger brother of Starling Burgess of Burgess-Dunne airplane fame, his training had been as a civil engineer; but during the war he entered the Navy Department and became closely associated with aeronautics. During 1922–1924 he was a special lecturer at M.I.T. on airship structures, and in 1927 he published the only American textbook on the design of rigid airships. Ray "Helium" Brown was Burgess' engineering partner in the LTA Design Section, and BuAer's enduring authority on helium gas.

Nine parties entered the competition, but only three provided material which could be given serious consideration; these were Goodyear-Zeppelin, Brown-Boveri, and Schütte and Company of Germany.

Goodyear-Zeppelin, as in 1927, submitted a package of three designs; but these were not the same as those of the previous summer. Goodyear's new proposals were in fourteen volumes of data which presented its designs as Project I, Project II, and Project III; all described airships of 6,500,000 cubic feet.[24] Project I is the most significant because its essentials eventually took to the air as the *Akron* and *Macon*; but the others are of more than passing interest. Project II was similar to Project I, but it had only six engines, and there were significant variations in its hull structure and gas cell arrangements. Project III, however, was wholly different; it was a "conventional" design which, to the eye, was simply a very much-enlarged *Los Angeles* which had an airplane compartment inside its hull.

The Brown-Boveri and Schütte designs are an interesting study in economic conflict. They were almost identical. But the Brown-Boveri proposal was sloppily done and was wholly wanting in the technical verification which the Schütte design so obviously had.

Wilder had not found it as easy to round up a staff of airship design engineers as he had boasted. Brown-Boveri sent agents to Germany to make a deal with Dr. Johann Schütte, designer of the wartime Schütte-Lanz airships, but there was no accommodation. Then they simply went ahead and pirated as much Schütte data as was available and used it to paste up an airship design, working in a few of their own variations. As for Schütte, he never had a hope of winning the competition; he was not prepared to build his design, and the Navy in any case wanted nothing to do with an overseas contractor. Schütte entered his design expressly to expose Brown-Boveri. But this served no practical end, because neither Brown-Boveri nor Schütte offered what the Navy wanted.

In grading the designs, the board of judges gave the highest figures of merit to the Goodyear-Zeppelin designs, Projects I, III, and II, respectively. Schütte's was considered fourth best, and Brown-Boveri's came last.

If it was not clear in 1928 it should be clear in retrospect that, from the beginning, there was only one serious contender for the airship contracts—Goodyear-Zeppelin. The fact that Brown-Boveri was prepared to build but did not have an adequate design, and that Schütte had an adequate design but was not prepared to build, obviated each as competitors. In the end, this hocus-pocus of "competition" boiled down to that among the three Goodyear designs; but even here there was little doubt in the matter. After a relatively brief study of these, the judges decided unanimously for Project I.[25] In short, the men in the Bureau of Aeronautics knew what they wanted in the way of a rigid airship, and knew exactly where they could get what they wanted, but were obliged to go through these charades to salve the prejudices of the gentlemen on Capitol Hill. The result was that the first of the airships which Garland Fulton discussed in 1925, which could not fly before 1929, did not fly until 1931.

Of greatest significance was that Goodyear-Zeppelin represented an effort to found an airship-building industry in the United States. This was largely due to Goodyear's president, Paul W. Litchfield, who believed that the rigid airship would have a prominent place in commercial aeronautics. The interests of the Navy and Goodyear coincided here. The Navy was as interested in obtaining a regular supplier of rigid airships as much as Goodyear was interested in becoming that supplier.

On Saturday morning, 6 October 1928, in the office of the Secretary of the Navy, the contracts were signed between Goodyear-Zeppelin and the Navy for the construction of the two airships. The price of the first one, to be delivered within thirty months, was $5,375,000. The price of the second was $2,450,000; it was to be delivered within fifteen months of the first, and was subject to cancellation at the government's discretion.

It had been four and one-half years since the Truscott Memorandum and three years since the black days which followed the *Shenandoah* tragedy. The hopes and expectations embodied in the specifications of Design No. 60 had moved a long way toward realization. Half of Fulton's proposal for a farsighted development for the airship stood near accomplishment. The future of the rigid airship in the Navy and lighter-than-air transportation in America stood at the dawn of a new day of promise. That promise was represented in Goodyear-Zeppelin's Project I, which would become the ZRS4&5.

CHAPTER TWO

The Men on the Flying Trapeze

The *Akron* and the *Macon* encompassed several aspects of design that set them apart from other rigid airships. One of these made their design unique—not only among airships, but among all aircraft. This feature, which occurred behind a T-shaped door in their lower hull between frames 125 and 147.5, was their airplane trapeze and the hangar space provided for four airplanes.

This was the essential difference between the ZRS4&5 and all previous military airships. This was their *raison d'etre;* if their design had not provided for this airplane-carrying ability, their construction would have had no military justification in the environment of the 1930's. As Garland Fulton would remark to the members of the General Board in 1937, "The justification of a military or naval airship is the fact that she can carry airplanes."[1]

The *Akron* and the *Macon* were the only aircraft of any type which were originally designed for an airplane-carrying mission; and although other aircraft have carried "parasite" airplanes, none of these—before or since—have ever approximated their capabilities. As flying aircraft carriers the ZRS4 and ZRS5 were embryonic: at most they represented a prototype which never experienced development; but they stand in the history of technology as the only machines which ever approximated the role of flying aircraft carrier.

Flying airplanes from, or to and from, airships did not originate with the Navy's Bureau of Aeronautics, nor was it new to the 1920's. At the dawn of aeronautics, would-be inventors and aeronauts used balloons to hoist gliders and various contraptions which were supposed to fly into the air for testing. In 1905, Professor John J. Montgomery of Santa Clara College launched a man-carrying glider from a balloon, and a year later Santos Dumont used one of his dirigible envelopes to lift an airplane into the air for testing. In 1915 the Brit-

ish sought to create a composite aircraft by attaching a B.E.2c airplane to the envelope of a "Sea Scout" type blimp—with fatal consequences for the innovators.

The year 1918 saw three efforts to combine airship and airplane. In January the German rigid airship L35 carried aloft an Albatros DIII fighter which was released in flight, an operation which was duplicated a few months later by the British, using their rigid airship R23 and a Sopwith 2F.1 "Camel." And a few weeks after the Armistice the experiment was tried successfully at Fort Tilden, New York, using the Navy blimp C-1 and an Army JN4 airplane. But none of these efforts proved to be a first step toward anything.

These 1918 experiments were so isolated, and relegated to such obscurity, that most of the persons who were concerned with the development of the airplane trapeze for the *Akron* and *Macon* were unaware of them. What is more, none of these 1918 efforts contemplated the airplane returning to the airship; a means for retrieving the airplane on board had to wait upon the genius of Lawrence B. Sperry.

At a conference of Army Air Service officers at Bolling Field in September 1921, the problem of operating airplanes from airships entered into the discussion. The Army was interested in developing a means of operating an airplane or two from its semirigid airship *Roma.* Lawrence Sperry, head of the Sperry Aircraft Company and son of Elmer Sperry of gyro-compass fame, was at the meeting, and he proposed to mount a hook on the upper wing of a plane, which would engage the bar of a "trapeze" suspended from the airship.[2] A contract was let, and there followed three years of off-and-on experimentation which produced a practicable hook-on apparatus in 1924.[3]

Monday, 15 December 1924, was a crisp, clear winter day at Scott Field, Illinois, and the mercury in the

19

SPERRY-GYROSCOPE COMPANY

Lawrence B. Sperry, president of the Sperry Aircraft Company and designer of the first airship trapeze and skyhook. Sperry was killed in a plane crash in 1923 and never lived to see the success of his project, which produced a practicable hook-on apparatus in 1924.

thermometer stood below freezing. In the bitter air 1,500 feet above the field, First Lieutenant Clyde V. Finter jockeyed his hook-equipped "Messenger" biplane into the slipstream of the blimp TC-3. This was his second bout with the trapeze suspended from the blimp's control car. His first try was on Saturday; but the air was rough, and his plane was thrown up against the trapeze, shattering its propeller.

While First Lieutenant Frank McKee piloted the TC-3 along a steady course at 1,500 feet, Finter flew in under the blimp, fought his little plane through the airship's prop wash, and put his skyhook over the trapeze. But instead of coming to rest on the trapeze, he kept right on going. His skyhook was equipped with a pressure-impact safety feature which automatically released it when the plane made contact with the trapeze with a speed differential of more than 5 mph. It worked too well. On his second pass he again got his hook onto the trapeze; but once more the hook released him.

Finter discovered that when he got his plane within about two or three feet of the trapeze the turbulence around the airship's hull and control car literally stopped his plane, and that it was necessary to give the plane an extra burst of power to break through this barrier. This power had to be applied delicately, or it would give the plane too much speed, and cause the hook to release itself.

While circling for a third pass, he decided that instead of making his approach level with the trapeze, he would come in several feet below it, and then climb to the trapeze to make his hook-on. This way he would remain outside the area of turbulence until the final moment. This approach was a success, and Finter flew in to hang the "Messenger" on the TC-3's trapeze, and to become the first man to "land" an aircraft aboard another aircraft in flight.[4]

The Army's success proved to be an end in itself. There was some subsequent hook-on flying with the trapeze rigged to the blimp TC-7; during 1926 there was discussion of installing a trapeze on the semirigid airship RS-1; and in 1930 the Army briefly considered the procurement of a very large Metalclad airship which would have carried airplanes; but there was never a program of further development.

At this point in time interest in hook-on flying shifted across the Atlantic briefly. After the Army's success, the British displayed a fleeting interest in a skyhook project. During the winter of 1925 a hook-equipped DH.53 monoplane was used in a short series of experiments with a trapeze on the airship R33. And a year later the R33 carried aloft a pair of Gloster "Grebe" fighters which were released in flight; but not being equipped with skyhooks, the Grebes could not return to the airship. And after this, British interest evaporated.

Under the supervision of the U.S. Navy, the airplane-trapeze system and the art of hook-on flying from airships was destined to reach its ultimate degree of development. In the fall of 1928, the Navy announced that the *Los Angeles* would begin airplane hook-on experiments "soon." But the trapeze was not installed on board the airship until December 1928, and the flying work did not get under way until the summer of 1929.

Shortly after midnight, in the small hours of 3 July 1929, the *Los Angeles* took off from her Lakehurst base for what was to be more than just another routine training flight. The *Los Angeles* was now under the command of Lieutenant Commander Herbert V. Wiley, who had relieved Rosendahl in May. It is appropriate that Wiley commanded the airship on this flight. He was an airship man and had had no experience with airplanes; he would nevertheless prove himself the most resourceful and successful of the Navy airship captains through his recognition of the hook-on planes as the airship's key to success. Aside from Commander Frank C. McCord, whose career was terminated by the *Akron* disaster, Wiley is the only airship skipper who appears to have been of the early conviction that the airship's success had to depend upon its hook-on planes. And now he was flying the *Los Angeles* to her first hook-on.

A few hours later, as the summer's early daybreak spread across the New Jersey coast below, a Vought UO-1 flew out of the still-dark western sky. At 0415, Wiley ordered Lieutenant George F. Watson, officer of the watch, to bring the airship about into the wind.[5] In the cockpit of the Vought, Lieutenant A. W. "Jake" Gorton swung his plane in on the tail of the *Los Angeles* and lined up the skyhook on his upper wing with the trapeze suspended from the airship's frame 100. Six minutes later, after a great deal of aggravating "fishing" with his hook, Gorton finally got his hook onto the trapeze's yoke—but only for a moment.

The Navy's skyhook had the same safety release as the Army's; Gorton was experiencing Clyde Finter's frustrations of 1924. He would scarcely get the Vought onto the trapeze when the hook would release. And when he finally got the plane on the trapeze his hook experienced a mechanical failure, and he fell off. The morning's tests ended with only four out of fifteen pass-

First Lieutenant Clyde V. Finter of the U. S. Army Air Service stands on the cockpit coaming of his skyhook-equipped Sperry "Messenger." He became aeronautic first "trapeze artist" and the "Messenger" the world's first hook-on plane.

On 15 December 1924, over Scott Field, Illinois, First Lieutenant Clyde V. Finter flew his skyhook-equipped Sperry "Messenger" to a successful hook-on aboard the Army blimp TC-3.

es resulting in a contact with the trapeze yoke, and one aborted hook-on.[6]

Jake Gorton was no novice. He was a three-year veteran of the Navy's racing team, and most of his career had been spent as a test pilot; among his several assignments was participation in the first night carrier landings aboard the USS *Langley*. After the first day's disappointments some voices claimed that maybe the trapeze idea was wrong, or too complicated. Gorton disagreed. He told Lieutenant Calvin M. Bolster (CC), Lakehurst's Experimental Officer and one of the principal figures in the trapeze project, that he thought the existing gear was good. He could make a successful hook-on with it—but the pressure-release business in the hook would have to go.

Gorton also felt that a change in his flying approach was necessary. On 3 July, he made his approaches level with the trapeze and "fished" with his hook. This called for delicate stick and throttle control, which was almost impossible in the turbulence created by the *Los Angeles'* hull, the prop wash of her No. 4 and No. 5 engines, and from eddies created by the trapeze structure. To avoid this and the frustrations of "fishing," he suggested what he called a "reverse carrier approach" to the trapeze.

Until the mirror landing system became operational in 1957, airplanes usually approached a carrier's flight deck in a stalling attitude, and stalled out with their tail-hooks in the carrier's arresting gear. Gorton would reverse this procedure and approach the trapeze from below, climb to the trapeze in a stalling attitude, and "stall out" with his skyhook on the trapeze. This was essentially the same approach which Finter found necessary with the TC-3; but being an Army pilot, he was unable to articulate it in these terms.

A few of the airship men objected to the reverse carrier approach, and very loudly. They were afraid Gorton might not come to rest on the trapeze, that he might fly on into the airship—and the *Los Angeles* was the only rigid airship they had. But Jake Gorton had been flying airplanes too long to be deterred from a good idea by "gas bag" men.

On 20 August, Gorton was back under the *Los Angeles* with the UO-1, trying his new approach. The pressure-release feature had been removed from the skyhook, too, and his first pass at the trapeze resulted in a successful hook-on. He missed on a second approach, but a third ended in another successful hook-on. The next day he flew the Vought to another landing

on the trapeze, and then turned over the plane to Lieutenant Commander Leslie C. Stevens (CC), a Bureau officer, who had little difficulty in flying his first hook-on. Then Lieutenant Commander Charles A. Nicholson (CC), who was handling the Bureau end of the trapeze project, took the Vought up for a couple of hook landings. After this there was no longer anything tentative about the airplane trapeze. After Nicholson made his report to Admiral Moffett, the Admiral publicly announced that the tests were a success, and remarked that the ability of the two forthcoming airships to carry airplanes would greatly increase the airships' value to the Fleet.

On 28 August 1929, at the National Air Races in Cleveland, Ohio, the *Los Angeles* gave the first public demonstration of her hook-on evolution. The 100,000 persons in the stands that afternoon watched Colonel Charles Lindbergh perform aerobatics with two pilots of the Navy's High Hat Squadron, Amelia Earhart do spins in a glider, and Professor Juan de la Cierva demonstrate his novel Autogiro; but when the *Los Angeles* plodded down the field, escorted by a swarm of insect-like planes and a pair of Goodyear advertising blimps, she stole the show with her trapeze act.

As the airship came over the field, Gorton climbed into the Vought and flew up and hooked onto the trapeze. Inside the airship, seamen cranked away at the trapeze-hoisting mechanism and swung it and the plane up against the *Los Angeles'* hull.[7] Then Bolster, without a parachute, climbed out of the airship into the 45-knot slipstream, onto the Vought's upper wing, and swung himself into the front cockpit. The trapeze was lowered, Gorton slipped his hook, and flew off to land Bolster on the field—the first passenger disembarked from an airship in an airplane. This had its stunt value, but its purpose was to prove that the plane had actually "landed" on the airship, and that such a transfer of personnel was a simple matter.

Trapeze experiments were dormant until 8 October, when Chief Boatswain E. E. Reber, a pilot from the Naval Aircraft Factory, put the Vought through a series of hook-ons; and the next day Chief Aviation Pilot John J. O'Brien, a Lakehurst pilot, tried his stick work on the trapeze. Until the spring of 1931, when the first of the ZRS4&5's hook-on pilots arrived at Lakehurst, O'Brien flew most of the experimental trapeze work. Nicholson, however, would come up from the Bureau periodically to check on progress and to take a plane up for a hook-on landing or two.

Chief Aviation Pilot John J. O'Brien labors the weary old Vought UO-1 for an approach to the Los Angeles' trapeze, somewhere in the vicinity of the Lakehurst Air Station. Until Harrigan arrived at Lakehurst, O'Brien flew most of the experimental hook-on work with the Los Angeles.

Between trapeze acts, the *Los Angeles* had a brief affair with a glider. In the fall of 1929, Admiral Moffett became interested in using a glider to transport a mooring officer from the airship to the ground, and he called in Lieutenant Ralph S. Barnaby to discuss a glider launch from the *Los Angeles*. Barnaby had long been a prominent figure in American gliding circles. In July 1921, he had carried out a series of experiments with unmanned target gliders launched from the Navy's Italian-built, semirigid airship O-1, and in 1929 was correcting the proofs of his book, *Gliders and Gliding,* a technical discussion of the subject.

Barnaby assured the Admiral that it was practicable, and suggested that the Bureau procure a Prüfling glider to try it out. Thus on the morning of 31 January 1930, the *Los Angeles* was towed from her hangar, 196 pounds of Prüfling glider were attached to special fittings at frame 100, and the airship took off. While the *Los Angeles* circled the station, Barnaby climbed into his glider, slipped its moorings, and flew off to hold the air for 13 minutes before skidding in on the snow-covered Lakehurst field. The launch was a success, but the glider's value for landing a mooring officer proved to be questionable, and the motorless aircraft experienced only one more flight from the airship.

The *Los Angeles* was a very busy airship during the final days of May 1930. On the twentieth she flew out to sea to join in a Presidential review of the Fleet off the Virginia Capes. While President Hoover looked on from the bridge of the cruiser *Salt Lake City*, Nicholson flew the Vought off the *Saratoga's* flight deck and climbed to the *Los Angeles'* altitude. Inside the airship, crouched over a hatch at frame 100, N.B.C. announcer George Hicks described Nicholson's approach to his radio audience: "He did it—no, no, he didn't! Yes, he did! He's on! He's on!" The Vought was still oscillating on its skyhook while Hicks was lowering a microphone to Nicholson, who gave N.B.C.'s listeners a brief dissertation on the art of hook-on flying.

A week and half later, on Memorial Day, the *Los Angeles* flew to Washington, D.C., to put in an appearance at the Curtiss Marine Trophy race. On this flight the glider was in new fittings at frame 120, but Barnaby was not on board to take it down. At the last minute he was unable to make the flight, and Lieutenant T. G. W. "Tex" Settle volunteered to fly the glider. Settle was a lighter-than-air man, and one becoming well known by 1930 for his free balloon exploits. During the late 1920's he decided to try his hand at airplanes, and

when the Navy rejected his application with the excuse that it could not economically afford to train personnel for airships and airplanes, he obtained a civil pilot's license. In 1930, he was in charge of the Navy's inspection force at the Goodyear-Zeppelin plant where the ZRS4 was under construction. There he was introduced to glider flying by Dr. Wolfang Klemperer, Goodyear's aerodynamicist, who had been an authority on gliders in Europe.

Two miles south of Anacostia, Settle climbed into the glider and was away for ten minutes of silent flight over the Anacostia and Bolling airfields. But the 15,000 spectators on the ground did not watch his glider for very long. As soon as the glider fell away from the airship, Nicholson flew in with the Vought to hook onto the trapeze. It was a big day for everyone. Captain Arthur Page of the Marine Corps took the Curtiss trophy in a Curtiss F6C fighter, and a special trophy for another racing event, put up by Assistant Secretary of the Navy for Aeronautics David S. Ingalls, was won by Lieutenant D. Ward Harrigan.

That day at Anacostia was the first time Harrigan witnessed the airship-airplane trapeze act. It was not to be the last. And 13 months later he was at Lakehurst flying his own hook-ons, and later became the first squadron leader of the *Akron-Macon* "trapeze artists."

While the trapeze was being tested, BuAer was trying to find an operational hook-on plane for the *Akron,* and Goodyear-Zeppelin was insisting upon the plane's details so it could complete the design of the airship's airplane compartment. Not just any airplane would do. The T-shaped door in the *Akron's* belly dictated no more than a 30-foot wingspan, 10-foot tailplane, and 24-foot over-all length. To accommodate a larger one, additional longitudinal girders would have to be cut away in the airship's hull, and this was considered objectionable.

The requirement was exotic; no one knew what characteristics were desirable in an airship-based airplane. Nor could funds be spared to experiment with a special design. Several expedients were studied: shaving the dimensions of a Boeing F3B or Curtiss F7C, modifying a Vought O2U-1 with an O2U-2's wings, or developing Design No. 104, a triplane design BuAer had on paper. But no decision was reached. The Bureau finally had to approve Goodyear's generalized hangar layout with the assumption that an airplane of the proper dimensions would be available by the time the *Akron* was completed.

Two competitors of the XF9C-1 for the role of hook-on prototype were the Berliner-Joyce XFJ-1 and the Fokker XFA-1. Like the XF9C-1, they simply happened to be small enough to pass through the Akron's hangar door.

Test Pilot Lieutenant Ralph A. Oftsie climbs out of the XF9C-1 after a mishap during carrier arresting-gear tests at Hampton Roads, Virginia, in June 1931. Finally judged unsatisfactory for carrier service, the XF9C-1 was made available for hook-on experiments, and inadvertently became the prototype of the F9C-2 "airship fighter."

The final decision belonged to BuAer's Plans Division, the most influential policy organ outside of Admiral Moffett's office, at this date ruled by Commander Marc Mitscher, who held a very dim view of the rigid airship's naval future. Mitscher came up with six Consolidated N2Y-1 training planes scavenged from Pensacola, and an offer of any cast-off experimental planes which might be suitable—specifically, the Berliner-Joyce XFJ-1, the Fokker XFA-1, and the Curtiss XF9C-1. It was believed that the N2Y's would temporarily serve the *Akron* and *Macon* as operational planes; the rejected fighter types would be used only to compile data for a high performance hook-on plane of special design, to be executed in the future.

The F9C was eventually put into production, but only as an expedient. It was judged unsatisfactory as a carrier plane; it would be less satisfactory as an airship plane. The airships needed a lightweight, high-speed scout plane with exceptionally good cockpit visibility and range, and so stable that it would almost fly itself. This was not the F9C. But the options of 1930 were very few; it was a stroke of luck that a high performance airplane of the correct dimensions was available at all. And although the F9C was ill-suited to the airship mission, it was a good, solid airplane, far superior to its XFJ and XFA competitors. In 1933 BuAer prepared a preliminary study of its Design No. 124, a sleek, all-metal monoplane to replace the F9C's; but it never got off paper.

In late 1930 the Bureau of Navigation announced that billets were open in hook-on flying and the response was phenomenal; 41 requests were received from pilots in the Scouting Fleet alone. The Bureau's initial action resulted in a set of orders which arrived at the U.S. Naval Air Station, Hampton Roads, Virginia, on the morning of 19 January 1931. They were addressed to Lieutenant Daniel Ward Harrigan, flight instructor at the station, and ordered him to Lakehurst to assist in the development of the airplanes which would operate with the *Akron*. These orders were unusual in their result; they created the nucleus of a group of men who are unique in the history of aeronautics. These were the pilots of the *Akron*'s and later the *Macon*'s Heavier-Than-Air Unit, who operated a miniature squadron of airplanes from a hangar in the sky.

Ward Harrigan graduated from the Naval Academy with the class of 1922, and after four years of sea duty went to flight training at Pensacola where he received his wings in 1927. From Pensacola he was ordered to further training with the pilots who were to form the squadrons of the uncompleted carriers *Lexington* and *Saratoga*. He was a member of the Experimental Landing Unit which developed landing techniques to be used on board the new carriers, and was the first pilot of the Pacific Fleet Air Squadrons to land aboard the *Lexington*. After two years with the "Red Rippers" of Fighting Squadron Five aboard the *Lexington,* he was sent to flight instructor duty at Hampton Roads. This quickly palled on Harrigan. After only 90 days at Hampton Roads he was looking for channels into experimental flying work; he found one in the orders to Lakehurst.

Although Harrigan was strictly a heavier-than-air man, he had a dynamic appreciation of the rigid airship's potential. Because of his experiences on board the *Lexington,* he saw the airship for what it had to be —a high-speed carrier of airplanes. His viewpoint was not unique. This was a carrier pilot's natural reaction to a close association with the big airship, and the other hook-on pilots developed similar appreciations. Harrigan stands out because he was one of the few who analyzed the airship's mission in terms of military aeronautics of the 1930's. The concept of the ZRS4 and ZRS5's operations which he sketched out in 1931 and presented in greater detail in 1932, outlined the tactics which guided the *Macon* to her scouting successes in late 1934. But because of personal politics, general inertia, a shortage of development funds, and a variety of uncontrollable circumstances, three years slipped by before the essence of Harrigan's 1931 thesis was translated into action—and then it was too late.

When Harrigan arrived at Lakehurst in February 1931, there was no XF9C-1 at the station, nor any of the six N2Y's—only the old Vought. The *Los Angeles* was in Panama, and the trapeze was at the Naval Aircraft Factory for modifications. The first hook-equipped N2Y was delivered in March, but the trapeze was not re-installed on board the *Los Angeles* until June. In the meantime, for the lack of anything to hook onto, Harrigan went through Lakehurst's course in lighter-than-air flight training and qualified as a pilot of free balloons and blimps.

John J. O'Brien introduced Harrigan to trapeze work; on 17 June, he made his first flight to the *Los Angeles'* trapeze, and had few difficulties in running through ten hook landings. He discovered that after only a little practice it was easier to hang the N2Y onto the trapeze than it was to set a plane down on a concrete runway, much less on a carrier's flight deck.

In the spring of 1932, Commander Philip D. Seymour, the Lakehurst Air Station's executive officer, congratulates three of the primary figures in the airship trapeze development. Left to right, hook-on pilots Lieutenant Howard L. Young, Lieutenant D. Ward Harrigan, and Lieutenant Calvin M. Bolster, Lakehurst's experimental officer, who was in charge of research and development on the trapeze.

REAR ADM. D. W. HARRIGAN, USN (RET.)

There was a consensus among the hook-on pilots that landing on the trapeze was unusually simple. This was because airship and airplane were moving in the same medium, their relative speed was approximately zero, and the pilot's only concern was getting his hook onto the yoke of the trapeze. In a conventional landing, however, the concrete runway was a fixed surface and the carrier's flight deck was a surface in motion relative to the sea, while the airplane's motion was always relative to the air through which it was moving. On the trapeze there was no problem of an icy or wet runway, nor of missing the carrier's arresting gear. And if a pilot stalled out in his approach to the trapeze, he usually had at least 1,000 feet of altitude in which to recover— a luxury in short supply during a stall in a conventional landing.

At Lakehurst, Harrigan became acquainted with the blueprints of the *Akron*'s airplane compartment and its full-scale mock-up, and he felt that the internal stowage of the planes would impose serious limitations upon the hook-on planes' military effectiveness. Taking his troubles to Calvin Bolster in order to get an engineer's viewpoint, he found him interested. Together they devised an arrangement by which the planes could be hung outside the *Akron*'s hull and could be launched simultaneously, instead of having to be lowered on the trapeze, one by one, through the airship's hangar door.

Harrigan was convinced that the primary mission of airplanes operating from an airship—which he called a "lighter-than-air carrier"[8]—was to determine the presence or absence of enemy forces within a given area or along a given front. In short, if the airship were going to be the eyes of the Fleet, then the hook-on planes would have to be the eyes of the airship. The airplane scouting line would have to be as continuous as possible, using a maximum number of planes, and this would depend upon the planes' endurance and the speed with which they could be serviced upon returning to the "carrier." Because the *Akron* would carry only four planes, and at least one of these would have to be held in reserve, the need for rapid servicing was all the more important. The *Akron*'s internal hangar was desirable for extensive servicing, repairs, and in-flight stowage, but under combat conditions its use would be awkward.

To avoid the bottleneck created by the *Akron*'s hangar door, the Harrigan-Bolster scheme proposed a monorail along the airship's outer hull with trolleys to accommodate three or four planes. The monorail would serve as the airship's "flight deck," and would be used for all extensive flight operations. The internal hangar would be reserved for repairs, in-flight stowage, and independent flights by the planes. This "flight deck" would also permit airplanes from ashore, or surface carriers, to be equipped with skyhooks for operating to and from the *Akron*. They could be used to supplement —in fact, double—the airship's ordinary force of planes; and their larger dimensions would not be an obstacle because they would not have to be brought through the hangar door.

Harrigan's expression "lighter-than-air carrier" had a vital semantic importance for the *Akron* and *Macon*. It implied that the airship was useless without its airplanes. No longer would the airship be a direct means of scouting; it would support the direct means—the airplanes would do the searching and the airship would do its best to remain out of sight of the enemy and act as the planes' service and communications center. This view was not popular with some of the airship men, who at this early date resented the notion of their airship taking a "back seat" to a flock of airplanes—if not to say a bunch of cocky airplane pilots.

It would make a great deal of difference for the future if the *Akron* and *Macon* were going to be considered "lighter-than-air carriers" or simply as scouting airships in the image of the German naval Zeppelins of World War I which incidentally happened to carry airplanes. The former concept anticipated the challenges of the future; the latter was a dream which military aviation of the 1930's would not tolerate.

The Harrigan-Bolster scheme was received with enthusiasm at the Bureau, and Garland Fulton recommended an experimental installation be made on board the *Los Angeles*. The project was begun, but was temporarily lost in the press of work which swamped Lakehurst's small staff when the *Akron* brought her teething problems to the station in October. It was lost for good when the *Los Angeles* was decommissioned.

Neither the *Akron* nor the *Macon* were to have this elaborate outside monorail system; but a compromise of sorts was realized in the "perch." This was a small, fixed, auxiliary trapeze which accommodated one plane on the outer hull at frame 102.5. It was anticipated that four or five of them would be spotted along the airships' undersides, but neither of the ships ever had more than one such perch.

In the summer of 1931, Harrigan was joined at Lakehurst by Lieutenant Howard L. "Brigham" Young,
the second charter member of the *Akron*'s hook-on club. On 18 August, Harrigan and Young were in the air, each in an N2Y, taking turns at the trapeze. It was Young's first swing on the trapeze, but he had no difficulty in running through eight hook landings.

By the end of September, Harrigan and Young decided that it was time to find out how hooking-on worked at night. The N2Y's were not yet equipped with navigation lights, so they carried flashlights with them in their cockpits in order that, from time to time, they could flash to let each other know about where they were in the darkness surrounding the trapeze yoke. To illuminate the trapeze, the mechanics in the *Los Angeles'* Nos. 2 and 3 power cars were given flashlights to aim forward at the yoke. Later, aboard the *Akron,* a headlight scavenged from a Model-A Ford was used to illuminate the trapeze; but with the *Los Angeles* on this night of 29 September it was hook-ons by flashlight. Except for the shortcomings of the lighting system, the pilots discovered that night trapeze operations were no different from those in daylight. In fact, the night operations were a bit more pleasant because the calmer conditions of the night air made for easier flying, and they had no difficulty in running through a dozen landings.

In mid-October, Harrigan went to the Naval Aircraft Factory and took delivery of the Curtiss XF9C-1, which had finally been equipped with a skyhook, and on 23 October he and Young put the fighter through its paces on the trapeze. The plane gave Harrigan no trouble during five landings, but when Brig Young took it up he discovered a serious "bug" in the hook mechanism. The XF9C took Young through two landings nicely, but on his third Young was pained to discover that he could not get the plane *off* the trapeze. The XF9C was equipped with the same hook system as the N2Y trainers. But the fighter was a heavier machine, and under the strain of its weight the cable between the pilot's lever in the cockpit and the releasing gear in the hook had stretched—only a fraction of an inch, but enough so that Young could not pull it through its complete action.

The *Los Angeles* could not land with the plane on its trapeze, so it had to be removed. For half an hour she circled Lakehurst while Young struggled with the distorted mechanism as much as he dared. Aboard the airship, Lieutenant George Calnan decided that the only way that the plane was going to get off the trapeze was for someone to go down and knock it off. While the *Los Angeles'* skipper, Commander Alger Dresel, killed the power on two engines and slowed the other three to cruising, Calnan slipped a wrench into his back pocket and climbed down the lattices of the trapeze girders to a position on the yoke. After ten minutes of Calnan's pounding, the hook flipped open and the plane fell free.

Young's being stranded on the trapeze may seem a bit humorous in view of the early difficulties in getting planes onto the trapeze. But to Harrigan and Young it was very disturbing. A similar occurrence on board the *Akron* could be dangerous. If a relief plane being swung out on the trapeze had its hook jam and could not get off, an incoming plane might exhaust its fuel while waiting for the trapeze to be cleared, and have to ditch at sea. This cable in the hook-releasing system continued to give trouble on the F9C's until it was re-engineered in 1932. In the meantime, this condition underscored the need for a second trapeze.

After the XF9C was landed, a new release wire was installed, and Harrigan took off in the plane to meet the *Los Angeles* over Jersey City's municipal airport where a three-day air meet was in progress, and the Navy had scheduled a trapeze exhibition. Three days later he was again in the air with the fighter, pushing it toward western Georgia to rendezvous with the *Los Angeles* for a Navy Day exhibition over Atlanta. And while the *Akron* was being groomed for her commissioning that evening in Lakehurst, he flew the fighter to two hook landings on board the *Los Angeles*.

These were the last hook-ons to the *Los Angeles'* trapeze, and they were the last hook-ons made anywhere for the next seven months. The *Akron* did not have her trapeze installed until January 1932, and did not receive her planes on board until May. During the months which remained in 1931, the *Los Angeles* had her trapeze cannibalized to provide parts for the *Akron*'s. This was a "temporary" measure; but the nation was sliding deeper into the Great Depression, and on 30 June 1932, the *Los Angeles* was decommissioned in the interest of "economy." That, too, was "temporary"; but the *Los Angeles* never flew again.

With the conclusion of the *Los Angeles'* trapeze operations, the strictly experimental phase of hook-on flying came to an end, and trapeze work embarked upon its operational phase. The word "operational" is here construed loosely, because there was continual experimentation during the hook-on flying with the *Akron* and the *Macon,* and it was still in progress when the *Macon* was lost in 1935. But on board the *Akron* and *Macon* experimental work was complicated by operational demands, and often the latter could not be fully met without first working out certain aspects of their solution by further experiment with the trapeze, the plane-handling gear, or the planes themselves. On this count alone, the decommissioning of the *Los Angeles,* lighter-than-air's flying laboratory, was a great loss.

The success of the rigid airship in the U.S. Navy was going to be in the hands of the men on the flying trapeze; but their success in turn depended upon recognition of their vital role. At bottom, everything depended upon recognition of the *Akron* and *Macon* as "lighter-than-air carriers," and conducting their operations on this premise. Unfortunately for the future, this recognition would not be fully given until the latter part of 1934. Perhaps the long delay in the installation of the *Akron*'s trapeze was an omen of the immediate future.

The *Akron* was not going to be a "lighter-than-air carrier," but only a rigid airship which happened to carry airplanes.

CHAPTER THREE

ZRS4: "Our Hearts, Our Hopes . . ."

If there was ever a bright future for the rigid airship in the United States it was between 1928 and 1931. Five days after the ZRS4&5 contracts were signed, the *Graf Zeppelin* took off from Friedrichshafen on its celebrated first flight to America. During the next three years the *Graf* put the rigid airship on the front pages of the world's press whenever it took to the air on its several voyages. The Germans were organizing an airship passenger line between Europe and South America; American interests were planning a transpacific airship line to Asia; and there was to be a German-American organization to provide transatlantic service. For two weeks in August 1930, the British airship picture appeared equally as bright when the R100 flew to Canada. But British hopes vanished in a grim October moment when the R101 crashed and burned en route to India. In the subsequent reaction, the successful R100 was cut up for junk—which was the end of the rigid airship in England.

In these years, too, the first of the two Navy rigids became a massive and intricate duralumin skeleton inside Goodyear-Zeppelin's airship dock—and was covered, completed, flown, and commissioned, and work was begun on its sister ship. As 1931 came to an end, the Aeronautical Chamber of Commerce reflected lighter-than-air's bright prospects when it titled its annual report: "America Takes the Lead in Airships."

The construction of the ZRS4, the *Akron,* stands as one of the most remarkable performances in the history of American industry. It was not an isolated instance of building a big airship, but a highly involved effort on the part of the Navy and Goodyear to found a new industry. In the two years, eleven months, and twenty-eight days between the moment when the ink dried on the airship contracts in Washington, and that when the *Akron* was cast off from her mooring mast at Akron,

Ohio, not only did a hangar to house the erection work have to be built, but a corps of technicians and production personnel had to be developed around the cadre of German engineers; hundreds of workmen had to be recruited and trained to an art almost unknown in America; and thousands of drawings had to be translated into patterns and jigs for what was to be the largest airship in the world.[1] In order to build these two airships Goodyear was obliged, in one leap, to create an industrial plant of a magnitude which the airplane industry required almost a quarter of a century to develop.

The hangar which sheltered the ZRS4&5's construction excited almost as much public interest and engineering comment as the airships themselves. Variously referred to as a shed, airship dock, or air dock, this hangar remains one of the most unusual buildings of its type in the world, as a structure and by way of its accommodation to the airship.

One of the most difficult things to keep in mind about the airship is that, in spite of its phenomenal size, it really was *lighter-than-air*. Because of this, the most difficult moments of its handling occurred on the ground. An especially dangerous moment was while the airship was being moved in and out of its hangar; here a sudden gust of wind might slam the airship and its relatively delicate structure against the hard steel of the hangar's doorway. The Navy's studies of wind currents around the hangar at Lakehurst—a squarish building with straight-sliding doors which stood into the wind like Mickey Mouse ears when open—had shown that air currents whipping around its sharp corners experienced a venturi effect which often gave them a velocity twice that of the prevailing wind. In the design of the Goodyear hangar this problem was minimized; not only were flat surfaces practically eliminated, but also conventional hangar doors.

The first arch of Goodyear-Zeppelin's airship dock is being hoisted into position.
GOODYEAR AIRCRAFT CORPORATION

A crowd of thousands gathers inside the uncompleted hanger on 7 November 1929, to watch Admiral Moffett officially initiate the ZRS4&5's construction by driving a golden rivet in the ZRS4's first main ring.

Admiral Moffett drives the golden rivet, while Goodyear's president, Paul W. Litchfield, looks on.

Prior to the first World War, two small airship sheds of semi-parabolic shape, with hemispheric "orange-peel" doors, had been built in Germany. These unusual doors opened into the contour of the building, creating a minimum of air disturbance. With these essentials in mind, Dr. Arnstein initiated wind tunnel tests at the Guggenheim School of Aeronautics at New York University, using a 1/240 scale model of the proposed building. This data was correlated with Dr. Arnstein's and Dr. Klemperer's studies of suction pressures as a reaction of wind pressures, and Paul Helma worked this into a stress analysis and preliminary design, which was turned over to William Watson and Associates, who developed the final structure.

The spring of 1929 began to see structural steel frameworks sprouting out of the rural landscape adjacent to the Akron Municipal Airport, and on 21 May the hangar's first arch stood completed. B. E. "Shorty" Fulton, the airport's manager, was on the site that day, and expressed a burning desire to fly a plane under the arch—as Lieutenant Al Williams had flown through the Lakehurst hangar. But William C. State, Goodyear's engineer in charge of the work, was having none of this, and was careful to see that cables were hung from the arch to discourage anyone from "accidentally" flying through it. Ten more arches remained to be erected; of the total of 11, spaced 80 feet apart, only the center arch was anchored in the building's foundation. The other ten had their footings on rollers to permit a lateral movement of four inches in the hangar's longitudinal direction. This allowed not only for thermal expansion, but also for sudden changes in atmospheric pressure—which on a building of its size could amount to thousands of pounds.

On Tuesday, 29 October 1929, workmen had almost finished roofing the hangar and were erecting the steel of the south doors. While construction proceeded, workers trucked in the subassemblies of the ZRS4's first main ring, which had been prefabricated at Goodyear's Plant 3. The hangar was virtually finished a week later on 7 November, when 30,000 persons assembled under its north arch to watch Admiral Moffett officially begin the ZRS4's construction by driving a golden rivet in the main ring.

When Admiral Moffett drove the golden rivet, the airship was still "ZRS4"; but there was no lack of suggestions as to a name. The Admiral wanted to name the airships "Maxfield" and "Lansdowne," but found official opposition to naming them after individuals. In the fall of 1929, John S. Knight, publisher of the *Akron Beacon-Journal,* suggested to Francis Seiberling, Akron's congressman, that it would be appropriate if the ZRS4 could be named after the city of its construction. A few weeks later, Seiberling announced that he and Senator Simeon D. Fess (Republican, Ohio) would try to have the airship named "Akron," which would be a "deserved tribute to the world's new lighter-than-air capital."[2]

At this same moment, Assistant Secretary of the Navy Ernst Lee Jahncke was suggesting names of his own to Secretary Adams. Jahncke concluded: "I believe you will agree with me that the naming of these dirigibles 'Honolulu' and 'Alaska' will at least keep us out of political hot water."[3] But the political waters of Northern Ohio became very warm indeed; and in May 1930, Jahncke informed Seiberling, Senators Fess and McCulloch, and J. R. McNutt, treasurer of the Republican Party, that when the ZRS4 flew she would be known as the *Akron.*

The erection of the ZSR4's hull structure began in March 1930 and proceeded apace; sixteen months later she was complete. As is the case with all prototype aircraft, work on the ZRS4 was punctuated by a variety of difficulties. Physical problems were resolved by a letter, a conference, or a bit of slide rule work; but the psychological problems proved to be extremely thorny. These manifested themselves in the press, the public mind, and politics—and here there were no satisfactory solutions.

The brunt of these difficulties fell upon Dr. Arnstein and the Goodyear-Zeppelin engineers, and the Navy's inspection force headed by Tex Settle. From his office in Goodyear's Plant 3, with Lieutenant George V. Whittle as his assistant, Settle kept his finger on the subassembly work in Plant 3 through Lieutenant C. V. S. Knox, and upon the erection work in the air dock through Lieutenant Roland G. Mayer. With the exception of Settle, all were Construction Corps officers. It was expected that a naval constructor of captain's rank would head the inspection force; but when none was available, the title of "Inspector of Naval Aircraft, Akron, Ohio," fell to Settle by virtue of his seniority.

Although Settle was not an engineer, he was no stranger to the mechanics and physics of the rigid airship. He graduated from the Naval Academy second in the class of 1919, which in fact graduated in 1918 because of wartime acceleration. After the usual tour of sea duty he entered lighter-than-air aeronautics in

Dr. Karl Arnstein, designer of the Akron *and* Macon *and Goodyear-Zeppelin's chief engineer, and Lieutenant T. G. W. Settle, Navy Inspector in charge of the* Akron-Macon *construction, examine one of the* Akron's *box girders.*

Men at work on a main frame during construction of the Akron.

1924, served on board the *Shenandoah,* and was engineering and executive officer on board the *Los Angeles.* Settle's position as head of the inspection force held a certain measure of psychological value: the assurance that the "operator's viewpoint" would be represented, and not be sacrificed to engineering expediency, a grumbled complaint which usually attends this type of construction work.

As work on the ZRS4 progressed, it became clear that various alterations in structure and in internal layout might be desirable. Small alterations were usually executed on the authority of Settle's office; but large changes involving a change in costs, the airship's weight or performance, or a delay in construction, had to be handled through a change order approved by the Bureau.[4] There were several temptations toward experimentation, to change this or that aspect of the airship; but discipline was exercised, and there were less than two dozen of these change orders. The only one of any great interest is Change Order No. 2, which slightly altered the appearance of the airships by changing the configuration of their fins.

Every year of the *Akron*'s rather unhappy career was a crucial one, in one respect or another, and 1931, the year of her completion, christening, and commissioning, was the pacemaker. In that year there was hatched a farrago of trivial events which would make the *Akron* an object of public controversy, and harass the airship even beyond her tragic end.

The first of these events was triggered by the arrest of Paul Kassay, a riveter who was accused of sabotaging the airship. In fact, it seems that his only real offense was a love affair with the sound of his own voice. Kassay was a Hungarian by birth, an admitted communist, and was wont to thrill his co-workers with wild tales of his participation in Bela Kun's terror of 1919. When two FBI undercover men who had him under surveillance asked him why he always spit on the rivets he put into the airship, he allegedly told them it was in anticipation that the saliva would freeze, leave a gap when it melted in the spring, and thus weaken the airship's structure.

Kassay's arrest was front-page news, but the *Akron Beacon-Journal* questioned its significance. Nevertheless, the damage had been done. By the time the press associations trimmed the story of its dull qualifications and put it on the national wire, it had become part of a vast Bolshevik plot to wreck the whole American aircraft industry. In Washington, Congressman Hamilton

Fish, Jr. (Republican, New York), who had recently organized a congressional "Red Hunt," seized upon the "*Akron* plot" as evidence of a fearful conspiracy. Of course, he was going to expose it all.

Dr. Arnstein and Settle issued a statement which insisted that under the overlapping inspection systems of the company and the Navy, it was impossible for anyone to sabotage the *Akron.* As a precaution, all of Kassay's work was carefully re-examined—and found faultless. But these remarks did not make headlines outside of Akron, Ohio. Kassay was indicted, but Judge Walter Wanamaker threw the case out of court, citing the Holmes dictum that talk by itself cannot be considered a crime. But it was not Kassay's talk that damaged the *Akron,* and the "talk" did not end in Judge Wanamaker's court. From coast to coast, the *Akron* had been "sabotaged."

The Kassay affair had hardly blown over when another fiasco was in the making. Two workmen employed on the *Akron*'s construction contacted the Navy Department with information that the airship was a victim of inferior materials and shoddy workmanship. This resulted in a confidential investigation by Commander Ralph D. Weyerbacher and Lieutenant Karl Schmidt. Both were Construction Corps officers: Weyerbacher, manager of the *Shenandoah*'s construction; Schmidt, an inspector on Fulton's staff in Germany. They contacted the two workmen, Underwood and MacDonald by name, and after a week of conversations concluded that the two had little idea of what they were talking about. MacDonald claimed to have been a supervisor on the *Shenandoah*'s construction, but Weyerbacher knew better. The two officers later spent five days climbing through the *Akron*'s structure, but found nothing amiss. His investigation concluded, Weyerbacher had the informers sign a statement which declared that they were not engineers, were not competent to judge airship design, and accepted the results of his investigation.

This should have been the end of it, but it wasn't. Underwood faded from the scene, but MacDonald, who felt that he was not receiving the right kind of cooperation from the Navy, would later seek the aid of the politicians, and drag the *Akron* into a congressional investigation in 1932.

The day after Weyerbacher wrapped up his investigation, the Navy announced that the *Akron* would be more than 20,000 pounds "overweight." An unusual storm of criticism unleashed itself from the pages of the press. First the *Akron* had been "sabotaged." Now she

Inside the Akron's hull, looking forward from main frame 57.5. In this view the nose and forward hull areas are having their outer cover applied.

The nose of the Akron takes shape inside the huge Goodyear-Zeppelin hangar.

The Akron's Bay VI stands completed in June 1930, with its gas cell installed and inflated. The quilt effect on the face of the gas cell is from the cord netting of the elastic bulkhead. This gas cell installation was only for temporary "fitting" and testing; normally the cells were among the last installations made in the airship. The free balloon serves as a "surge tank" during inflation.

was "overweight." This may have been startling news to jaded editors who were in need of something they could blow up into good copy, but it had been common knowledge within the Bureau for more than a year.

The expression "overweight" was unfortunate; it suggested that a great blunder had been made. What it meant was that the *Akron* as constructed in 1931 exceeded the weight of her paper specifications of 1928, an occurrence not at all unusual in a prototype. What made it worse was that 22,282 pounds seemed to be such a lot of *over*weight. The less exciting details show that this was 7.94 per cent in excess of the 1928 specifications, and reduced the airship's gross lift by 4 per cent. Of the 22,282 pounds, 3,532 were authorized by the Navy, the balance was the responsibility of Goodyear-Zeppelin. This was undesirable, but no cause for alarm; the *Shenandoah,* the *Los Angeles,* and even the much-touted *Graf Zeppelin* were 3 to 5 per cent "overweight." The Navy recognized Goodyear's position, that the airship must be built strong enough, but felt that the company's weight-control measures had not been sufficiently stringent.

The headline writers, however, were not interested in these details; nor were certain politicos who faced an election in 1932 and who needed an issue to pommel for the sake of the folks back home; and neither was MacDonald. They would become a noisy chorus of malevolence in 1932.

With the ZRS4 taking shape in the Goodyear-Zeppelin air dock, one-half of the essentials of Garland Fulton's memorandum of 1924 was in the process of being realized. With the prospect of two new airships the Navy was faced with an airship housing problem which made the West Coast base a necessary corollary of the ZRS4&5's construction. Thus in January 1929, the Secretary of the Navy asked Congress to provide for an investigation of sites for the new air station. This was the first substantial move toward the establishment of the Naval Air Station at Sunnyvale, California.

A board of officers headed by Admiral Moffett was appointed to make the investigation, and on 15 May it met to study 97 locations between Puget Sound and the Mexican frontier. The members of this so-called Moffett Board were Rear Admiral Joseph M. Reeves, ComAirBatFor (Commander Aircraft, Battle Force), Garland Fulton, Rosendahl, and Lieutenant Commander Edward L. Marshall, an officer of the Civil Engineering Corps.

The several sites were soon reduced to two in Cali-

fornia: one, a square plot of 1,700 acres in the Santa Clara Valley near Sunnyvale; the other, known as Camp Kearny, was a rectangular area of 2,032 acres on the arid coastal plain about 11 miles north of San Diego. Both would eventually be acquired, but at this moment the board decided on Sunnyvale.[5] The decision was not unanimous, and here occurred a significant division which serves to illustrate the gap between the airship organization and the Fleet.

Admiral Moffett, Fulton, Rosendahl, and Marshall recommended Sunnyvale because of better meteorological conditions, and it would provide naval aviation with facilities in the San Francisco area. At Camp Kearny, however, it was known that severe temperature inversions[6] were common; 692 acres of it was unusable canyon land, and there was a problem getting sufficient water. But they recommended that if Sunnyvale were selected, Camp Kearny should also be purchased, for use as an airplane base and a secondary airship facility.

Admiral Reeves disagreed; he felt that the San Diego site was at least the equal of Sunnyvale, and its strategic position was overwhelmingly superior because it was near the center of the Fleet's exercise area, whereas Sunnyvale was from 350 to 550 miles away. Pointing implicitly at lighter-than-air's isolation from the Navy at Lakehurst, he felt that the airship and its personnel should be located in the immediate vicinity of the Fleet, its heavier-than-air units, and their thinking, instead of being hidden away in a remote area.

Reeves's tough logic did not prevail; it was felt that Sunnyvale was more suited to the peculiar needs of lighter-than-air, and that the airship's great range would compensate for the base's distance from the Fleet operating area. No one could foresee how that distance would artificially bedevil the *Macon*'s operations; nor that three years later Admiral Moffett would no longer be an actor in the airship drama; nor that in five years it would be Reeves, as Commander in Chief, U.S. Fleet, who would certify the end of the *Akron* and *Macon* epoch of naval aviation. All that was in the future. In the meantime, Congress provided for the development of Sunnyvale; and on 7 August, the day before the *Akron* was christened, the Navy invited bids on the construction of the base's hangar.

As the first week of August got under way in Akron, the city became alive with a carnival-like atmosphere as its citizens prepared for the moment when Mrs. Herbert Hoover would christen their lighter-than-air namesake. The public library was distributing free posters and

Rear Admiral William A. Moffett, Lieutenant T. G. W. Settle, and Commander Garland Fulton at a civic function in Akron, Ohio, during the Akron's construction.

Right: more than half a million persons were present to witness Mrs. Herbert Hoover christen the airship ZRS4 "Akron," on 8 August 1931.

banners which said "Welcome First Lady," and Mayor Lloyd G. Weil declared that the day of the christening would be a legal city holiday. The press claimed that it would be one of the greatest days in the city's history.

A banquet was being planned for more than a thousand persons, and Amelia Earhart, Frank Hawks, and Jimmy Haizlip were among the aviation celebrities who would fly in to join in the festivities. Jimmy Doolittle was expected, but he proved to be too busy tuning up his Laird "Solution" for the close-at-hand National Air Races, and sent his regrets. Captain Sam Williams of the Akron police would direct traffic from a Goodyear blimp, while the National Guard, American Legion, and the Boy Scouts were recruited to help the police handle traffic on the ground. At the airport, Shorty Fulton was hurrying arrangements for 50 railroad gondola carloads of ashes to provide temporary parking for 60,000 automobiles, while downtown the R.K.O. Keith-Palace made it a point to bill the Navy melodrama "Dirigible," starring Jack Holt, and the East Market Gardens Ballroom announced a "Christening Dance," featuring special Zeppelin decorations.

One of the final touches was provided by Miss Nellie Glover, music supervisor of the city's schools, who wrote a special song to be sung by the schools' glee clubs at the christening ceremonies. It was entitled "Ode to *Akron*":

> *Akron,* beautiful airship,
> Speed on your way;
> *Akron,* beautiful airship,
> Greet lands far away.
> May you carry the message,
> "Brotherhood of Man";
> *Akron,* beautiful airship,
> As the world you span.[7]

When it was revealed that the 48 racing pigeons loaned by members of the Akron Racing and Homing Pigeon Club for use at the christening had been successfully flight-tested, everyone felt good. And when word came from Washington that, contrary to rumors, the construction of the ZRS5 would not be canceled by the government's economy program, everyone in Akron felt even better. In the composing room of the *Akron Beacon-Journal,* compositors slipped in their last corrected slugs and hurried to tighten their quoins on the special "Zeppelin Edition," and the airport weatherman Leo Fangman, who had earlier predicted showers, announced that the eighth would be "a hot, dry day—and

no rain!" It was going to be a real "Zeppelin holiday."

The sun was still a dark red ball loitering on the eastern horizon when automobiles began filing into the parking lots around the Goodyear-Zeppelin air dock. By mid-morning streams of traffic were converging upon Akron from Pittsburgh, Cleveland, Toledo, Erie, and countless rural communities, flowing into the city's streets to infiltrate the local traffic and move along with it, bumper-to-bumper, to the municipal airport. In the air the show was already under way. Lieutenant Colonel H. H. "Hap" Arnold flew in from Wright Field, leading a squadron of two dozen Army fighters, while Major George H. Brett led in thirty-eight fighters from Selfridge Field. The Navy was represented when scout bombers from the USS *Langley* appeared over the city and put on a display of aerobatics. Massillon Road, which led around the airport to the airship dock, had been transformed into a veritable circus midway by a rash of souvenir and refreshment stands. On the airfield raucus-voiced hawkers, armed with peanuts and popcorn to generate a thirst and with soda pop to quench it, moved among the agreeable crowd of thousands. There was no ferris wheel, or a parade of elephants; but for those who had a dollar to spend, the Goodyear blimp fleet was present, prepared to give them a lighter-than-aerial view of Akron.

As two o'clock approached, the air activities ceased, and the perspiring crowd of more than a quarter of a million persons began shuffling off toward shade provided by the steel vaulting of the airship dock where the ceremonies were about to begin. Inside the hangar five brass bands from the Akron high schools were taking turns at challenging the building's miserable acoustics, while James Wallington of N.B.C. and Ted Husing of C.B.S. threaded their way among the crowd, trying to outdo each other with superlatives in describing to their radio listeners the wonders of the great "battleship of the skies" whose hull arched out over their heads, and which in a few minutes would be known as the *Akron*.

As Mrs. Hoover and the official party mounted the speakers' stand under the airship's bow, Rosendahl and his officers and crew fell in before the control car, and all the bands swung into "Anchors Aweigh." Paul Litchfield was the first speaker, and after paying tribute to such pioneers of lighter-than-air as Vaniman, Maxfield, Scott, and Lansdowne, who had bought airship progress with their lives, he introduced Rear Admiral Moffett.

The Admiral thanked Mrs. Hoover and the crowd

for attending the ceremonies, and interpreted their presence as evidence that, at last, lighter-than-air aeronautics had come into its own. He regretted that the United States did not lead the world with its merchant marine, nor with its Navy; but with the construction of the *Akron* America now led the world in airship development. The *Akron* was a military airship, but through her construction the Navy had laid the foundation of a new industry which would make it possible for private capital to carry on and build commercial airships to carry the flag around the world. He hoped that the nation would take advantage of this great opportunity, and that within a few years a fleet of American commercial airships would be carrying freight and passengers to points all over the globe. In concluding his address, which was a dedication to the past and future, the Admiral employed a metaphor which underscored the essence of the new airship:

> I know you will all join with me in saying as Longfellow said of our ship of state:
> "Sail on, nor fear to breast the sea.
> Our hearts, our hopes, are all with thee;
> Our hearts, our hopes, our prayers, our tears,
> Our faith triumphant o'er our fears,
> Are all with thee—are all with thee."[8]

As Admiral Moffett's words faded in the public address system, Mrs. Hoover picked up the microphone and said, "I christen thee *Akron!*" She reached above her and pulled a red, white, and blue cord which opened the *Akron*'s bow hatch; the 48 racing pigeons dashed out. All the bands struck up the National Anthem, and as workmen slacked the airship's tethering cables, the *Akron* silently floated off the hangar floor to complete her "launching."

With the ceremonies attended to, work was resumed to prepare the *Akron* for her first flight. Every morning after reveille at the Anthony Wayne Hotel, the *Akron*'s crew mustered at Akron's YMCA where Lieutenant Commander Herbert V. Wiley, the airship's executive officer, held school for them. In the afternoon the classes were held at the air dock on board the *Akron*. And at the air dock, Goodyear engineers and Settle's staff were working a 16-hour day to put the *Akron* through a series of "shop flights" which were necessary before she took to the air.

Before the airship was flown it had to be put through a series of tests which could yield accurate information only when she was completed, inflated, and in a condition of flight readiness. These tests included general and particular overloadings, hogging and sagging, a strength test of the "bridge" across the airplane compartment; final ground testing of rudder and elevator controls, engines and transmissions, fire extinguishing systems, electrical bonding, and the airship's two 8-kilowatt, 110-volt, D.C. generators and their transmission system. Aside from these technical matters, Wiley, Lieutenant Rodney Dennett, and Goodyear's Art Sewall were busy training 250 civilians, all greenhorns, to act as a ground crew for the *Akron*.

The public found it impossible to appreciate the necessity for this work. The *Akron* would not fly until the last week of September; but the excitement generated by the christening had hardly begun to fade when the nation became impatient for the airship's first flight. As days became weeks and the weeks became three, the press began grumbling. Then Goodyear naively announced that the maiden flight would be delayed because strains incurred by overload tests (to be expected in proof testing), had made it desirable to build greater localized strength into the ship. Public impatience soured to skepticism; new life was breathed into the old rumors: something must be "wrong" with the *Akron*. A further aggravation occurred on 26 August when calm weather permitted Dennett to put his ground crew through a dress rehearsal; the air dock's doors rolled open, and the crew was drilled in moving the *Akron* in and out of the hanger—no mean operation. But why didn't she fly?

Labor Day, 1931, provided a macabre illustration of this strangely intense negative public attitude toward the *Akron*. While Rosendahl and some of his officers and crew were enjoying themselves as official guests at the National Air Races in Cleveland, the public address system blared Rosendahl's name. He had an urgent phone call. Upon reaching the wire, he was told that Rodney Dennett had been seriously injured in a glider crash at the Akron airport. The word "crash" was linked to the urgent phone call, "Akron" was confused with the *Akron*, and before the afternoon ended, word-of-mouth had it that the *Akron* had crashed. That evening and all through the night the switchboards of Goodyear-Zeppelin and the *Akron Beacon-Journal* were tied up with phone calls from all over the United States, asking for details of the "crash."[9]

With Dennett out of action, Lieutenant Scott E. Peck was sent from Lakehurst to take over the *Akron*'s ground crew. Having entered naval aviation before

1917, Scotty Peck was among lighter-than-air's old old-timers. He had assisted with the flying of the DN-1, the Navy's first blimp; and later went to Wingfoot Lake, Ohio, where he became an airship pilot. During the war he flew antisubmarine blimp patrols out of Montauk, Long Island, and in 1919 was relief pilot on board the blimp C-5, which was wrecked at St. John's, Newfoundland, before it could jump off on a transatlantic flight. When LTA operations were terminated at San Diego's North Island in the early 1920's, Marc Mitscher "strong-armed" him into heavier-than-air training, and made him one of the few airship men who was also a qualified airplane pilot. During 1923–1927, Peck put in a tour of sea duty and then returned to airships. On board the *Los Angeles* he was instrumental in modifying the principles of marine navigation to the airship's peculiar needs; during the *Akron-Macon* epoch he would be navigator on board both the airships, and wrestle with the several navigation problems which cropped up during the *Macon's* operations.

All during the morning of 23 September the suspense had been building up as the wind continued to blow a dismal overcast across the airfield. In the thousands of cars parked on the hills around the field, in the hangar where crew and ground crew had been alerted since 0900, and in the office of Leo Fangman in the municipal airport where Rosendahl and his aerology officer, Lieutenant Anthony L. Danis, studied the latest weather data—everyone wondered: would the *Akron* fly today?

The first trial flight had been planned for Monday, the twenty-first; but the sudden visit of 20-knot winds caused its cancellation. Now everyone was ready for a second disappointment. But the 1400 weather report indicated clearing. When the two officers returned to the air dock, Rosendahl told Wiley that they would take off as soon as possible, and Wiley passed the word to "stand-by for flight."

The *Akron* moved out of the darkness of her hangar into the dull afternoon light stern first. She was pushed by a tractor-drawn mooring mast which held her fast at the nose, while her tail rolled along on a taxi wheel attached to her lower fin. From frame 35 hung a tail drag, consisting of a pair of artillery wheels with weights across their axle, which rolled along the ground and served to hold down the airship's tail. On both sides of her 785-foot length Scotty Peck's ground crew moved along with her, tensely gripping their handling lines and creating the effect of an army of Lilliputians who had just captured an awesome and exotic monster.

On hand to make the flight were Secretary of the Navy Charles Francis Adams; his assistant, David S. Ingalls; Admiral Moffett; and the Board of Inspection and Survey,[10] which would determine the airship's acceptability. With the Admiral were Paul Litchfield and other Goodyear-Zeppelin officials, while passengers of a more technical bent were present in the persons of Garland Fulton, Dr. Arnstein, C. P. Burgess, and Ralph Weyerbacher.

When the airship had been moved about a hundred feet onto the field, word was passed to drop the tail drag and for the ground crew to slack their lines; the *Akron*'s tail was permitted to vane around with the four-knot wind. The passengers embarked, and Rosendahl proceeded to "weigh-off." This consisted of determining the airship's static condition, and discharging water ballast fore-and-aft to bring the ship into a state of equilibrium in which her weight was literally zero.

When word came from forward that the ship was about 600 pounds light, Rosendahl ordered, "Stand by." A few seconds later, at 1537, he gave the order, "Up ship!" Atop the mooring mast, Lieutenant Charles F. Miller unlocked the airship's nose spindle and cast her off from the mast, the ground crew pushed up on her underside, and the *Akron* rose statically. As she floated away from the earth the Stars and Stripes were broken out at her stern, Ohio's 135th Field Artillery boomed a 21-gun salute to the colors, and from the more than 200,000 spectators on the field and perched on the surrounding hills there came a chorus of cheers and automobile horns. At 200 feet the airship's engines roared to life, and she began moving under her own power. Then the sun broke through the dirty overcast to create a dazzling effect on her aluminum pigment, making the *Akron* appear as the silvery "Queen of the Skies" that she was.

The purpose of the maiden flight was simply to find out how the *Akron* flew, and in this it was a success. After leaving the ground Rosendahl circled the field and headed off toward the city. As he took the airship over City Hospital, whose roof was packed with airship-watching employees, he dropped a "tough luck" note to Dennett, who was immobilized in 50 pounds of plaster of paris. Then the *Akron* headed north to Cleveland, trying out various combinations of her engines en route. The only serious trouble discovered was with the elevators and rudders, which proved to be quite overbalanced, so that at high speeds two men were needed on the control wheels to return the controls to

GORDON S. WILEY

The Akron is ready to be swung around for movement into Lakehurst's Hangar No. 1, on the evening of 3 November 1931, after a nine-hour local flight.

neutral. This fault was easily corrected for later flights.

As the big airship droned over the countryside, people on the ground dashed out of their homes to see it; cars stopped along the highways; and telephone exchanges became paralyzed as people phoned friends to tell them about the *Akron*. In larger communities traffic became a hopeless tangle as motorists stopped on the spot and got out to gape at the great aircraft. The excitement inside the airship was even greater; but it was a very different kind. To the slack-jawed spectators on the ground the *Akron* was a phenomenon; but to the 113 men riding inside her hull she was the object of a personal pride which defies definition. She was the product of their thousands of hours of thought, speculation, argument, and labor, which they had wrought in spite of those dire moments which occurred in the wake of disaster; the *Akron* was the instrument with which they expected to prove the efficacy of their vision, which would prove the rigid airship to be an effective means of navigating the air, and gain for lighter-than-air aeronautics an assured place in the future. Their hearts, their hopes, indeed, were all with her.

This was the first of ten trial flights, including her delivery flight to Lakehurst, which totaled 124 hours and 11 minutes. Most of these flights took place in the Akron-Cleveland-Pittsburgh area, where studies were made of fuel consumption at various speeds using different engine combinations, of the water-recovery apparatus, and of the functioning of the automatic gas valves; and data was compiled on her speed, turning, climbing, and diving characteristics, and her deceleration. The *Akron*'s ninth flight was a 48-hour endurance trip which took her down the Ohio Valley to St. Louis, across Illinois to Chicago and Milwaukee, and back to Akron, a course of about 2,000 miles. This may not sound like much in the so-called jet age; but it was considerable in 1931, when a Ford Trimotor did well to fly 500 miles on a tank of fuel, and when night flying was still a hair-raising adventure.

As could be expected in a structure so large and complex, there was a rash of minor troubles which had to be detailed to pick-up work. The only serious shortcomings appeared in the water-recovery system and in the airship's not meeting her required speed. Water recovery was a mechanical means of condensing moisture from the engines' exhaust gases to replace the weight of fuel consumed. The system's troubles were primarily in plumbing, distribution of the exhaust gases, and metallurgy, and were never completely resolved. The novel skin-type condensers on the *Akron* were partly responsible for this; but the water-recovery problem as a whole remained the *bête noire* of the helium-inflated rigid airship. The failure of the *Akron* to make the 72-knot (80 mph) contract speed was more serious. This was due to inadequate propellers. Goodyear had two sets of wooden, two-bladed propellers made for the *Akron,* one scientifically designed by the National Advisory Committee for Aeronautics, the other ordered from the Hartzell Propeller Company. Ironically, it was the Hartzell airscrews that turned in the better performance; but neither brought the airship up to her contract speed. Nor did a third set of two-bladed props which were subsequently supplied. The propeller problem was not solved until three-bladed, metal propellers of adjustable pitch became available in 1933.

In the meantime the *Akron*'s maximum speed was given as 69 knots. This was only a 2 per cent deficiency, but it put another scar on the *Akron*. Announcement that she did not attain her contract speed caused all the old skeletons to be hauled out of the closet, and they were given such a noisy rattling by the press that Secretary of the Navy Adams and Admiral Moffett felt obliged to take the unusual step of making a direct rebuttal, stating that the Navy had no cause to apologize for accepting the airship.

Late in the afternoon of 21 October, the *Akron* was undocked stern first through the north door of the Goodyear-Zeppelin air dock for the last time. At a word from Rosendahl, propellers 3, 4, 7, and 8 were tilted through 90 degrees to point downward, and at his order, "Up ship!" the *Akron*'s four engines came to life and pushed her into the air. After circling the city several times, she was laid on a course for Pittsburgh, destination Lakehurst. When she arrived at Lakehurst with the sunrise, there was no 250-man ground crew to greet her; here she was introduced to mechanical ground-handling equipment which gripped her firmly at both ends and hustled her into the hangar alongside the *Los Angeles* with a minimum of trouble.

The seventy-third anniversary of Theodore Roosevelt's birthday, 27 October 1931, was Navy Day, and at Lakehurst it was the day of the *Akron*'s commissioning as a vessel of the Navy. At eight o'clock that evening, in the presence of several thousand spectators, the *Akron*'s officers mustered the crew at quarters beneath her hull in Hangar No. 1. At this time radio was much bewitched by the novelty of remote broadcasting, and N.B.C. was on the spot with a four-way hookup to facilitate the ceremonies. After announcer Graham McNamee had questioned Rosendahl about the airship for the benefit of the radio audience, Paul Litchfield spoke from New York City, to be followed by Secretary Adams who spoke from the quarterdeck of the recently renovated frigate USS *Constitution* in Baltimore Harbor. Then Admiral Moffett spoke from Washington. Finally, Assistant Secretary Ingalls gave a brief speech at Lakehurst and turned over the ceremony to Captain Harry E. Shoemaker, the station's commanding officer.

Captain Shoemaker read the orders by which he was delegated to turn over the airship to its commanding officer, and asked Rosendahl if he was ready to accept the command. Rosendahl replied, "I accept the ship, Sir," and ordered Wiley to set the watch. A bosun's pipe shrilled through the hangar, and as the crew marched aboard, a band played the National Anthem; fore and aft, in the control car and along the keels' gangways, the USS *Akron*'s lights came on to signal her new status.

As the crowd milled around beneath the airship's hull on this exciting Lakehurst evening, to all appearances the *Akron* was a formidable vehicle of the air prepared to join the Fleet. The press had been highly critical of the *Akron* in its news and editorial columns; but on its feature pages it had not hesitated to exploit the airship's novelty for the sake of good copy. No claim seemed too fantastic to make for the airship: newspaper and magazine writers, publicists and airship enthusiasts, had tagged the *Akron* with such superlatives as "battleship of the air," "cruiser of the clouds," "*Leviathan* of the skies," and similar hokum. In fact, the *Akron* was something less than this; she was an experimental prototype aircraft, and however serene she may have appeared, the spaces inside her hull were full of minor mechanical bugs which required hundreds of hours in the air to iron out. But because of circumstances peculiar to the airship in 1931 this was not—perhaps could not be—fully appreciated.

The rigid airship scene, from beginning to end, was attended by a rosy smoke screen of emotional and promotional ballyhoo which continues to obscure the realities of the airship's predicament to this date. By 1931 this had become an intellectual miasma producing that dangerous condition in which even the propagandists come to believe their own propaganda. There can be no disillusionment without first a flight from reality to unwarranted expectations. In the twilight of 1931, in too many minds, the rigid airship was navigating a world of make-believe. The return to reality, in terms of Fleet needs, was close at hand.

The bright future which appeared to exist for the rigid airship in America between 1928 and the end of 1931 had achieved a great measure of its brilliance from glowing promises. A new period loomed in prospect. Even exorbitant promises will be called upon for performance. In 1932 the *Akron* was called upon for the performance which she was not capable of giving until 1933, which she did not ever give, and which finally had to be provided by her sister ship.

CHAPTER FOUR

Too Much, Too Soon

The commissioning of the USS *Akron* marked the passing of an important mile in the progress of the rigid airship in the Navy. The past had not been easy, marked as it was by the early crashes and relatively heavy losses in veteran personnel; the struggles to obtain authorizations and appropriations from a penurious administration; and irrational criticism. The future would be no easier. It held even more formidable difficulties, and the urgent and unsettled character of the 1930's would not be as relatively benevolent toward the airship as the decade past.

During the seven months between her commissioning and the summer of 1932, the *Akron* was hastily put on trial and found wanting. The trial was premature and the evidence incomplete, and while the verdict was not unfavorable, it scarred the *Akron,* compromised the *Macon,* and permitted critics of the rigid airship an "I told you so."

The *Akron* was the seventh rigid airship built in the world since 1919; the second built, and the third flown in the United States. In her condition of 1931–1932, she was little more than a prototype for the projected squadron of ten rigid airships contemplated by war plans. Under these circumstances it should seem incredible that while her builder's trials were still under way a fantastic operating schedule was being prepared for her.

On 16 October, while the *Akron* was on her 48-hour endurance test, the Navy Department queried Rosendahl on the feasibility of the airship undertaking a 7,000-mile flight around the rim of the United States during the next 60 days. In view of the *Akron*'s subsequent troubles during her West Coast flight of 1932, it is probably very fortunate that the plans for this "rim flight" were eventually dropped. But it is a typical example of what was at the heart of the troubles that afflicted this new and untried machine: too much was expected of it, and much too soon.

The distance of this rim flight posed no problem to the *Akron,* but the geography was something else. The *Akron* was not a high-altitude aircraft—in fact, was exactly the opposite; she had been designed for operations between 2,000 and 5,000 feet over the sea. Flying over 10,000-foot mountain ranges was a secondary consideration for a naval scouting airship. There was also the problem of logistical support for the airship during a long-distance barnstorming venture such as this proposed rim flight.

The problem of maintaining a rigid airship away from its home base for extended periods was a formidable one that was never completely solved. This was essentially an economic problem. An airplane could be landed and serviced almost anywhere; but an airship needed a mooring mast on a site with a generous supply of water for ballasting, and facilities for helium storage. In 1931 there were only six mooring masts in the United States, including the one on the Navy tanker *Patoka,*[1] and only four airfields which had gassing facilities adequate to the needs of a large airship.[2] Except for the establishment of the Sunnyvale base and secondary mast facilities at Camp Kearny, Opa-locka, Florida, and Guantanamo Bay, Cuba, this situation had not improved by 1935.

Also in October the Chief of Naval Operations was planning to hustle the *Akron* into 1932's Fleet Problem; she was to fly to the West Coast in January, from there to Hawaii, and during February and March participate in Grand Joint Exercise No. 4, Fleet Problem XIII, and subsequent tactical exercises during the Fleet's concentration on the West Coast. To accommodate the *Akron* in Hawaii the mooring mast at Ewa, which had been erected in 1924 for a flight the *Shenandoah* never made, would be rejuvenated; helium would be provided from the *Patoka.* It was gradually realized that the *Akron* was having problems, and this ambitious

The Akron *is undocked at Lakehurst, nose locked in the mooring*
mast, and tail lashed to the stern beam which rides the railroad-
tracked circle. Right: The rail mast and beam have moved
her from the hangar to the hauling-up circle. The beam has
been transferred from the hangar's tracks to the circle's
tracks. After being brought parallel to the wind,
the mast will tow her to the mooring-out circle.

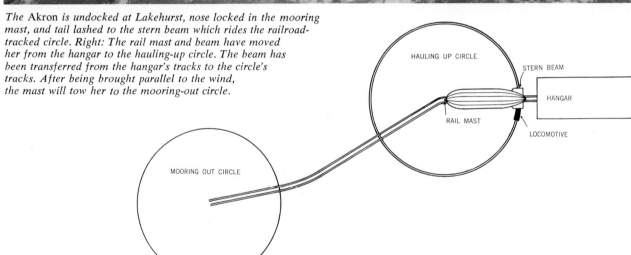

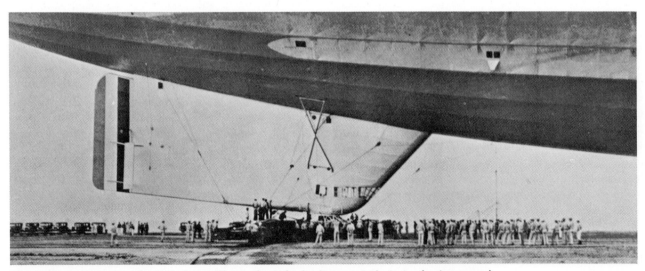

The Akron *is secured to the stern beam. The track of the hauling-up circle is in the foreground.*

schedule was reduced to the Fleet Problem in March. This was a small concession to reality, but it did little to ease the pressure on the men at Lakehurst.

The small group of engineers and technicians at Lakehurst which was available to help the *Akron* with her teething problems had their hands full. They faced problems which ranged from the installation of the trapeze to deciding where to locate the enlisted men's smoking room. Leaks in the water-recovery apparatus were reducing its efficiency; there were air distribution problems in cooling the four after engines, and it was discovered that four engines on the same axis using the same pitch propeller created undesirable vibrations in the aftermost engine rooms. But these problems were academic as compared to the trapeze and hangar installation. With the *Akron* due to join the Fleet in March, the completion of her hook-on plane accommodations was vital. Four months earlier, Fulton had tried to have Lakehurst speed up the *Akron*'s trapeze, but with very little success.

Because of the experimental status of the trapeze the Navy had elected to make its installation. In late December a rush order for its manufacture was placed with the Naval Aircraft Factory with a deadline of 15 February 1932, and the *Los Angeles'* trapeze was shipped to N.A.F. so it could be cannibalized. The *Akron*'s trapeze was delivered eight days before the deadline and Lakehurst went on a 24-hour day to get it installed before the airship was due to leave for the West Coast. But after the events of 22 February this would make little difference.

While Washington was making its optimistic plans for the *Akron,* the airship was logging hours in the air. Most of these were spent in trouble-shooting by her crew, Goodyear-Zeppelin guarantee engineers, and Lakehurst technicians. But not all of these flights were strictly work.

At 0430, 2 November 1931, the general assembly siren sounded across the air station and the *Akron*'s officers, crew, and ground crew hurried to their stations in Hangar No. 1 to prepare the airship for her first flight as a commissioned vessel of the Navy. Engines were warmed up, controls tested, and 715 pounds of food put aboard; the airship was loosed from the spring balance scales which tethered her in the hangar, and her nose was locked in the cup of the mobile mooring mast. An hour later Admiral Moffett arrived, accompanied by a party of the nation's leading aviation journalists and four N.B.C. men who were to make a remote broadcast from the airship.

At 0614 a small diesel locomotive began moving the mooring mast forward on its 64.5-foot-gauge rails, towing the *Akron* behind it. The airship's lower fin rested on what appeared to be an extraordinarily long—186.5 feet—railroad flat car. This was the "stern beam," an invention of Calvin Bolster's[3] which complemented the mast by providing mechanical control of the airship's stern during its ground handling. By eliminating the need for uneconomically large ground crews and making it possible to handle an airship in and out of its hangar in 20- to 25-knot winds, it was a signal advance over the practice of manhandling airships. Unfortunately, it could not eliminate enough of the human factor, and there were some trying moments during its early employment.

The beam rolled along under the lower fin, its wheels riding on the 64.5-foot-gauge rails. From both ends of the beam, cables reached up to reinforced points on the *Akron*'s main frames 35, 17.5, and zero, and held the airship on the beam's center. The mast and stern beam were connected by spreader gear so the airship's structure would not have to tow the beam's 133-ton weight.

When the mooring mast reached the center of what was called the "hauling-up circle"—a circle 1,300 feet in diameter with a standard gauge (4 feet 8½ inches) railroad track around its circumference—it stopped towing. Here the beam was transferred from the 64.5-foot-gauge hangar tracks to the railroad track around the circle. This was simply done by a pair of standard gauge railroad trucks being cranked down to the circle's tracks, which lifted the beam's other wheels clear of the hangar tracks. When this was done, a small diesel locomotive was coupled to the beam and towed it around the circle until the airship was parallel to the wind. Now the cables were disconnected from the airship, the beam was drawn out from beneath the fin, and the airship was ready for takeoff. As a rule the airship did not take off from Lakehurst's hauling-up circle, but was towed farther out on the field to a similar layout called a "mooring circle." This double circle system was necessary because the Lakehurst hangar had not been built on an axis with the prevailing wind. For towing to the mooring circle a temporary pneumatic taxiwheel was attached to the lower fin.

At 0657 the *Akron* was cast off from the mast, and with four of her propellers tilted for vertical thrust, she took off for a pleasant day of cruising down the coast to Washington, D.C. It was all in a day's work for the airship people, but it was a new experience for most of the newsmen, and a good time was had by all. There was a

On 3 November 1931, the Akron *took to the air with 207 persons on board, which set a world's record for the greatest number of persons carried by a single aircraft. Here the Akron's passengers line up beneath her hull. This demonstration was to prove that in an emergency airships could provide a limited but high-speed airlift of troops to outlying possessions. In 1931 the airplane was incapable of providing such transportation.*

Rear Admiral William A. Moffett, Chief of the Bureau of Aeronautics, and Lieutenant Commander Charles E. Rosendahl, commanding officer of the Akron, on the Akron's bridge in early 1932.

holiday flavor to this flight, but the journalists' presence on board was not without calculation. Admiral Moffett arranged the trip to give them an opportunity to become familiar with the airship, in the hope that it might stem some of the unreasoned criticism of the *Akron*. It was a hope which would not be realized.

By the end of 1931, the *Akron* had logged slightly more than 300 hours in the air. Forty-six of these were spent on an endurance flight across the South Atlantic states to Mobile, Alabama, returning to Lakehurst via the Mississippi and Ohio river valleys. But her most important hours were still ahead of her, most immediately the 60 hours and 13 minutes of January she was to spend working with the Scouting Fleet.

The morning of 9 January blew into Lakehurst with gusty winds full of rain. The *Akron* had orders from Vice Admiral Arthur Lee Willard, ComScoFor, to be off Cape Lookout, North Carolina, at daylight on the tenth, to begin a search for a group of destroyers en route from Charleston to Guantanamo Bay. The *Akron* was to locate and shadow this "enemy" force, and keep ComScoFor informed of its position, course, speed, and disposition. At 1600 the mast and beam moved the *Akron* out of her hangar into a 14-knot, cross-hangar wind; the ceiling fell lower and the rain fell harder. When she took off half an hour later, visibility fell to zero at an altitude of only 600 feet.

When the airship reached 1,000 feet, Rosendahl set a course for Philadelphia, Richmond, and Greensboro. Just before takeoff the *Akron* had received a storm warning; Cape Hatteras was enveloped in a low which was moving between an area of high barometric pressure in Missouri and a similar high over Bermuda. Because storms in the Northern Hemisphere blow in a counter-clockwise direction, and on the Eastern Seaboard usually move from west to east, Rosendahl took the airship on a westerly course for Greensboro in order to fly around behind the storm. At the same time he could use the air circulation on the storm's fringes as a tail wind.

As the *Akron* flew over Baltimore, the air became filled with blinding snow, and ice began forming on her hull and fins. At 2000, dim lights were seen below; after circling them a few times, glimpses through the driving snow permitted their identification as Richmond. In the meantime, crewmen phoned the control car that ice and snow was continuing to collect on top of the airship and on its control surfaces. In some places the ice was six inches thick. Suddenly, after

2200, near Crewe, Virginia, the sky cleared, and good weather remained with the *Akron* for the rest of her flight. It was calculated from her static condition that more than eight tons of ice had formed on her hull and fins; yet at no time had there been difficulty in controlling her. During the next forenoon, as the *Akron* cruised through the warm convections over the Gulf Stream, chunks of ice were still falling off her hull.[4]

The *Akron* arrived over Cape Lookout at 0330 on the tenth and circled the area until daylight. At 0700 battle lookouts were posted and she headed out to sea on a southeasterly course, sweeping out in a shallow arc which would bring her back in a southwesterly direction, almost within sight of the Bahamas. The sky was overcast at 1,200 feet with few breaks, so Rosendahl flew immediately below the cloud base, which gave the lookouts visibility of about 35 miles from the airship to the horizon. Aside from lookouts in the control car, pairs of men with binoculars were stationed in the auxiliary control room in the lower fin, and in the gun stations on top of the airship at frames 57.5 and 170. But from the moment the *Akron* left the coast until about 75 miles north of Green Turtle Cay in the Bahamas at 1700, her lookouts did not see the enemy. And the enemy was present.

At 1140 the *Akron* departed from her search course and flew west for a few minutes to give the navigator a favorable bearing for his noon sight. Rosendahl also wanted to check his ground speed by flying a different heading for awhile. At 1230, while returning to her original track, the lookouts on top of the airship reported three vessels on the eastern horizon. A false alarm. Then at 1240 the *Akron*'s radio room intercepted a message from the enemy destroyers, reporting engine trouble in one of their ships. The signal was strong, its transmitter very close; but the *Akron* had not yet been equipped with her radio direction finder and was unable to trace the signal. And she flew on toward the Bahamas.

The enemy was in the vicinity, and he had his eyes open. At 1350 the bridge watch on the destroyer *Dickerson* (DD-157) reported the *Akron* in sight, ten miles away to the northwest. A few minutes later lookouts on the *Leary* (DD-158) also had her spotted.[5] The destroyer squadron held its breath from 1350 to 1410 while the *Akron* flew across its wake and disappeared into the southwest.

At 1700 the *Akron* reached the end of her search curve and reversed course to the northwest at a leisurely speed until 2200, when she resumed a southeasterly

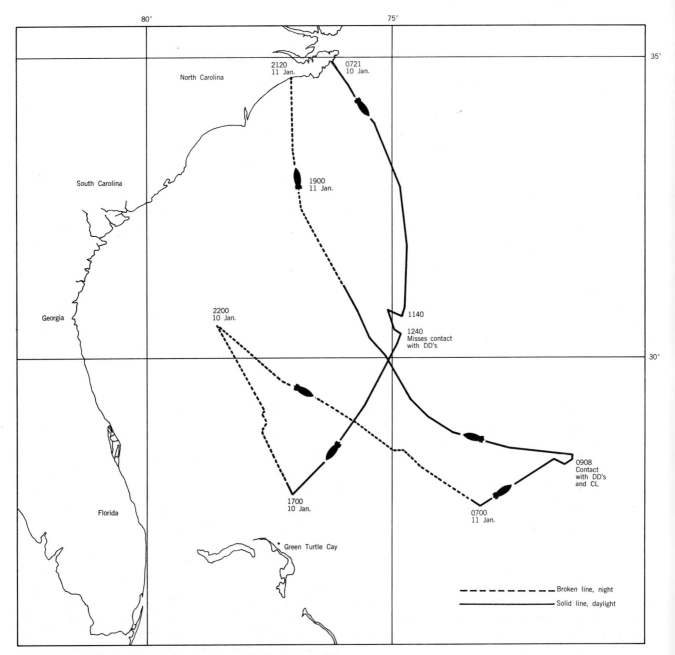

Track of the USS Akron *during her operation with the Scouting Fleet, 9–12 January 1932. The exercise was a success for the Akron. She had only one more opportunity to work with the Fleet before she crashed.*

course toward the point where she would resume her search at daylight. At 0700 on the eleventh she was about 200 miles east of her previous day's track, and began her second sweep on a course northeast-by-east. It was another overcast day. Suddenly, at 0908, a large group of ships was reported on the eastern horizon. Two minutes later positive identification was made of the cruiser *Raleigh* and 12 destroyers.

Rosendahl swung the *Akron* in behind the formation and slowed his engines in order to shadow it from beyond gun range. The sea was rough, so he did not feel that he had to worry about the *Raleigh* sending up its seaplanes. At 0957, a second group of destroyers was sighted. A few minutes later ComScoFor released the *Akron* from the exercise, and after circling the formations of ships she headed back to Lakehurst.

The exercise was a qualified success for the *Akron;* but Admiral Willard pointed out that the problem was framed so that the airship should have made contact with the enemy on the tenth. A division of cruisers was searching for the same enemy formation, but it was impossible for them to make contact on the first day of the exercise. The cruisers made contact at 1605 on the eleventh, seven hours after the *Akron.* The airship had beaten the cruisers, but according to Willard she was already 12 hours late.[6] There was also the fact that the airship had been in the presence of the enemy for 20 minutes without seeing him. But this could not be blamed on the machine.

Although Admiral Willard's judgment of the airship was reserved, after Fleet Problem XIII in March he remarked his disappointment in not having the *Akron*'s services, and said "her short but effective service in a minor problem . . . last January under adverse weather conditions gave promise of her efficient employment in the Pacific."[7]

Rosendahl thought he may have missed the enemy at 1140 when he swung west to check his navigation. He was correct; it appears that if the *Akron* had been held to her track she would have flown directly over the destroyers at about noon. Nevertheless, the enemy had passed within 15 miles of the *Akron*'s dozen lookouts during 1350-1410, and had passed unseen.

This should have been the outstanding lesson of the exercise. Of course, if the *Akron* had had the excellent RDF equipment she was to receive later, she certainly would have zeroed in on the destroyers when they broke radio silence. But her greatest material deficiency was in Bay VII where there were no trapeze and no air-

planes. With a plane on each flank during this exercise, even if they had loitered on the horizon within sight of the airship, vision would have been doubled and the enemy would not have gone unseen.

Rosendahl noted these material deficiencies, and the hook-on planes' potential in this regard; but the airplanes were regarded as auxiliaries on a par with the spy basket. Even at this early date, these "near-miss" results should have demonstrated the bankruptcy of tactics which anticipated the airship doing its own searching. But this 1914–1918 mode of operating, to which the Germans had no alternative, remained a brake on the airship's search tactics until 1934.

"Might-have-been's" aside, and consideration given to the weather, duration of flight, a track of more than 3,000 miles flown, her material deficiencies, and the rudimentary character of aerial navigation at that date, the *Akron*'s performance was remarkable. There was not a military airplane in the world in 1932 which could have given the same performance, operating from the same base. But it is unfortunate that the *Akron* did not turn out a performance which could be considered a "brilliant success," because not only was she the *Akron,* but at this moment *the* rigid airship. And as a result of all the ballyhoo of the previous seven years a "miracle" had been promised, and in the Fleet an "airship miracle" was expected. The *Akron* would have only one more opportunity to prove herself to the Fleet. In the meantime she had to prove herself to the politicians.

In January 1932, Representative James McClintic (Democrat, Oklahoma), of the Committee on Naval Affairs, instigated an investigation of what he declared to be the *Akron*'s military worthlessness. His motives are by no means clear. During debates on the Five Year Program he had been among the noisiest proponents of the rigid airship, and it is curious that six years later he should try to destroy with innuendoes what he had helped call into existence. But in the background there lurked the informer MacDonald and the problem of McClintic's re-election in November.

At the investigation, McClintic resorted to all the devious tricks of a politico who is determined to stomp up a cloud of publicity. He claimed to have documentary evidence of "poor workmanship" in the *Akron,* but refused to produce it; he expected two former Goodyear-Zeppelin employees (obviously, MacDonald and Underwood) to produce evidence against the *Akron,* but who never showed up; and he wanted to know why the *Akron* always flew so low, why she never went up to

The Akron *leaves the USS* Patoka's *mooring mast off Hampton Roads, Virginia, 17 January 1932. The* Patoka *was a Navy oiler which was converted to a mobile airship base. The Los Angeles* used the Patoka's mast *extensively, but the* Akron *used it only twice, and the* Macon *not at all. Use of the mast was dependent upon a large body of sheltered water, with the airship being "flown" while moored to the high mast, to prevent the airship's tail from dipping into the water. Otherwise it was a straight-forward operation.*

20,000 feet, and if she was as good as the Navy said, why were so many Goodyear engineers still hanging around Lakehurst?

Garland Fulton explained that the *Akron* was designed for low-altitude work; a scout had to be down where it could see things. It was impossible for her to fly to even 16,000 feet, except as a free balloon, and in this condition she would have no crew, fuel, ballast, nor any military load. Fulton pointed out that the *Akron* was only the third rigid airship operated in the United States, and expressed confidence that the third, or even the thousandth, airplane had not been subjected to such destructive criticism from uninformed sources as had the *Akron*.

Admiral Moffett complained to the committee about the press being hypercritical, and was surprised that knowledgeable persons chose to credit what were obviously rumors. On the whole, the Admiral's aircraft program was a remarkable success, and the vicious gossip which assailed the *Akron* clearly caught him off balance. There is a measure of pathos in his remark to the committee that "instead of [the *Akron*] being regarded as something that we could all be proud of, it has seemed to me that there has been a rather widespread desire to say that there is something wrong with it."[8] And in support of the *Akron* he quoted the famous German airshipman, Dr. Hugo Eckener, who had called the *Akron* "a masterpiece of American engineering and workmanship."

Acting on the theory that seeing is believing, Admiral Moffett invited the committee to make a flight on board the *Akron*. Thus on the morning of 22 February, Lakehurst was busy preparing the airship for flight, and at 0938 the mast began pushing her out of the hangar stern first. Four congressmen, including McClintic and Patrick J. Boland (Democrat, Pennsylvania) had arrived at the station the night before and were on hand to watch the undocking. The rest of the committee was expected to fly in from Washington around noon.

A brisk northwest wind of from six to fourteen knots was blowing as the *Akron* came out of the hangar. Walking alongside the control car were Rosendahl and Wiley so they could have easy oral communication with the mast and stern beam crews. Ward Harrigan, who was on the field as a spectator, noticed that the wind was listing the *Akron* six degrees or more, and that the wind was under her horizontal fins working her stern section against the cables which secured her to the stern beam. The man operating the mast's diesel locomotive

noticed it, too, and shoved his throttle wide open to hurry the airship clear of the hangar doorway in case something happened. The mast had barely passed over the door's sill when there came a loud snapping noise. And someone cried, *"She's loose!"*

The *Akron*'s tail had broken loose from the stern beam. Freed from the calculated grip of the beam, she slipped into the capricious grasp of the wind, and her tail soared upward. In the control car, Lieutenant George Campbell grabbed the ballast toggles and released a couple of tons of water aft in the hope of softening the blow when the stern came down. But the *Akron* came down on her lower fin with a sickening crunch, and the tail bounced back into the air. In the meantime, Rosendahl ran to the control car and managed to swing aboard, but the situation was long past remedy. There was nothing anyone could do except ride her out and grimace at the terrible sounds of the lower fin banging its way around the field, until the *Akron* had pivoted almost 150 degrees around her nose-hold on the mooring mast, and finally came to rest parallel with the wind.

The heavy damage was concentrated in the lower fin, and there was minor damage in the airship's main structure where the ground-handling fittings had pulled out of the main frames. The outer cover and one gas cell had been slashed by the flailing cables. This spoke well for the *Akron*'s heavy but rugged three-keel construction and deep-ring main frames. A similar accident to an airship of "conventional" design, such as the *Los Angeles* or the *Graf Zeppelin,* would probably have resulted in a severely mangled tail section. The physical damage was relatively light, but the psychological damage was incalculable. The rumor mongers now had a dramatic fact to build upon.

Representative McClintic put his tongue in his cheek and remarked what a sad but thrilling sight it was to see such a great ship so helpless in the wind. The other committee members, who had no axe to grind, retained their perspective. When they met three days later to draw up a report of their investigation, Representative John J. Delaney (Democrat, New York) said that he thought the *Akron* was as good an airship as there could be, and wished that he could be a passenger during her projected flight to the West Coast. There was a "me too" from William H. Sutphin (Democrat, New Jersey) followed by a chorus of "so would I's" from other members. McClintic and Patrick J. Boland were not among these voices.

The Akron *emerges from the clouds over Maxwell Field, Alabama, en route to the West Coast in 1932.*
Because of their clean hull lines, the Akron *and* Macon *were unquestionably the most beautiful airships ever designed.*

Boland had witnessed the tail smashing; but unlike other committee members he did not go aboard afterward to inspect the airship. He did not have to. Predicating his judgment upon his experience as a building contractor in Scranton, Pennsylvania, he announced that the *Akron* had been knocked out of alignment from stem to stern, and would never fly again. But McClintic and Boland were a minority of two. More typical was the reaction of Leonard W. Schuetz (Democrat, Illinois) who had been certain that the *Akron* was a grand boondoggle. After seeing the airship and inspecting its interior, Schuetz changed his opinion; he was convinced that she was among the most remarkable pieces of engineering he had ever seen. The Committee on Naval Affairs chose to go on record with Dr. Eckener, that the *Akron* was a masterpiece of engineering and workmanship.[9]

The *Akron*'s tail-smashing act had not hurt her with the politicians, but it did hurt her with the Navy. Because of her injured tail she was unable to join in Fleet Problem XIII. This was probably just as well. If she had gone into the Problem without a full complement of planes her performance would probably have been less brilliant than that with the Scouting Fleet. The *Lexington, Saratoga,* and *Langley* and their squadrons were active participants in Fleet Problem XIII, and the *Akron* would not have had the air to herself.

On the other hand it may be regretted that the *Akron* was unable to join the Fleet. It seems likely that she would have committed some conspicuous "blunders," been "shot down" more than once, and elicited some caustic but instructive comments from the Fleet. A "bloody nose" at this early stage of the game might— just might—have been a chastening and enlightening experience. But this did not happen; it was left to the *Macon* to take the "bloody nose" in 1934.

But the *Akron* did not completely miss the Fleet Problem; she was there in the speculations of Admiral Moffett and the Commander in Chief, U.S. Fleet. At the end of the exercises, the CNO queried Admiral Frank H. Schofield, CinCUS, for his opinion of the *Akron*'s possible value during the maneuvers as they had developed. Schofield replied with a dispatch which landed in Admiral Moffett's office like a bombshell. It tersely discussed what the *Akron* might have done, what certainly would have been done to her, and concluded with the emphatic statement that "the need of aircraft for the Fleet is not more *Akrons* but more carriers [and] his latter need is acute."[10]

Moffett immediately circulated Schofield's dispatch among the airship officers in the Bureau and at Lakehurst for comment. These were correlated with the Admiral's own views, and were synthesized in a letter to CNO which sought to refute Schofield's judgment. But both pro and con in this paper fracas could only speculate in the light of their respective prejudices; the fact remained that the *Akron* had yet to be proved.

Through March and most of April the *Akron* sat in her hangar, minus her lower fin, with her tail up on cradles. Her lower fin was rebuilt, the handling points in frames 35, 17.5 and zero were beefed up, and the trapeze installation was completed. On the evening of 28 April she was towed out on the field to fly again. Secretary of the Navy Adams and Admiral Moffett were on hand to go up as passengers. After nine hours of cruising the New York–New Jersey coast, she touched down to disembark her passengers, and took off again. On this flight occurred the first test of the airship's "spy basket."

The spy basket, sometimes called the "angel basket" or "sub-cloud observation car," had been used by the Germans during the first World War. It resembled a miniature airplane fuselage and was lowered out of the airship on a cable. The observer in the basket's cockpit had telephone communication with the airship. With this device trailed about 1,000 feet below, it was possible for the airship to cruise above a layer of clouds, invisible from the ground, while the man in the basket acted as the airship's eyes. The spy basket was one of those gadgets which had more appeal to the imagination than application to reality. The Germans discovered this and soon abandoned its use.

On this first test with the *Akron,* the basket was weighted with sandbags and lowered out about 1,000 feet. It proved to be frighteningly unstable. A few minutes after it had been lowered, the men in the control car looked out to see the spy basket flying along beside them—at least for a moment. The basket had zoomed up, dragging its hoisting cable along in bight behind it, as high as the *Akron*'s equator. It appeared that it was going to fly a loop over the airship. But it stalled and fell away—and then zoomed up on the other side! The *Akron* was slowed, the basket hauled in, and this was the last use it experienced with the *Akron.*[11]

The morning of 3 May saw the *Akron* cruising down the New Jersey coast with Rear Admiral Day and the Board of Inspection and Survey on board to observe the ship before her formal acceptance. On this flight Harrigan and Young flew the first hook-ons to her trapeze with N2Y trainers, and later with the heavier XF9C-1. The rest of the flight was consumed by engineering and performance tests for the board. The next day she was in the air again, this time with 12 members of the Committee on Naval Affairs on board. Patrick J. Boland was not among them. The congressmen were treated to a nine-hour ride during which Harrigan and Young gave them a hook-on demonstration.

The Akron's projected "rim flight" had been canceled by her teething problems, and her participation in the Fleet Problem had been canceled by the wind. But the Navy Department was determined to send her to the West Coast. The flight would serve to show off the airship to the taxpayers, and permit her to join in some minor exercises with the Scouting Fleet, which was still in the Pacific. Thus in the dawn of 8 May the Akron, her ballast bags bulging with 15 tons of water and fuel tanks topped off with 40 tons of gasoline, was towed to the mooring circle for takeoff. Her destination was the uncompleted airship base at Sunnyvale.

After the airship took off, Harrigan and Young scrambled after her in their planes, and while she moved down the coast they hooked on and were hoisted into her hangar. It became practice to have the planes hook on after the airship was airborne. This was because the planes were so many thousands of pounds which did not have to impose upon the airship's static lift during takeoff, and which could be easily absorbed by her dynamic lift once she was moving through the air. With her planes secured on board, the Akron continued down the Eastern Seaboard to sweep across central Georgia into the Gulf Coast plain, and toward the mountain passes of Texas and Arizona.

To the man in the street who picked up his morning paper and read of the Akron's departure for the West, the flight probably seemed like an idyllic adventure. The men aboard the airship had no such illusions. Nor did those who shaped public opinion. A friend of Harrigan's who worked for Paramount News told him that Paramount had alerted its cameramen along the Akron's route in the expectation that she would crash. For the Akron's crew, this flight was a challenge, not only to cheat the newsmen of a macabre thrill, but to prove their airship. This challenge became especially sharp as the Akron flew into western Texas.

Trouble first announced itself when a fuel tank burst and filled the port keel with gasoline fumes, a fire hazard which lingered on board for more than an hour.

Greater troubles were outside the Akron in the wads of fog which plugged the mountain passes ahead of her, and in the network of thunderstorms which closed in around her near San Angelo. For six hours Rosendahl maneuvered the Akron through the lightning-filled air over San Angelo, dodging thunderstorms while waiting for the fog to disperse. He was in need of weather information, which might show him a path to better conditions; but in 1932 the Weather Bureau sent out only two comprehensive reports a day.

Finally, at daylight of 10 May, he took the Akron south to Langtry on the Mexican frontier, in the hope of finding the Rio Grande Valley clear. But a few miles west of town the valley became filled with fog, visibility fell to zero, and he was forced to fall back on Langtry. Here he picked up the Pecos River and was able to grope his way over the obscured ground—and equally obscured mountain peaks on both sides of the airship—to a better sky over the town of Pecos. But the weather remained poor and the weather reports few as the Akron flew out of Texas and into New Mexico. Here, and across Arizona, the capricious convections boiling off the deserts made the air extremely turbulent, and sandstorms harassed her passage almost all the way to California.

At 0800 of the eleventh the Akron was circling fog-blanketed San Diego, preparatory to landing at Camp Kearny. She had received orders to land and refuel, and to take off to join the Scouting Fleet in the Pacific. The Akron's hangar door was opened and Harrigan was lowered out in the Curtiss fighter; Young followed him in the N2Y, with Scotty Peck in the front cockpit. Peck was the Akron's navigator, but in this instance was being flown down to act as mooring officer. No Navy rigid airship had visited the West Coast since the Shenandoah's transcontinental flight in 1924, so there were no experienced ground crew personnel available to service the Akron; nor were the mechanical mooring facilities on hand adequate to handle the Akron's size. What was even less promising was that Camp Kearny's ground crew had been assembled from raw recruits at the San Diego Naval Training Station.

The Akron nosed into the fog at 0925 and a few minutes later, at 1,200 feet, came out over the Pacific and turned inland. An hour later she was over the field and drifting down to the mooring mast to drop her trail ropes. The ground crew was supposed to seize the two ropes and shackle each of them to a "spider," which provided about two dozen lines with which the ground crew could steady the airship and guide her to the mast. But when the ropes hit the earth the ground crew did nothing. In spite of Scotty Peck's shouting at them, they stood frozen, gaping at the huge apparition floating above their heads. The *Akron* had to circle for a second approach. It was not until 1131 that the ground crew was holding her between their spider lines and her mooring cable was connected to the mast.

The *Akron* left Lakehurst with 55 tons of fuel and ballast; upon arrival at San Diego she had only five tons of fuel, ten tons of ballast, and was 40 tons lighter. The launching of her planes removed a further two and one-half tons. During the hour she was maneuvering to a landing, the sun's heat, intensified by the prisms of the water particles in the fog, had been superheating her helium, and by 1150 she had become extremely light. Now, held at the bow by her mooring cable, the *Akron*'s stern began to rise sharply.

Rosendahl tried to bring down the tail by using vertical propeller thrust, but the rapidly steepening angle cut off the gravity flow of fuel and the engines sputtered uselessly. He was valving helium when some of the emergency ballast bags accidentally discharged themselves and, as their five tons of water spewed out, the *Akron* became uncontrollably light. In a few more minutes she would be standing on her nose at the end of the mooring cable. Rosendahl shouted for the ground crew to let everything go. At the mast, Peck cut the mooring cable, and the *Akron* snapped away to an altitude of 1,000 feet. But three of the ground crewmen had failed to let go their lines and were carried up by the airship. Two of them lost their holds and fell to their deaths; but the third made himself fast to his line, and two hours later was hauled on board the *Akron*.

It was not until 1900 that evening that the *Akron* was finally riding at Camp Kearny's mast. While trying to bring the *Akron* down during the emergency, and later in an effort to save the men on the lines, Rosendahl had valved a considerable amount of helium; now when the gas temperature was normal, the airship's lift was sharply reduced. But there was no helium at Camp Kearny. Joining the Fleet was now out of the question. The ship had to be lightened even for her short hop to Sunnyvale. Harrigan and Young were ordered to fly north independently, and two of the *Akron*'s officers and ten crewmen were loaded into a pair of Sikorsky amphibians and flown to Sunnyvale. The public took these necessary actions at face value. No one was about to consult a book on aerostatics, and there was only one

In an aborted attempt to moor at Camp Kearny, California, 11 May 1932, the Akron *carried up three ground crewmen on her mooring lines. Two lost their grips and fell to their deaths. The third, Apprentice Seaman Bud Cowart, made himself fast to the lines and hung on for dear life during the hour it took to winch him aboard.*

conclusion to be drawn: the *Akron* was not only uncontrollable, but she could not even carry the load she was supposed to carry.

Most of the *Akron*'s operations on the West Coast consisted of "hand-waving" flights into the Sacramento and San Joaquin valleys; she had a much-hurrahed mooring to the mast on the *Patoka* in San Francisco Bay, and a flight to Bellingham, Washington, on the Canadian frontier, to show the airship to the citizens of the Northwest. The value of these operations is questionable. The crew was getting experience in what was still a new aircraft; but there is no evidence that on any of these flights there were military preparations for the *Akron*'s most important flight on the West Coast, working with the Scouting Fleet.

At 0820, 1 June, the crew began gassing the airship, and by 1030 had topped off her cells with 140,000 cubic feet of helium. At 1740 she cast off from her mast and turned her nose down the San Joaquin Valley for San Diego and the Fleet's exercise area off Baja California. The *Akron* was part of the GREEN forces which were searching for the enemy WHITE forces.

The morning of 2 June dawned cloudy and overcast, but rapidly cleared. At 0500 the *Akron*'s lookouts were posted around the ship, and she began a southward sweep in an arc away from the coast in the direction of the island of Guadalupe, a lonely hunk of mountain sticking out of the Pacific about 300 miles due south of San Diego. During the morning a merchant ship was spotted, and several of the GREEN forces; but at 1521 a large formation of WHITE ships was discovered creeping along the western horizon. The *Akron* swung around to take up station in their wakes.

The sea was rough, so Rosendahl did not believe that the enemy would risk launching his seaplanes in an effort to drive off the airship.[12] He had left his own planes back at Sunnyvale. But this was the same enemy which the *Akron* had tracked in the Atlantic in January, and the enemy had been doing some hard thinking. The commander of these WHITE forces was Rear Admiral William H. Standley, who was very skeptical of the airship's value, and he had planned a reception for the *Akron*. Standley had ordered half of his cruisers' force of Vought O2U seaplanes to be on their catapults, ready for launching on ten minutes' notice; the others ready to be shot off within 30 minutes. Thus he had two flights of eight planes to send up against the *Akron*. The rough sea upset Standley's calculations because it complicated recovery of the seaplanes; but by way of an experiment he decided to launch two, and at 1600 planes were catapulted from the cruisers *Chicago* and *Salt Lake City*.

The two O2U's did not seem to be a threat, so Rosendahl held the *Akron* to her contact, assuming that the airship's guns could fight off the attack. The O2U was a two-place, single-float observation plane which had a top speed of about 135 mph. Their "attack" was brief, and within 30 minutes of their launching the O2U's were back on board their cruisers. The *Akron* clung to the enemy until 2000, when a tail wind raised her speed above that of the surface ships, making shadowing difficult; to remain beyond their gun range she had to fly in circles behind them. During the night the cruisers managed to lose the *Akron;* and on the morning of 3 June she got a navigation fix on Guadalupe Island, and set out through a series of rain squalls on a new search course.

By 1500 the *Akron*'s lookouts had the cruisers in their glasses again, and Rosendahl took up station between the ships and the sun. As a result, the ships did not spot the *Akron* until after she had been shadowing them for 14 minutes.

On this second contact Admiral Standley really had his cruisers' claws sharpened for the airship, and, within ten minutes of sighting her, 13 planes were launched against the *Akron*. When Rosendahl saw the cruisers deploying to catapult their O2U's, he took the *Akron* up into the broken cloud base. This confused the planes; they had planned to attack en masse, but while chasing the airship through the clouds they lost formation. At 1540 two O2U's swept over the *Akron* in dive-bombing runs and broke off engagement. After half an hour of hiding, Rosendahl reckoned that he must have shaken the other planes, and sought to resume contact with the cruisers. Then, at 1622, five other O2U's popped out of the clouds on the *Akron*'s tail to make a series of dive-bombing passes.

Lieutenant John Lockwood Pratt, who flew one of the *Richmond*'s O2U's in this exercise, reflected the general bias of fleet aviation when he later remarked that because the *Akron* was such a huge target she could be easily destroyed by dive bombers.[13] This notion in turn reflected the idea of "vulnerability," rooted in the image of Zeppelins falling out of English skies in a blaze of hydrogen. But the helium in the *Akron* would not burn; in fact it would suffocate fire. If a bomb-hit on the *Akron* struck a main frame, a keel structure, or an engine room, its explosion would probably mark the beginning of the end. But unless it hit one of these "solid" areas it would probably pass right through the airship without exploding. Later experience by the hook-on pilots in simulated attacks on the airship suggested that ordinary dive-bombing attacks by 150–250-mph airplanes against a 65–75 knot airship which chose to take evasive action were often ineffective.[14]

As for vulnerability to machine-gun fire, a great amount of it would have been required, distributed among the upper areas of the gas cells, to bring down the airship. The gas in the cells was not under pressure in the ordinary sense of the term; the pressure was so slight that it was measured, not in pounds per square inch, but in inches of water. Except in the case of large rents in the tops of the cells, gas loss would be relatively small, at a slow rate, while a huge hole in a cell bottom would inflict a negligible loss. So it is to be wondered if the twin .30-calibre armament of any six Navy fighters of the early 1930's was capable of destroying the airship.

Rosendahl assumed that the Akron would be able to beat off her attackers with her own armament. This would have had a harder ring to it if even her one XF9C had been among her armament that day. It might have mitigated Admiral Willard's subsequent concern for the airship's "vulnerability"; and just might have served to mitigate some of Admiral Standley's subsequent bias against the Macon.

In the January exercise the Akron was not able to carry planes; in this exercise Rosendahl pleaded the inadvisability of bringing them along because of difficulties with the hook-on gear. The N2Y would have been practically useless anyhow; it had no radio, no compass, and, if it had to be ditched at sea, it had no flotation gear. But when the Akron returned to Sunnyvale the XF9C was flown aboard so she could have the plane's 2,500 pounds as ballast to assist her landing. In any case, Rosendahl thought it was "perfectly apparent" that the hook-on planes could have repulsed the O2U's; and, if carried, the planes could have been used to expand the airship's scouting line.[15]

At 1895 the Akron was released from the exercise and returned to Sunnyvale. There was a critique after the exercise, and comments by the cruisers' commanding officers were generally favorable toward the airship.

Admiral Willard thought the Akron had conducted her search in a "very creditable manner," and observed that "under most conditions a dirigible is a most efficient scout, insofar as making a first contact is concerned." After the initial contact he felt the airship's destruction was certain, especially if carriers were in the enemy force, and concluded "the sacrifice of a dirigible under these conditions may well be worth the information gained."

Rear Admiral W. T. Cluverius, Commander, Cruiser Division 4, agreed; and Admiral Standley conceded that, "This exercise indicates that ship-based seaplanes cannot drive off an airship and keep her off." The most Rear Admiral William D. Leahy, Commander, Destroyer Scouting Force, flying his flag in the Raleigh, could remark was "the ease with which a dirigible is sighted at long range is noticeable."

It was Captain Laurance N. McNair of the Richmond who went to the heart of the matter by pointing out that "the outstanding fact in these operations . . . is that the Akron left Sunnyvale at 1800 on 2 June and in less than 22 hours had found the Fleet." And he believed that the large airship had a valuable function in two wartime situations:

(1) As a long-distance scout in extensive over-sea strategical search operations when the location of enemy force is vital to success of our plans. Of course, an airship of this type would probably be destroyed or run grave risk of destruction shortly after contact; but nevertheless she would have been able to provide the CinC with information vital to his success.
(2) As a long distance patrol from Fleet Operating Bases such as Hawaii, the Philippines, and the Panama Canal. . . . Her presence in Hawaii prior to and during a sortie of the Fleet from that base en route westward would be of tremendous value in that she could undoubtedly greatly hamper and possibly completely nullify [surprise by] enemy submarines. . . . It is probable that she would be of little or limited use in a fleet battle as she would undoubtedly be destroyed during early stages, or even before the battle. However, when we consider that the cost of the Akron type is about equal to . . . a modern destroyer's, I believe that they are well worth developing for use in the situations above outlined.[16]

But when Admiral Willard drafted his report to the Chief of Naval Operations he chose to emphasize the airship's vulnerability and to complain about the Akron's apparent inability to operate away from hangar facilities. He did not feel justified in recommending further expenditures for rigid airships until future operations demonstrated their dependability under a variety of circumstances.[17] Willard failed to understand the airship's base predicament; but under the circumstances,

The Akron, *moored to the mast at Sunnyvale in 1932, just before departing for Lakehurst, New Jersey.*

While the younger generation looks on in wonder, the Akron's *crew board the control car to prepare her for departure from the Parris Island mast, where she moored en route to home base and Lakehurst.*

his was a reasonable and reserved judgment. No one could know then that the *Akron* had participated in her last Fleet exercise, nor that the rigid airship had enjoyed its last strategic search problem with the Fleet.

The *Akron* had been away from her home base for a month, a fact appreciated only by the airship men. The aluminum elements in some of her water-recovery condensers had corroded badly and needed replacement, and some engines needed work. It was later discovered that much of this work could be done at a mooring mast; but in 1932 it was felt that a hangar was required. The Chief of Naval Operations was anxious to have the *Akron* remain on the West Coast into the summer and return east with the Scouting Fleet, via the Panama Canal. But for the safety of the airship, Rosendahl insisted that she return to Lakehurst as soon as possible.[18] Admiral Willard thus recommended her return to the East, and he did it with a shrug which was indicative of his lack of understanding of the airship's logistics problems.

It was fortunate that the weather held good during the *Akron*'s flight east, because in all other respects it was worse than the flight west. Four hours after leaving Sunnyvale on the morning of 11 June, the propeller on No. 3 engine carried away. Damage to the airship was slight; but she was now short one engine.

The *Akron*'s biggest problem was her static condition. Flying west-to-east she would reach the mountains and have to begin climbing too soon. East-to-west, she enjoyed 1,600 miles between Lakehurst and western Texas in which she consumed 20 tons of fuel before having to climb into the mountains. But from Sunnyvale to the mountains at Phoenix, Arizona, is only 700 miles, and when she arrived over Phoenix she had consumed only five tons of fuel.

Upon arrival over Phoenix at midnight the airship was flying about three degrees up by the nose, maintaining herself in the air dynamically—and she faced a 3,000-foot climb. Rosendahl circled the area for two hours, jettisoning six tons of fuel to lighten ship. When the *Akron* left Phoenix and began her climb to Tucson, she was only one degree heavy, but her heaviness increased. She was flying close to pressure height too; her cells were 100 per cent full, and she would periodically bob above pressure height, where her automatic valves would blow her lift-giving helium to the atmosphere. The *Akron*'s static condition became worse, and by 0430, over the frontier town of Douglas, Arizona, she was 4.5 degrees heavy. Rosendahl decided that some-

thing else had to be thrown out as ballast. It was going to be Harrigan and Young and their 4,200 pounds of airplanes.

At 0415 George Campbell held reveille on the pilots, and told them they were getting out. It was urgent—not even time for a cup of coffee! Harrigan went to the control car and asked Scotty Peck for a chart, but Peck had only one of the area and needed it to navigate the airship. Peck pointed at the Southern Pacific's railroad tracks below, and told Harrigan that they would take him and Young into the heart of El Paso. They were told to fly on to Pecos, where the *Akron* would pick them up; so they climbed into their machines, were swung out on the trapeze, and got on the Iron Compass for El Paso.

Upon release of the planes, the *Akron*'s static condition improved 1.5 degrees. At Douglas, Arizona, she was over the hill, and as she flew "down" into Texas she was flying only two degrees heavy. But when she arrived over Pecos and her planes flew up to meet her, she treated them like a plague of locusts and refused to open her hangar door. The N2Y's engine had been giving trouble, and Harrigan tried using it as an excuse to get aboard. But the airship was having none of that; he got no response to his radio calls. Upon landing back at Pecos, Western Union delivered a message from the *Akron*; the two pilots were instructed to proceed to Lakehurst independently, and were told that if the N2Y was unsafe to fly they could have it put on a flatcar and sent to Lakehurst by rail.

As senior man, Harrigan took the uncertain N2Y, gave Young the fighter, and they were off for Lakehurst. For lack of a compass, Harrigan flew the railroads all the way back. Their flights were without incident; but Harrigan had a moment of wonder when he was low on fuel and the tracks went into a tunnel. He had to spend several precious minutes circling to find where they came out, and made his next fuel stop with only a few drops left in his tank.

Even after the relief obtained by dumping the planes and descending out of the mountains, the *Akron* was in sore shape. While crossing the mountains she had lost about a million cubic feet of helium through her automatic valves and had dumped 12,300 pounds of fuel. She had enough fuel to take her to Lakehurst, but an inadequate reserve if bad weather prevented landing immediately. So a course was laid for the mooring mast at the Marine Base at Parris Island, South Carolina, where she landed on the evening of 13 June. The

Akron's visit was longer than anticipated, and it was not pleasant.

Immediately after her mooring, there came a torrential downpour. The storm included sudden wind shifts which sent the *Akron*'s tail careening around the mooring circle, and the heavy rain waterlogged her outer cover. The next day, too, was filled with rain squalls. No helium was available at Parris Island, but there was fuel. During the afternoon 12,100 pounds of fuel were pumped aboard, the crew was embarked and ordered to flight stations, and the engines warmed up—but the airship was so short of helium and so logged with water, that she refused to lift herself off the field. That evening 4,200 pounds of fuel were pumped back ashore, and at 1000 on the fifteenth she took off for Lakehurst. Ten hours later, after an uneventful flight, the *Akron* was snug in Hangar No. 1, her long and sometimes harrowing voyage at an end. Seventy-nine weary men climbed down the gangway in the after end of the control car, more than glad to be back.

The *Akron*'s first nine months of operations came to an end with a wheeze. From her first flight in Ohio to her return from the West Coast, a minimum of allowance had been made for her status as a quasi-experimental aircraft. The *Akron* had been pushed unreasonably hard, with unreasonable expectations, and her inability to score a smash hit which corresponded to the airship propaganda of 1926–1931 made her performance appear as something of a failure.

The *Akron*'s less than brilliant performance had many aspects; among them were her material deficiencies, the primitive base facilities on the West Coast, the Fleet being unable or unwilling to understand the airship's predicament at this date; and there was the *Akron*'s deplorable goldfish-bowl existence during these months, attended by the hullabaloo created by the press, public, and politicos.

Closer to home, and probably at the heart of the matter, was the *Akron*'s own lack of military preparedness. The airship's log and the commanding officer's reports of this period indicate a marked preference for hand-waving flights over population centers, instead of drilling lookouts and running problems at sea, and drilling the hangar-deck crew in expeditious handling of the hook-on planes. Nor was an attempt made which indicated that a process had begun to integrate the planes with the airship's scouting doctrine. Instead, there was a reliance upon tactics which the ZRS4&5 airship had rendered obsolete.

These presumptuous approaches to the airship in general, and to its military problems in particular, were about to end. In the months ahead the *Akron* would take her first faltering step toward fulfilling her potential as a "lighter-than-air carrier."

CHAPTER FIVE

Training and the Harrigan Report

The summer of 1932 held an almost inevitable turning point in the *Akron*'s career. The feverish and premature efforts to force the airship to prove herself came to an end, and there began a cautious program of training which was aimed toward the development of search tactics which corresponded to the original promise of the airplane-carrying airship.

Most important, these tactics began to focus upon the exploitation of the airship's hook-on airplanes. This shift in emphasis coincided with four more pilots joining the Heavier-Than-Air Unit, the delivery of her F9C-2 airplanes, and a change in command. This new approach did not have a signal influence on what remained of the *Akron*'s existence—her military career was already over; but it would affect the *Macon*'s operations. The lessons of these months were digested in a comprehensive report by Ward Harrigan, which was both a report of past operations and a prospectus of those for the future.

This turning point in the *Akron*'s operations was officially marked on 22 June when Commander Alger Dresel relieved Rosendahl of command, so Rosendahl could take his normal tour of sea duty. Dresel graduated from the Naval Academy with Lansdowne and Weyerbacher in the class of 1909. For the next 20 years he served mostly with the Fleet, in battleships until the First World War, during which he held a command with the Queenstown destroyer squadrons. In 1919 he was on Admiral Sims' staff and did other staff duty in Europe, after which he returned to destroyers. In 1924 he was ordered to the Asiatic Station where he held various commands until 1927, when he was assigned to the staff at the Naval Academy. He volunteered for airship duty in the spring of 1929, and after going through the lighter-than-air course, and spending a year on board the *Los Angeles,* he took command of her in April

1931. In the spring of 1932 he was ordered to the *Akron* as prospective commanding officer, and made her West Coast flight as an observer.

Dresel was a modest man who loathed publicity, and this personal characteristic was reflected in his command. Not only did the *Akron* do most of her operating at sea, far from the tumult and the shouting, but he was successful in discouraging the Navy Department's requests for politically-inspired hand-waving flights. Always solicitous of the welfare of those under his command, he was revered by his officers and crew, and was probably the most popular of the airship skippers.

Also during June, Commander Frank C. McCord reported to the *Akron,* for duty under instruction as her prospective commanding officer. The *Macon* would be completed in early 1933 and Dresel was to become her commanding officer; McCord would take his place on the *Akron.* Dresel and McCord were of the so-called "third-generation" of airship officers. The first generation consisted of Maxfield, Lansdowne, Emory W. Coil, Laverne Pope, Scotty Peck, Charlie Bauch, Raymond F. Tyler, Joseph P. Norfleet, Jacob Klein, Frank McCrary, and George Steele, among others. They had gone into airships during the war or immediately thereafter; by the 1930's most of them had given up on the airship, out of disgust with its politics or concern for their Navy careers, and many of their ranks were dead.

The second generation consisted of Lewis Hancock, Rosendahl, Wiley, Roland G. Mayer, Calvin Bolster, Maurice Pierce, Tex Settle, Joe Arnold, Earle Kincaid, Bert Rodgers, and Vince Clarke, among others, who went into airships during 1923–1928. Those who had not dropped out in the meantime were the core of the Navy's airship experience by the 1930's. The third generation was called into being around 1930 as a result of lighter-than-air's expansion, to help fill the new billets

The Akron's *Heavier-Than-Air Unit* in the fall of 1932. Front row, l. to r.: Loren A. Alford, AMM1,
Francis J. Ferry, AOM2, William F. Germain, AMM2, James F. Kane, Sea/1c, Charles E. Jones, Sea/2c,
Harry T. Cudd, Sea/2c, William H. Clarke, Sea/1c, and Vincent J. Feigenbutz, AMM1.
Second row: Lt. (j.g.) Frederick N. Kivette, Lt. (j.g.) Harold B. Miller, Lt. D. Ward Harrigan, senior
naval aviator, Lt. Frederick M. Trapnell, Lt. Howard L. Young, and Lt. (j.g.) Robert W. Larson.
Rear: Hugh Ross, AMM1, John M. Robonic, AMM1, D. O. Maconaghie, ACM2, Ralph E. Kreps AMM1,
William C. Cody, ACMM, R. R. Davis, AMM2, Clyde Green, AMM2, K. H. McArdle, AMM1,
and Howard E. Aemissegger, Sea/1c. Absent: Emery E. Sherman, AMM3, and Arthur F. Glowacki, Sea/1c.

REAR ADM. D. W. HARRIGAN, USN (RET.)

A Curtiss F9C-2 inside the Akron's
airplane compartment. Above the plane
can be seen portions of the overhead monorail system and one of the
trolleys by which the planes were
moved around the hangar.

created by the *Akron* and *Macon* and the Sunnyvale base. This group included a small number of commanders and captains; as regards lighter-than-air, this was done to get heavier rank into airships, so they would "draw more water" in the Navy.[1]

As a stroke to further establish the airship's political position within the Navy this was a step in the right direction. But it was a *faux pas* as it affected the airship's internal politics. These senior officers were given billets commensurate to their rank, which blocked the advancement of more junior officers who had been through the airship's most bitter pioneer years. A lieutenant commander could command the *Los Angeles* in 1930, and a lieutenant could fill the executive officer's billet. But on board the *Akron* in 1932, command called for full commander's rank, and executive officer for a lieutenant commander. The airship organization at Lakehurst tended to be a hotbed of personal politics even in its happiest moments; the senior officers of this third generation introduced an additional frustration into an already frustrating environment.

Most important for the future, it was during June that Harrigan and Young were joined by Lieutenants (junior grade) Harold Blaine "Min" Miller, Robert W. "Swede" Larson, and Frederick N. "Knappy" Kivette, who reported for duty with the HTA Unit. A sixth pilot, Lieutenant Frederick M. Trapnell, arrived in July. It was during June, too, that the first F9C-2, the production model of the XF9C-1 fighter, was received at Lakehurst for trials. Thus by July 1932, the *Akron* was only beginning to receive the elements which she should have had before being thrown into Fleet exercises. But these elements only represented potential; it would require several hundred hours in the air to work them into a scouting machine and this would not be fully realized with the *Akron*.

During the two weeks subsequent to the *Akron*'s return from the West Coast, her crew was busy replacing corroded water-recovery condensers, overhauling the Allison propeller-tilting gears, renewing ballast bags, checking out her control systems, and inspecting her whole structure. An experimental steel, three-bladed propeller was installed on No. 3 engine, and the first Navy-designed Mark IV water-recovery unit was installed on No. 7 engine. The Mark IV proved to be highly satisfactory; eventually it was installed on all the *Akron*'s engines, and its competent employment contributed to further improvements in the *Macon*'s water-recovery system.

During July the *Akron* was ordered out on a three-day emergency flight to search for the sailing yacht *Curlew,* which had supposedly become lost during a New London to Bermuda yacht race. The *Curlew* was not found; she turned up safely in port, quite unaware of the commotion she had caused. Aboard the *Akron* as an observer on this flight was the British airship pioneer, Squadron Leader Ralph A. Booth, R.A.F., who commanded the R100 during her transatlantic flights. A few days later he was again on board, to witness all six of the *Akron*'s hook-on pilots exercise on the trapeze, and was greatly impressed by the Navy's progress in lighter-than-air aeronautics.[2]

After their arrival at Lakehurst the new pilots were introduced to the trapeze by Harrigan and Young, who explained the vagaries of hooking-on, and showed them motion pictures of the evolution. On 14 July they were all in the air in N2Y's for their first tries at the trapeze. After watching Harrigan and Young make a few landings, the new pilots took their turns, and at the end of the exercise had made a total of 54 hook landings. During one of these hook-ons an N2Y's hook seized, and Roland G. Mayer climbed down the trapeze from the airship, slid into the plane's front cockpit, and knocked the hook's cam loose. More weight to the case for a new hook-releasing system.

Admiral Moffett visited Lakehurst on the evening of 20 July for a flight on board the *Akron*. Hours later, as the airship cruised off the coast conducting an eight-hour test of its water-recovery apparatus, the wind suddenly rose to 40 knots, and pommelled the airship with violent gusts. Lightning filled the southeast. The *Akron* had flown into a small but violent storm which had not been indicated in the evening weather data. Reports coming into the radio room told of thunderstorms breaking over the Washington and Baltimore area; then static became so bad that the *Akron* was cut off from the world for the next hour.

Because these storms usually blew eastward and out to sea, Dresel swung the *Akron* around on a westerly heading, to circle around it. The *Akron* moved inland, across the Maryland peninsula and swept around Fredricksburg and Manassas, Virginia, and flew into Washington, D.C., in the storm's wake. Because of the many ugly storms which formed over the Midwest and blew out to sea via the Cumberland Gap, this stratagem of flying west to get out of the storm's path, and flying around to the storm's "safe semicircle" had become standard practice with the airship operators. Lakehurst and their operating area were smack in the path of just about every big wind that hit the Eastern Seaboard.

It was the airship operators' practice to make their landings and takeoffs around sunrise and sundown, the hours of the day when the wind was usually at a minimum. Evening takeoffs also permitted the airship to take off with the day's superheat in her helium, which gave her extra buoyancy in the cool evening air. Conversely, landing shortly after sunrise allowed the airship to land in the warming morning air while her helium was still cool from the night's operations.

By noon of the twenty-first, Admiral Moffett became restive and was anxious to get back to his work at the Bureau. But he knew of these preferences for evening and dawn landings, and it was his rule never to meddle in routine operations. So Dresel ordered the hangar crew to ready the N2Y, which was carried on board as a "running boat." With Harrigan at the controls and Admiral Moffett in the front cockpit, the plane was swung out on the trapeze, Harrigan slipped his hook, and flew the Admiral to Lakehurst where his Ford Trimotor was waiting to return him to Washington.

Local flights to sea continued to be the rule in the *Akron*'s operations. Although these flights were "local" in the sense that the airship returned nonstop to her point of takeoff, they usually involved several hundred miles of flying conducted within a triangle bounded by Lakehurst, Cape Hatteras, and Nantucket. Extensive tests were run to compile data on engine wear and performance; fuel consumption at various speeds using various engine combinations over eight-hour periods; and the effect of the water-recovery apparatus on engine performance, fuel consumption, and speed. This data was important so that alterations could be made in the *Macon* before her completion, and to establish criteria for the "next airship," a project always high on the priority list in Garland Fulton's office. These working flights also allowed for drilling the hook-on pilots on the trapeze, and for training the "*Macon* Detail," the officers and crew who would man the *Macon* when she was completed. Toward the end of August these operations were suddenly suspended.

A balmy four-knot wind was stirring the evening air of 22 August when the mast and stern beam moved the *Akron* out of her hangar into the hauling-up circle. Everything proceeded smoothly until a premature order was given for the mast to begin towing the airship out to the mooring circle. The stern beam had not yet been moved clear of the lower fin, and the fin fouled on the

beam's 133-ton mass. Within a second, shouting from the stern-handling crew halted the mast. But the damage was done, and the *Akron* had to be taken back into the shed. Ballast was dropped aft to lighten the stern, and the tail was floated back onto the beam and secured in place. While moving the beam around the tracks of the circle to realign it with the hangar's rails, the beam was derailed and its tethering cables inflicted unusual torsional stresses on the *Akron*'s after-hull structure, causing further damage. Half an hour later she was safely inside the hangar, somewhat the worse for wear.

The damage was serious enough to cost $8,000 and require three weeks' time to restore members in the lower ring girders and longitudinals between frames − 6.25 and 28.75, and some members in the lower fin. But as in the case of the 22 February tail smashing, this accident underscored the value of the *Akron*'s heavy but rugged structure.

While the *Akron* was having her tail nursed, Harrigan and his pilots were busy ferrying her six F9C-2's from the Curtiss factory in Buffalo. This made a total of seven F9C's, including the XF9C-1; An eighth, the XF9C-2, was delivered to Lakehurst in January 1933. The Bureau warned the *Akron* to take good care of these planes, because there were not going to be any more, and four of them would have to be transferred to the *Macon* when she was commissioned.

A further improvement in the *Akron*'s material condition occurred when Trapnell modified the trapeze. The mechanics of the *Akron*'s trapeze were substantially the same as the *Los Angeles*'. After a plane had hooked onto the yoke, and before it was swung into the hangar, the yoke and airplane had to be cranked up at the end of the trapeze and locked into the mechanism of the "third pole." In this same action a pair of steadying arms swung down from the trapeze, behind the plane, and moved into a pair of open jaws on the plane's upper wings. This provided a three-point grip on the plane while it was being swung into the hangar. But it was awkward. With the plane wobbling on its skyhook it sometimes required 15 minutes to get the steadying arms lined up with the jaws on the plane's wings. During military operations, when four planes with almost empty fuel tanks might be in the air, each pilot anxious to refuel, this would be intolerable.

Trapnell's modification eliminated the third pole, its system of steadying arms, and the need for steadying points on the plane's wings. In their place he substituted the "saddle" and "fork"; the former was a padded yoke which was lowered over the airplane's after fuselage to arrest oscillation and swaying; the latter, a pair of prongs at the end of the trapeze which were lowered after a plane landed, thus centering its skyhook on the yoke. These not only accelerated the retrieving of planes on board, but by eliminating the third pole and its gear, lightened the airship by 300 pounds.

At about this same time, work was begun on the perch, which was an auxiliary trapeze only five feet away from the hull, installed at frame 102.5. Besides providing an emergency landing facility, a plane could be kept on the perch ready for takeoff at a moment's notice. Perches were also planned for main frames 57.5, 80, and 147.5, but they never got off paper.

The *Akron*'s biggest airplane headache proved to be the lack of equipment for securing the planes in their stowage positions inside the hangar compartment; lack of catwalks for use of personnel servicing the planes; and lack of stowage facilities for ammunition, spare parts, and auxiliary gear. Theoretically, five planes could be stowed in the hangar, one in each corner on the overhead monorail system, and a fifth on the trapeze in the hangar's center. In the *Akron,* however, two girders obstructed use of the two after-corner positions. The Bureau gave permission to hinge these struts so they could be swung out of the way while handling planes, but the *Akron* was lost before this work could be accomplished.

Because of these obstructions, the *Akron* never carried more than three planes. This deficiency was corrected in the *Macon* while she was under construction. And although the *Macon* could house five planes, the fifth plane was seldom carried, and with good reason. The fifth had to be left on the trapeze, and if it had engine trouble, the other four planes would be trapped in their corners until the one on the trapeze could be repaired or jettisoned.

Between 21 September, when the *Akron* took to the air again after her repairs, and the end of the year, she made eight extended flights to sea which were devoted to intensive hook-on practices and to drilling battle lookouts; and, while the F9C's simulated attacks on the airship, her gun crews were trained with camera guns.

These operations saw the first attempt to use the scouting technique of maintaining two planes out on the airship's flanks, and of a mathematical system for prenavigating the planes beyond the horizon. The latter system was devised by Lieutenant Donald M. Mackey, a station officer. Previous to his airship duty he had spent a year at the Naval Academy's Postgraduate School where Lieutenant Commander Richard Harwood Knight was teaching a course in the problems of relative motion.

During World War I, Knight was navigator on board the USS *Nicholson* (DD-52) of the Queenstown squadron, and was faced with practical problems of interception relative to radius action. These were escorting outward-bound convoys as far west as possible, and then intercepting an eastbound convoy to St. George's Channel, with careful attention to the destroyer's fuel. This was essentially a problem in relative motion, and he devised methods of solving it and others by means of vector analysis of the relative motion. The problems created by the speeds of aircraft were even greater, and Knight gave Mackey's class intensive drilling in relative motion and maneuvering board problems which concerned ships and aircraft. Knight's unique methods proved to have a special application to the airship-airplane combination.

The technique of using two planes at the limit of visibility extended the airship's vision well beyond the horizon. But when combined with Mackey's mathematical system of prenavigation, it permitted the planes to fly beyond the horizon with assurance of returning to the airship. Even in this first cautious use of the system, it permitted the *Akron* and her planes to sweep a path 100 miles wide.[3] On 18 November, when it was tried for the first time, the *Akron* began her sweep at Scotland Light, south of New York City, and flew southward along the coast. The airship and only three planes were able to maintain their scouting line for seven hours. During the afternoon, when Swede Larson flew to the trapeze to refuel, there was a failure in its hoisting mechanism and Larson had to find his fuel at a village in Maryland. The trapeze was back in commission within 20 minutes, but it might have been an hour or two, and Larson could not afford to hang around in speculation. This experience underscored the need for an auxiliary trapeze.

This first experiment was necessarily cautious. Both pilots and planes had been exposed to what was for that day a rigorous flying schedule. Thus the flight had been made along the coast, so if one of the planes had troubles and could not get back to the airship, it could—as Larson had to—find relief at a shoreside field. Also, the planes had to be flown relatively close aboard to the airship, within 25 to 30 miles, because of their inadequate radios. But at Lakehurst, in paper games set up

Lieutenant Harold B. "Min" Miller at the controls of his F9C over Moffett Field. In 1934, Miller became the HTA Unit's senior aviator and was co-developer of the radio equipment which "homed" the pilots back to the airship.

The USS Akron *passing over lower Manhattan Island.*

by Wiley and participated in by Dresel, Peck, Harrigan, Mackey, and other officers, an even broader sweep was anticipated. It was calculated that with adequate radio communications, and a reliable radio homing device to bring the planes back to the airship, the airship and two planes could sweep a path 200 miles wide. At a rate of advance of 60 knots during 12 hours of daylight, this sweep would cover more than 165,000 square miles of ocean. This system, however limited, and however compromised by the human factor and that day's technology, provided a scope of vision to very-long-range, air-sea search during the 1930's, which did not become available again in a single aircraft until the huge airborne radar systems of the 1950's.

The exploratory operation of 18 November was a qualified success, and rather clearly pointed the way in which the airship had to develop its tactics. Upon its conclusion Harrigan recommended to Dresel that the billet of "Flight Control Officer" be created, and that Mackey be ordered to fill it.[4] This request did not receive favorable action; by happenstance, Mackey was reserved for the *Macon*.

Two major factors inhibited a rapid development of the 200-mile airship-airplane scouting screen—navigation and communications. The F9C was the smallest operational fighter plane the Navy had in the 1930's, and by the time six-footers like Harrigan, Trapnell, Miller, and Kivette had shoehorned themselves into its cockpit, there was hardly space to study the most artfully folded chart, much less the most elementary gadgetry of navigation. And although the F9C was a wonderful aerobatic plane, its general flying characteristics demanded the full attention of its pilot.

At this date the F9C's were equipped with radio homing gear which was supposed to be able to home on a radio signal from the airship. But it was a sometime thing; it was not until 1934 that a reliable homing system was developed. The F9C's radio sets were no more inspiring. Until these deficiencies were remedied it was dangerous for the planes to stray out of sight of the airship while operating at sea, except for brief moments.

For quite awhile Harrigan had pondered an appropriate insignia for the HTA Unit. During the *Los Angeles'* trapeze experiments the name "Belly Bumpers" caught on at Lakehurst, and the motto *Ventram Semper Impengentes*—those always bumping the belly—was suggested. But this lacked the combination of humor and dignity that he wanted. Lakehurst punsters hit upon the name "Little Oaks" for the HTA Unit by twisting the old expression into "Little Oaks From Great *Akrons* Grow." Others suggested a kangaroo or shark-and-pilot-fish motif. Min Miller suggested a stern view of a horse with half a dozen flies buzzing around it, but the airship men did not think it was at all appropriate—or funny.

Harrigan finally went to an art school in Philadelphia where a student drew up an insignia for him which became a classic among the colorful and imaginative Navy squadron insignia of the 1930's. It showed a burly and smiling acrobat in red tights and yellow shirt hanging by his knees from a trapeze, reaching out for a skinny fellow performer who is flying through the air with a worried look on his face. The insignia and its flavor stuck, and from that day to this the pilots of the airships' Heavier-Than-Air Units have been "The Men on the Flying Trapeze."

In the first week of November, Garland Fulton visited Lakehurst and made a 23-hour flight aboard the *Akron*. Also on board was Captain Ernest J. King of the Naval War College. King did not have any enthusiasm for the rigid airship, but he could not dismiss its potential as the only available instrument of very-long-range reconnaissance. He was especially impressed by the possibilities in the demonstrated airplane-carrying ability of the *Akron*. On this flight King was able to witness the first tests of the Trapnell-modified trapeze, which were highly successful.

The *Akron* had another distinguished visitor a few weeks later when Admiral Frank Schofield turned up at Lakehurst in the company of Admiral Moffett. Schofield had just been relieved as CinCUS by Admiral Daniel F. Sellers, and was in Washington preparing for retirement. Admiral Moffett could not resist inviting this bitter critic of the airship, his former Annapolis classmate, for a ride aboard the *Akron*.

After dinner, while the airship cruised down the New Jersey coast, the officers gathered in their smoking room and Schofield made some very critical remarks about airships. Wiley felt he was so junior that he had nothing to lose and took the Admiral's remarks as a challenge. Wiley raised a question about Schofield's caustic dispatch of March 1932, and soon everyone was in the argument. It appears that Admiral Moffett enjoyed the controversy and made a point of encouraging the airship men.[5] When the *Akron* landed the next day, Admiral Schofield had been exposed to every argument in the book which supported the airship's case; but it is doubtful if he had become a convert. In any case, as far as the airship was concerned, Schofield was a figure of the past. Daniel F. Sellers was the man the airship would have to face up to in the future.

In mid-December Dresel received an item of correspondence which is one of the most significant documents of the *Akron-Macon* epoch. It was a letter from Harrigan which enclosed a 42-page report on the HTA Unit's operations, progress, and projects.[6] It was more than a routine report, or even an unusually long one; it was a prospectus for the "lighter-than-air carrier."

The Harrigan Report summarized the history of hook-on development and described the technical aspects of the *Akron*'s airplane-handling facilities; it discussed hook-on technique, doctrine for training pilots to trapeze work, possible hazards during trapeze operations, and the need of an arrangement for rescuing pilots downed at sea. Attention was given to fire hazards and fire prevention inside the *Akron*'s airplane compartment, to cold-weather operations from the airship's hangar, and the HTA Unit's gunnery status. The most significant topics, however, were under the headings of "Scouting," "Communications," and "Future Projects."

There was nothing radically new in Harrigan's dissertation on scouting, but it elaborated in some detail upon his thesis of 1931. Once again the expression "lighter-than-air carrier" experienced wide usage, and the *Akron* was usually referred to, not as an airship, but as a "carrier." This portion of the report opened with a restatement of the 1931 thesis, that the mission of airplanes operating from a lighter-than-air carrier was to expand the scouting operations of the carrier, and that providing fighter protection was incidental. The airship's most important means of protection was to have her planes far out on her flanks and ahead of her, as pickets, where they would make the first contact with the enemy and warn the airship so it could turn away and remain unobserved. The possibility of the airship establishing contact with the enemy was considered highly undesirable.

Stress was placed upon lack of adequate radio equipment in the areas of communication and navigation. The difficulties experienced by the pilots in flying their F9C's, keeping the horizons under surveillance, checking on their fuel consumption and time in the air, and keeping track of their navigation were also emphasized. As a step toward resolving the navigation problems— which were at the heart of the scouting problem—the creation of a "Flight Control Officer" aboard the airship was again recommended. This officer would be sta-

tioned in the airship's navigation compartment and, like the present-day Combat Information Center's personnel, would maintain a plot on the planes' positions, do their navigating for them, and direct their courses by radio. This would not only simplify flying for the pilots, but would give the airship positive control over its planes and complete freedom in its own movements. The airship could correlate the navigation of its planes with its own, and, in the event a radical change in course was necessary, it could do so immediately and direct the planes to a new rendezvous instead of first having to wait until they came home to roost.

The Flight Control Officer clearly anticipated future developments, and of a type which transcended the *Akron* and *Macon;* but he did not become a reality until 1934, and even then he was an embryonic figure. The report noted that the Flight Control Officer's efficacy depended upon good radio communications, and especially good voice radio, over 200 to 250 miles. The F9C's could communicate with the airship over this distance under most circumstances by telegraphic key; but only under the most favorable atmospheric conditions could their radiotelephone sets be relied upon for more than 35 to 50 miles. None of the F9C's had their radio sets shielded from the interference created by their ignition systems; until this was done airplane scouting doctrine would have to be developed within visibility of the airship.

By way of future projects the report looked forward to more perches, improvement of servicing facilities for the planes inside the *Akron*'s hangar compartment, and development of a reliable radio homing device. An experimental installation of wing slots or flaps was desirable on one of the F9C's; by reducing the planes' landing speed, the airship's own speed could be reduced during recovery operations, thus effecting an economy in its fuel consumption.

A flight test of an F9C from the airship with its landing gear removed was anticipated. Wheel landing gear was unnecessary during trapeze operations and useless in over-water flying; its removal would reduce parasite drag and increase the F9C's performance. The weight of the landing gear could be replaced with an auxiliary belly fuel tank which would provide an appreciable increase in range and endurance; furthermore, the absence of undercarriage would make a forced landing at sea less hazardous to the pilot. As for ditching at sea, a pilot rescue system was under study by which the airship could lower a bosun's chair to a pilot in the water and hoist him aboard with the mooring winch in the airship's nose. Development of this system and practice in its use was urgent so that the hook-on pilots would have some assurance of being fished out of the water if they had to ditch. The F9C's had flotation gear and inflatable rubber rafts, and the pilots had life jackets, but this was not the same as being rescued. For the next two years the pilots would complain about the need of this simple accommodation; it was finally tested in 1934.

A further item of lifesaving gear proposed in the report was a combination parachute-boat harness. During the 1930's, Navy planes carried an inflatable rubber boat; but if a pilot had to leave his plane via parachute, he had to leave the boat behind. Harrigan proposed that a collapsible rubber life raft be integrated with the pilot's parachute harness, with a separate ripcord which would open the CO_2 bottle so the pilot could inflate the raft during descent, before he hit the water.

Harrigan finally developed this arrangement himself.[7] Just about every American pilot who flew in extensive over-water operations during World War II sat on the Harrigan parachute-boat pack, more than a few of them were delighted with its performance, and naval aviators are still sitting on the security of its principles today.

One of the more speculative projects in the report was a large service and utility plane for the airship. This idea was not new in 1932. Rosendahl mentioned the desirability of a plane to service the airship in 1929;[8] and the idea had been revived in 1931, when Harrigan explored the possibility of equipping a Bellanca "Airbus" with a skyhook and using it as a cargo and tanker plane.[9]

If the airship arrived at its base short on fuel and during bad weather which made a safe landing questionable, the tanker plane could shuttle between the ground and the trapeze and keep her supplied with fuel until a landing was practicable. Because of its size and weight the plane could not be swung into the hangar; it would hang on the trapeze and pump cargo fuel up to the airship. Other planes of this type could be used to ferry dry stores and personnel, permitting the airship to be provisioned and her personnel exchanged without the airship landing. The trapeze would have to be modified to include a hoist for handling stores, piping and hoses for fueling, and a ladder for personnel. By these means the airship could be serviced from any field which could accept the utility planes, or from aircraft carriers at sea. The idea of the service and utility plane

was revived in 1934; but it remained an interesting might-have-been.

In view of the fact that the HTA Unit had had only four months of intermittent experience with the *Akron* by December 1932, the Harrigan Report was comprehensive indeed. It was not exhaustive, but it is doubtful if it could have been at this early date. It was groping for equipment which did not have physical existence until 1934, and for modes of operation which did not become fully practicable until the realization of radar. Nevertheless, in spite of its sometimes nebulous character, if there was going to be a military future for the rigid airship during the 1930's, the Harrigan Report pointed the way.

It should not be imagined that Harrigan's was a lonely and unappreciated voice crying in a wilderness. The other pilots of the HTA Unit, too, immediately saw the *Akron* for what she was—the means of extending the range of their airplanes. Nor was this idea the monopoly of the hook-on pilots; by the end of 1932 this was also the thinking among some of the airship men.

What makes the report significant is that it went to the heart of the rigid airship's military future—assuming it was going to have any; and that two years later its essence became the operating doctrine of the *Macon*. More significant perhaps is that in the meantime it was virtually ignored.

One of Dresel's last acts as the *Akron*'s commanding officer was to forward Harrigan's report to the Bureau. Fulton received it with enthusiasm and remarked that "great credit is due this H/A unit for their zeal, and to them should go most credit for progress."[10] But when the report passed out of Fulton's hands to other Bureau divisions, it encountered only myopic resistance and indifference.

Most others conceded that it was a good report, and then pounced upon Harrigan's insistence that the primary mission of the hook-on planes was scouting. The F9C's were fighters, so how could they be used for scouting? The F9C's *were* fighters and they would have to remain fighters and be employed as such. It was forgotten that Marc Mitscher offered the F9C as an expedient. Even Mitscher himself forgot.

Lieutenant Commander Andrew C. McFall of the Flight Division thought the F9C's might extend the airship's vision somewhat, but not much; however, he thought the idea worth a trial. But Commander Harry B. Cecil of Plans insisted that the planes' primary mission should be protection of the airship. Lieutenant

One of the Consolidated N2Y-1 "running boats" is being lowered out of the
Akron's airplane hangar for a taxi trip to Cristobal, Canal Zone, 15 March 1933.

Commander Harold B. Sallada, also of Plans, expressed conviction to Mitscher that the planes were essentially fighter protection and that the F9C's would never get very far away from the airship. Mitscher agreed; he did not think the mission of the planes should be changed until experience proved the necessity. Mitscher dourly noted that "this thing"—the expression he reserved for the *Akron*—was not officially called an "LTA carrier," and added that he would prefer the airship as a "bomb carrier."[11] In spite of Plans' want of imagination and love of medieval hair splitting, the men on the flying trapeze continued to use their F9C's as scouting planes, because they were convinced of the efficacy of their own concept—and because they were given nothing else to fly.

When the *Akron*'s crew returned from holiday leave on 2 January 1933, they immediately turned-to to put the airship in flight readiness, to put a fresh press in their blues, and touch up the shine on their shoes for a change-in-command ceremony. At 1300, 3 January, Commander Frank McCord relieved Dresel, who had been ordered to the Goodyear-Zeppelin plant as prospective commanding officer of the *Macon*. On this date, too, most of the officers and men of the *Macon* Detail were detached from the *Akron* with orders to the new airship in Akron, Ohio.

Frank Carey McCord graduated from the Naval Academy in the class of 1911, and the next 14 years of his career were spent almost entirely at sea, mostly in destroyers. Although technically one of the third generation of airship officers, he went into lighter-than-air aeronautics in the spring of 1925 and qualified as a pilot of free balloons and blimps. After two years at Lakehurst he was ordered to the carrier *Langley*, and in January 1929 was transferred to the new *Saratoga*. But McCord was anxious to return to airships, and nine months later he was back at Lakehurst. For awhile he was the station's executive officer, but was soon assigned to the *Los Angeles*. He was her executive officer when he was ordered to the *Akron*.

Two years' duty with the *Langley* and *Saratoga* provided McCord with experience which was unique among airship men, and airship commanding officers in particular. He was the only one who had had an extended exposure to carrier aviation, and as navigator aboard the *Langley* and *Saratoga* his experience with fleet aviation was not of a pedestrian nature. McCord was not intellectually or emotionally wedded to the idea of the airship being something in itself, a sort of naval

panacea; for him it was simply a means to an end. It was easy for him to accept the idea of a "lighter-than-air carrier"; his acceptance is given evidence by the trend of operations under his tragically short command.

Under Dresel's benevolent command a bewildered and exhausted *Akron* had learned how to crawl; McCord was determined to see that she got up and walked. And he was a man in a hurry. Two hours after the change-in-command ceremony the *Akron* was weighed-off and had her fin lashed to the stern beam. At 1620 she was towed out of the hangar, and at 1719 was on her way to Florida. Shortly after she took off, Harrigan, Young, and Trapnell were in the air with two F9C's and an N2Y, and while the airship moved down the New Jersey coast its trapeze hooked the planes out of the sky and tucked them away in the hangar compartment. With the planes on board, the *Akron* slowed her engines to a 50-knot cruising speed and continued south for an inspection of mooring facilities which had a more pleasant climate than Lakehurst's.

The next afternoon the *Akron*'s massive shadow was gliding across thousands of upturned faces on the streets and countryside between Palm Beach and Miami. That evening she was swinging from the expeditionary mast at the Naval Aviation Reserve Base at Opa-locka, outside Miami. On the morning of the seventh she was refueled, her cells were topped off with 6,000 cubic feet of helium, and at 1355 she took off for Cuba. Early the next morning, while the *Akron* circled Guantanamo Bay, Harrigan operated a taxi service with the N2Y, ferrying Garland Fulton, Wiley, Scotty Peck, and a civil engineering officer from the Bureau to the ground so they could inspect the local real estate for a mooring site. The inspection ended in the afternoon, and when Harrigan wrapped up the day's taxi service he returned not only with the four officers, but with the front cockpit full of lobsters for the general mess.

The *Akron*'s return to Opa-locka and thence to Lakehurst was uneventful. The flight to Cuba was fruitful, at least for the immediate future. For several months there had been discussion in the Bureau of establishing a system of secondary airship facilities—mooring masts and their auxiliaries—to permit an expansion of operations. Admiral Moffett recommended the development of a railroad-tracked mooring circle on Fisherman's Point near Guantanamo; the project was executed, but no rigid airship ever rode its mooring circle.

On 18 January the *Akron* resumed her schedule of extended local flights to sea. Navigation problems were conducted, hook-on drill intensified, and the perch was given its first workout with the F9C's. It was first tested with an N2Y en route to Florida; now it proved satisfactory with the heavier fighters. And toward the end of the month the *Akron* began a program of assisting in the calibration of radio direction-finding stations along the East Coast.

During the last week of January the *Akron* flew two F9C's aboard and went out to sea on an overnight navigation problem. Nine officers from the Navy Department were on board to observe these operations. This flight proved to be more unusual than anticipated; and in view of McCord's decisive handling of the airship during this difficult moment and the popular criticism which was directed against him after 4 April, this flight has a singular significance.

Upon returning to Lakehurst, McCord was obliged by an order from the Navy Department to take the airship over Philadelphia because the citizens of that community were in a fevered fit to see the *Akron*. There was a storm moving in from the west, so after a quick sweep around the city McCord opened his throttles wide and ran for the barn. But he was too late. When the *Akron* arrived at Lakehurst the wind was up to from 10 to 12 knots, and the field was alive with 30-knot gusts. The ground crew was unable to get the airship under control, so McCord decided to meet the storm in the air. It was following the usual storm course out of the west, heading along the East Coast to spend itself at sea. So he laid a course to the north which would take the airship out of the storm's path and permit him to circle to westward, around behind it.

The airship faced a long, disagreeable flight; she had been in the air for 43 hours, so engine speeds were kept low in order to conserve fuel. She crept north during the rapidly darkening afternoon, up the Hudson Valley, just ahead of the storm. By sundown the *Akron* was over Lake Ontario in the vicinity of Rochester; but heavy rain drove McCord to seek better weather further west, over Lake Erie. From midnight to 0900 on the twenty-sixth, while tons of ice formed on her hull, the *Akron* probed her way through dense fog over the lake. Because airplanes never got off the ground in this kind of weather there was no danger of a collision with other aircraft. At 0935, in the vicinity of Cleveland, McCord swung the ice-covered *Akron* eastward and put her on a course along the commercial airway to Trenton.

The weather remained thick. In the radio room above the control car, Miller and Kivette were taking turns at the headphones, guiding the airship along the radio beam of the commercial airway. Four hours later, halfway across Pennsylvania, Lieutenant (junior grade) Wilfred Bushnell, who had relieved Peck as navigator, spied the town of Bellefonte through a break in the fog. This was his first visual fix in more than 12 hours. Thereafter, the fog began to break up into scattered cumulus, and the way was cleared to Lakehurst, where McCord brought the *Akron* to her mast just before sunset.[12] The observers from Washington had more of an airship experience than they had bargained for; they had witnessed a remarkable test of the airship and of airship command, and a performance by which both passed the test admirably.

For the *Akron*'s February operations McCord pressed for a second flight to Florida. He was impressed by the fact that the *Akron*'s Florida–Cuba flight had afforded the airship twice the operating hours she could have expected in Lakehurst's winter, and he wanted to exploit the promise of the Opa-locka facilities. But Garland Fulton, who was usually one up on the future, had a conference with McCord and Lakehurst's new commanding officer, Commander Fred T. Berry, and had him resubmit his request in terms of a March flight to Panama.[13] So the *Akron*'s February operations were local, and these were abbreviated by a two-week overhaul period and inclement weather; she got into the air only once for a 48-hour flight.

March, however, was a very active month. On the first she took three of her F9C's out to sea where the planes were drilled to speed up recovery operations with the trapeze. The best time obtained with three planes, from opening to closing of the hangar doors, was 15 minutes. This left something to be desired; the delays occurred in transferring the planes from the trapeze to the hangar trolleys, and in getting them clear of the trapeze so it could be swung out for the next plane. On 4 March the *Akron* put in an appearance over Washington, D.C., where, on the Capitol's steps, Franklin D. Roosevelt was taking an oath to the nation and telling a bewildered America that it had nothing to fear but fear itself. And a week later she was on her way to Panama.

Departure for Panama was planned for 8 March, but 60-knot gales kept the *Akron* locked in her hangar until the eleventh. And then takeoff was delayed by the oil in the stern beam's locomotive having frozen. But at 0249 she was undocked into a 18- to 25-knot cross-hangar wind, and at 0405 took off for the Canal Zone. Immediately after her takeoff, Harrigan and Larson flew a pair of N2Y's aboard. Eighteen hours later the *Akron* had her tail on the riding-out car at the Opa-locka mast, preparatory to jumping off for Panama. It would have been a simple matter for the *Akron* to have flown nonstop to Panama—even the *Los Angeles* was capable of this performance—but there was practical importance in this stopover. Opa-locka was looked forward to as a winter operating base for the *Akron*; it was desirable to give the crew experience with the field, and necessary for the field's personnel to have experience in handling the airship.

The flight was continued on the fourteenth—a routine operation similar to the Cuba flight. Fulton and two civil engineering officers from the Navy Department were on board, again to inspect mooring sites. The Navy had received a parcel of land on the Balboa end of the canal, and Admiral Moffett wanted to use part of it for a mooring base. So, while the *Akron* cruised back and forth over the Canal Zone, Harrigan and Larson ferried the inspecting party to the ground. On their return flights they brought with them officers from Coco Solo who wanted to see the *Akron* firsthand. There was apparently only curious brass and no lobsters in the Canal Zone.

En route back to Lakehurst the *Akron* spent six days at Opa-locka, taking advantage of the fine weather to make several local flights during which her gun crews were exercised at camera-gun practice, using the N2Y's as targets. On the twenty-second she took departure for grim New Jersey. North of Cape Hatteras winter flight gear quickly became the uniform of the day, and the *Akron* fell in with a blinding snowstorm which accompanied her all the way to Lakehurst. Only one more flight was made in March, a 23-hour operation at sea in which a navigation problem was run, and the F9C's were flown in radio homing drills which used their inadequate homing gear and the airship's RDF set. The results of the homing tests were inconclusive.

When McCord summarized the *Akron*'s operations for 1933's first quarter, he emphasized the value of her two southern flights and the desirability of Opa-locka as a winter operating base. It would also provide the airship with a base at the other end of the Eastern Seaboard from which airship patrols could cover the Panama Canal's Caribbean approaches. He proposed another Florida flight in mid-April with a week's operations at Opa-locka; but the operating schedule which he outlined for May and June was vague.

This vagueness was not unusual; it reflected a longstanding practice. Because of the airship's experimental status, quarterly schedules were usually framed in elastic terms. Now the Bureau took exception.[14] Airships had reached a point where they should operate with specific objects in view—scouting doctrine for its planes, perfection of internal organization in general quarters conditions, and casualty control. The trend of the *Akron*'s operations had been in this direction since June 1932; but from now on the pace was to be accelerated. In short, the *Akron*'s necessary breather was over; she now faced a period of exacting training and drilling on an operational basis, directed toward developing her success with the Fleet.

The *Akron*'s second nine months had been everything that her first nine should have been. There was a demonstrated conviction that the airship had to be "sold" to the Navy, and not an amorphous "public opinion"; and that this could be achieved only by means of military flights, not publicity flights, much less by rhetorical flights. This had been a period of hard work; most of the *Akron*'s water-recovery system was rejuvenated by the new Mark IV units, her trapeze was re-engineered, and installation of the perch doubled her plane-handling ability. Two experimental metal, three-bladed propellers were in use by 1933 and promised to become standard equipment; RDF gear was installed on board, and deficiencies in her planes' radio systems were evaluated and steps taken to remedy them. The airship's machine gun armament was unsatisfactory, but camera guns had been obtained, the crew had been drilled with them, and the films were available for evaluation. Most important, the *Akron* had received her full complement of planes and pilots, and exploratory efforts were made toward fusing airship and airplanes into an effective instrument of very-long-range sea reconnaissance.

Even after 18 months, more time was necessary for working out airship-airplane search doctrine, and especially the material improvement of communications gear. Nevertheless, by the spring of 1933, the *Akron* had assumed the appearance of a modern military airship, and held the promise of becoming a "lighter-than-air carrier."

But on 30 March, as Frank McCord sat at his desk in the Lakehurst air station scheduling the *Akron*'s operations for the second quarter of 1933, he, Admiral Moffett, 71 other persons, and the *Akron,* had less than five days remaining to them.

CHAPTER SIX

The Beginning of the End

On the evening of 3 April 1933, the USS *Akron* left her Lakehurst base and flew out to sea on a routine training mission. The *Akron* and most of the men on board her were never seen again. Among the 73 persons lost with the airship was Rear Admiral Moffett. In loss of life and property, the *Akron*'s crash was the greatest disaster aeronautics had experienced, and it had a stunning effect upon the world of 1933.

The *Akron* disaster was more than a collection of black newspaper banners, sensational headlines, and tragic statistics; it was the crippling blow to the Navy's development of the rigid airship. In a single sweep, one-half of the 1926 airship program and almost one-third of the Navy's experienced airship operating personnel were wiped out. This was in addition to the great loss of Admiral Moffett to naval aviation and the Navy in general. The shock upon the public, Congress, and the Navy seriously undermined confidence in the rigid airship's future; and in a material and psychological sense, it seriously complicated the operations of the *Macon*. A few men sensed it in 1933, but we know in retrospect that the *Akron* disaster marks the beginning of the end of the ZRS4&5 epoch, and of the rigid airship era of naval aviation.

The morning of 3 April crept in from the Atlantic under a lead-colored sky, and throughout the morning the ceiling proceeded to lower. In Lakehurst's Hangar No. 1, the *Akron*'s crew was preparing her for an evening takeoff. She was scheduled for an extended flight to Newport, Rhode Island, and other points on the New England shore, to assist in the calibration of RDF stations.

At 1100 the phone rang in McCord's office; it was Admiral Moffett, who was expected for the flight. While McCord spoke with the Admiral, Wiley phoned the *Akron*'s aerologist for an estimate of the weather

and the probability of making the flight. Lieutenant Herbert M. Wescoat told him that it would be possible to take the *Akron* out of the hangar at sunset, when the wind should be down; but he doubted if visibility over Newport on the fourth would be suitable for calibrating operations. This was of no immediate importance. A two- or three-day flight was planned, and if visibility was not good on the fourth, it might be by the next day; in the meantime the airship had a number of training missions and engineering tests to execute. Wiley passed the word to McCord, who told the Admiral, and Moffett said that he would be at Lakehurst for takeoff.[1]

In the station's aerology office, Wescoat and Lieutenant Frederick Dartsch, the station's assistant aerology officer, were discussing their weather maps. The 1000 report from the U.S. Weather Bureau had recently come over the teletype, and they had just finished charting its data. Wescoat anticipated eventual clearing, but Dartsch interpreted showers. Wescoat granted the possibility, and remarked that if they occurred they would probably be thunder showers. Neither saw an unusual threat in the data.[2]

Within the hour McCord and Wiley conferred with Wescoat, and after examining the disposition of the isobars on the maps, decision was made for the flight. McCord designated 1800 as the hour for general assembly, and told Wiley to have three of the F9C's ready for a hook-on drill immediately after takeoff. He also wanted an N2Y flown aboard for a running boat.

During the afternoon, the day's relatively high winds moderated enough so that Trapnell could take out the ZMC2 for a training flight. But visibility— the range of horizontal vision—continued to deteriorate, and the ceiling fell lower. Late in the afternoon, Harrigan returned to Lakehurst from Washington in an F9C and the ceiling had kept him on the tree tops all the way. At

1600 McCord and Wiley again visited the aerology office, to inspect the weather data which came over the teletype at 1600. This did not seem to hold any menace; however, McCord noted the ceiling and told Wiley to cancel the hook-on drill. But, weather permitting, he still wanted an N2Y ready to fly aboard.

At 1830 the mooring mast and stern beam moved the *Akron* into the failing light on the field. In the darkness overhead the ceiling hung at 300 feet, and fog was rapidly forming. Trapnell was designated to fly the N2Y aboard, and he told McCord that there were probably breaks in the fog through which he could find his way up to the airship after her takoff. But McCord wanted him to wait until the *Akron* had ascended through the fog and its thickness could be determined. If it was unsafe for the plane, he told Trapnell to be on stand-by to meet the *Akron* off the New Jersey coast in the morning.

The Akron was cast off from the mast at 1928, and within a minute her great bulk had dissolved into the murk over the field. She climbed out of the fog at 1,500 feet, where her engine telegraphs jangled six of her engines to standard speed, and she climbed to a 2,000-foot flying altitude. McCord radioed Lakehurst to order Trapnell not to attempt takeoff, and reported that he was flying to the Delaware Capes via Philadelphia, and then south along the coast. It was only a three-hour flight from Lakehurst to Newport, but the area between was blanketed by fog, and the *Akron* was not due at Newport until morning. McCord evidently planned to circle south of the known fog area and cruise along the coast until morning, by which time the fog might possibly have dissipated.

Aboard the airship, in addition to her regular complement, were Admiral Moffett, Commander Fred T. Berry, Lakehurst's commanding officer, and Commander Harry B. Cecil, who was acting as the Admiral's aide. And the Admiral had a guest with him, Lieutenant Colonel Alfred F. Masury of the U.S. Army Reserve. In civilian life Masury was vice-president of the Mack Truck Company; he had flown as a passenger aboard the *Graf Zeppelin* and was among those men interested in the commercial future of the rigid airship.

The *Akron* was over Philadelphia by 2010, and McCord told Lieutenant (junior grade) Cyrus Clendening, officer of the deck, to follow the Delaware River for about 20 minutes. While passing Wilmington, Delaware, sharp flashes of lightning were observed in the south. The *Akron*'s two idle engines were started, she was

brought up to eight-engine standard speed, and course was changed to eastward across southern New Jersey. Wiley remarked that they might find better weather by flying west and getting on the safe semicircle of the storm. But McCord had seen lightning in the west.

Lightning began to fill the southern sky, and seemed to be moving closer. The *Akron* edged away from it with alternating 15-degree course changes. Near Vineland, New Jersey, McCord ordered the course changed to approximately northeast, directly away from the lightning. As a precaution against attracting lightning, altitude was reduced to 1,500 feet, where the *Akron*'s mass skimmed the lower cloud layer. Now the *Akron* was moving back over the fog-covered area along the coast, and shortly after leaving Vineland the ground became obscured.

The weather had taken a radical and unexpected change. Unknown to the men on board the *Akron,* they were flying ahead of one of the most violent stormfronts to sweep the North Atlantic States in ten years. It would soon envelop them.

As the *Akron* sped northeastward at an estimated ground speed of 70 knots, lightning became more extensive and was observed with increasing frequency in the west. At about 2145, in what was calculated to be the vicinity of the seaside resort town of Asbury Park, the fog was beginning to rise above the airship's 1,500-foot flying altitude, so it was increased to 1,600 feet. The *Akron* was between a lower cloud layer at 1,500 feet and an upper layer at 6,000 feet; the latter acted as a diffusion screen for the lightning, making it impossible to determine its source and direction. McCord and Wiley frequently exchanged positions, moving from one side of the bridge to the other, in hopes of obtaining fresh impressions of the lightning's direction. The question which frequently passed between them was, "Was that flash on your side?"

At about 2200, course was changed to 83 degrees true,[3] almost due east, and a few minutes later the *Akron* crossed the coast to the sea. Lightning seemed to surround the airship; efforts to obtain weather information by radio were frustrated by intense static. McCord had recently spoken with Wescoat; now he sent Wiley up to the aerology office to examine the new weather map. The aerology office was near the radio room, above the control car. Wescoat told Wiley that he had received only two-thirds of the data broadcast on the 2000 weather report. Wiley noticed that the map did not appear to have its usual number of symbols; but he could see a low pressure area centered upon Washington, D.C., and took it to be the storm's center.

Among the pertinent data evidently missing from Wescoat's map was the wind's direction and force in the New Jersey area.

When Wiley returned to the bridge, McCord told him that he intended to continue eastward and ride out the storm at sea. He understood McCord's plan was to fly east, across what seemed to be the storm's path, then turn southeastward and circle around behind it. But the weather became even more wild; the lightning surrounding the *Akron* appeared to be closing in on her, and it seemed as if she were flying directly into the storm's center. Thus at 2300 McCord ordered the course changed to 268 degrees, almost due west, and headed back toward the coast.

Shortly before 2400 a row of lights was observed through the fog below, which were taken to be the lights of a coastal town's boardwalk. This disturbed Lieutenant Commander Harold E. MacLellan, the *Akron*'s navigator: the airship had arrived at the coast much sooner than he expected, which indicated that her speed over the surface was boosted by a tail wind. He told Wiley that he had been assuming a southeast wind of light velocity; but now he was obliged to estimate a northeast wind of 20 to 25 mph.

The ground had been obscured since Vineland, about two hours before, which made it almost impossible to calculate the airship's drift, track and ground speed. The 1600 weather data, which the *Akron* had on board at departure, indicated south and southeast winds of from 7 to 10 mph in the New Jersey area. MacLellan's last drift angle south of Philadelphia corresponded to this information. But the data assembled in the Weather Bureau at 2000 and broadcast between 2005 and 2130 indicated a wind shift created by the storm, and showed winds of from 12 to 14 mph in eastern New Jersey. The *Akron* very evidently had not received this information, and MacLellan had not reckoned with a wind shift in the storm's path.

According to MacLellan's information, the *Akron* should have had a light to moderate tail wind during the leg of her flight from Vineland to what was thought to be the vicinity of Asbury Park. But in fact she was flying into a relatively strong head wind. Thus when she crossed the coast at about 2200 she was not near Asbury Park, but at some point 30 to 35 miles south, near Barnegat. Now, with the shore dimly visible below, MacLellan set about getting a drift angle. But then the airship's course was changed to 120 degrees, about southeast, and back to sea. If MacLellan succeeded in obtaining a drift angle and discovering the error in his dead reckoning, it would make no difference during the next half hour. A few minutes later men on duty at the Coast Guard station at Barnegat Inlet observed the airship flying out to sea. It was the last time anyone ashore ever saw the *Akron*.

After leaving the coast the *Akron* was frequently submerged in the fog tops. Lightning continued to fill the sky, and bursts of heavy rain became more frequent. For awhile the air was strangely smooth, but at 0015 it became extremely turbulent, and the elevator man reported that the airship was falling rapidly. Afraid that he had lost control of his wheel, Wiley rushed to assist him. The elevator man had the situation well in hand, but the altitude was 1,100 feet, and the *Akron* was still falling.

McCord rang up full speed on the engines and told Wiley to dump ballast. He pulled open the toggles on the storage ballast amidships, but these bags emptied rather slowly and there was no immediate effect. The *Akron* was still falling, and in a nose-down attitude, so he pulled the releases on the forward emergency ballast at frame 187. Immediately, these bags were turned inside-out, discharging 1,600 pounds of water, and the *Akron*'s nose began to come up. She leveled out at 700 feet, and began to rise rapidly. The elevator man was ordered to reduce the rate of climb, and at 1,300 feet the airship was under good control and was gradually returned to her cruising altitude at 1,600 feet. But now the air became even more violent, and the *Akron* was drawn into her second and last descent.

Caught in a descending current of air, the *Akron* was carried downward again. The sequence of events during those last few minutes was rapid. Sensing a moment of danger, Wiley sent five long signals out of the howlers of the 18 telephones located throughout the airship, which was the signal for "landing stations." Curiously, the *Akron* had no regular general alarm signal; but in the air over the sea, "landing stations" sufficed for an emergency signal. Or so it might seem.

In response to "landing stations," Lieutenant George Calnan, who had been roaming the hull structure on a round of inspection, appeared on the bridge and took his station at the ballast controls. Wiley told Calnan of the ballast he had dropped, and returned to his station by the man handling the rudder. Lieutenant Richard F. Cross, the engineering officer, took his station at the engine telegraphs. Meanwhile, the *Akron* was falling through the fog at about 14 feet per second.

During her first descent, the *Akron* was in a diving attitude; now she was falling with her nose slightly up. More elevator was applied to increase her climbing attitude; as a result, her tail went down further and the *Akron*'s inclination increased. And it began to increase alarmingly, varying between 12 and 25 degrees.[4]

Wiley heard Calnan call out "800 feet!" and a few seconds later a gust of terrific force shook the *Akron*. The rudder man reported that there was no response from his wheel, and Wiley noticed that the cable to the lower rudder had been carried away. Wiley rushed aft to the officer of the deck's desk to get a flashlight. The airship seemed to be leveling out now, but the air was full of unusually jerky gusts and bumps. Returning to the controls, he quickly unclutched the lower rudder and told the helmsman to see if he could steer with the upper rudder. There was no response from it, either.

The airship's angle began to increase alarmingly. Then the upper rudder's control cable carried away. The air became more violent. As the *Akron* climbed to a 45-degree angle, Wiley had to cling to a girder in order to remain on his feet. The carrying away of the rudder cables suggested to him that the *Akron* had broken in two. Perhaps with the *Shenandoah*'s experience in mind, he imagined that the 785-foot-long *Akron* had jackknifed, and was now plunging toward the sea with her nose and tail pointed skyward. He braced himself for the impact of the after section hitting the sea. It was a sensation which never came.

The fact is, the *Akron* was already in the sea. The unusually violent "gust" which shook the airship so severely and carried away the lower rudder's controls was not a gust. It was the impact of the *Akron*'s lower fin striking the sea. And the strange gusty and bumpy air which Wiley felt was the action of the sea pouring into the fin and lashing at the airship's after-hull areas, dragging her stern into the ocean. The *Akron*'s eight engines labored to make her airborne again, but they could not prevail against the submerged fin's sea-anchor effect; they could only drag her floundering through the water and pull her nose up in a grotesque attitude—where the *Akron* stalled and surrendered to the sea.

Clinging to his girder, Wiley saw McCord and Cross hurriedly conferring; the cables between the telegraphs and the engines had carried away. The *Akron* continued to rise sharply by the nose—and then began to fall rapidly. Someone called out "300 feet!" Then she dropped through the bottom of the fog. Upon sighting the waves, Wiley shouted, "Stand-by for crash!" And the control car hit the sea.

While the *Akron* was in her final moments, the German motorship *Phoebus* was creeping through patches of fog and curtains of rain on the surface. On the tanker's bridge, Captain Karl Dalldorf and his second mate strained their eyes against the poor visibility. At 0023, Dalldorf saw a bright, flickering light in the western sky, then a second and a third. The lights were almost in a straight line and seemed to be pitched at 45 degrees to the horizon, and were falling toward the sea. Ten degrees above the horizon they vanished, and three minutes later reappeared, blinking on the water.[5]

The lights at first mystified them; but now Dalldorf assumed it was an airplane crash. He swung the ship to starboard, rang up full speed on the engines, and ordered the crew to man the lifeboats. By 0048 the *Phoebus* was maintaining way in a sea littered with wreckage; the air was oppressive with gasoline fumes. There was no sign of the airship floating on the surface.

While the *Phoebus* was getting away her first boat at 0055, a man was seen clinging to a piece of wreckage; a line was thrown to him and he was hauled on board. It was Wiley. The boat found three more of the *Akron*'s crew hanging onto a fuel tank, and took them aboard. These were Robert W. Copeland, chief radioman, Richard E. Deal, boatswain's mate second class, and Moody E. Erwin, aviation metalsmith second class. All were suffering from shock, exposure, and having swallowed gasoline and sea water. Copeland never recovered consciousness and died on board the *Phoebus*. The remaining three were the *Akron*'s only survivors.

Dalldorf had a second boat away at 0110. He was still under the impression that an airplane had crashed. In view of the rescue of four men, and that his boats reported that four or five others had slipped beneath the waves before they could reach them, it is surprising that at this point he did not recall his boats from the wild night. It was a rare airplane in the early 1930's which carried more than a dozen persons.

It was not until half an hour later, when Wiley recovered consciousness, that Dalldorf discovered that the world's largest airship with 76 men on board had crashed. A few minutes later the *Phoebus*' radio flashed the news to the world. The tanker's boats continued to search the gale-swept sea until 0600, when the Coast Guard cutter *Tucker* arrived on the scene. After the *Akron*'s survivors were transferred to the *Tucker,* the *Phoebus* resumed her voyage to Tampico.

The first effect of the *Akron*'s disaster upon America

GORDON S. WILEY

The German motorship Phoebus *picked up the Akron's survivors—Wiley, Erwin, Deal, and Copeland—and flashed the news to the world that the huge airship had crashed with 76 men on board. Copeland died on board the* Phoebus.

and the world was stunned disbelief. The world has long since become jaded to six or seven dozen persons falling out of the sky in multimillion-dollar aircraft, but in 1933 this was a wholly new and peculiarly awesome phenomenon. And the crash could not have occurred at a worse moment. On the morning of 4 April the nation was in the very depths of the depression. The banks had been closed, political and financial circles were horrified by rumors that the United States might go off the gold standard, unemployment estimates ranged from 12 to 16 millions, while overseas Hitler had recently become chancellor of Germany and was already making the world uneasy. The *Akron* disaster had the psychological value of a knockout punch.

At the Lakehurst Air Station, the offices were crowded with the dazed wives of the *Akron*'s men, who could not believe that they were widows. In Washington, in the Bureau of Aeronautics, it was difficult to believe that Admiral Moffett had been so suddenly removed from the controls of naval aviation. In Akron, Ohio, Dr. Arnstein and others of Goodyear-Zeppelin were speechless with disbelief; and the Navy men who were preparing the *Macon* for her trials pondered the fate of their friends lost with the *Akron,* and their own luck. Many of the *Macon*'s officers and men had swapped duty with men lost with the *Akron,* simply because they wanted the newer airship, or because they knew the *Macon* would be based on the West Coast. Then the *Akron*'s tragedy was compounded when the blimp J-3 crashed at sea off Beach Haven, New Jersey, while searching for *Akron* survivors. Two more lives were added to the *Akron*'s toll.

The nation as a whole was dumbfounded by the disaster, but within 24 hours the gentlemen on Capitol Hill were able to find their voices. An immediate cry went up for an investigation of the crash, and the congressmen fell to quarreling among themselves about who should do the investigating. The Committee on Naval Affairs was determined upon an investigation—and rightly so—but congressmen not of the committee were suspicious of their fellows who were associated with the Navy, and shrilled that it would be a "whitewash." They wanted an "unbiased" investigation. The matter was further complicated by factions in the House and Senate, each determined upon running its own investigation.

While the congressmen wrangled, the press had a field day. All the airship crashes of the previous 30 years were reviewed, and all the old skeletons in the

Akron's closet were hauled out for a noisy rattling. There was Kassay's "sabotage," the "overweight," the 1932 investigation of her "military worthlessness," and all the rumors that the *Akron* was "unsafe." The tail smashing of February 1932 was rehashed, and the macabre details of the Camp Kearny tragedy were revived. It was recalled that in the summer of 1912 a small airship, also named the *Akron* and also built by Goodyear, had exploded and crashed at sea off Atlantic City, in approximately the same area as did the Navy's *Akron* in 1933. This hodge-podge of highly-colored facts was squeezed together into what the newswriters called "the *Akron* jinx."

The editorial pages were wringing wet with tears for the 73 dead "heroes of the *Akron*." Then the editorial writers hurried on to wring their hands over the taxpayers' dollars lost with the airship. The fact that the "heroes of the *Akron*" left behind five dozen widows, many with children, and that the Economy Act of March 1933 had slashed service death benefits and widows' pensions, was ignored. That had nothing to do with "heroism," and to mention it would have been trespassing in the sacred realm of the taxpayers' dollars.

On Monday, 10 April, the congressmen and senators succeeded in compromising their jealousies and decided upon a joint investigation by a special committee. It would probe not only the *Akron*'s loss, but *all* airship crashes. On this same day a naval court of inquiry appointed to determine the causes of the *Akron*'s crash convened at Lakehurst.[6]

During the 11 days in which the court met between 10 April and 1 May, a determined effort was made to establish the causes of the crash. The structural integrity and general airworthiness of the *Akron* were examined in great detail, the circumstances of the weather and the wisdom of making the flight were studied, and the final events which led to the *Akron*'s destruction were reconstructed. The only condition which the court did not adequately reconstruct was the *Akron*'s navigation. But here it was in a large sense stopped even before it convened, for one reason: too few survivors. Nevertheless, with regard to navigation there occurred a noteworthy oversight.

There were five primary and six secondary figures in the *Akron*'s crash. In order of importance relative to the information which each could have provided, they were McCord, the commanding officer; MacLellan, the navigator; Wescoat, the aerologist; Clendening, officer of the deck from 2000 to 2400; and Lieutenant (junior

GORDON S. WILEY

In loss of life and property, the Akron's crash was aeronautics'
greatest disaster up to 1933. The only survivors were Lieutenant
Commander Herbert V. Wiley, foreground; Moody Erwin, aviation metalsmith
2nd class, left; Richard E. Deal, boatswain's mate 2nd class, right.

grade) Morgan Redfield, officer of the deck from 0000 to 0030. These were the persons immediately concerned with the airship's navigation. Secondly, there were Wiley, the executive officer; Calnan, the first lieutenant; Cross, the engineering officer; Joseph J. Zimkus, boatswain's mate first class, and Tony F. Swidersky, coxswain, who were handling the elevators; and a third enlisted man who was handling the rudder. Wiley had been in the control car during the whole flight, and all these secondary figures were on the bridge during the Akron's final descent. Of these 11 persons, Wiley was the only survivor.

As executive officer and second in command, it might be supposed that Wiley should have been closely associated with the airship's navigation. This is not necessarily true. In the navigation of a Navy ship, the executive officer can be almost a supernumerary. In problems of navigation the commanding officer confers directly with his navigator, and for weather information directly with his aerologist. He may in turn discuss these problems with his executive officer, or he may not. This may explain Wiley's vagueness on many salient points.

On the other hand, the other survivors, Erwin and Deal, had nothing to do with navigation and were not in the control car at the time of the crash. Their presence in the port keel's passageway during the crash provided a limited, but important, amount of information on the condition of the Akron's main structure. But they could not see outside the airship, and were unable to correlate events inside with what they might have, under other conditions, been able to see outside.

On the court's first day two things stand out in Wiley's testimony: his belief that the Akron had been in the vicinity of Asbury Park; and that she must have experienced a major structural failure and broken in half in the air.

The error in the Akron's navigation, and its probable causes, have been observed. On this first day it is understandable why Wiley assumed that the airship had taken her 2200 departure from the coast near Asbury Park. But he was not sure. The track which he reconstructed for the court holds erasures which illustrate his uncertainty as to the Akron's exact whereabouts.[7] His most significant erasure shows the Akron heading out to sea at 2200 from a point four miles south of Asbury Park, and returning to the coast at 2400 at a point about ten miles south of Asbury Park. Here he must have realized that he was in error, because he did not continue his construction to the point at sea where the Akron crashed at 0030. If he had, it would have shown the position of the crash at a point due east of Toms River, and this contradicted his belief that the Akron crashed due east of Barnegat Inlet. So he reconstructed the track accordingly; but even here he was in error.

In later sessions, evidence was introduced that the Akron was seen over Barnegat Inlet's Coast Guard Station at 2400, and that her wreckage was discovered at a position about 31 miles southeast of Barnegat. This contradicted Wiley's track with a discrepancy of at least 20 miles, and should have opened the Akron's navigation to intensive study. But it was overlooked by the court, and by Wiley. Indeed, on 22 May, giving testimony to the congressional committee, Wiley was still convinced that the Akron had been near Asbury Park at 2400 and had crashed off Barnegat. This error may well have been an important factor in creating a false environment relative to the weather of 3–4 April, which led to the Akron's destruction.

Wiley's testimony of the first day corresponded to his report to the Secretary of the Navy[8] and statements to the press.[9] He was by no means certain, but was of the feeling that the Akron, like the Shenandoah, must have broken up in the air. But when questioned in detail on the character of the "gust" which shook the airship so severely, he hesitated, became vague, and somewhat confused and contradictory. But it was not Wiley who was contradictory; it was a case of the "gust" contradicting his past experience.

On the court's second day he changed his testimony. He was now convinced that the "gust" was in fact the impact of the Akron's lower fin striking the sea, and he based his change of opinion upon several observations:

1. The shock was too sudden and short to have been a gust. [He later compared this to running along with a rope dragging on the ground, and having someone suddenly step on it.]
2. There was no sudden wind through the control car's windows, which usually accompanies a gust.
3. Immediately after the "gust," the lower rudder's control cable carried away.
4. Even before the lower rudder's controls carried away, the helmsman received no response from either of the rudders—which would be the case if the airship was held at her stern by the sea.
5. Erwin and Deal, who had been inside the main structure, were unshakable in their conviction that the main hull structure was intact until the airship hit the sea, and the lights went out.
6. Deal had heard Chief Petty Officer Carl Dean pass

the word "all hands forward" at the moment the *Akron* began her steep inclination; perhaps Dean realized she had her tail in the sea, perhaps he even saw it.

7. Although anticipated, the shock of the airship's tail hitting the sea never came.

8. Finally, when the control car hit the sea, the airship had no forward motion over the water.[10]

Wiley's testimony was confirmed a few days later by evidence from the bottom of the sea. On 18 April the fishing trawler *Olympia* accidentally found the *Akron*'s wreck, when her trawls fouled in the wreckage. The *Akron* was down in 105 feet of water about 30 miles due east of Little Egg Inlet. Divers from the submarine rescue vessel USS *Falcon* were sent down with explicit instructions to determine if any major portions of the *Akron*'s main structure were missing, but not to enter the wreck; the tangle of girders and wires was too great a hazard to their air hoses.

The divers found the wreckage of one piece, so far as the main hull structure was concerned; but it was badly mangled by the sea. The *Akron* was 132.9 feet in diameter; on the ocean floor her wreckage stood barely 25 feet high. The forward section of the control car was found about 100 feet away from the main wreckage; but the only major piece of the *Akron* which had become separated from her main structure was, significantly, the lower fin. It was found about 510 feet behind and to the side of the main wreckage. And this consisted of the fixed, vertical stabilizer only; the fin's movable surface, the rudder, was nowhere to be found.

The fin was hoisted aboard the *Falcon,* where it was discovered that it had not experienced any severe damage. Its leading edge was in reasonably good condition; damage was confined to the after portion of its underside. This suggested that the trailing edge and rudder struck the water first, and it was calculated that the *Akron* was flying about 25 degrees up by the nose when she dragged her fin in the sea. The fact that the rudder could not be found supported this theory.

The most unusual aspect of the information from the *Falcon* was that which indicated that the *Akron*'s lower fin was not immediately torn off by its impact with the sea. Along the hard ocean bottom between the fin's position and the main wreck the divers found deep ridges and ruts which indicated that the main wreck had shifted away from the fin. When the wreck came to rest on the ocean floor the fin was evidently still attached to the hull, however tenuously, and only the shifting wrenched it loose. The disposition of the wreckage indicates that the main wreck pivoted about 40 degrees on its midpoint; the arc made by the bow dragged loose the control car section, and the arc made by the stern dragged off the lower fin.[11]

These findings suggest the *Akron*'s ground speed could not have been very great when the fin hit the sea. The wind's direction and force within this storm between 0020–0030, and at this position at sea, is impossible to know; but if the *Akron* did encounter a sudden head wind of from 40 to 50 knots, she would have been moving at no more than from 10 to 20 knots. Also suggested is that the airship was at the point of pulling out of her descent. Perhaps if she had been only 100 feet higher the newspaper banners of 4 April would have been more concerned with the legalization of 3.2 beer than the circumstances of the USS *Akron*. And the history of the rigid airship in the U.S. Navy might have been somewhat different.

The *Akron* had literally flown into the sea. The how and why of the matter is less easily explained than determining that she did. The *Akron* must have been flying at an altitude considerably lower than the men in the control car supposed. Wiley said the second descent began at 1,600 feet, and cites subsequent altitudes of 800 and 300 feet. But he obtained this information through the eyes of others; at no time did he see the altimeter. But no matter, there is a question if the altimeter was correct.

An altimeter is simply an aneroid barometer geared to read in hundreds of feet instead of inches of barometric pressure. As an aircraft rises above the earth, atmospheric pressure decreases and the altimeter indicates altitude according to the pressure changes. Under certain conditions of weather, however, an altimeter will give a false reading. An atmospheric "low" moving into an area, bringing with it a 0.1″ change in pressure, will make an altimeter indicate 100 feet of "altitude," even though the aircraft is on the ground and locked inside its hangar.

When the *Akron* left Lakehurst at 1728, the barometer was 29.7″. The atmospheric low, or "storm center," shown on the 2000 weather map was 29.5″. The differential of 0.2″ represents 200 feet on an altimeter. By 0030 part of this low pressure area was northeast of Atlantic City and the *Akron* was flying in it. The basic setting on her altimeter was now changed by 0.2″, making it read 200 feet "high." As she flew deeper into the storm this differential may have become as much as 0.25″. Compounding this, there is a question of altime-

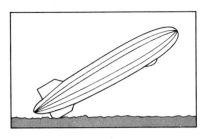

Wiley: "It [the angle of inclination] got gradually larger and larger, and before the after controls of the [lower] rudder carried away. At that time [of the shock] it must have been 20 degrees or perhaps more—20 or 25 degrees—up by the bow . . . the lower rudder control had carried away. . . . The feeling was like you were pulling a line [along the ground] and running with it, and someone stepped on it momentarily."

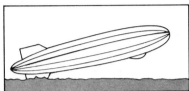

Wiley: "The angle immediately after this shock was somewhat less—the shock that I think was the stern hitting the water—because I walked back to the officer of the deck's desk in the control car to get a flashlight to unclutch the rudder . . . and it was not difficult for me to walk back there."

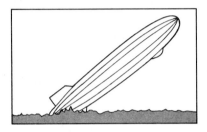

Wiley: "After that it was gusty and bumpy . . . my other rudder control carried away at this time. . . . The noise made by the sheaves carrying away in the ship indicated . . . the ship's structure had broken someplace . . . the angle up by the bow increased. After the second rudder control broke, the angle was large. . . . I was waiting for the shock of the stern hitting the water, but it never came."

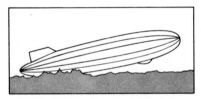

Wiley: "I inquired the altitude and looked out my window. I could hear structure breaking in the ship. The answer to my inquiry [was] '300 feet.' I think it was exactly at that moment we descended through the ceiling. I sighted the waves and sang out, 'Stand by for a crash!' "

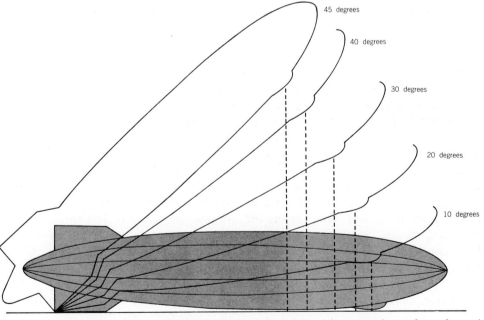

The Akron at various angles of inclination, showing the height of her control car above the surface with the trailing edge of her lower rudder touching the surface. At an angle of 10° the control car would have been about 70 feet above the surface; at 20°, about 160 feet; at 30°, about 250 feet; at 40°, about 330 feet; at 45°, about 365 feet. It appears that a margin of only 50 to 100 feet of altitude would have spared the Akron the disaster at the end of her second descent.

ter lag during her descent, but it is doubtful if this was very great.

In a very acute study of the *Akron*'s crash, Rosendahl questioned the "rapid rise" she experienced between 700 and 1,300 feet after her first descent. Was all of this altitude, or was some of it due to the airship passing into an area of unusually low pressure in the storm's center? This can only be conjectured; but without consideration of a false reading on the altimeter, it is virtually impossible to understand the *Akron*'s low altitude, unless the men in the control car were unconscious of the reading on the altimeter, and this seems unlikely. Flying aircraft into the surface because of a false-reading altimeter was not without precedent. Nor is it a novelty even today.

Thus when Wiley heard Calnan call out "800 feet!" the *Akron*'s control car was probably about 500 or 600 feet above the surface. A few seconds later the "gust" shook the airship. With the 785-foot-long *Akron* inclined 30 degrees and her lower fin's trailing edge touching the ground, the control car would be 350 feet above the surface. And with a 0.25" error in the altimeter, the indicated altitude would be 600 feet. This is the only logical explanation of what brought the *Akron* so low. On the other hand, in view of what has become known of the almost incredible energy unleashed within a thunderstorm, it cannot be dismissed as a possibility that a powerful downdraft carried her within dangerous proximity to the sea.

One more question remains, and that is, what took the *Akron* into what seemed to be the storm's center? The court of inquiry implicitly censured Frank McCord for "having committed an error in judgment in not setting such courses as would have kept him in the safe semicircle [of the storm], thereby probably avoiding the severe conditions finally encountered." And it was of the opinion that "this error in judgment was a contributory cause of the loss of the *Akron*."[12] But it was not this simple.

There was a tendency in 1933, among press, public, and the investigating congressmen, to imagine McCord as stupid, blundering, and inexperienced. In even very recent years he has been pictured as someone who became an airship pilot almost by accident, and who spent his Navy career "learning to be a master mariner."[13] Frank McCord was considerably more than this. By virtue of his duties as navigator of the *Langley* and *Saratoga*, a billet of vital importance on any ship but especially so aboard a carrier, he was far from being a novice at the art of navigation. He had only 2,256 hours' experience in airships, as compared to "old-timers" like Rosendahl and Wiley, who had logged around 4,000 hours. But, relative to most airship officers, this made him a veteran. Tex Settle, who put McCord through a refresher course when he returned to airship duty, found him to be an excellent pilot of free balloons—and in this peculiar aircraft a man had to know his weather. But in the uproar of 1933 the mob demanded a scapegoat for the *Akron* disaster. As her commanding officer, this had to be Frank McCord.

In 1933 and thereafter it was deplored that McCord had not taken the *Akron* west, and got on what was supposed to have been the storm's "safe semicircle." In the daylight of 4 April everyone knew what few supposed on the evening of 3 April. Even the Weather Bureau's forecaster who assembled the data for the reports on 3 April admitted that he had no suspicion of a storm, until he was sitting on his back porch that evening and saw the lightning.[14] The Bureau's principal meteorologist remarked that he had never before seen such a general storm area as that of 3–4 April. What is more, he pointed out that the storm did not have a "safe semicircle." It was not the usual type of squall thunderstorm, which is an entity in itself; the conditions of 3–4 April were dictated by a cold front which extended across the whole Eastern Seaboard, and every mile of it was charged with thunderstorms of unusual violence.[15] The *Akron* did not know this.

At 2030, near Wilmington, lightning was sighted in the south. This was the first indication of the storm, and it had just passed Baltimore. Wiley, from instinct, suggested flying west to get on what was ordinarily considered to be the safe semicircle of a storm in that area. But McCord had seen lightning in the west. The weather data received by 2145 was incomplete, but it showed a low pressure area centered upon Washington, which was moving northeastward. This "low" suggested a conventional storm center.

McCord's critical moment occurred at 2200 when the *Akron* arrived at the coast in what was thought to be the vicinity of Asbury Park. He could run north, as he had in January, and certainly escape the storm by hiding out over the Great Lakes. But the *Akron* was due at Newport in the morning, and she would not make it if she spent the night over Lake Erie. On the other hand, he could run east, and try to fly around the storm. For that matter, the *Akron* had enough fuel on board to run all the way to the Azores—and back.

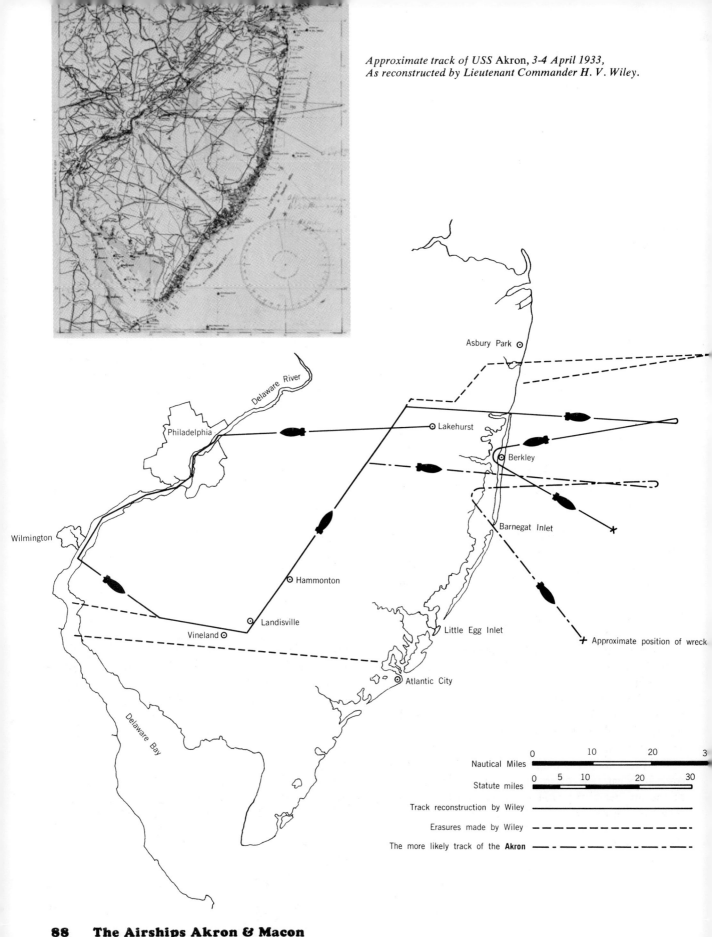

Approximate track of USS Akron, *3-4 April 1933,*
As reconstructed by Lieutenant Commander H. V. Wiley.

Asbury Park ⊙

Delaware River

Philadelphia ⊙   ⊙ Lakehurst

Berkley ⊙

Wilmington

Barnegat Inlet

⊙ Hammonton

⊙ Landisville
Vineland ⊙

Little Egg Inlet

✛ Approximate position of wreck

⊙ Atlantic City

Delaware Bay

0		10		20		3
Nautical Miles

0	5	10		20		30
Statute miles

Track reconstruction by Wiley   ——————

Erasures made by Wiley   — — — — —

The more likely track of the **Akron**   —·—·—·—

Believing the *Akron* to be in the vicinity of Asbury Park (approximately 30 to 40 miles north of her actual position), and estimating the storm's speed at 35 to 40 mph, McCord had good reason to believe that he had more than enough time to fly east, across the storm's path, and then turn south and fly in behind it. At 2200 the storm was about to break over Atlantic City, 60 miles south of Asbury Park. It is not known if McCord was aware of this; but he should have been able to estimate it. If he did, he had good reason to believe that he had almost two hours in which to fly the *Akron* 120 miles across the storm's front. But at 2200 he was not near Asbury Park, he was only from 20 to 25 miles north of Atlantic City, and the storm would be upon the *Akron* in less than an hour.

After leaving the coast the weather became worse, and by 2300 air conditions were extremely violent, the airship surrounded by lightning. The storm was moving at a much faster rate than he had estimated. According to Wiley, at this point they seemed to be near the storm's center, and one course seemed to be as good as another in order to get out of the area as quickly as possible. Thus at 2300 McCord swung the *Akron* around on a heading of 268 degrees and ran back to the coast. It may be significant that this course is almost due west. Believing he had stumbled into the storm's center, McCord now thought he knew where to find the safe semicircle.

Upon reaching the coast at 2400, McCord swung around to the southeast, on what Wiley recalled as 120 degrees true.[16] Wiley suggested that this sudden turn away from the coast may have been because they were not sure of the *Akron*'s dead reckoning, and there was a possibility of their flying over the high buildings of New York City, which was not desirable in a thunderstorm. This may have been a reasonable assumption *if* the *Akron* had taken her 2200 departure from Asbury Park. It seems more likely that McCord revised upward his estimate of the storm's speed and, preferring to remain in the air conditions over the sea, struck off to the southeast with the assumption that the storm was moving rapidly away to the northeast, and that he would swing in behind it.

But the *Akron* was never near Asbury Park; she was over Barnegat. The storm was not moving rapidly away to the northeast; the cold front was progressing at its previous rate of about 35–40 mph. The *Akron* was not on the safe semicircle of the storm; in the conditions of the night of 3–4 April 1933 the safe semicircle, as

such, did not exist. Wholly unaware of the cold front, unaware of the wind shift until it was too late, and decoyed by the low pressure area indicated on his weather map, McCord was reacting correctly to the information he had, but to circumstances which did not exist. The error in dead reckoning created a false environment in which the decisions were made, the incomplete 2000 weather data held just enough information to be dangerous, and the *Akron* was flown back into what was probably the heart of the storm.

These decisions behind the *Akron*'s navigation, as set out in the preceding five paragraphs, are only interpretive conjecture, and offered by way of a probable explanation. Only Frank McCord could know.

The congressional investigation of airship disasters in general was an anticlimax to the Naval Court of Inquiry. It determined very little about the *Akron*'s loss which was not known before. One thing it did produce was sufficient circumstantial evidence to indicate that there were no life jackets and only one rubber raft on board the *Akron* during her last flight, a factor which doubtlessly contributed to the heavy loss in lives. The scope of this investigation was broader than the naval court's, and its 12 days of hearing 56 witnesses compiled a 944-page document which is fundamental to the history of aeronautics in the United States.[17]

The chairman of the joint committee was Senator William H. King (Democrat, Utah), one of those pre-1914 political intellects who may have represented everything that was good about nineteenth-century America, but who resented the disorderly pressures of the 1930's. A grass-roots gentleman of the old school of string tie and silver tongue, King was an arch isolationist, a pious foe of "militarism" in general and an expensive Navy in particular, and at this moment he had donned his shining armor of self-righteousness to do battle against the rigid airship. There were three other senators and five representatives on the committee, however,[18] and they more than balanced Senator King's prosecutor's approach to the subject. Their questions, however naive at times, were advanced in a sincere effort to enlighten themselves on an alien and very technical subject, and in this they were to a large degree successful.

Because of the congressmen's unfamiliarity with the subject, there were many occasions on which the hearings became a virtual hullabaloo. Complementary to Senator King's many moments in the pulpit, Patrick Boland appeared to tell of his witnessing the *Akron*'s tail smashing. He had predicted that the airship would never fly again; now the *Akron* had crashed and he was proved correct. And Representative Hamilton Fish, Jr., burst in to babble about Kassay, sabotage, and the *Akron* being a victim of a Bolshevik plot.

Besides these publicity seekers and axe-grinders, there appeared a broad spectrum of officer personnel from the Navy Department, the Bureau of Aeronautics, and the Navy's airship organization, as well as the principal figures of the Goodyear-Zeppelin Corporation, former Assistant Secretary of the Navy for Aeronautics Edward P. Warner, Colonel Charles Lindbergh, and the principal figures of the U.S. Weather Bureau. These persons gave the proceedings their value. And the agent for bringing forth this value was the committee's able counsel, Colonel Henry Breckenridge, who prevented the sessions from degenerating into a three-ring circus with Senator King as ringmaster.

The principal value of the congressional investigation to a study of the airships was in obtaining the airmen's opinions on the military employment of the airships. Their testimony is revealing, and provides a measure of insight into the operations of the *Akron* and the *Macon*.

There were two extremes of opinion, Harrigan at one, Rosendahl at the other. Harrigan was of the conviction that an airship's primary purpose was to carry some instrument which would enlarge its area of search, and at the same time provide it with a measure of invisibility to the object of search. This "instrument" was the airship's hook-on planes, and he bluntly remarked that without its hook-on planes, the airship had no wartime utility.[19] Rosendahl, however, flatly disagreed. He felt that the planes were of some benefit, but that the airship had missions it could perform without using any airplanes. These several missions were expressed in terms of 1914–1918 precedents. Under certain conditions he thought the airship would make an effective bomber, but conceded its probable destruction as a result of the effort. And he had a few words on the alleged effectiveness of the spy basket as an auxiliary in the airship's search mission.[20]

Tex Settle qualified Harrigan's description of the airship as a "carrier." It carried planes for the same purpose a scout cruiser did, and not like a conventional aircraft carrier, which used its planes as artillery. But he thought it possible to build an airship which would be a "carrier" in the strict sense of the word, and not an airplane-carrying scouting vessel.[21]

Lieutenant Commander Bert Rodgers remarked on the great possibilities in the airplane-carrying airship, and looked forward to one which would carry eight or ten planes. He was especially interested in increasing the number of perches on the *Macon,* so more planes could be carried.[22] Ralph Weyerbacher thought that the airplane-carrying mission would be the primary consideration in the design of future naval airships.[23] Trapnell agreed with Harrigan, but added that an airship could be an effective long-range scout even without planes. This would almost guarantee its destruction upon contact with the enemy, but under certain circumstances its sacrifice might be worth the information gained.[24] Colonel Lindbergh, who denied any familiarity with airships, expressed belief that the airplane-carrying airship made possible the search of a large area at lower cost than could be achieved by any other means.[25]

Alger Dresel, who had just taken command of the *Macon,* thought that the planes greatly increased the airship's scouting value; but the system which he envisioned was conservative. He thought the airship should do the scouting and make the contact with the enemy force, then retreat from the scene and launch her planes to maintain and develop the contact.[26] The only limitation in this concept was that it obliged the relatively conspicuous airship to come in visual contact with the enemy, thus running the risk of revealing its presence and, perhaps, subsequent destruction.

It was Wiley who held a view which most closely corresponded to the "carrier" image. The airship was the means of extending the range of its planes, and the planes did all the scouting. He described the *Akron*'s first experiment in maintaining an airplane scouting line, and mentioned some of the scouting problems which had been worked out on paper, which sought a practicable system of search for the combination.[27]

The most significant testimony here is Rosendahl's, Dresel's and Wiley's, because they were the only ones who had commanded the airships. Their remarks accurately reflected their appreciation of the airship-airplane combination as each of them employed it in practice. During the one military exercise in which the *Akron* could have carried an airplane, Rosendahl had not carried it; and his statements to the congressmen indicate his reluctance to accept the hook-on airplane as the airship's necessary partner. Dresel's rather conservative view of the hook-on planes' employment with the airship would be given illustration in his handling of the *Macon* during 1933 and early 1934. Similarly, Wiley's view here in 1933 coincided with his imaginative handling of the *Macon* after he took command of her in the summer of 1934.

On 14 June 1933, Senator David I. Walsh (Democrat, Massachusetts) presented the committee's report and recommendations.[28] It was a clean bill of health for the airship. The immediate question was if the Navy should abandon its airship experiments and liquidate its 40-million-dollar investment in airships and facilities for lighter-than-air craft. In view of the inhibited character of the airship's past circumstances and experiences, and the fact that it had not yet been exhaustively tested by the Fleet, the committee did not feel this was justified. It was remarked that epic disasters have usually been the price of progress—in steam navigation, railroads, the development of gun turrets, and the submarine, not to mention the airplane—and the airship's troubles should not be considered as unique. They noted that the airplane-carrying airship diminished the scouting obligations of surface vessels; and accurately summed up the airship's position in the terse remark: "It supplants nothing. It supplements all."

The committee recommended retaining Lakehurst as a training center, the commissioning of the *Macon,* and immediately building an airship to replace the *Akron.* This replacement was vital in order to fulfill the requirements of the Five Year Program, which contemplated two fleet-type airships. Also recommended was a rigid airship of moderate size for training purposes and, until it was built, the *Los Angeles* should be recommissioned to serve this function.

The committee's favorable and constructive recommendations would have it appear that the airship was given a rather powerful reassurance. But the committee was not Congress, words are not deeds, and deeds on behalf of the rigid airship cost money. Lots of money. And congressional skepticism and the Navy Department's prejudices provided very little in the way of funds for the future of the rigid airship.

Of the many voices heard speaking about the *Akron* and the airship in general at the Naval Court of Inquiry, the congressional investigation, and in the columns of the newspaper and magazine press, one familiar voice was missing: Admiral Moffett's.

During his 12 years as Chief of the Bureau of Aeronautics, Moffett spoke and wrote frequently on the subject of airships, and he had good reason to do so. Relative to the airplane's progress, the airship's development was very slow; it was a subject of widespread misunderstanding which tended to harden into prejudice,

THE CHICAGO DAILY NEWS, TUESDAY, APRIL 4, 1933.

and it was an object of considerable abuse rooted in ignorance, and in jealousy motivated by fiscal considerations. He realized that a situation involving these elements required an active and articulate defense, and at the highest level.

In 1933 there was a pronounced tendency to picture Admiral Moffett as a sort of martyr in the airship's cause. But Moffett's "cause" was always naval aviation, not the airship *per se*. He held a remarkably clear and realistic view of the air weapon in general, and its place in naval aviation in particular. This has been too well obscured by the smoke screen laid down by the "air-power" apostles of the 1920's and their publicists of the three succeeding decades. Moffett's view of the air weapon was an organic one, in which it was a vital part of the Fleet; the airship was only one part of the organism as he saw it.

While the Admiral maintained a vigorous public defense of the airship, he was not without private criticisms. Indeed, he was very reluctant to prosecute the construction of the *Shenandoah* until Lansdowne convinced him that the mooring mast would give the airship a flexibility in operations approximating the airplane's. On more than one occasion he almost reached the end of his patience with a measure of inertia he thought he detected in the Lakehurst operating organization;[29] the unusual number of trips which he made from Washington to Lakehurst during 1926–1933 were not simply for the sake of going for a ride on the *Los Angeles* or the *Akron*. His occasional dissatisfaction is illustrated in his remark of 1931 to Lakehurst's commanding officer: "I have a feeling, and I have had it for a long time, that the [air] ships have not been operated as much as they should have been."[30] And he concluded that unless they could operate as required, the Navy should abandon them.

The Admiral's defense was essentially a delaying action, to provide the airships with the time necessary for a shakedown and exhaustive trials with the Fleet. When the end came in 1933 he had decided that the shakedown period had ended, and that the *Akron* and *Macon* were ready for their workouts with the Fleet. Unfortunately for the rigid airship, neither Admiral Moffett nor the *Akron* survived to participate in this second, vital stage of putting the airship to its military test.

Under happier circumstances, Moffett would have retired at the end of 1933, and the *Akron* and *Macon* would have been operating with the Fleet. It may be assumed that he, like Admiral Pratt, would have continued to speak and write on behalf of naval aviation and the airship. In view of the *Macon*'s performance during the latter part of 1934, it is probable that the performances of the two airships together would have eventually justified his defense. But the *Akron* was lost, and Admiral Moffett with her—not to mention the talents and skills of the 72 other persons. Time would prove these losses irreparable.

Prior to 4 April 1933 there was a general increase of confidence in the rigid airship's future. The *Akron*'s condition of material readiness had been greatly improved, and her Florida-Panama-Cuba flights had a healthy effect upon naval opinion. Concurrently in the commercial realm, the German *Graf Zeppelin*'s passenger and mail flights between Europe and Brazil were becoming routine affairs, and the McNary-Crosser legislation in Congress held the promise of an American "merchant marine of the air," made up of passenger- and cargo-carrying rigid airships.[31] The *Akron*'s crash smashed this hopeful picture.

The *Akron*'s disaster seemed to repeat what too many suspected should have been the "lesson" of the *Roma, ZR2, Shenandoah,* and R101 crashes. The objectivity of the congressional committee was not expanded to a general outlook; its recommendations were never acted upon. The psychological damage of the *Akron*'s crash defies estimate, but it was great. It affected not only the press and public, but Congress, the Navy Department, the Bureau of Aeronautics, and even the Navy's airship organization.

It could not be known with certainty in 1933, but the forecast of the future was in the words of Representative Carl Vinson, chairman of the House Committee on Naval Affairs, when he remarked, "We've built three and lost two; you can take it from me, there won't be any more airships built."[32] The loss of the *Akron* was the beginning of the end.

CHAPTER SEVEN

ZRS5: Off to the Wars

With the exception of a few minor changes, the ZRS5, USS *Macon,* was a reproduction of the *Akron;* but the nature of her career made her a very different airship. There were no Kassay's, MacDonald's, or Mc-Clintic's to afflict the *Macon,* and the noisy fanfare which badgered her sister ship was wholly absent from her 22 months of operations. The *Macon*'s career was a much happier one than the *Akron*'s and although her end was only a little less violent, she at least spared most of her crew from sharing her tragedy.

The *Macon*'s career was different expressly because the *Akron* had preceded her, and she was the beneficiary of all her sister ship's troubles. When she left the Goodyear-Zeppelin plant she was more ready to meet the challenges which the rigid airship had to face than the *Akron* had ever been. Her officers and crew were trained aboard the *Akron,* so she was not something new to them; her airplane hangar and trapeze installation were complete when she left the factory; and perhaps most important, she had the experience of the *Akron*'s HTA Unit at her disposal. This was aside from the many advancements, a few large but most small, which had been worked into her structure, which were developed the hard way with the *Akron.* Thus it was not unreasonable when, only four and one-half months after her commissioning, the Chief of Naval Operations ordered the *Macon* off to the "wars" which the Pacific Fleet was fighting off the coast of Southern California.

There was one experience, however, which the *Akron* was not able to pass on to her sister ship, and that was military experience with the Fleet. The *Akron* participated in two operations with the Scouting Fleet, but in neither was the airship challenged by the muscle of naval aviation, the Fleet's carrier squadrons. The *Akron* would have had this enlightening experience in 1932's Fleet Problem XIII, or 1933's Fleet Problem XIV; but the first opportunity was lost in a gust of wind, and the second in the sea off Little Egg Inlet. The *Macon* had to face this problem alone, and without precedents to guide her. She had to take the "bloody nose" which the *Akron* would have otherwise received; and the hard lessons which might have been learned as early as 1932–1933 did not come under study until 1934.

Although the *Macon* was practically a replica of the *Akron,* there was a moment during her gestation when she might have presented a very different appearance. The *Macon*'s was basically a 1926 design; the *Akron* was built in strict accordance with the original specifications. It was felt that the second airship should represent a step forward; thus in the spring of 1931, Bu-Aer's LTA Design Section proposed increasing the ZRS5's size 930,000 cubic feet by inserting an additional 22.5 meter bay at main frame 57.5.

The proposed enlargement was technically feasible and operationally desirable. The additional gas volume would increase her useful lift by 40,000 pounds to a total of 210,000 pounds. Speed would be reduced by 1.5 knots; but at a cruising speed of 50 knots, range would be extended by 25 per cent, to 11,500 miles. The alteration would increase her total gas volume to 7,430,000 cubic feet, and over-all length to 859 feet. The Sunnyvale hangar was big enough for an airship this long, but Lakehurst's was 60 feet too short; by installing orange-peel doors on the latter, however, it was calculated that it would be more than long enough.

Admiral Moffett had mentioned his desire for enlarging the ZRS5 at the *Akron*'s christening ceremony, and in January 1932 he officially recommended it to the Secretary of the Navy. Secretary Adams and Admiral Pratt, Chief of Naval Operations, thought it an excellent idea, except for the added cost of $400,000, which

93

The Macon's hull structure from frame 170 aft. Frame 170 has only recently been put in position and has yet to be joined to frame 147.5 by keel girders and longitudinals. On floor, right: Frame 187.5 under construction. Foreground: An intermediate frame under construction.

would carry the total for the two airships over the statutory limit of cost. This meant that Congress would have be asked for more funds, and Admiral Pratt was opposed to this. Goodyear's engineering staff favored the enlargement, but management had doubts. The company had lost money on the *Akron,* and it looked askance at projects which might possibly cause delays in the ZRS5.[1]

The proposed enlargement may seem to be of scant importance. But it would have had a significant effect upon the *Macon*'s performance, and the *Macon* would have been the world's largest rigid airship.

Another change which the Bureau hoped to realize in the ZRS5 was in the engines. The Maybachs performed very well, but the Navy did not relish dependence upon a foreign contractor for its airship engines. Excellent airplane engines were available in the United States, but an airship needed an engine fundamentally different from the airplane's high-speed engine.

An airship maintained itself in the air by virtue of its buoyant gas and, although it could fly dynamically when necessary, it usually used its engines only for locomotion, and did not depend on high speed to keep it aloft. In fact, a high-speed engine was undesirable. The long periods between overhauls with an engine of slow speed were especially important, because when an airship took to the air it usually remained airborne for two, three, or even four days. Reversibility was another important factor in an airship engine, but of no consequence in an airplane's.

During the 1920's, the Bureau tried to interest American manufacturers in developing an airship engine, but received only lukewarm response. No big profits could be foreseen in an airship engine, and the Navy did not have the funds to subsidize private industry in a research and development program.

By the end of the 1920's, the Bureau had coaxed the Allison Engineering Company into accepting a development contract, and it was hoped to have this engine ready for the ZRS5. But there was much foot-dragging on Allison's part, and its VG-1710 airship engine had only reached the test stand when the *Macon*'s German-built Maybachs took her on her last flight in 1935. In the meantime the Bureau was considering other possibilities. One was to use a Junkers diesel engine then under development in Germany; the other was to replace two or four of the *Akron*'s liquid-cooled Maybachs with air-cooled Wright "Cyclones." But the diesel proved to be prohibitively expensive in its engineering

costs, and funds were lacking for experimenting with the air-cooled engine installations, which had not excited any enthusiasm at Lakehurst anyway.[2]

In May 1931, while the finishing touches were being applied to the ZRS4, the smaller subassemblies of the ZRS5's structure were begun in Goodyear's Plant 3. Concurrently, several communities across the United States began beating the drum to have the ZRS5 carry the name of their fair cities. But 1932 was an election year, and Representative Carl Vinson faced a difficult campaign in the Georgia primary.

Vinson had been on the House Committee on Naval Affairs since 1914 and became its chairman in 1930. An advocate of national preparedness and a good friend of the Navy's, he usually steered a course between the extremes of the committee's "Little Navy" faction and its "Navy-Second-to-None" group in an effort to achieve the possible. His attitude toward the airship was somewhat ambivalent. During the 1920's he was an active partisan of the airships' construction; but after the *Akron*'s crash he became highly skeptical of its future.[3] And although after the loss of the *Macon* he had practically dismissed the rigid airship as a military possibility, in 1938 he assented to the Navy procuring a small rigid for training purposes, and remained very favorably disposed toward the blimp.

During the campaigning in the Georgia primary, Vinson's opponent mentioned that in spite of his seniority on the Naval Affairs Committee, he was unable to have any ships named for cities in his constituency, and sought to blow this up into an "issue." The Navy's practice is to name cruisers after cities, and in the early 1930's there were several cruisers being built, but all the hulls had already been assigned names. But the airship being fabricated in Akron, Ohio, was nameless. The ZRS5 carried the name of Macon, Georgia, the largest city in Carl Vinson's congressional district.

The city was delighted with the honor, and was even more delighted in the summer of 1932 when Goodyear invited a delegation from the city to assist in the ZRS5's construction. Thus on the Fourth of July three-score Maconites were enjoying a place of honor among the 15,000 persons assembled in the Goodyear-Zeppelin airship dock. Mayor G. Glen Toole remarked with awe at the ZRS5's structure—it was taller than Macon's Hotel Dempsey! Then Susan Myrick, a reporter from the *Macon Telegraph,* blew a whistle, and workmen hoisted the airship's 65-foot bow section into place. This act completed the ZRS5's main structure.[4]

Inside the Macon's *hull. The tarpaulins were to catch tools dropped accidentally.*

Applying the Macon's *outer cover.*

One of the fins having its outer cover applied. The fin weighed 2,700 pounds, as much as one of the F9C fighter planes. The gaps where the cloth is laced to the girders can be seen; they were covered by sealing strips of fabric before the painting was begun.

The city of Macon was less happy when it was announced that Mrs. William A. Moffett, the Admiral's wife, would christen the airship. In early 1933 the Democratic hottentots of Macon were reveling over Franklin Roosevelt's recent election and the Democrat Party's return to power after 12 years in the political wastelands, and they wanted Eleanor Roosevelt to christen "their" airship. After all, Mrs. Coolidge had christened the *Los Angeles,* and Mrs. Hoover had done the honors for the *Akron.* The City Council adopted a unanimous resolution to invite Mrs. Roosevelt to christen "their" airship, and Mayor Toole shot off notes to Carl Vinson and Senators Walter George and Richard B. Russell, asking them to put pressure on the Navy.[5] Because the christening would occur after Roosevelt's inauguration, the good mayor was especially outraged; he thought the Republican Secretary of the Navy was usurping power. Vinson put his foot down on this; the airship was still Goodyear's property, and it is customary for the builder, not the Navy, to choose the sponsor. And with this the matter was settled.

In the meantime the citizens of Macon speculated about the cost of a mooring mast so their airship could visit them during the Georgia Bicentennial in May 1933; they talked up Macon's fine qualities for a Navy airship base, and set about selecting eight of "the city's most beautiful girls" to represent Southern Womanhood at the christening. A Dirigible Gift Committee was appointed, and a silver service set was purchased for the airship. It was hoped that the airship would fly to Macon to receive its gift, and send down one of its hook-on planes to pick it up. The Central of Georgia and Southern railroads extended special rates to christening-bound Maconites, and by 9 March everyone who was going was on his way to Akron.[6]

The eleventh of March 1933 was a bitterly cold day in Akron, Ohio. A howling wind hurled blinding snow across the municipal airport, while a 325-piece band played for the 5,000 persons gathered inside the airship dock. The huge hangar had no heating plant, so the spectators shivered and anxiously shifted their discomfort from one foot to the other during the thoughtfully short gamut of speeches.

In his last public speech on lighter-than-air matters, Admiral Moffett had stated that the Navy now had two fine airships, but having them was not enough: they had to demonstrate their usefulness to the Fleet. He called attention to the successful use of airplanes with the *Akron* and how greatly they increased the airship's

naval value; he looked forward to airships larger than the *Akron* and the *Macon,* which would be capable of carrying a much larger complement of planes.

The Admiral took to task the critics of airship development and explained the airship's relatively small cost as a naval scout, and as a vehicle of commercial air transportation. He looked forward to the successful passage of the McNary-Crosser merchant airship legislation in Congress which would establish commercial airship operations. The Navy had no intention of asking for more airships at that time, but he hoped that as soon as funds became available both the *Akron* and *Macon* would be enlarged by a million cubic feet. And until the Navy could order more airships, he hoped that the construction orders for commercial airships would keep airship building active.

Then Mrs. Moffett christened the ZRS5 "Macon" and the ceremony was over. As the band played the National Anthem, Admiral Moffett was handed a telegram from President Roosevelt which congratulated him upon his 12 years as Chief of the Bureau of Aeronautics, and the completion of his Five Year Aircraft Program, which was marked by the *Macon*'s christening.[7]

Early on 21 April 1933, the *Macon* was undocked into a fresh northeast wind. At 0602 Alger Dresel gave the command for takeoff, and she was cast off from the mast for her first flight. Immediately after takeoff she rose into a steep temperature inversion, lost her superheat, and had to tilt four of her propellers for vertical thrust to climb through it. Then she was off to the air over Lake Erie for preliminary trials.

This was the first of four test flights the *Macon* made at Akron between 21 April and 14 June. These totaled 82 hours, the last of which was a 48-hour endurance flight into northern Illinois, eastern Wisconsin, and across lower Michigan. The *Macon* began her trials with her engines turning two-bladed wooden propellers, but by her third flight she was completely outfitted with three-bladed metal Hamilton Standard propellers which had an adjustable pitch. These should not be confused with the automatic variable pitch propeller; the *Macon*'s props were only adjustable, and the pitch settings had to be made with the engines stopped. Nevertheless, this was a great improvement on the past; these three-bladed airscrews improved the *Macon*'s performance considerably over that of the *Akron.*

At 1400, 23 June 1933, Lieutenant Commander Joe Arnold, the *Macon*'s executive officer, mustered officers and crew at quarters in the Goodyear hangar. Lieuten-

On 7 July 1933, two weeks after her commissioning, the Macon meets two of her Curtiss fighters over New Egypt, New Jersey, and drills them for the first time on her trapeze. The pilot of the first plane is Lieutenant D. Ward Harrigan, senior HTA aviator; of the second, Lieutenant (j.g.) Frederick N. Kivette. The "stripes" or "windows" partly around the airship's circumference are the condensers of her water-recovery apparatus.

Left: With the green flag clearing him for landing, Harrigan hangs his F9C-2 onto the trapeze. After the fork is dropped over the skyhook to center it on the trapeze's yoke, and the saddle lowered over the after fuselage, the plane will be swung up into the hangar.

ant George Whittle, who was acting in Settle's place as inspector of naval aircraft,[8] informed Alger Dresel that he had taken preliminary acceptance of the airship, and had given Goodyear-Zeppelin a receipt for it. Then Rear Admiral Ernest J. King, the new Chief of the Bureau of Aeronautics, placed the USS *Macon* in commission. Dresel read the orders which placed him in command, the colors and commission pennant were hoisted, and the watch set. The setting of the watch was not simply a formality in this instance; the watch that went aboard the *Macon* went aboard to prepare her for flight, and within six hours the *Macon* was on her way to Lakehurst.

Admiral King made it a point to be on board the *Macon* during her delivery flight. For more than a decade Admiral Moffett had vigorously defended the rigid airship and its promise. King had only recently stepped into the office of Bureau Chief, and he knew the rest of the Navy was watching him and his attitude toward airships. He felt that the airship had a function in the Navy, and he refused to cast aside anything which held promise of a peculiar value, without first exhausting its possibilities by trial. Even beyond the *Akron* and *Macon*, King continued to believe that the big airship had a place in the Navy. But general skepticism, the airship's chronic experimental status, and the several urgent matters which crowded his career after he left the Bureau in 1936, never permitted him a clear picture. His presence on this flight was a public vote of confidence for the rigid airship.

At Lakehurst the *Macon* was berthed in the double hangar next to the decommissioned *Los Angeles*. The older airship's status was supposedly "temporary," but in July 1933, Rear Admiral George C. Day and his Board of Inspection and Survey officially ended her flying career. She could have been restored to flying condition at a cost of $15,000, but the board did not believe the expense was justified and recommended her disposal by sale or scrapping. Her scrap value was estimated at $2,500. It seemed that time had run out on the *Los Angeles*; but she possessed remarkable powers of survival, and even as a nonflyable airship managed to resist the burners' torches until 1940.

Meanwhile, the *Macon* was continuing her trials at Lakehurst. On 7 July, returning from an overnight flight to sea, she rendezvoused over New Egypt, New Jersey, with Harrigan, Trapnell, Larson, and Kivette, and the F9C's were flown to her trapeze for the first time. A week later, upon return from a night of engine

and water-recovery tests off the Delaware Capes, the *Macon* appeared over Floyd Bennett Field, Long Island, to join in New York City's noisy welcome for the Italian flier Italo Balbo and his 23 flying boats. The week before, Balbo captured the world's attention by leading his squadron of sleek, double-hulled flying boats from Orbetello, Italy, to Chicago, for the "Century of Progress" world's fair. While the Italian planes bobbed at anchor in Jamaica Bay, the *Macon*'s HTA Unit gave them a demonstration of their trapeze work.

During the last two days of August, the *Macon* performed for Admiral Day and his board. These were her official trials, and she was formally accepted. The *Macon*'s speed performance was more than gratifying. The contract called for 72.4 knots; the *Akron* was able to make only 69, but the *Macon* logged 75.6. This was due to a particular cleaning up of her hull protuberances and the efficiency of her three-bladed propellers. A perch was installed at frame 102.5 a few days before this flight, so the board was able to witness the planes make perch landings, as well as on the trapeze.

With her trials completed in the fall of 1933, the *Macon* was ready for the West Coast. As early as the summer of 1932, it was planned that the *Akron* would remain at Lakehurst and the *Macon* would go to Sunnyvale. Various experimental projects were under way or anticipated with the *Akron,* and it was considered best to keep her close to the Bureau. Also, the *Macon* was anticipated as an improvement over her sister ship and the more suitable to operate with the Fleet.

In the twilight of 12 October the *Macon* made her good-byes to Lakehurst, and at 1805 was cast off from the mast for the flight to her new home on the West Coast. After the ground crew stowed their gear and rolled the doors closed on Hangar No. 1 that autumn evening, the air station never again handled a commissioned rigid airship of the U.S. Navy. An era of naval aviation had already ended at Lakehurst.

As the *Macon* headed down the New Jersey shore, Trapnell flew one of the N2Y's aboard for a running boat, and got a free ride to the coast. The other pilots flew their planes cross-country. None of them minded this, especially Min Miller; it gave him the opportunity to refuel and spend the night at Newton, Iowa, his hometown, and show the folks his strange-looking little airplane. But when the trapeze artists lit out for the West Coast, one F9C was left behind at Lakehurst. Under happier circumstances Ward Harrigan would have flown this plane.

A section of one of the two fore-and-aft passageways. The two tanks held fuel.

The ladder leads from the corridor to the upper catwalk.

Telegraph for bow mooring gear.

Harrigan did not fly west with the HTA Unit. In the fall of 1933 he was stricken with what appeared to be a very serious illness that threatened to invalid him out of the Navy. This proved to be a false alarm; but after his recovery he was not returned to the *Macon*. In the spring of 1934 he received a commendation from the Secretary of the Navy for his "contribution to the successful operation of heavier-than-air craft from dirigibles," and his "zeal and energy . . . evidenced by the present high degree of efficiency of such operations."[9]

In anticipation of the *Macon*'s flight west, and because of the known difficulties of the airships in crossing the North American continental divide, Lakehurst made a study of alternate routes. The only one with a minimum of mountain obstacles—without going all the way to Panama—was the isthmus of Tehuantepec in Mexico. It was 130 miles wide, only 20 miles involved flying through mountain passes, and the maximum altitude the airship would have to attain was 2,500 feet. From Lakehurst to Sunnyvale via Tehuantepec was 4,131 miles, as compared to 2,488 miles via Texas.[10] But the study was received with mixed feelings in the Bureau, and decision was made for the Texas route.

The *Macon* departed Lakehurst with a little more than 46 tons of fuel and about six tons of ballast on board. Her static condition varied during the night, according to fluctuations in her superheat;[11] but by 0700 the next day over Milledgeville, Georgia, Carl Vinson's hometown, she was in equilibrium. A few minutes later, when she passed over Macon, most of the city's population was crowding the streets, perched on rooftops, and hanging out of windows, to see their airship.[12] They had been waiting for the *Macon* since sunrise. It was their first and last look at the silver-sided namesake.

By 1400, as the *Macon* crossed the Mississippi, her helium had acquired seven degrees of superheat and she was flying 7,500 pounds light. If her engines were stopped while she was in this condition, she would free balloon upward to an altitude where the lifting forces of her gas came into equilibrium with the weights on board. Thus, in order to maintain her altitude, she had to fly with her nose inclined slightly down to use the motion of her hull against the air to counter the lift of her helium. But by 2100 she was in West Texas, that land of airship troubles, and as she passed ten miles east of Brazos she was flying dynamically to carry 7,500 pounds of heaviness; and by the time she began her climb into the mountains near Sweetwater this had increased to 11,000 pounds.

In the mountains west of Midland, the *Macon* ran into scattered fog and a storm whose vertical gusts repeatedly tossed her above pressure height, which caused her automatic valves to open and bleed helium to the atmosphere. A ton and a half of fuel was jettisoned to lighten ship, but an increase in the atmospheric temperature reduced the value of her helium's superheat, and by the time she arrived over Pecos she was 18,000 pounds heavy. Still, conditions were not so bad that Trapnell and his 2,000-pound airplane had to be thrown out. It should not be misunderstood that something was wrong with the airship when it was flying heavy. A small measure of heaviness was desirable to give the airship aerodynamic stability. But it was not desirable to have upwards of 10,000 pounds of heaviness, which had to be carried by the airship at full power, for long periods, especially when in turbulent air.

The changing static condition of an airship relative to its altitude, gas and atmosphere temperatures, gas loss from bobbing over pressure height, and rain, snow, or ice accumulating on the hull, was anticipated by the airship operators and accepted among the facts of life of airship flying. But these conditions could complicate flying, especially in the fickle air masses of land, and while negotiating mountain passes in which the earth was only a few hundred feet away on three sides and there was scarcely room in which to turn around a 785-foot-long airship.

Shortly after noon on 15 October the *Macon* arrived over Sunnyvale and Brig Young flew aboard in an F9C, by way of welcome and to provide 2,700 pounds of ballast to assist her landing. Between Lakehurst and Sunnyvale the *Macon* had consumed more than 38 tons of fuel.[13] This is approximately the gross weights of five Ford Trimotors, which were still standard commercial airliners in 1933. At 1622 she moored in Sunnyvale's south circle, and at sunset was towed into the station's sleek-looking Hangar No. 1.

The U.S. Naval Air Station, Sunnyvale, which in the spring of 1933 had been named Moffett Field, was probably the finest airship base in the world. Its futuristic Hangar No. 1 dominated the scene, but the pseudo-Spanish colonial architecture of its administration buildings and living accommodations loaned a measure of charm from the past. Beyond both of Hangar No. 1's orange-peel doors was a mooring circle. Because of careful attention to prevailing winds on the site, the Sunnyvale hangar was oriented on an axis with them, and the double circle system necessary at Lakehurst

*While Lieutenant (j.g.) George Campbell and Chief Bosun William A. Buckley look on from
the windows of the auxiliary control room, Lieutenant Commander Bert Rodgers (pointing) directs
the ground crew in securing the lower fin to the mooring circle's riding-out car.*

was eliminated. East of the hangar were three runways for airplanes. But from the day the *Macon* arrived, Moffett Field had only 16 months in which to serve its planned function: a complete servicing facility for rigid airships.

Shortly after the *Macon* arrived on the West Coast, Admiral William H. Standley, who in July 1933 relieved Admiral Pratt as CNO, informed Admiral David F. Sellers, CinCUS, that the *Macon* was to be employed to the fullest extent possible in fleet exercises so her military value could be determined. Standley requested a report from CinCUS, by the end of September 1934, which would give his conclusions on her performance and recommendations for the Navy's future airship policy. This gave the *Macon* a little more than ten months in which to prove herself.

Between her arrival in California and her first fleet exercise, the *Macon* made only two flights. One was a 50-hour operation around San Diego and the Channel Islands to give her officers a brief acquaintance of the area in which the exercises were held. The other was a short hop over San Francisco with Admiral Sellers and his staff on board. This was imaginative diplomacy on Dresel's part. But however much Sellers enjoyed the flight, and the hook-on exhibition put on by Young and Kivette, he was reserving his judgment for the *Macon*'s performance with the Fleet.

During 1933–1934, Admiral Sellers and his staff created two war situations along the California coast which are rather interesting in the light of what is known of War Plan ORANGE and World War II. In one, San Francisco represented a large harbor on a large island in the extreme Western Pacific, which was held by the BLUE forces at the end of a long line of communications. The coast between Point San Luis and San Diego represented part of another large island in the same area, but held by the BROWN forces. The ports of San Diego and San Pedro were well developed BROWN bases, but at San Francisco BLUE had only a big harbor. BLUE was contesting BROWN for the ownership of some small islands between the two big ones; these were represented by the Santa Barbara Channel Islands and some points on the coast of the mainland. It takes no stretch of the imagination to visualize the BLUE base as Manila or Lingayen Gulf, and the BROWN bases as Kirun (Keelung), and Takao (Kaohsiung), on what was then Japanese-held Formosa.

The second situation was a Caribbean problem which reflected the Navy's historic concern for the Isthmus of Panama. Here the BLUE forces were trying to dislodge the GRAY forces from islands they had somehow seized in the Antilles. These islands were represented by various points along the California coast and the Channel Islands. The GRAY forces were supposedly a coalition of European powers, seeking a foothold in Central America that would permit them to outflank the Panama Canal's defenses.

These were the general contexts of the "wars" in which the *Macon* operated as a scout for the BLUE forces until the spring of 1934.[14] The geographic frameworks of both problems enclosed relatively small areas which dictated tactical situations, much to the *Macon*'s disadvantage. These exercises proved what everyone knew in advance—by logic or prejudice—that the airship was practically useless in tactical situations. The "war" was already in progress when the *Macon* arrived on the coast; however, she arrived in its opening phases. Her baptism of fire came in mid-November, in Exercises D and E.

Late in the afternoon of 14 November the *Macon* took off from Moffett Field's south circle, two F9C's were flown aboard, and course was laid for the Pacific via the Golden Gate. At 0500 on the fifteenth, when the gun went off on Exercise D, she was circling beneath a layer of broken cumulus off Point Arguello, with instructions from the BLUE commander to make a sweep south in a westerly arc, to cover BLUE's right flank. The *Macon* was under way less than two hours when she blundered out of a cloud to find herself looking into the main batteries of a BROWN cruiser, which immediately opened fire—simulated by blinking searchlights. The airship was almost directly over the cruiser, the range was point-blank, so the umpire on board the *Macon* faced the obvious conclusion that under combat conditions she would not have survived. Because there was nothing to be gained by sending her back to Sunnyvale after being "destroyed," the *Macon* was ordered to remain in the exercise as the hypothetical "ZRS6."

With her upperworks brushing a 1,600-foot overcast, the *Macon* continued south. At 0917 two curious enemy flying boats closed with her, and Kivette was launched in an F9C to fight them off. At 1125 a ship was spotted on the western horizon, and Trapnell was sent out to investigate. It proved to be a BLUE cruiser; but over the horizon—beyond visibility from the airship and the cruiser—Trapnell reported a division of BROWN cruisers. Shortly after retrieving Trapnell's F9C, the *Macon* again wandered out of the broken clouds

Rear Admiral George W. Laws, Commandant of the Twelfth
Naval District, welcomes Commander Dresel to Moffett Field.
D. J. BELLEW

Lieutenant Howard N. Coulter, the Macon's
communications officer, at navigator's chart table.
GOODYEAR AEROSPACE CORPORATION

The entrance to the airship's forward control car from the ground.

and into the antiaircraft fire of a division of enemy cruisers and their destroyer escorts. She was again ruled "shot down" and instructed to remain in the exercise as the "ZRS7."

By 1543 she was patrolling a wide circle around San Nicholas Island where BLUE's amphibious forces had made a landing and were consolidating their beachhead. She remained in this area until the end of the exercise, reporting BROWN forces which sought to approach the island. During these hours the airship took it upon herself to do all the scouting; no planes were used, and she was frequently assessed damaged from her contacts' antiaircraft fire. The Macon was released from the exercise at sundown and flew to San Diego, where she circled the area until Exercise E began the next morning. The Macon could have landed at Camp Kearny, been refueled and serviced overnight at its mooring mast; but this secondary mast facility was used very seldom.

In the predawn of 16 November, Scotty Peck checked the Macon's position with landmarks on Coronado and Imperial Beach and gave Dresel the course to the BLUE Fleet rendezvous off San Clemente Island. At 0753 the airship checked her position with the BLUE carrier Saratoga, and flew off into the low visibility to find the enemy. At 0835 her lookouts reported ships in the west. Trapnell and Young were in their planes, one hanging on the perch and the other on the trapeze, and they were launched immediately. A few minutes later they radioed back that they had located what appeared to be BROWN's main body; in fact, it proved to be his advance forces.

When the planes returned, the Macon broke off contact with the enemy and hid in the clouds until 1010, when it was decided to intercept the enemy again. But the enemy was gone. No BROWN formations were sighted again until 1315, and a few minutes after she radioed off her contact report she was jumped by enemy fighters. And she was again ruled "shot down."[15]

In these exercises the F9C's experienced very little and limited use. A complication here was ComAirBatFor's instruction that the airship's planes should not be risked more than 25 miles out of sight of any fleet unit. In view of the poor state of the F9C's navigation at this date, this was not an unreasonable limitation. And it more or less corresponded to Dresel's belief that the airship should do the preliminary scouting and use her planes only after the contact had been made.

The umpire on board the Macon, Lieutenant Donald M. Mackey, immediately pointed out in his report to CinCUS that tactical scouting was not the function of a rigid airship. But he thought the exercises were an enlightening experience for the Macon. He pinpointed her troubles as being navigation and vulnerability in close contacts with enemy forces. Heretofore, the airships were used mostly in point-to-point flying over great distances, and this flying was conducted in a fashion to facilitate the navigator's work. But the constant maneuvering in response to friendly forces, or in reaction to the enemy's, during these exercises demonstrated a need for a radically new approach to the Macon's navigation.[16]

With the airship dodging in and out of clouds and making changes in course from minute to minute, it was extremely difficult to obtain sights, determine wind direction, and obtain drift angles. The result was an accumulation of small errors which over a period of hours left the navigator with a dead reckoning position which was frequently in error by several miles. And it was vitally important for the airship to have a correct position for reference when making a contact report.

Mackey's lucid reports as umpire during these and subsequent exercises provided fresh insight into the airship's problems, and a remarkable willingness to call a spade a spade. Don Mackey entered the Navy during the first World War and spent the war in European waters aboard sub-chasers. During 1920–1924 he served in destroyers, after which he went to submarine school. He spent four years in submarines, during which time he was commanding officer of the submarine O-10, part of SubDiv 8 based at Coco Solo in the Canal Zone. During 1928–1929, he spent a year at the Naval Academy's Postgraduate School, followed by a year at the Naval War College. After a year aboard the battleship Arkansas he received his orders to airship duty.

In July 1931, Mackey arrived at Lakehurst among the more junior officers of the "third generation." After qualifying as an airship pilot he and Lieutenant Commander Harold E. MacClellan, another War College graduate, were assigned to draw up a massive document called the "Force Operating Plan." This was an apologia to justify the expenses of the Lakehurst Air Station, whose funds were forever under the threat of being sacrificed on the altar of "economy." On their own time, however, he and MacClellan discussed airship and airplane scouting problems, and especially how Dick Knight's systems of vector analysis could be applied to them. This led to their working out rather detailed search problems, and some speculation as to exact tactics, which drew the pilots of the HTA Unit into the discussions. But these investigations had nothing to do with their primary duties. In early 1933, MacClellan was ordered to the *Akron* as navigator and was lost with her, while Mackey was ordered to Sunnyvale.

In November 1933, Mackey was Moffett Field's communications and intelligence officer, and was not yet a member of the *Macon*'s complement. His position aboard the airship was somewhat anomalous, and certainly difficult. As umpire he was responsible to Cin-CUS for true and critical reports on her performance. At the same time he was anxious to see the *Macon* do well, and desperately wanted a billet on board. As the man who decided when the *Macon* was "shot down," he had to render some hard judgments against her. But his reports to CinCUS, copies of which went to Dresel, also analyzed the airship's problems and prescribed the direction in which answers might be found. Not content to merely prescribe, after he became the *Macon*'s tactical officer in 1934, Mackey was the central figure in devising the techniques which liberated the F9C's from the need of constant visual contact with the airship.

With regard to the airship's vulnerability, Mackey informed CinCUS that there was only one solution: the airship had to remain out of sight and let her planes do the searching.[17] A pair of planes should always be out in front of the airship when she was operating in an area where contact with enemy forces was imminent. If the airship was going to realize any success, it had to stop behaving like a 1914–1918 Zeppelin and begin to perform like a "lighter-than-air carrier."

In his report to the Fleet, Admiral Sellers credited the *Macon* with two good reports. He refrained from direct criticism, but the record seemed to speak for itself.[18] The *Macon* was "shot down" three times. When Sellers reported the exercises to CNO he enclosed Mackey's report, which eventually reached Admiral King. He took notice of the *Macon*'s tactical employment and suggested that she would turn in a more creditable performance if used in strategic work.[19] This was the *Macon*'s only plausible use; but it was never to be her experience in a fleet exercise.

Between her commissioning and the end of 1933, the *Macon* and the men who flew her experienced a very busy six months. The future would be even more exacting on their time and efforts, and Exercises D and E pointed the direction in which the effort had to be applied. The *Macon*'s navigation had to be tightened up, a system for navigating her planes away from the airship had to be worked out, and the still inadequate communications between the airship and her planes had to be improved. But here it is important to recall the rather rudimentary character of the technology of radio and aerial navigation in the early 1930's. The *Macon* would have to break new ground in these areas, and the remedies for her military shortcomings were more easily prescribed than worked out to practical solutions.

The entire burden of these necessary developments fell upon the *Macon*'s officers, of whom there were less than two dozen, including the pilots of the HTA Unit. And the only one whose primary duty involved tactics was Mackey. Although he had the active assistance of Scotty Peck, Lieutenant Howard N. Coulter, the airship's communications officer, Trapnell, Miller, and the other hook-on pilots, what this small group seemed able to achieve without transcending their times appeared to be limited.

What they in fact did achieve was considerable, and they almost transcended their times in the achievement. But this was not realized until after mid-1934 and did not become clear until early 1935. In the meantime, everything they tried was new. There was no body of reference, much less any broad experience, to draw upon. But no matter what fine schemes were worked out on paper, they had to be tested in practice and made effective through training. This required many hours in the air. In the months ahead, the *Macon* flew very seldom except for her participation in exercises with the Fleet.

The November exercises were not only the curtain-raiser to several more "combat" experiences for the *Macon,* they also established the pattern of her performance in the immediate future. A stumbling progress would be made, but it would not become evident until the end of the year. In the meantime, between January and June of 1934, the *Macon*'s performance would not be enough to meet the demands of what Admiral King recognized as the crucial year for the acceptance of the rigid airship and its possible role in the Navy.

CHAPTER EIGHT

The Crucial Year

During the first six months of 1934 the *Macon* was put on trial six times. In each instance, like the *Akron* before her, the results were inconclusive. But unlike the *Akron*'s case, the Fleet found the *Macon* wanting in performance and judged that she had failed to demonstrate the airship's military usefulness. There is a paradox in the sister ships' military predicaments which warrants consideration.

When the *Akron* flew off to her exercises with the Scouting Fleet she was materially deficient, her crew was new to the airship and had little training in the airship's military mission, and the only attention the hook-on planes received was lip service. But the *Akron* operated in search problems over large areas of ocean suited to her capabilities. These represented the opening phase of a naval conflict: the presence of the enemy is not known, only suspected; he is "lost" in a vast ocean and it is the airship's mission to find him.

On the other hand, the *Macon* was in excellent material condition, almost all of her crew were acquainted with their general quarters duties, and the importance of the F9C's was at least recognized. But she was pressed into a series of congested tactical problems in which the air was thick with airplanes, and in which an airship had no place at any time. These tactical donnybrooks bypassed the opening phase of the battle. Not only was the presence of the enemy known, but also his general intentions. The distances between the opposing fleets were rarely more than two or three hundred miles, which involved such small units of time that they demanded an aggressive employment of airplanes, not an airship. The *Macon*'s dilemma was that the fleet exercises of 1934 were framed with the purpose of developing the offensive qualities of carrier aviation, and gave no consideration to the uses of an airship. Nevertheless, it was in this environment that the *Macon* was supposed to demonstrate her military capabilities and general usefulness.

Across the continent from the Pacific battleground, Admiral King sensed the problem, and expressed his concern in a personal letter to Dresel. He put his finger on the heart of the matter with his observation that "this is a crucial year for airships, with the *Macon* carrying practically all the hopes for the future of airships in the Navy."[1] He thought a strenuous operating schedule would be necessary during the next nine months in order that a highly favorable report would be forthcoming from the Fleet.

In view of a general skepticism in the Fleet and Congress, King was convinced that an indifferent performance and a lukewarm report would not be sufficient to save the airship. And he warned Dresel that Commander Holloway Frost was on Admiral Sellers' staff. Frost had gone out of his way to ridicule the German Zeppelins in his study of naval warfare during 1914–1918,[2] and during a recent visit to the Navy Department was heard to remark that airships were useless. And many in the Department were inclined toward agreement. Thus the *Macon* would be performing before an audience which was probably not favorably disposed toward her.

At the same time King wrote Dresel, he sent off a letter to Rear Admiral John Halligan, ComAirBatFor (Commander Aircraft, Battle Force), which displayed his deeper concern for the airship:

This is to be a critical year for airships. We have only one airship. We must not be reckless, but if airships are to justify themselves, the *Macon* has got to show more than she has shown.

I am trying to keep an open mind on the airship question, but the more I see of airships the more I can visualize a useful field for them in searching operations, especially in conjunction with their airplanes, provided we can get the airships to perform.[3]

The yaw guys are out and taut, the main mooring cable has been connected and is being taken up, and the
Macon floats over the mobile mast, in the process of mooring. Her two forward propellers have been rotated
downward for vertical thrust; the engines will be brought up to speed, the mast's winch will take
up on the mooring cable, and the airship will have her nose spindle brought to the mast and locked in its cup.

Because fleet problems were few, he suggested to Halligan that special problems should be arranged for the *Macon* between exercises. She could search for fleet units in transit between the West Coast and Hawaii, or make a nonstop round trip to Hawaii, and the airship and her planes could be used to test the West Coast's air defenses upon their return. In his conclusion, King came directly to the point:

Summarizing them, this letter is a personal plea for (a) wider operation of the *Macon* directly with the Fleet and on additional problems which might be framed to suit her special characteristics; (b) a square deal all around for the *Macon* during this crucial year, so that at its conclusion when we come to total up the ledger, no one may say she has not had a fair test.

King's letter to Halligan, and a similar one he sent to Admiral Sellers, are ample proof that in spite of the passing of Admiral Moffett, the airship still had at least one proponent in the higher echelons of the Navy. It also suggests that the airship's test was political as much as military.

At 0734, 3 January 1934, the *Macon* was towed out of her hangar and moored in Moffett Field's south circle in preparation for her flight to Fleet Exercises F and G. Through the morning she rode the circle to let her helium absorb the sun's heat, and at 1421 took off. After she was in the air, Trapnell and Miller flew two F9C's aboard. A third plane would have been carried, but after leaving the ground she ascended into a steep temperature inversion in which her helium lost its superheat, and she had to dump 2.5 tons of ballast to climb through it. To carry a third or fourth plane she would have been obliged to dump more ballast, which was undesirable, or to fly dynamically at full speed to carry the planes' weight, and Dresel was concerned for the airship's fuel consumption.

The *Macon* had to have sufficient fuel to take her through two days of exercises and return to Sunnyvale with a reserve to allow circling for a few hours in case bad weather prevented an immediate landing. She usually returned to base with enough fuel for 48 hours, but fuel also had a value as ballast. If she consumed too much fuel she would return to base light and it would be necessary to valve relatively large quantities of helium in order to bring her down to the mast.

Under the depression economy the Bureau of Mines' helium plant at Amarillo was operating only intermittently. This caused the extraction process to operate at insufficient volume, making its costs artificially high, and the Navy's helium funds were limited. It was a vicious circle dictated by depression economics. Thus it was cheaper to consider fuel as ballast than to valve helium in the course of ordinary operations. In the long run it may have been wiser to have carried less fuel in order to carry more planes during fleet operations, and valve gas as necessary. But there was no assurance of extra helium funds, and with no helium there was no flying.

On the evening of the third, the *Macon* was off San Pedro Harbor with orders from Rear Admiral Joseph M. Reeves, ComBatFor (Commander, Battle Force), and commander of the BLUE forces, to search an area between San Nicholas and the Santa Cruz Islands. Her search began at 0600 on the fourth. The situation was a continuation of Exercises F and G; BLUE was advancing from its bases in the San Francisco area and trying to gain footholds in the Channel Islands in order to outflank BROWN's base at San Pedro and drive him back upon his main base at San Diego.

When the *Macon* set out, visibility was excellent and remained good all day. At 0649 nine enemy flying boats were sighted headed for the *Macon*. She turned tail to avoid them, and they passed clear by two miles. In spite of this distance, these planes of Patrol Squadron 21 optimistically claimed damage on the airship with machine-gun fire. At 0733 lookouts reported a concentration of ships in the northwest, and Trapnell and Larson were hoisted out in F9C's to investigate. By 0835 they reported 12 cruisers, four transports, and a swarm of destroyers. This was a BROWN convoy en route to reinforce San Nicholas. The *Macon* relayed her planes' reports to Admiral Reeves, with the result that he was able to launch an air strike which almost "wiped out" the convoy.

The *Macon* enjoyed unusual circumstances in this exercise because all the carriers[4] were assigned to BLUE. Nevertheless, by mid-morning the air activity launched from enemy shore bases had reached such a pitch that the airship felt obliged to limit her operations to the vicinity of a BLUE cruiser division, in order to have the "shelter" of its antiaircraft batteries. She remained here for the rest of the day. As darkness approached at 1725, the *Macon* decided to track the fleeing BROWN forces. But 30 minutes later she flew directly over a division of BROWN cruisers at point-blank range—with all her lights on—and was "shot down."[5]

During the night the *Macon* cruised around San Clemente Island, and at 0700 on the fifth was on station off the island's China Point when Exercise G got under way. Again, visibility was very good. This time the F9C's were put into the air immediately. The planes were directed to cover the western portion of her assigned area of search, while the *Macon* flew off to cover the eastern part. This sortie saw the first employment in a fleet exercise of the mathematical system of prenavigation devised by Mackey, which liberated the planes from their need of visual contact with the airship. This system had been neglected since it was first tried with the *Akron* in November of 1932.

The planes were sent out on a course which diverged from the airship's track at 60 degrees, with instructions to maintain a speed exactly twice the speed of the airship. On this course the planes generated a *relative* motion to the airship's track which was equal to the airship's speed; no matter how far they flew on, they would maintain a constant 90-degree bearing on the airship. Wind was of no concern so long as both aircraft were at the same altitude, because they were moving within the same medium. At any point along their divergent course of 60 degrees the planes could execute a

120-degree turn which converged with the airship's track at 60 degrees. On this homeward leg they would return to the airship in the same amount of time flown on the outbound leg.

Reflection on the airplane's position over this 60–60 course will show that its motion, *relative* to the airship's track, is zero. As far as *relative motion* is concerned the plane is simply "sliding" back-and-forth over a course 90 degrees to the airship's position.

Elementary? The application was novel in 1933–1934. Two years later, after trying other methods without success, the British physicist Henry T. Tizard, director of the development of England's prewar radar network, hit upon a similar system to solve the Royal Air Force's problems in directing interceptions. It proved to be the basic means by which ground controllers, working from radar intelligence, directed fighters against incoming bombers, and was a singular success in the Battle of Britain.[6]

The 60–60 system had the disadvantage of committing the airship and F9C's to a fixed speed and course until their rendezvous. But it was nevertheless a "break-

Vector Diagram of Relative Movement: ZRS airship and two airplanes.
Right: 60–60-degree Search System: ZRS airship and two planes for five hours.

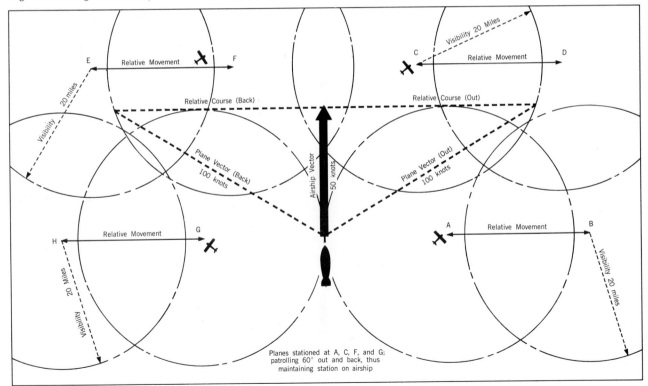

CAPTAIN D. M. MACKEY, USN (RET.)

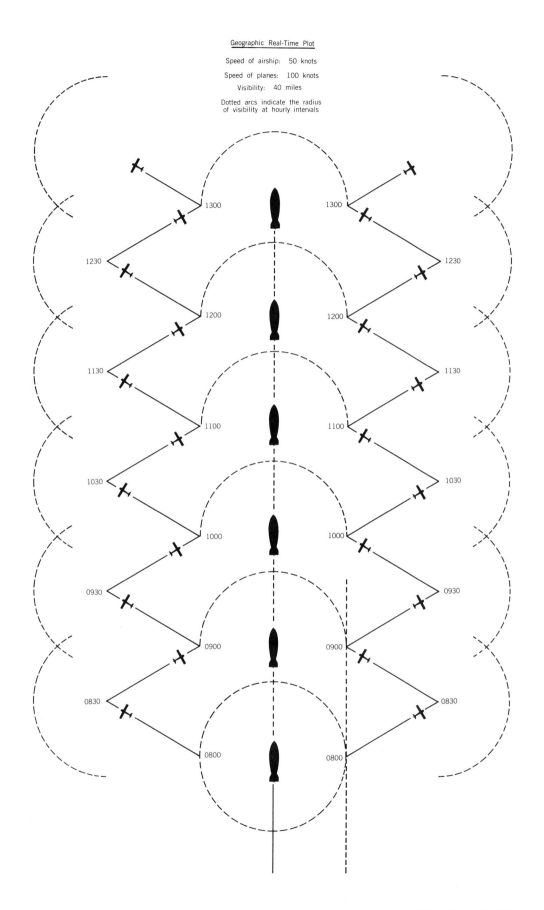

Geographic Real-Time Plot

Speed of airship: 50 knots

Speed of planes: 100 knots

Visibility: 40 miles

Dotted arcs indicate the radius
of visibility at hourly intervals

through." Its formula gave the F9C's a means of operating beyond the airship's horizon with assurance that they would find the trapeze where they expected it to be when they returned.

In this first practical use of the 60–60 system, the F9C's were operated together over the same course. Using the F9C's in pairs was a standard precautionary measure during these early over-the-horizon operations, in case a plane was forced down in the sea. On this sortie, however, it was the *Macon,* not the planes, which found the enemy. A few minutes later her planes returned and were sent ahead to investigate; their information, relayed by the *Macon,* provided the BLUE commander with visual confirmation of an enemy course change his radio had intercepted.

The F9C's proceeded to track the enemy force, but troubles in their radiotelephones forced them to use key transmission, which was poor. Reports came into the airship slowly, and often had to be repeated several times. Here it is important to visualize the pilot flying his cranky F9C with one hand, working his radio key with the other, while attempting to interpret the movements of the enemy ships from a cockpit which afforded miserable visibility, and at the same time keeping an eye open for enemy aircraft!

At 1135 the *Macon's* topside lookouts reported a formation of planes above the airship which seemed to be preparing for an attack. Fifteen minutes later 18 enemy fighters swept in around the *Macon* and "shot her down." The exercise did not end until darkness, so the *Macon* continued to operate as the "ZRS7." At 1535, however, Admiral Sellers released her from the exercise and she headed north at a leisurely speed to arrive over the Farallon Islands on the morning of the sixth. The rest of the day was spent around the Farallons, assisting in the calibration of the islands' RDF installation. By 1635 she was back at Moffett Field. She had been in the air for 74 hours and 14 minutes, flown 3,439 miles, and had 33,430 pounds of fuel on board upon mooring.

In summarizing the *Macon's* performance in these exercises for Admiral Sellers, Mackey observed that the excellent visibility and operations in sight of the Santa Barbara Islands had greatly simplified the airship's navigation. But he thought the accuracy of the positions given in the *Macon's* contact reports was doubtful. Bearings were accurate, but distances only estimates. And he reported that the airship was learning to be more cautious about approaching unidentified ships, and the handling of her planes was improving.

Mackey's report illuminated several of the F9C's troubles. None was new. The Harrigan Report anticipated most of them in 1932; but now they existed in fact and could be articulated in detail:

Experience to date seems to indicate that maneuverability, strength, and high speed are characteristics not required of an airship's planes. Prime considerations should be long endurance, good reliable communications *by voice* up to at least 100 miles, and a speed of 110–120 knots. . . . These planes can protect the airship most efficiently by giving her ample warning of enemy approach. It is further felt that the airship planes should not engage in combat except as it is forced upon them, or in an effort to give the airship a chance to escape when seriously threatened. They are too valuable to lose. The planes must be navigated from the airship as accurately as possible to do. This should be the sole task of one officer. It will facilitate determining the position of contacts reported, as well as relieve the strain on the pilot, who has all he can do otherwise.[7]

When Admiral Sellers made his report to the Fleet he saw fit to quote several passages from Mackey's report, including the above paragraph. The Admiral remarked favorably upon 13 valuable contact reports the *Macon* made in Exercise F, and 11 in Exercise G. But he was caustic about her loitering around the BLUE cruisers for antiaircraft protection. This made the *Macon* an aerial signpost which would draw enemy aircraft to her, and permit them to locate the surface units. And if she was hiding behind friendly antiaircraft batteries, she was not doing any searching. The *Macon's* "destruction" as a result of flying over the enemy at night with her lights on led Sellers to the precipitate conclusion that "it is not thought that the airship is suitable for tactical scouting at night."[8] And the Admiral fell into the same confusion experienced by too many congressmen, by complaining that the *Macon* was flying too low; he wanted her to develop as a tactical scout by operating at high altitudes.

In these same exercises, the carrier *Langley* had sneaked close inshore and launched a devastating surprise attack on the "enemy" airfield at San Diego. But the *Langley* was in turn "destroyed" by an enemy counterattack. The carrier *Lexington* was ruled completely out of action as a result of dive-bombing attacks. But Sellers optimistically observed that "our carriers, however, have one great advantage: they will be very difficult to sink [and] even if their upper works and flight deck were completely wrecked, they could continue to act as 8-inch [gun] cruisers."[9]

This apologia employed casuistry as fatuous as that used by some of the airship men in their efforts to promote the airship. But no similar apologia was forthcoming from Sellers to explain away the *Macon's* difficulties. The difference was that the aircraft carrier was already acknowledged naval hardware, and had been for almost a decade. And the carrier enjoyed a wonderfully broad political base, in naval aviation and in the Fleet. The airship, however, was an alien thing which had been cooped up in Lakehurst for too long and had yet to be worked into the over-all scheme of naval operations. Nor was it destined to be.

The Fleet's reports of this period suggest that the *Macon* was being tolerated until she spent herself, and then the Fleet could go on about its business. There is a further suggestion that in these exercises she was dealt out like the queen of spades in a hand of hearts—an impediment to the side which received her services.

Except for a brief flight to San Diego on 8–9 February, the *Macon* did not fly again until she was obliged to take part in Exercises H and I. Exercise H began at 0500 on the twentieth, but a squall delayed takeoff until 1157, and she did not arrive in the exercise area until early evening. By this hour Exercise H was almost concluded. She carried three F9C's but none were used. The weather was wretched—the surface covered by large patches of fog, the ceiling only 200 feet, and the air filled with drizzle.

At twilight the "enemy" battleships *Texas* and *New York* spied the *Macon* about 13 miles away, groping through the murk. Between 1815 and 1825 they watched her fly toward them, until the range was within 12,000 yards, and then "opened fire" with their searchlights. Aboard the *Texas,* Rear Admiral T. T. Craven remarked that she made a "splendid target." The *Macon* continued to close the range until 1831, when she finally turned away. Admiral Sellers remarked on this with a disgusted shrug.[10] But Sellers was not on board the *Macon.*

Just as the *Macon* closed the battleships, Dresel was observing his aerologist, Lieutenant Anthony Danis, assemble the evening weather map, the data for which had just come over the radio. Early that day the weather had been bad, then miserable, and now a line squall threatened. Dresel was no daredevil. By his own admission, his ideas of airship operation were "very conservative,"[11] and he had a healthy respect for weather. He knew that he was responsible for the *Macon's* performance, but also that he was responsible for the safety of officers and men on board. The lines which Danis was drawing on the weather map could be a grim reality within hours; the searchlights flashing from the ships below were only a political threat to the *Macon.*

Dresel ignored the enemy contact; his mind was on the squall in prospect and the weather map's indication that the fields at Camp Kearny and Sunnyvale would probably be socked in during the next 48 hours. For the next two hours the *Macon* continued south, then at 2205, in the vicinity of San Nicholas Island, turned around and headed back to Moffett Field, where she moored at 0746 on the twenty-first. In view of the *Macon's* exposed political position, this was not an easy decision for Dresel to make. He knew there would be criticism. But he had the satisfaction of having the next three days' weather prove his judgment correct.

The *Macon* was late for Exercise H, and was back in her hangar when Exercise I got under way. This did not set very well with Admiral Sellers, in spite of his judgment that the "weather was particularly unsuitable for all aircraft operations."[12] The Admiral's notion of "all aircraft" was evidently limited to airplanes, excluding the F9C-2, because he felt that the weather conditions were well suited to the *Macon's* employment. She could have remained above the clouds and sent her planes down under the 200-foot ceiling, where visibility was less than 1,000 yards, to search for the enemy. But Rear Admiral Frank H. Brumby, ComScoFor, remarked that he thought the low ceiling and poor visibility would have rendered the *Macon* and her planes useless. The *Macon* was evidently damned if she did and damned if she didn't. This was a tough audience to perform for, indeed. Even when there was no performance.

The *Macon* did not put her nose out of her shed for the next 28 days. When she did, it was to exercise her F9C's on the trapeze and at gunnery drill, and to try out a new hook-on plane. By the summer of 1933, it was clear that the N2Y trainers were inadequate for utility planes. The service types available were too large to pass through the door to the airship's airplane compartment, so Ward Harrigan canvassed the civilian airplane market. He came up with the Waco UBF, a three-place sport biplane.

There was some hemming and hawing on the part of the Plans Division about the purchase of these planes; but Garland Fulton convoyed them through the Bureau to a contract. Thus on 16 March 1934, two skyhook-equipped Wacos, with the Navy designation of XJW-1, were delivered to Moffett Field. On 20 March, upon the *Macon's* return to the bay area after exercising the F9C's at sea, the Wacos were flown to the trapeze for

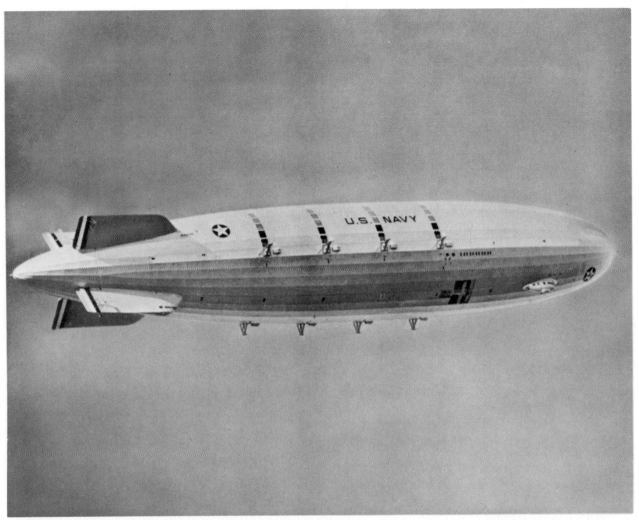

Loafing along on six engines somewhere in the vicinity of Moffett Field, preparatory to mooring, the Macon's hangar deck crew has readied one of her N2Y "running boats" for a mail run to the ground.

In early 1934, two Waco UBF's, a three-place sport plane, were procured from the civil airplane market as replacements for the obsolescent N2Y's. They were used as "running boats" to ferry mail and personnel.
JOHN C. MITCHELL

the first time. Some minor difficulties were found in stowing the new planes inside her hangar, but these were eventually ironed out.

Since the first of the year a radical modification had been under study: removal of the *Macon*'s No. 3 and No. 4 engines. Their removal would relieve the airship of 15,044 pounds; this could be converted to fuel capacity which would extend her range at 50 knots by almost 2,000 miles. Her top speed would be reduced by four knots, but the increase in range more than compensated for this. Dresel responded enthusiastically to the proposal and requested the Bureau's permission to temporarily remove the propellers, outriggers, radiators, and other protuberances, to clean up her hull in order to determine the airship's speed with six engines. But the Bureau wondered if the *Macon* would have sufficient speed for retrieving planes if one or two of the remaining six engines failed. Authorization was given to remove the water-recovery condensers on No. 3 and No. 4 engines, and this was done in March. But the engine removal idea was still under discussion when the *Macon* was lost.

In April the Fleet was preparing for its annual concentration and joint exercises of the Atlantic and Pacific Fleets. In 1934 this was Fleet Problem XV, which was simply a combination of Exercises M and N of the alphabetical series; it was to be held in the Caribbean, in order to determine how quickly the Pacific Fleet could be moved through the Panama Canal to the Caribbean perimeter of the Antilles. Exercises J, K, and L would be conducted en route to Panama, but the *Macon* would leave the Fleet after J.

The *Macon*'s participation in the Caribbean operations had been planned for since late 1933, and it was an event which none of her complement looked forward to. The exercises posed no difficulties, but in order to reach the Caribbean the *Macon* would again have to struggle through the canyons of the continental divide. There were the alternate routes, however; the one across Tehuantepec, and there was a possibility of her accompanying the Fleet via Panama.

Dresel aptly described the transcontinental route as the hardest flight possible for an airship of the *Macon*'s characteristics. He preferred to follow the Fleet or Tehuantepec as the alternatives. Panama was not only the easiest, but would permit the *Macon* to move with the Fleet and join in all the exercises. But lack of mooring and servicing facilities in the Canal Zone made this out of the question; the Army had prevented the Navy from developing an airship base on its Balboa site.

The CNO offered to recommission the *Patoka* and have her sent to Panama to service the *Macon*, but Dresel would have none of that. He had been umpire on board the *Los Angeles* in 1931 when she operated for several days from the *Patoka*'s mast in the Gulf of Dulce. On more than one occasion she had dunked her tail while moored to the tanker's mast. The *Macon* was a much larger airship; the prospects of her putting her tail in the sea were not only greater, but because of the auxiliary control room in her lower fin it would be more serious. The State Department obtained permission from the Mexican government for a Tehuantepec passage; but Admiral Sellers had already made up his mind —the *Macon* was going to the Caribbean via the canyons of the continental divide.

In the meantime there was Exercise J. At 1501, 9 April, the *Macon* took off and headed down the Pacific coast to rendezvous with the BLUE Fleet near Guadalupe Island, about 200 miles off the coast of Baja California. The exercise got under way at 0500 on an overcast 10 April; the ceiling varied between 2,000 and 3,000 feet, with only a few breaks in the cloud layer. During 0540-0715 and 0840-1005, the *Macon* had her two planes in the air, searching her assigned area to seaward of Guadalupe. She found nothing. In other words, she was able to inform the BLUE commander that there was no enemy to his west, and that he could concentrate his attention on threats from the south and east. At 1055 she was instructed to make a sweep between Guadalupe and Point San Eugenia on the Mexican coast. On this new track she quickly found action.

Shortly after 1300 the *Macon* was jumped by a pair of enemy dive bombers. In an effort to lose them by diving into the overcast, she flew out beneath the ceiling into the face of a division of enemy cruisers, which immediately opened fire on her. An hour later a squadron of enemy dive bombers brought her under attack; she was ruled "shot down" and instructed to continue as the "ZRS6." As the hypothetical ZRS6, the *Macon* lasted about 90 minutes, when she was again destroyed. She continued in the exercise as the "ZRS7" and managed to survive until the afternoon of the eleventh, when she was released from the operations.[13] The Fleet continued on to Panama, and the *Macon* returned to Sunnyvale to prepare for her struggle through the mountains.

At 0937, 20 April, the *Macon* cast off from her mast and took off for Opa-locka, Florida, her base of operations during the Caribbean maneuvers. The 54.5-hour flight between Sunnyvale and Opa-locka was one of the wildest flights a rigid airship ever experienced. It almost

The navigating bridge of the Macon's control car.
Directly in front of the rudderman's wheel is a mag-
netic compass; on the girder above, a clinometer.
Inside the vertical girder at left is a voice tube to
the radio room, and an altimeter and airspeed indicator
for the OOD. The dark rectangle hanging over the windows
at left is a variometer. To the right is a "black
box" whose gauges give the airship's static condition
while moored. On the small blackboard, upper right,
are recorded the barometric reading at takeoff, and
total fuel. To its right is a telegraph used in mooring; directly below, a voice tube to the captain's cabin.
The canvas bag at right contains life jackets. In the
deck at right is a circular plug, which is a mount
for a drift meter. Rigid airships were not flown;
they were commanded.

Right: Inside the Macon's control car,
looking aft from the bridge.

brought the *Macon* to a disastrous end in a Texas canyon, and it inflicted upon her the structural malaise which erupted in crisis ten months later and triggered a series of events which sent her to the bottom of the Pacific off Point Sur, California.

The *Macon*'s problem on her flight east was the same as the *Akron*'s in 1932. Both were low-altitude aircraft, both had to cross a mountain range which obliged them to fly at or above pressure height, and both had to begin their climb into the mountains before they were able to consume enough fuel to lighten themselves for an easy crossing. The *Macon* had an advantage in 1934, however; she was not carrying any airplanes. It was originally planned to carry one of the Wacos as a "running boat"; but the utility plane was finally sent cross-country with the F9C's.

When the *Macon* departed Sunnyvale she carried about 21 tons of fuel and eight tons of ballast. As she cruised down the coast she was flying in equilibrium, but when she swung east and into the warmer air masses over land she became increasingly heavy. After fighting her way with full power through unusually violent air in San Gorgonio Pass, she flew into the hot, thin desert air of the Imperial Valley where she became 22,000 pounds heavy. By the time she arrived over Yuma, Arizona, at 2030, she had dumped more than half of her ballast and about 2.5 tons of fuel.

At about 2300, over Phoenix, she circled to await daylight of the twenty-first before entering the mountainous territory between Phoenix and Dragoon, Arizona. The route was lighted by airway beacons, but they were for airplanes, and were placed on the mountain peaks; they could not serve the airship, which had to hug the valley floors between the peaks in order to remain below pressure height. The most difficult passage here was Dragoon Pass, only little more than half a mile wide, whose 4,400-foot elevation forced the airship to frequently fly over her pressure height. After clearing the Dragoon Mountains at about 0600, the *Macon* sped across New Mexico with her shadow following the tracks of the Southern Pacific Railroad.

El Paso was in sight from the bridge at about 1050, and as she flew into West Texas her troubles began again. The desert sun had raised her helium's superheat to ten degrees and the cells' automatic valves were chattering in their seats from the pressure of the expanded gas as she flew along at pressure height. The desert sand reflected the sun's rays back into the atmosphere where their heat accelerated the air into violent

eddies. The writhing air whipped up the desert's sand in "dust devils," each an evanescent cyclonic storm in miniature, which raced alongside the *Macon* and threw themselves against her hull.

Around noon on 21 April the 785-foot-long airship was snaking her way through a pass in the vicinity of Van Horn, Texas, with her eight engines turning at full power. On both sides, the hard faces of the Sierra Diable range looked down from a thousand feet upon her passage. She had been flying under full power for almost two hours. The airship was about 15,000 pounds heavy; the full power was necessary not only for dynamic lift, but for control in the narrow canyon's increasingly turbulent air.

By noon the air conditions had become extremely violent, and the *Macon* was rising and falling at rates of from 24 to 36 feet per second. The men on board had to grope their way hand-over-hand along her keels' passageways. Two men were necessary to work the elevators' controls, and they had to be relieved at ten-minute intervals because of exhaustion. In the chartroom aft of the bridge, Don Mackey clung to the chart table for balance, and during one fall he looked up in surprise to see a pair of 7×50 binoculars and his dividers and parallel rules "floating" in the air before his eyes—for a moment. Then the *Macon* went into a steep dive and a gust of terrific force slammed into her.

At this moment Chief Boatswain's Mate Robert J. Davis was at the after end of the port keel's corridor, inspecting the structure around frame zero. When the gust hit the *Macon* he heard a terrible grinding noise, and discovered that one of the diagonal girders in frame 17.5 had broken. He immediately ran forward to muster a repair gang. Lieutenant Walter Zimmerman, who was in the upper keel at the instant of the gust, also heard the sounds. By the time he climbed down from the top of the airship a second diagonal girder had broken. By this time Davis was back on the scene with half a dozen men and damage control materials.

The repairs to the two broken girders were completed within half an hour. In the meantime, signs of buckling began to appear in some of the main ring's other girders. This, too, occurred between longitudinals 8 and 9, where the port fin was bolted to frame 17.5. By 1400 all repairs and reinforcements were completed. In view of the progressive rate of structural damage, it seems likely that within a relatively short period frame 17.5's diagonal girders near the fin junction would have failed completely, and the violent air condi-

 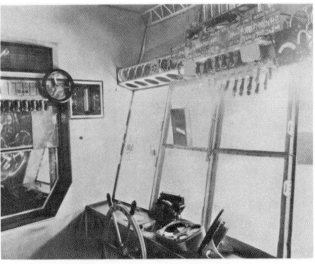

There was no direct control of the engines from the bridge in the Akron and Macon. The OOD signaled speeds to the engine rooms by means of a telegraph, and machinist's mates on watch in the engine rooms executed the signals. The four telegraphs direct the eight engines. Each telegraph has two handles and two "jingle" bell pulls. The handles at extreme upper left allow remote control release of trail ropes, port, starboard, forward and aft, for mooring. Right: navigator's chartroom.

The port side of the Macon's bridge, opposite the telegraphs. The wheel controls the elevators. Forward of the wheel: elevator angle indicator and two bubble-type inclinometers. At right: altimeter, airspeed indicator, and a rate-of-climb meter. The large gauge tilted at 45° is a German altimeter. Rectangular box in the middle of window: variometer. High row of handles: water-ballast releases. Lower row: fuel dump tank releases. Far right: superheat meter. Far left: handles for individual gas valve controls.

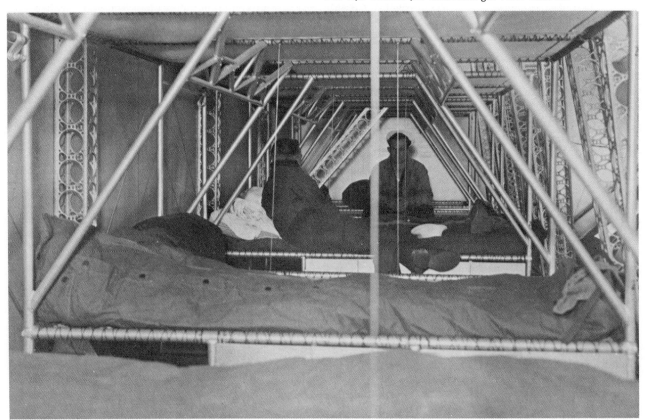

Crewmen relax in the Macon's bunk room.

tions would have torn away the *Macon*'s port fin. Davis' conscientiousness, quick thinking, and quick actions probably saved the *Macon* from a dismal ending in the wastelands of West Texas.[14]

From Van Horn to Florida the flying was downhill, the flight became progressively easier, and by the evening of the twenty-second the *Macon* was riding in Opa-locka's mooring circle. But this was only a temporary respite. On 5 May she was due in the Caribbean for the fleet problem, and could not fly into the middle of the Caribbean for two or three days of operations with her bandaged tail. But Alger Dresel had already made arrangements for a more permanent repair.

On the evening of the twenty-first, shortly after finishing dinner, Garland Fulton was called to the phone by the Navy Department's duty officer who had a confidential message from the *Macon*. Upon arrival at the Navy Department, Fulton was given a dispatch from Dresel which described the *Macon*'s damage and requested immediate repairs.

Within the hour Fulton was on the phone to Akron, Ohio, speaking with Dr. Arnstein. The next morning the doctor had V. W. "Red" Coffelt, Goodyear-Zeppelin's general foreman, and a mechanic aboard Goodyear's Fokker transport, en route to Florida. A day later, stress analyst Kurt Bauch, two more mechanics, and repair materials were on a train for Miami. For nine days the Goodyear men and the *Macon*'s crew worked 16 hours a day to effect a more permanent repair to the damaged girders. These days were none too pleasant.

The day after the *Macon* arrived at Opa-locka a 40-knot thunder squall overloaded with rain blew into the base, the first of several torrential downpours experienced at Opa-locka. As rain water accumulated on and in the *Macon* she became heavier, and ballast had to be discharged to prevent the weight of the rain—which amounted to tons—from putting a sagging strain on her hull. When the rain stopped and the sun dried her out, ballast had to be pumped back aboard. On some occasions ballast alone was insufficient to compensate for the rapidly changing static condition, and fuel, too, had to be pumped to and from shore. Then another squall would blow in and the cycle was repeated. The squalls included sudden wind shifts, some of which sent the airship's tail hurtling around the mooring circle's railroad tracks at unbelievable speeds. A mooring-mast watch on board the *Macon* at Opa-locka was frequently a busy and exciting four hours.

While at the mast, the *Macon*'s bow hatch at the mooring spindle had to be left open for gas, fuel, and ballast hose connections. Rain ran off her outer hull, poured through the hatch, and ran down inside her fabric cover to flood the control car and collect in the lower hull spaces. Rain swept through the louvered gas valve discharge openings along the top of her hull and into the upper keel's passageway; it flowed along the keel's narrow catwalk as if in a canal until it reached the end of the walkway at frame 17.5, where it cascaded down between gas cells I and zero, into the lower fin. Crewmen noticed some unusual bulges in the fabric of the *Macon*'s elevators; holes were drilled in their aluminum trailing edges and a few hundred pounds of water drained out.

The effects of these heavy rains were unusual; in flight, her motion would have swept most of the rain off her hull. But the experience was an enlightening one. It provided the crew with a series of intensive lessons in mooring-mast operations under unfavorable and rapidly changing conditions, and revealed some minor considerations for future airship design.

Opa-locka, in 1934, was in the middle of a swampy waste. The *Macon*'s officers and crew were berthed and messed in tents on the field. Everything was damp, and the evening air was crowded with ferocious mosquitoes. The heavy rains churned up the nests of animal life in the palmetto around the field, and among those disturbed was a group of owls who sought shelter inside the airship. The *Macon* had had owl troubles at Moffett Field; but the Sunnyvale birds were content to roost among the steel girders of Hangar No. 1 and harass the crew by whitewashing the *Macon*'s upper strakes. The Opa-locka owls, however, were setting up housekeeping between the *Macon*'s gas cells and her outer cover, and there was danger of their clawing holes in the cells. Far more threatening than the owls were the rattlesnakes which the rains had driven out of the ground. Everyone was very careful where he walked around the field at Opa-locka. In spite of several good liberties in Miami, all hands were just a little glad when the time came to shove off for Exercise M.

On the morning of 5 May, the *Macon* left Opa-locka to join the Fleet in the Caribbean. After her takeoff, Trapnell and Miller flew two F9C's aboard. But besides her F9C's the *Macon* had on board another winged creature—an owl which was homesteading at the top of No. VIII gas cell. A careful watch was kept on the bird for fear of its holing the cell, and by 2300 the stow-

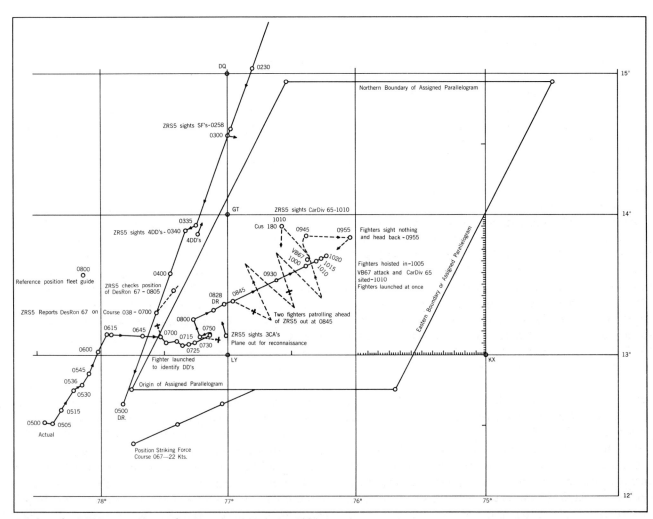

Track of the USS Macon *during Fleet Exercise "M," 6 May 1934.*

away was captured and launched over the side as the airship crossed Point Morant, Jamaica.

In Exercise M an enemy GRAY fleet had seized Puerto Rico and the Virgin Islands. The BLUE fleet, which had just transited the Panama Canal, had the task of destroying the GRAY fleet and retaking the islands. The *Macon* was part of the BLUE forces. By 0500, 6 May, after running an obstacle course of thunderstorms southeast of Jamaica, the airship was at 77° 30′ W. 12° 15′ S., a point roughly midway between the Canal Zone and Kingston, Jamaica. Here she was ordered to begin a search to the northeast.

At 0722 the lookouts discovered a group of destroyers on the northern horizon. Trapnell took off in an F9C for a close look while the *Macon* turned tail to the south to open the gun range. Within half an hour Trapnell had identified them as GRAY forces and had his plane back on its trolley inside the *Macon*'s hangar. After this contact the sky blackened, the air filled with squalls, and visibility fell to less than ten miles. Thus at 0745 the *Macon* emerged from a cloud into the face of three strange cruisers. In anticipation of their launching seaplanes, Dresel promptly turned downwind, and sped away from the ships at 90 knots. As she made her turn an F9C was launched to investigate the ships, which proved to be GRAY forces.

Visibility remained poor. This created difficulties; it increased the chances of the *Macon* stumbling onto enemy forces at close range, and it restricted the use of her F9C's. At 0845 the planes were launched to fly a 60–60 patrol about ten miles wide back and forth across the airship's track at the limit of visibility ahead. For the next hour nothing was seen, and at 1005 the planes returned aboard to refuel. And then the *Macon* flew into a hornets' nest of enemy aircraft.

While the F9C's were being secured on their trolleys everything happened at once. The airship's radio monitor picked up enemy planes talking on their command sets. They were directly above the *Macon* at 12,000 feet, reporting her to the *Lexington,* and informing the carrier they were about to attack. The F9C's were immediately ordered back into the air. In the same instant a hole appeared in the weather and the control car spotted the *Lexington* 20 miles to the north, and the topside lookouts reported enemy fighters overhead, diving on the *Macon*. Trapnell cleared the trapeze, but Kivette and his F9C were only being swung out of the hangar when the air around the *Macon* became alive with Grumman FF-1's. The carrier pilots had a field

day buzzing around the big airship, "shooting it down," and Mackey ruled that the *Macon* was destroyed.

Between the moment the *Macon* spotted the *Lexington* and the airship's "destruction," the *Macon*'s radio was able to send out the carrier's position, but not its course and speed. But ComAirBLUE demanded the information in spite of her being shot down. Mackey had to stretch a point and permit the information to be sent out, supposedly by Trapnell's F9C, which had survived the attack.

The *Macon* was disengaged until 1048, when she was told to resume operations as the "ZRS6," and was given specific instructions to find the *Lexington*. At 1158 Dresel reckoned he was about 30 miles astern of the carrier, and launched his planes; but it had made some radical course changes, and they did not find the *Lexington* until 1307. The F9C's shadowed the carrier until 1442 without being discovered. Their reports, frequently garbled by static and repeated many times, were relayed by the *Macon* to the BLUE fleet. This information permitted ComAirBLUE in the *Saratoga* to launch a highly successful attack against the *Lexington*.[15]

After 1442 the *Macon* was told to return to her originally assigned area of search. About half an hour later she came upon a large group of cruisers and destroyers, which her planes identified as GRAY forces. During the rest of the afternoon she found nothing, and at 1847 was released from the exercise to return to Opa-locka.

The Bureau had made considerable effort to prepare the newly finished mast and mooring circle at Guantanamo Bay for the *Macon*'s use in these exercises. The Fisherman's Point mast was about 500 miles closer to the Caribbean exercise area than Opa-locka; but the *Macon* had information that the fuel there was low octane and contaminated with water, and thus felt obliged to return to the more distant base. This was annoying to the Bureau, and did not please Admiral Sellers.

During her return to Opa-locka, her No. 1 engine burned out a bearing. Immediately after mooring on the evening of the seventh,[16] Chief Warrant Machinist Emmett Thurman had his machinist's mates removing the engine. While the airship swung at the mast, her engineers hoisted out the defective engine, lifted in a spare, and by midnight had it almost completely installed. This was not only valuable experience, it also proved that some large repairs could be made at a secondary mast facility, and that an airship did not always have to rely upon availability of a two-million-dollar hangar.

At 0855, 11 May, the *Macon* took off for Exercise N

which concluded the fleet problem. Two planes were flown aboard, and Dresel put the airship on a great circle across the Bahamas for Mona Passage and Puerto Rico, 1,000 miles to the southeast. This operation continued Exercise M, with BLUE trying to destroy GRAY's naval forces and isolate his armies in Puerto Rico. The action occurred off the southwest quarter of the island, between Cape Rojo and Point Figuras.

The *Macon* was circling Cape Rojo at 0955, 12 May, when the exercise began, and struck out on a sweep to the southeast. As usual, her mission was tactical scouting; but Admiral Sellers also thought she might be useful for collecting weather data for the BLUE forces. On these searches she began to experiment with several new procedures which had been under study for a few months.

At 1050 her lookouts reported a huge formation of ships dead ahead; the *Macon* swung away to the east and launched her planes. Thus far her response to the contact was conventional. But at this point she broke with her old habits. The ships were identified as the enemy's advance forces; but instead of having her planes shadow them, Larson and Young were directed to fly southeast for about 40 miles, on a track which angled across the wake of the advance force in anticipation of their discovering the enemy's main body. After flying 40 miles, they were told to turn east and rendezvous with the *Macon* 30 miles off Point Figuras. Thus for a second time the F9C's were thrown out to shift for themselves.

The planes had barely disappeared over the horizon when, at 1107, a tube burned out in the *Macon*'s radiotelephone set, and she had no voice communication with the F9C's for the next half hour. In the meantime, information came in on her main radio from other BLUE units that GRAY's main body was located and was making a series of course changes. When this data was correlated with the directed track of the F9C's it became obvious that the planes would miss the enemy. But the *Macon* could not recall her planes; she had to make the rendezvous at Point Figuras. By 1215 Young and Larson were back on board, and the *Macon* returned to Cape Rojo to begin another search.

This second search employed yet another new tactic, in which the planes were *controlled* from the *Macon*. At 1310, while the airship circled Point Brea, Miller and Young were sent out with exacting instructions to maintain a constant speed over a search course to the southwest. They would be navigated by radio from the

airship. Maintaining a constant speed was of vital importance in this first experiment. It would allow Mackey, who was handling their navigation, to keep an accurate plot of their flight on a maneuvering board and know where they were at all times. After the F9C's were launched, the *Macon* returned to Cape Rojo and circled until the planes returned to roost at 1430.

During the first half hour the F9C's flew southwest. Then at 1335 they began receiving instructions from the *Macon* to take off on a series of dog-legs to the east, then southeast, then south, and again southeast. The *Macon* was directing these courses from information overheard in BLUE's radio traffic and from intercepted enemy radio calls. Mackey plotted this information on his maneuvering board, which showed the positions of the enemy units relative to the position of the F9C's, and allowed him to direct an interception. At 1400 Miller and Young saw a large group of ships over their cowl rings. It was GRAY's carrier divisions. The two pilots throttled their F9C's back to the horizon to shadow the carriers and develop the contact, and at 1410 made a streak for the *Macon*.

This experiment was executed in a limited area with the airship in a relatively stationary position. Nevertheless, the F9C's were successfully navigated for more than an hour, over a varying track of 165 miles, and a maximum distance of 60 miles. The "Flight Control Officer" whom the Harrigan Report anticipated was now more than a few typewritten lines buried in the files of BuAer. Harrigan had failed in his effort to have Mackey assigned to the *Akron;* now Mackey was becoming the airship's "Flight Control Officer" anyhow, but on board the *Macon.*

After recovering her planes the *Macon* resumed her old habits and flew off to scout by herself. At 1508 she came upon GRAY's main body, and swung away from the contact to make a complete report of the formation. Fortunately for the airship, the enemy had no aircraft carriers in his main body.[17] Shortly after this she was released from the exercise and returned to Opa-locka, where she moored at 0545, 13 May.

In his report to Admiral Sellers, Mackey included certain observations which form a postscript to the Harrigan Report, and which illuminate the progress in airship search tactics as of the spring of 1934:

I believe that the concept of a rigid airship, of itself, being a scout is false. It is more on the order of an aerial carrier. The attached planes must accomplish the scouting.

The airship's sole function . . . is to impart mobility and endurance to her planes. This concept then, should be the basis on which we start to build airship tactics. A skillful development along these lines may prove that the airship is of equal value in tactical scouting situations to what we believe is its value in strategical scouting.

The employment of the airship in tactical problems has been of value, not so much to prove its worth to the Fleet, as it has to provide a school for airship officers in studying airship tactics. I respectfully submit that the inherent capabilities of the airship can be demonstrated only when the operating personnel have attained perfection in the utilization of this instrument.[18]

Mackey's report noted that the *Macon* had tried four methods of search with her F9C's: (1) having them maintain a constant bearing at a constant distance off the airship's beam; (2) flying them on station ahead, either with two planes straddling the airship's track or flying a 60–60 pattern back and forth across it; (3) flying the planes out and back a certain distance beyond the horizon using the 60–60 system, or having them rendezvous with the airship at some predetermined geographic position; and (4) navigating the planes from the airship by radio.

The first method had the advantage of allowing a very broad sweep, but was suitable only for patrol work. The second, which insured that the planes would make the initial contact, was considered best for general scouting when an enemy contact was imminent. The third held a number of possibilities, but also limitations: it could be used only when the enemy's position was more-or-less known and it was desired to keep him under intermittent observation. But the 60–60 method held promise in combination with the first method, to expand its sweep. The use of a geographic rendezvous was contingent upon operations close to land and having a prominent landmark available. In both cases of the third method, the airship was inflexibly committed to her course and speed until the planes were recovered, and this could prove disadvantageous. The fourth method, by which the planes were navigated from the airship, was regarded as the best; it was the most elastic, and could be combined with the better features of the other methods. But it was contingent upon improved radio communications, and a reliable means of homing the planes to the airship in the event the system broke down.

During the Caribbean operations the *Macon* had experimented with these methods, but the core of her tactics remained those of the immediate past. The airship was still a too prominent figure on stage in the scouting act; but at least she was no longer trying to hog the show. The conservative and spasmodic approach to the experiment, however, cloaks a transition. The *Macon* had taken her first step toward becoming a "lighter-than-air carrier."

Two days before the *Macon* left for California, Admirals Standley and King visited Opa-locka to inspect her. This was partly a diplomatic effort on King's part, prompted by Standley's disdain for the *Macon*. King himself may have had some doubts at this moment. The next day, when Trapnell flew into Jacksonville to refuel his F9C while en route back to Sunnyvale, King's plane was on the field being serviced. The Admiral recognized the F9C and made it a point to have a few words with its pilot. King, of course, was noncommittal, but Trapnell thought he was visibly worried by the *Macon*'s damage and lukewarm reports he had received of her performance in the Caribbean.

Admiral King was definitely not pleased with the *Macon* returning to California. He wanted her to continue operations with the Fleet while it was in the Atlantic, and be present at the Presidential Fleet Review on 31 May. This would have necessitated dusting off the rigid airship facilities at Lakehurst, but King thought it was worth the expense in order to keep her operating with the Fleet. Dresel, however, was not enthusiastic about delaying return to the West Coast until October, when the *Macon* would have to negotiate the Texas canyons in the thunderstorm season. But it was the damage to frame 17.5 which finally decided her return to Sunnyvale.

On the morning watch, 16 May, the crew was busy preparing the *Macon* for her return to Moffett Field; 175,000 cubic feet of helium was piped to her gas cells, her tanks were topped off with 22,220 pounds of gasoline, and 1,200 pounds of food was stowed on board. At 0707 she was cast off from the mast and turned her nose across the Gulf of Mexico for El Paso. The usual troubles were encountered in the mountain passes of West Texas; but compared to her flight east, her return to Sunnyvale was a relatively uneventful 51 hours. She moored in Moffett Field's south circle at 0707, 18 May.

The *Macon* did not fly again until 19 June, when she made a 44-hour flight up the coast to the vicinity of Coos Bay, Oregon; no planes were carried. The more important events of June were not the airship's operations, but the turnover in her personnel. Lieutenant Commander Bert Rodgers, her executive officer, who

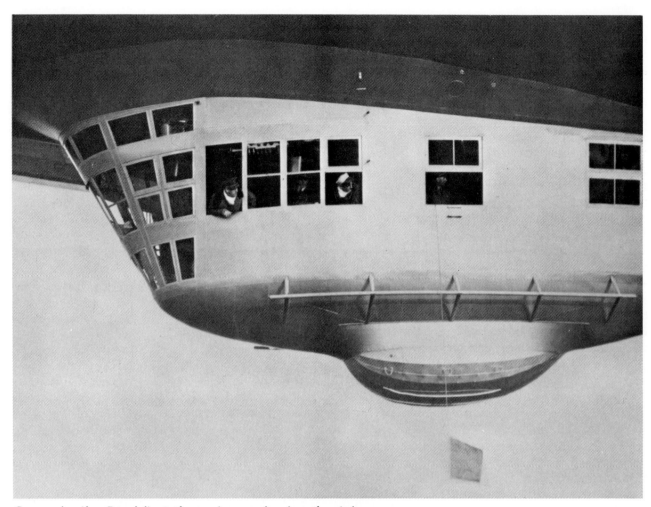

Commander Alger Dresel directs the mooring procedure from the windows
of the Macon's *control car. The bulge beneath the control car, which looks*
like a modern radome, is simply a bumper to serve as a cushion in landing.
Later it was used to house the antenna of the Fisher-Coulter radio compass.

had been engineering officer aboard the *Akron*, was transferred to sea duty. He was relieved by Lieutenant Commander Jesse L. Kenworthy, who was experienced in blimps, but new to the rigid airship. And the *Macon* lost three of her hook-on pilots. Trapnell, Young, and Larson were transferred to duty aboard cruisers.[19] In their places the *Macon* received Lieutenants (junior grade) Harry W. Richardson and Leroy C. Simpler. But the most important event of June was the ten-page report which Admiral Sellers prepared for the CNO on the *Macon*'s performance with the Fleet, and his estimate of the airship's place in the Navy.

The Commander in Chief's report was not due until September; it was accelerated by the *Macon* terminating her fleet operations when she returned to Sunnyvale. Whoever were the officers on Admiral Sellers' staff who assembled the data for his report, they evidently had no knowledge of airships or aerostation; they confused the *Macon* with the *Akron*, and their choice of materials reflected most of the fatuous prejudices which had dogged the airship since 1918. Be this as it may, Sellers was probably prepared to accept this information, and Admiral Standley was prepared to accept Sellers' interpretation of it.

The Sellers Report[20] complained that the *Macon* was 22,000 pounds "overweight," a defect which reduced her range and endurance. It was impossible to operate her at high altitudes; her maximum speed was only 74 knots, while her minimum was 38 knots. The *Macon* was "vulnerable" to weather, airplane attacks, and to antiaircraft ordnance. She was unable to operate in fleet exercises for more than an average of 12 hours without being "shot down," and in no case was she able to stay in the area of operations for more than 36 hours. To build another airship of her type would cost four million dollars, and in Sellers' opinion these funds would be better spent on 30 or 40 flying boats which had an operating radius of 3,000 miles.

Sellers admitted that the *Macon* showed constant improvement in her performance, which was "remarkable and commendable." He felt that reasonable argument could be made that her use in congested tactical exercises placed her at a disadvantage; but he flatly refused to speculate how else she might have been or might be used. He concluded that "the USS *Macon* has failed to demonstrate its usefulness as a unit of the Fleet"; and he was "decidedly of the opinion that the further expenditure of public funds for this type of vessel for the Navy is not justified."

When Ernest J. King read the Sellers Report, he bristled. King informed the General Board[21] that the *Akron*, not the *Macon*, was "overweight"; the range and fuel consumption figures in Sellers' report were confused; and although the *Macon*'s 74 knots was slow compared to an airplane's speed, it was very fast when compared to a surface ship's. And King pointed out that in any discussion of routine aircraft operations at sea which were more than 500 miles from a base, there was only one aircraft which could enter the discussion —the rigid airship. As for the *Macon*'s minimum speed, it was not 38 knots; when she was brought into equilibrium it was zero.

King admitted that the experiences of the *Shenandoah* and *Akron* seemed to support an unqualified notion of the airship's "vulnerability." But he insisted that this was a relative matter, especially under combat conditions, and was equally applicable to airplanes and surface vessels. As for the flying boats with a 3,000-mile radius which Sellers anticipated buying, King wryly remarked that airplanes of this performance did not exist in 1934, and that gaining information per square mile of ocean was quicker and cheaper by means of an airplane-carrying airship than by any other instrument. He underscored the *Macon*'s tactical employment, and insisted that this was not the airship's practical function, and it was not advocated by anyone acquainted with the airship's obvious shortcomings and unique capabilities. In conclusion, King observed that some of Sellers' information was very confused, and that in view of his recognition of the *Macon*'s remarkable progress, his final judgment seemed contradictory.

However sound were King's arguments, it was impossible for him to come to grips with the heart of the airship's problem. Since the days of the *Shenandoah*, there had been in the Fleet some skepticism about airships and little effort to find a place for them in the Navy's organization. This was not helped by the airship's chronic experimental status and the fact there was never more than one airship available for fleet operations. And to a certain extent this was due to myopic jealousy in high places which interpreted the millions of dollars for an airship in terms of one destroyer, half a cruiser, or so many airplanes, which would be lost from their own projects.

The *Akron*'s inconclusive performances and her untimely end, and the *Macon*'s somewhat dazed performances, did nothing to dispel the old skepticism. In fact, it appears that they only served to catalyze old prejudices into convinced disbelief. Nevertheless, the *Macon* had not been marking time. Even Admiral Sellers had to admit this.

During the eight months between her arrival at Moffett Field and the summer of 1934, the *Macon* participated in seven fleet exercises. She was scheduled to operate in two others, but arrived for one so late that her participation can be discounted, and bad weather made her turn back from the other. In these operations she was "shot down" nine times. Her baptism of fire in Exercise D was her sorriest performance; here she was "shot down" three times.

In view of the fact that she was not an aircraft designed for tactical use, that she was developing her tactics as she went along, and that she was terribly conspicuous as the only craft of her type in the Navy, this record is not as bad as it may first appear. In these same exercises other Fleet units had occasion to display their "vulnerability"; the carriers *Langley, Saratoga,* and *Lexington* were "sunk" or ruled out of action more than a few times, and airplanes were "shot down" in squadron lots. But there was a fundamental differential in value—real, calculated, and emotional—between these established elements of the Fleet and the *Macon.*

Aside from the Fleet's obvious prejudices, and aside from the fact that the carriers and their airplanes were accepted hardware and the *Macon* was on trial, it was much to her disadvantage that she was *the* airship. The *Macon*'s errors and failures were the poor performances of any rigid airships in prospect; on the other hand, if she turned in an occasional brilliant performance it could be credited to happenstance. There could be no overlapping or complementary performances, and no comparison of performances, as would have been the case if the *Akron* had been operating with the *Macon,* or against her. If both airships could have operated in

these exercises, or in separate ones, the good performance of one might have balanced or canceled the failures of the other. In any case, there would have been twice as much data by which to judge the rigid airship's place in naval warfare.

Everything the *Macon* did was the best, or the worst, because there was no other criterion. To the Fleet, the airship seemed a failure because of the *Macon*'s stumbling performances and there was nowhere else to look for a standard. And this worked both ways. Aboard the *Macon* it is likely that there may have been a tendency for the officers and crew to become overly impressed by her mild successes, because they had no standard of performance for reference except that which they were gradually establishing by themselves. If the *Akron* had not been lost, and two airships were available for these exercises, and two airship crews and two HTA Units were in competition with each other and able to compare their performances, there is little doubt that the rigid airship's association with the Navy might have been different. This is where the loss of the *Akron* hurt the *Macon,* and hurt her badly.

At the beginning of the year Admiral King doubted if a lukewarm report on the *Macon*'s performance could save the airship. He was correct; but it deserves wonder if even the hottest performance by the *Macon* would have drawn more than a reluctant, lukewarm applause from Admiral Sellers. But in July 1934, the crucial year seemed to be only half over. A great deal of experience and many insights into the *Macon*'s needs had been gained during the first half of the year. It now remained to consolidate this information, press it into a framework for operations, and test it in practice. This was reserved for the second half of 1934 and the new dynamics which began to move the *Macon* when Lieutenant Commander Herbert V. Wiley took command.

CHAPTER NINE

Wiley Takes Command

Admiral Sellers rendered a hard judgment; but it was premature, and based upon incomplete evidence. The *Macon* was a wiser airship for having been "shot down" nine times. She had learned much of what not to do, and had taken a rather long stride toward the creation of a system of search tactics which centered upon her airplanes. Her training efforts were not what they should have been, nor what they could have been; but relative to the past everything was progress.

The *Macon* had reached a point where it was necessary for her to subject her exploratory efforts to an extensive test and a practical analysis. This required an intensive use of her tentative tactics in an aggressive schedule of operations which would forge their more promising aspects into effective doctrine. In the remaining six months of 1934 this was the course and speed of the *Macon*'s operations. It was signalled on 11 July 1934, when Lieutenant Commander Herbert V. Wiley read his orders to the *Macon*'s officers and crew, and took over his new assignment as commanding officer of the airship.

Herbert V. "Doc" Wiley entered airship service with the "second generation" of airship officers in 1923, and was one of lighter-than-air's "old-timers." In spite of his long service in airships, aboard the *Shenandoah* and the *Los Angeles,* the seniority system kept him in a secondary position. After Rosendahl had the *Los Angeles* for three years, Wiley finally received her command for a brief period during 1929–1930, but when the new airships were built, he was relegated to the background.

Aboard the *Akron,* Wiley was executive officer to Rosendahl, Dresel, and McCord; and with the commanding officer's billet upgraded to require a full commander in 1932, his opportunity for command seemed very dim. The July moment in which he took command of the *Macon* was one which he looked forward to

without much hope for more than four years, and it should have been a satisfying experience for him. But it could not be Wiley's disposition to be satisfied in this summer of 1934; he had observed and heard too much for this. He had come to Moffett Field to make the *Macon* perform.[1]

Among the airships' commanding officers, Wiley was unusual in at least one respect. With the exception of Frank McCord, he was the only one who had been to sea with the Fleet in recent years. In the spring of 1930, in anticipation of being assigned to the *Akron,* he gave up command of the *Los Angeles* at his own request, and spent a year as tactical officer aboard the battleship *Tennessee.* After the loss of the *Akron* he went back to the Fleet as navigator aboard the cruiser *Cincinnati.* In the Fleet he sampled all the sour remarks about airships, and read CinCUS's reports of the *Macon*'s unhappy experiences in the fleet exercises. On occasion he was even able to witness the *Macon*'s activities from the *Cincinnati*'s bridge.

During these months Wiley enjoyed a detached position which allowed him to study the *Macon*'s operations and reflect upon the airship's predicament; and he produced an article for the *U.S. Naval Institute Proceedings*[2] which remains the best examination of the rigid airship's function in naval warfare that exists in the public record.

Wiley's argumentative study of the military airship was not exhaustive. It had many open ends. But this was typical of his approach to the airship's problems. Far from being dogmatic or emotionally wedded to any preconceived notions, he displayed a willingness to try any proposal which sounded practicable and held a promise of improving the *Macon*'s performance. An aggressive use of the airship's planes had interested him since the *Akron*'s days, and he was determined to exploit the F9C's. Toward this end he let the hook-on pilots off their leash. This came as a pleasant surprise to Min Miller and Kivette, and it was not the last Wiley had in store for them.

A rather austere personality, especially with his juniors, Wiley was not an unusually popular officer. Among the crew he had a reputation as a martinet, and some of the officers held reservations about him for a variety of personal reasons. He was especially suspect to the hook-on pilots, and Miller for one had not looked forward to his command.

Shortly after receiving his orders to the *Macon* in early 1934, Wiley visited Moffett Field. Miller observed that Wiley was "as conservative and reactionary as before." And he bitterly remarked that "we [the hook-on pilots] are about ready to turn in our flying suits and prepare the [planes'] engines for long storage."[3]

The pilots of the HTA Unit saw Wiley as one of the "old-timers," a group whom they regarded with impatience as "lighter-than-air and thicker-than-mud." But the men on the flying trapeze were due for a revelation; by the dawn of 1935 Wiley had the *Macon* performing like a "lighter-than-air carrier."

On 11 July the *Macon* was taken out for a flight down the coast to the Los Angeles area, so Wiley could put her and the F9C's through their paces in order to get an estimate of what he had to start with. After hook-on drill, the F9C's were exercised in flying the 60–60 search pattern. Wiley was familiar with this from the time it had been tentatively tried with the *Akron*. Now he watched, fascinated, across the cross-hair of the *Macon*'s pelorus as the F9C's smoothly faded away over the horizon, all the while holding a 90 degree bearing on the airship. Less than an hour later they reappeared, mechanically holding the same 90 degree bearing. And he watched as Mackey directed the planes' navigation by radio and plotted their courses on the maneuvering board.

At the end of the exercises, several tests were conducted with a new experimental radio homing device in the airship, and a similar one in the F9C's, with excellent results. On this flight, too, the new pilots Simpler and Richardson were given their first swing on the trapeze, using XJW-1's.[4]

This flight gave Wiley a rule-of-thumb judgment of the *Macon*'s capabilities and shortcomings. And it told the hook-on pilots that a radical break with the past was at hand. In fact, the first demonstration of the future's new dynamics was only a week away. As Miller later remarked, "Doc Wiley took over with a bang!"[5]

Having obtained an estimate of the *Macon*'s eyes, reflexes, and apperception, Wiley now wanted to try her legs on a long-range search problem. In mid-July he had his eye on the cruisers *Houston* and *New Orleans* which were en route from Panama to Hawaii, and presented an excellent search problem. It might be a good stroke of public relations, too, because the vacationing President Roosevelt was embarked in the *Houston*.

In this operation Wiley displayed the characteristics of an "old-timer" who entered airship flying during the ballyhoo years. He was not content to merely make a contact with the cruisers; he planned to have the *Macon*'s planes drop packages of the latest San Francisco newspapers and national news magazines for the President. Also in the packages were souvenir letters self-addressed by the *Macon*'s crew; and, with awareness of the President's interest in philately, some were addressed to him and Mrs. Roosevelt. They were given a special cancellation by the *Macon*'s mail clerk, marking the first delivery of mail via airship and hook-on planes to a ship at sea.

Preparations were made with some secrecy; Wiley did not want to commit the airship publicly, because there was a chance that bad weather might cause him to cancel the flight, or turn back in mid-Pacific. And he probably felt that ComAirBatFor would cancel the flight for him if he described its object in detail. Thus on 17 July he requested and received permission to make a "protracted flight to sea."

At 0925, 18 July, the *Macon* took off from Moffett Field's north circle and headed over San Francisco, through the Golden Gate and to the Pacific. For days prior to takeoff Wiley and his officers were following the cruisers' movements in the newspapers. They had sailed from the Canal Zone to Isla de Cocos, and then to Clipperton Island. From the times of arrival and departure their cruising speed could be estimated. They were scheduled to leave Clipperton on the afternoon of the seventeenth, so Wiley had Scotty Peck work out a course for a point 100 miles in advance of their estimated position at 1000, 19 July. Except for knowing the ships' destination, Wiley felt this information was comparable to what might be obtained of an enemy force from wartime intelligence.

From San Francisco the *Macon* flew south into an overcast Pacific studded with rain squalls. For the rest of the day, and all day the eighteenth, a thick, gray layer of clouds at 1,600 feet hung between the *Macon* and the sky, which necessitated dead reckoning. At 0600 on the nineteenth the sky cleared for a few minutes and Peck was able to get a navigation sight. He was pleased to discover that after flying more than 1,000 miles his dead reckoning was only 22 miles in error. Peck had hardly obtained his sights when the weather closed in again and became worse.

At 1003 Wiley turned the *Macon* off her southern track and to the southeast, to intercept the cruisers. By this time the air was thickening with rain squalls, and he decided that if the *Macon* did not make contact by noon, he would take her back to Sunnyvale.

When the *Macon* made her course change, Aviation Chief Machinist's Mate William C. Cody and his mechanics were busy in the airship's airplane compartment, removing the landing gear from her two F9C's. This was a development which had been a subject of conjecture since 1929, at least, and which the Harrigan Report looked forward to in 1932. But this was the first time it was done. The removal of the landing gear relieved the F9C of about 250 pounds and a massive area of parasite drag, which permitted an increase in the plane's top speed from 176 to 200 mph. From this date on it was standard operating procedure to fly the planes without their landing gear during trapeze operations over the Pacific.

Between 1032 and 1041, Miller and Kivette were swung out in their F9C's to scout ahead of the airship; and by 1145 Kivette had the cruisers in sight and was tracking them. On the bridge of the *Houston,* Lieutenant (junior grade) Wellington T. Hines, officer of the deck, was in the process of turning over the watch to Lieutenant (junior grade) Leonidas D. Coates when the F9C's were spotted. It was a startling experience to see two tiny airplanes appear out of nowhere so far at sea, especially when it was known that all the Navy's carriers were in the Atlantic. Someone remarked apprehensively that the planes were carrying bombs. But Hines was a naval aviator; he recognized the F9C's by their skyhooks, and their "bombs" as auxiliary fuel tanks. The holiday mood which attended the President's cruise aboard the *Houston* was greater than ever as all hands off duty crowded the decks to watch for the *Macon*'s appearance.

The airship picked her way between a pair of rain squalls to join her planes over the cruisers, and while the President and his party watched from the *Houston,* the F9C's flew aboard the airship. Then Miller and Kivette were swung out again, and buzzed down to deliver their packages. It was a good thing the packages were waterproofed and could float, because both pilots missed their target, and the *Houston* had to put over a

F9C-2 with undercarriage replaced by fuel tank. Lieutenant (j.g.) Kivette is at its controls.

FOX-MOVIETONE NEWS

FOX-MOVIETONE NEWS

After 19 July 1934, it became standard operating procedure to remove the
undercarriage of the F9C's after they had been hoisted aboard the Macon.
The undercarriage was useless in over-sea operations, and its weight was
replaced by an auxiliary fuel tank, increasing the plane's range by
50 per cent. Their "landing gear" was their skyhook.

motor whaleboat to pick them up. While the F9C's were being retrieved aboard the *Macon,* her radio operator handed Wiley two messages from the *Houston*:

THE PRESIDENT COMPLIMENTS YOU AND YOUR PLANES ON YOUR FINE PERFORMANCE AND EXCELLENT NAVIGATION 1210.

WELL DONE AND THANK YOU FOR THE PAPERS THE PRESIDENT 1245.[6]

It might seem that the *Macon* made an influential friend for the rigid airship on this day. But as the airship question passed into the years of confusion after 1935, Franklin Roosevelt proved to be only a fair weather friend.

Before taking departure, Scotty Peck obtained a position from the *Houston* as a check against his navigation. The *Macon* was at 13°51′N 123°W, about 1,560 miles due south from San Francisco, almost midway between Hawaii and Clipperton. It would have been a simple matter for her to have flown northwest to Hawaii and returned to California nonstop. And Wiley probably wished that he dared. But he was in enough trouble already, although unaware of it at this moment.

The *Macon* returned to the mainland at a leisurely speed, and exercised the F9C's in over-the-horizon, 60–60 searches en route. Everyone on board was feeling very good about the airship's operation until 2025, when the *Macon*'s radio room was suddenly filled with the angry voice of ComBatFor. By this time the news correspondents traveling with the President had radioed their stories of the contact to their newspapers, and the news was on the street. ComBatFor was in a dither. He wanted to know if the *Macon* had "actually" made contact with the *Houston,* and delivered mail, and if so by what authority. And he demanded a reply with that alarming Navy adverb, "Immediately!" Wiley was a worried lieutenant commander when he landed the *Macon* on the evening of 21 July.

The *Houston* contact created a great stir in the upper echelons of the Fleet. Admiral Reeves, who had relieved Admiral Sellers as CinCUS, remarked to CNO that the flight was "ill-timed and ill-advised," and was a display of "misapplied initiative." He complained that "the *Macon* was the only fleet unit which knew where the *Macon* was going and what she was going to do [and] not only was this embarrassing to all officers in the chain of command, but it comprised a breach of fundamental naval indoctrination." And he recommended stringent safeguards against a repetition of similar "secret operations" by the *Macon*.[7]

In view of what happened to the *Macon* in 1935, there is much to be said for Reeves' concern for not knowing her whereabouts. Taken in its entirety, however, the noisy paper storm was a tempest in a teapot. All the communications of CinCUS, ComBatFor, and ComAirBatFor on the matter have a strong flavor of pique in them: the *Macon* had put on a good show for which no one else but the *Macon* could take credit. In fact, the *Macon* had done no more than what King had asked Sellers and Halligan to arrange for her seven months before.

The criticism plainly worried Wiley. He was due for selection to commander in 1935, and was afraid that if all this unfavorable correspondence went into his record, he was "cooked for selection."[8] Promotions were painfully slow under even the most favorable circumstances in the Navy of 1921–1941. But Wiley had the Bureau on his side. He had worked an outstanding performance from the *Macon,* and no one was prepared to recognize this more quickly than Ernest J. King.

The *Macon* was very fortunate during the summer and fall of 1934 because the Fleet was on the East Coast. This allowed her to devote all her time to intensive training. During the three months between the end of July and the return of the Fleet in November, she made 14 flights, logging 404 hours in the air.

Compared to the past, this was a rigorous—if not to say almost fantastic—schedule. The *Macon* assisted in the calibration of almost all the Navy's RDF stations along the Pacific Coast, the crew was drilled at battle stations and gun pointing, flights were made to Camp Kearny in order to familiarize its personnel with the airship and the crew with the base, and she was frequently left on the field at night—at Camp Kearny and Sunnyvale—in order to keep the crew familiar with extended mast operations.

This was also a period of extensive experimentation. The pilot rescue gear for retrieving a pilot downed at sea was finally tried out, and Wiley revived experiments with the spy basket. The service- and utility-plane idea was also exhumed for intensive examination, and the development of a novel device for picking up ballast from the sea was begun.

The most important developments, however, occurred in the area of radio communications and navigating technique. In the last six months of 1934 progress was surprisingly rapid. By 1935 it had fused the

The Macon's nose locked in the cup of the expeditionary mast at Camp Kearny, California. At the airship's bow hatches there were connections for refueling, gassing the ship, taking on water ballast, and for receiving shoreside power.

airship and her planes into a single instrument of very-long-range search which exceeded the most sanguine hopes of 1932.

In January 1934, a Dr. Gerhard Fisher had visited Moffett Field and contacted Lieutenant Howard N. Coulter, the *Macon*'s communications officer. The doctor hoped that he could interest the Navy in having the *Macon* experiment with a low-frequency, radio direction-finding device he was developing. The instrument was unique in its simplicity, and Coulter immediately recognized that it held promise for the *Macon* and her hook-on planes.

Ordinary RDF sets gave the operator an aural signal which had to be translated into a bearing; the Fisher-Coulter set[9] gave the operator an easily read visual indicator, which made it a "radio compass" in every sense of the word. And not only could bearings be taken with it; when its loop antenna was locked in its neutral position it performed as a homing set. A pilot could home on any radio signal simply by flying a course which kept the set's visual indicator on zero. There was no danger of riding the signal in the wrong direction, as with aural RDF equipment, because the visual indicator showed 180-degree error. The Fisher-Coulter set was installed aboard the *Macon* with its loop antenna in the bumper bag beneath the control car.

At the same time, Dr. Fisher and Min Miller combined a 500-kc. homing set with a 4,000-kc. radio receiver which could be used simultaneously. It was installed in F9C's No. 9056 and No. 9058, the antenna being carried around the upper and lower wings in a huge loop. The Fisher-Miller set proved to be the answer to most of the F9C's communications and navigation problems.[10] And as if Miller did not have enough work to keep him busy, he was also writing the first of his "Bob Wakefield" aviation stories, a series for boys, and was assembling materials for a history of naval aviation.[11]

The new radio devices were a signal success. Minor modifications were necessary to increase range, and a great deal of practice was necessary so that a pilot was willing to stake his life on the set's reading. On every flight of the *Macon,* the F9C's were drilled in its use, and Wiley elaborated this into a game of hide-and-seek. The F9C's would not leave Moffett Field until the *Macon* was from 50 to 75 miles away; and it was the pilots' job to find her with their homing sets, which they invariably managed to do.

It had been a necessary rule not to operate the F9C's more than 25 miles away from the airship or other fleet units during operations at sea. But with the new radio equipment, the range of the F9C's was limited only by the amount of fuel they could carry. Min Miller had an answer to this. While operating from the trapeze at sea, the weight of the F9C's landing gear was replaced by a 30-gallon belly fuel tank which increased the plane's fuel capacity by 50 per cent. At a cruising speed of 105 knots, the F9C had a normal out-and-back range of 175 miles; the "range tank" extended this to 255 miles. During the *Macon*'s final weeks in 1935, the F9C's were operating at the limit of this radius.

The success of the Fisher-Coulter set on board the *Macon* was immediate. Scotty Peck used it successfully to check his position during the early hours of the *Houston* flight by taking alternate bearings on stations K.F.I., San Francisco, and K.F.S.D., San Diego. At that early date its range was only 500 miles; by the end of the year it was improved to the extent that the *Macon* could obtain accurate triangulations from stations 3,000 miles distant.

Since its wild performance with the *Akron,* the spy basket had been a minor source of irritation to the Bureau. Perhaps this was due to knowledge that the Army Air Corps was having a great deal of success in using a spy basket with its new blimp, TC-13. In the spring of 1934 the basket was shipped to Lakehurst where it was tested from Hangar No. 1's overhead cranes, and later beneath the blimp K-1. There was nothing faulty in its design, but the arrangement of its suspension bridles caused excessive yawing. This was corrected; but when it was streamed from the *Macon* for the first time, 8 August 1934, its behavior still was erratic.

The spy basket was sent to the Guggenheim Foundation's aeronautical laboratory at Stanford University where further testing resulted in the addition of a supplementary vertical stabilizer beneath its tail. Tested again, it was a complete success. In these tests the little car was weighted with 200 pounds of sandbags, but on 27 September it received its first passenger when Lieutenant Commander Jesse Kenworthy climbed into its cockpit and was reeled out 1,000 feet below the *Macon* for a 15-minute ride. After he was hauled in, Min Miller and Scotty Peck took their turns at riding it down, and the spy basket was judged operational.

A ride in the spy basket was an eerie experience, and especially for the F9C pilots. They were accustomed to riding behind a noisy engine and looking out at a pair of wings. But the spy basket had no wings, and trailing

The newsreel camera catches a close-up of LCDR Jesse Kenworthy "piloting" the spy basket. The spy basket was first tried with the Akron, 29 April 1932, but proved unstable. An alteration in the basket's suspension bridles and the addition of a ventral fin corrected the troubles. On 27 September 1934, Kenworthy was the first man to ride in the Macon's spy basket. Wiley never used the basket in Fleet exercises, but relied on his scouting planes.

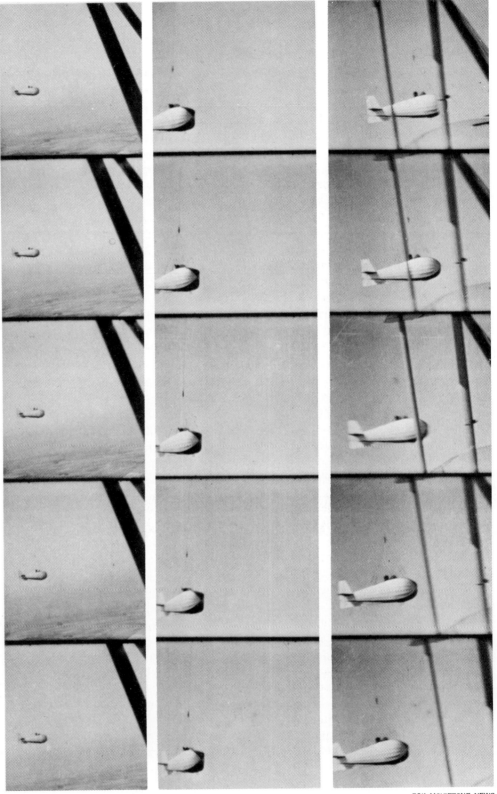

FOX-MOVIETONE NEWS

along 1,000 or 1,500 feet below and about 200 feet behind the airship, there was no sound except the sigh of the wind. The quarter-inch cable which joined the observer to the *Macon* faded away to a vanishing point, and the "spy" would be struck by a terrible feeling of loneliness—especially when the basket was lowered through a layer of clouds and the *Macon* was hidden by the ceiling. The man in the basket had a parachute, but its value would be questionable if the cable parted. The basket was usually trailed about 500 feet above the sea, and by the time the observer unfastened his safety belt and untangled himself from the car's wire suspensions, it is likely that the accident would have run a tragic course. But the operations of the spy basket were trouble-free in this respect.

There were several subsequent experiments with the spy basket; but however fascinating a gadget it was, it represented an idea which was 20 years out of date. For now the *Macon* had four "spy baskets," with 400-hp engines, whose "cables" reached out 250 miles to all points of the compass. The *Macon* was discovering this, and Wiley certainly appreciated it. Contrary to accounts which have been obsessed with producing an exciting story, Wiley never used the spy basket in fleet exercises; he always relied on his airplanes.

Another old object of speculation revived for study was the service and utility plane for refueling the airship. Rosendahl, who had recently returned from sea duty to take command of the Lakehurst Air Station, initiated this investigation. Admiral King approved of the project in principle and made available a Martin T4M-1 (No. 7640), an obsolete torpedo bomber, then in storage at the Naval Aircraft Factory, which was to be modified for the purpose. But then problems arose.

It was calculated that after the T4M was modified to a cargo-tanker plane it would have a gross weight of 5,900 pounds, including a cargo of 1,000 pounds, which was only 166 gallons of fuel. Difficulties were foreseen in pumping fuel from the plane, which would hang on the trapeze, against a pressure head of about 25 feet; the pumping operation might take so long that the airship conceivably might consume half the fuel while it was being delivered. But the crushing blow came from the limitations of the *Macon*'s structure.

Garland Fulton calculated that the lower part of the *Macon*'s frame 125, which supported the trapeze, could not accept an additional static load of more than 18,000 pounds. With a necessary factor of safety of four this was reduced to 4,500 pounds. So the T4M

was out of the question. Fulton did not think it could carry enough fuel anyway, and the whole idea was not worth the expense of strengthening frame 125. He thought such funds would be better spent on a good scout plane to replace the F9C's.

The Navy had no airplane with a 4,500-pound gross weight which included a 1,000-pound payload, so five commercial airplane types were investigated; but none of them could carry more than 160 gallons of cargo fuel. It was generally felt that the project was not worth its time and expense unless the tanker plane could deliver at least 500 gallons. After all possibilities were exhausted, Admiral King recommended that the project be dropped, and a fascinating prospect attendant to the *Akron-Macon* experiment came to an end.[12]

A new experiment was conducted by Calvin Bolster who looked forward to elimination of some of the airship's water-recovery apparatus. The water-recovery system was brought to an all-time high in efficiency aboard the *Macon*; but it was heavy and recovered water slowly. On the other hand, the airship's static condition was radically affected by airplane operations. When two F9C's were launched she immediately became 5,540 pounds lighter; with four planes, 11,080 pounds. In this condition she had to fly dynamically, nose down, to prevent rising over pressure height. It required hours for her engines to recover sufficient water to compensate for the weight of the planes—and by that time the F9C's would usually be back on board.

A quick means of obtaining ballast was needed, so Bolster developed a simple apparatus for picking up water from the sea. It consisted of a 2,900-foot loop of one-eighth inch steel cable which carried small cylindrical buckets, each to hold a few pounds of water. On 23 October, with the *Macon* making 40 knots at 1,100 feet, a model of it was tested. Instead of buckets the model used wooden blocks. The experiment proved that the airship's dragging the loop across the water imparted sufficient motion to the "buckets" to make the loop rotate, without fouling inside the airship or skipping on the water. It was not an absolute substitute for water recovery, but promised to be a highly efficient supplement. C. P. Burgess witnessed the tests and recommended further development. But the *Macon* was lost before any more work could be done.

The *Macon* and her F9C's were not without some minor problems. The F9C No. 9057 was having an especially hard time. On 27 July, while landing the plane during night operations, Roy Simpler stood it on

Ground crewmen haul on their spider lines to bring the Macon's *tail down to the riding-out car of Camp Kearny's mooring circle.*

its nose. And on 12 September, Kivette had the embarrassing experience of ground-looping the same plane during a takeoff from the Naval Reserve Aviation Base at Terminal Island. The F9C was a wonderful plane to fly when a pilot could give it all his attention, and it had a life of its own in aerobatics; but it was predisposed to be temperamental on the ground.

The plane was out of service for a few days with a fractured lower right wing. This was not serious, because the *Macon* had twice as many airplanes as pilots. And this was a condition which was becoming painful—her pilot shortage.

When Harrigan left the *Macon* he was not replaced. When three more pilots left in mid-1934, the *Macon* received only two as replacements. These were soon reduced to one. The day before the *Macon* left on her *Houston* flight, Harry Richardson was seriously injured in a plane crash. He had been teaching Lieutenant Clinton S. Rounds, an airship officer, how to fly. While practicing simulated emergency landings, their plane stalled and crashed in a field north of the air station. Rounds climbed out of the wreck with some bad cuts and bruises, but Richardson's ankles were fractured.

This accident reduced the *Macon*'s complement of pilots to three and marked the end of that veteran of hook-on work, N2Y-1, No. 8604. For the next three months Wiley's reports to ComAirBatFor and the Bureau insisted that his need for more pilots was urgent. He wanted two or three. He got one. And he did not see this pilot until Lieutenant (junior grade) Gerald L. Huff reported aboard on 19 October, three months after Richardson was put out of commission.

In the autumn of 1934 Admiral King arranged for Rosendahl and Anton Heinen[13] to visit Moffett Field to observe the *Macon*'s operations, and perhaps suggest improvements. By this time, however, Wiley, his officers, crew, and the *Macon* had practically rewritten the book, and they demonstrated it on an 80-hour flight over the Pacific.

After the *Macon* had taken off at 1755, 8 October, Miller, Kivette, and Simpler scrambled after her in their F9C's, homed their way to the trapeze, and landed their planes aboard within ten minutes. The *Macon* flew 450 miles northwest of San Francisco to begin a sweep at daylight, in search of a Japanese freighter en route to the West Coast. The search began at 0700, 9 October. The sea was obscured by fog, which presented an opportunity to use the spy basket. From 1130 to 1759 the spy basket was in constant use, the airship's officers

taking turns at two-hour watches in it. The ceiling beneath the fog was about 400 feet, and visibility for the man in the basket varied from a few miles to zero. The Japanese steamer was not sighted.

During the night the *Macon* retired northward to begin a new sweep to the south at daylight; this time the object of search was the Matson passenger liner *Lurline,* en route from Honolulu to San Francisco. At 0700, 10 October, lookouts were posted and the hangar crew was beginning to swing out the first F9C when, two minutes later, the *Lurline* was sighted 23 miles to the west. Having been on dead reckoning all night, a position was obtained from the liner, which permitted a check on the Fisher-Coulter RDF gear. Bearings were taken on several West Coast radio stations, and it was found that the instrument was accurate within one-half of one degree.

After circling the liner, Wiley broke off the contact and sped south until 0910, when he launched two F9C's to find the *Lurline.* The planes were operated sans undercarriage and with their range tanks in place. In accordance with a plan to have one plane on the scouting line relieved every hour, at 1015 the third plane was sent out and one of the others returned aboard. Five minutes after dispatch of the relief plane, the F9C's reported they were tracking the *Lurline.* The contact was broken, the planes retrieved, and the *Macon* retired to the south to repeat the search in the afternoon. In the meantime the F9C's were exercised flying 60–60 patterns and in the use of their homing sets. After airplane operations were secured at 1630, Rosendahl went for an 18-minute ride in the spy basket. Thus far it had been a big day for everyone. The next day would be even more eventful.

During the night the *Macon* moved closer inshore and by the morning of the eleventh was about 100 miles west of the Farallons. After a feeble sunrise the day degenerated rapidly; its 1,800-foot overcast began to lower, and heavy curtains of fog which reached down to the sea began forming. But there were clear areas, and at 0900 Miller and Simpler were launched for homing exercises. The ceiling continued to lower, rendering flying conditions dangerous, and at 0955 Wiley recalled the planes.

By this date everyone had confidence in the F9C's homing set being able to return them to the airship; but the homing set was not radar. It was not insurance against a collision of the planes in the fog, or their colliding with the airship. When the F9C's returned to the

*These rare views of the F9C's in operation sans landing gear were obtained
on 12 October 1934 when the* Macon *and her planes performed for a Navy Day
newsreel. The plane at left, piloted by Lieutenant Harold B. Miller, is
hanging on the main trapeze. Lieutenant Kivette's plane hangs on the perch, a
small, fixed trapeze on which a plane could be kept in combat readiness.*

Macon the ceiling was lowering rapidly, and Wiley had to take the airship down to 800 feet so the pilots could have clear visibility for their approaches to the trapeze.

As senior man of the *Macon's* miniature squadron, it was Miller's policy to be the last aboard, so Simpler flew to the trapeze first. As he made his approach, the *Macon* was almost wholly submerged in the descending cloud layer. As Simpler began his short climb to put his hook on the trapeze's yoke, he noticed out of the corner of his eye that the airship's No. 5 and No 6 engines had just been started in order to bring the *Macon* up to standard speed (58–60 knots) for airplane recovery, and at the same moment the landing flag was run down. As he closed with the trapeze he realized that the signal was premature: the *Macon* was not up to speed.

But it was too late.

Simpler was already under the trapeze, and a current of rough air threw his plane upward, against the trapeze, with an impact which caused the trapeze's yoke to slice through the F9C's guard tube a few inches forward of its hook. The guard tube was the only fore-and-aft member of the F9C's hook structure. Simpler was in a very ticklish position. His plane's hook structure was interlocked with the yoke, and there was only a gap of a few inches in the broken guard tube through which the plane could be flown out.

Simpler had to very careful. If he brushed the guard tube's broken end against the trapeze yoke as he flew out, he would tilt its forward tip into his propeller. So he favored the after end of the break, and reduced the plane's altitude an inch at a time until the broken ends passed clear of the yoke. But it could not be this smooth. In the process of disengaging his hook structure in the rough air, he banged up his hook badly, bending it back about 30 degrees. As a result, there was not much "hook" left in his skyhook.

Miller was watching Simpler's troubles from a position a few hundred feet aft and below the trapeze. He was watching his fuel gauge, too. Because of the local character of their flight, neither plane was equipped with its range tank. They had been in the air for more than an hour, and neither had sufficient fuel to reach shore. And if they did, they had no wheels to land on. Miller's plane could be taken aboard easily, so he ordered Simpler to clear the trapeze, and went in for his landing.

Roy Simpler was a very lonely man in this moment. Everything depended upon how much strength remained in his badly twisted skyhook. By this time the *Macon's* hull was completely hidden in the fog, and only her trapeze and lower fin stuck out beneath the clouds. The air was getting rougher, so Wiley did not dare to bring her any lower. He radioed Simpler that he would take the *Macon* above the overcast, which he estimated at 3,000 or 4,000 feet. But Simpler was too short on fuel; he had to do it now. By this time the *Macon's* eight engines had her up to her 75-knot full speed to make the landing easier. Simpler went in delicately and made it on his first attempt.[14] Miraculously, the hook held.

The plane was not swung all the way into the hangar, only to a level with the hangar door. If the hook failed, it was desirable that the plane fall clear of the airship. Lieutenant John Reppy climbed out on the trapeze and made fast some wire straps around the hook. Later several turns of wire were taken around the fuselage and over the hook, to relieve the strain on the hook's holding bolts, and the plane was brought all the way in. After Chief Cody's crew re-attached its landing gear, Kivette flew it back to Moffett Field.

In more than five years of trapeze operations, this was the only moment which held the prospect of a serious accident. It is doubtful if a shoreside airfield could make a similar claim. Not all of this unusual safety record, however, is due to the skill of the men on the flying trapeze. A very definite measure of credit belongs to Aviation Chief Machinist's Mate William C. Cody and his crew of 18 mechanics, who lavished mother-like care on the mechanical whims of the hook-on planes. In the several hundred hours of flying conducted from the airships' trapezes, the hook-on pilots had various causes for complaint; but none was of mechanical difficulties in their airplanes.

After receiving Simpler's plane aboard, Wiley took the *Macon* into the clouds, zeroed the Fisher-Coulter radio compass on station K.P.O., Oakland, and flew the airship into the San Francisco Bay area, blind. A large clearing in the fog was found over South Bay, and during the afternoon the F9C's were given further drill on the trapeze.

When the *Macon* returned to Moffett Field in the late afternoon, she was very light. She had consumed several thousand pounds of fuel and her helium had acquired considerable superheat while cruising around the bay. It promised to be a difficult landing, but Wiley had another trick up his sleeve. When Kivette returned to the *Macon* he came aboard in an XJW-1. Miller and Simpler were loaded into the Waco's front cockpit, and

Kivette flew them to Moffett Field so they could fly two more planes aboard. Thus when the *Macon* moored, she had five 2,800-pound airplanes for ballast inside her hangar. This use of airplanes to ballast the airship for light landings was not new; but Wiley was the first to exploit its possibilities to the fullest, and make it a standard part of landing procedure.

On this flight of 8–11 October the *Macon* gave a superb display of her new abilities. None was new; all had existed as latent abilities since the days of the *Akron,* and most were exercised with indifferent success in the past for want of aggressive development. It had required more than 350 hours of work in the air to bring together these diverse ideas and experiments of the past and forge them into successful operating procedures. Rosendahl and Heinen could not help but be favorably impressed by this flight. But it was one thing for the *Macon* to impress airship men, and quite another to impress the Fleet. And at this moment the Fleet was steaming across the Caribbean to the Panama Canal, en route back to the West Coast. The *Macon* would soon be back in combat.

Late in the afternoon of 7 October, the *Macon* took off from Camp Kearny's mooring circle and headed out to sea for Fleet Exercise Z. The miscellaneous Navy units on the West Coast were thrown together as the ORANGE forces, and were supposed to intercept the Fleet, which was steaming up the Mexican coast from Panama. At 0556 on the eighth, the *Macon* was 100 miles south of San Clemente Island, beginning a 400-mile sweep to the south to Guadalupe Island, in an effort to cover the enemy's western flank. But at this moment she received an urgent message from Admiral Alfred W. Johnson, ORANGE commander. His flying boats at San Diego were grounded by fog, and the *Macon* would have to search their assigned areas, too. So Wiley could not use the airship and its planes as a unit, but had to divide them in an effort to cover a ridiculously large area.

At 0555 two F9C's were launched to search the eastern sectors of the enemy's path, while the *Macon* tried to cover the western areas. The planes had instructions to search as far as Guadalupe, swing east and cover the area between Guadalupe and the mainland, and return to the island to rendezvous with the airship about 0830. By 0708 and F9C's were reporting a division of enemy cruisers northeast of Guadalupe, through heavy jamming of their radios. An hour later, when the F9C's were reporting the enemy's main body, the flying boats at San Diego were taxiing across the hazy harbor for takeoff.

The *Macon* arrived at Guadalupe at 0903, but discovered that she was not alone. A few minutes later the enemy carrier *Saratoga,* operating independently, steamed out of the haze in the southeast. Wiley wanted to run west, but he had to wait for his planes. So he flew the airship around to the west shore of Guadalupe in the hope of being able to recover the planes behind the cover of the island's mountains, and then dash west out of the carrier's range. But the *Saratoga* had spotted the *Macon* and was already launching a flight of dive bombers against her.

Shortly after 0930 the *Macon*'s topside lookouts were reporting six Vought SU-1 dive bombers overhead, maneuvering for an attacking position. A few minutes later they came screaming down from above. After all the planes were committed to the dive, Wiley ordered hard right rudder. The attackers did not expect this. The *Macon* had never before done anything like this, and to the carrier pilots she was probably not supposed to; the airship was supposed to be a sitting duck. As a result of the *Macon*'s radical maneuver, instead of sweeping over her length, the dive bombers came down off her beam with all of the airship's guns bearing on them. At this moment the *Macon*'s planes returned. Miller's fuel was almost gone and he went straight for the trapeze, while Kivette chased after the SU-1's.

After retrieving her F9C's the *Macon* ran west, and 20 minutes later had two F9C's again in the air, to track the *Saratoga.* While the airship held station about 60 miles south of the carrier, Miller and Simpler, flying at 16,000 feet, shadowed the unsuspecting carrier. Until the end of the exercise at 1600, planes from the *Macon* kept the carrier under constant surveillance.

For her performance in tracking the carrier, Admiral Henry V. Butler, ComAirBatFor, complimented the *Macon* on "her excellent scouting and [the] character of radio reports by [her] planes."[15] Nothing was said about the flying boat squadrons which proved to be "vulnerable" to a little bit of fog and were six hours late for the exercise.

At the end of the operations the *Macon* closed with the *Saratoga* and flew in company with the Fleet to San Pedro Harbor. During the 1930's, the Fleet was a vital economic factor in the life of the Los Angeles metropolitan area, and the governor of California and a host of lesser lights were on San Pedro's breakwater to welcome the Navy back to the West Coast. After she circled the Battle Fleet's anchorage for an hour, Admiral Reeves dismissed the *Macon* with a "well done," and she returned to Sunnyvale.

The conditions on board the *Macon* in this exercise closely approximated those of wartime. All her officers and crew were on watch continuously from 0500 to 1600; those manning lookout and gun stations even had the noon meal served to them at their stations, and the three hook-on pilots logged a total of 18 hours in the air. The *Macon*'s performance was impressive, and certainly reflected the efforts of the previous four months. But she was due for some unpleasant surprises in the next month's exercises.

In the meantime the airship continued her intensive drilling of lookouts, gun crews, and planes and the development of evasive action tactics. During 20–22 November, she flew to San Diego; en route her planes simulated dive-bombing attacks on her from different angles while the crew was drilled with camera guns, and the airship practiced taking evasive action. In the first week of December she flew to Camp Kearny where Admiral Butler made a formal inspection of the airship and her crew. When she returned to Moffett Field it was almost time for the December fleet exercises.

The operations of 6–7 December took advantage of the Fleet's movement from San Pedro to San Francisco, and thus occurred almost in the *Macon*'s backyard. Taking departure from a point about 50 miles west of Half Moon Bay at 0600 on the sixth, she began a sweep to the south. At 0655 Miller and Huff were sent out in F9C's on a sortie to the west. This was Huff's first flying from the *Macon* during a fleet exercise; and because she now had four pilots the *Macon* was carrying four planes, the first time in an operation. Forty minutes after the dispatch of the first flight, Kivette and Simpler were sent out on a search to eastward.

The second flight of F9C's found part of the enemy's scouting line and were recalled to the airship. In the meantime, at 0900, the *Macon*'s lookouts spotted an enemy battleship in the west, and Wiley swung the airship around to the northwest to circle around the enemy. At this moment the second flight of planes returned, were refueled, and sent out again. While circumventing the enemy, the *Macon* received reports from Kivette and Simpler that the battleship was trailed by a heavy escort. And then the first flight of F9C's returned aboard.

By 1058 the *Macon* was back on her original track, receiving reports from the second flight of F9C's: They

were tracking the enemy carrier *Lexington* and her cruiser escort. The *Macon* tried using the same tactic that she used with such success against the *Saratoga;* but the carrier pilots must have done some comparing of notes. At 1230 six Vought SU-2 dive bombers from the *Lexington* sneaked out of the sun for a successful attack on the airship, and the *Macon* was ruled "shot down."

The *Macon* continued in the operation as the hypothetical "ZRS6," but she did not last long. By this time the airship was again in an area highly congested with air activity. Within an hour of her first destruction, she was again "shot down."[16]

The next day's exercise was more successful for the *Macon,* and here she scored a very practical performance. Throughout the morning she and her planes located and tracked various enemy units, but had no success in finding the "big game," the enemy carriers. Then at 1325 the exercise was suddenly suspended. Two seaplanes from the cruiser *Cincinnati* had become lost, exhausted their fuel, and were down at sea.

The whole Fleet turned-to to search for the downed planes. At 1348 Kivette and Simpler were swung out of the *Macon* on a search to the south, and at 1507 Miller and Huff were sent out to the north. Within 35 minutes the *Macon* had a call from Miller; he and Huff were circling the downed planes and had dropped a smoke candle to mark the area. By 1600 the *Macon* had joined her F9C's. This was an ideal moment for a practical test of the airship's pilot rescue gear, but the seaplanes were still in good condition and could not be abandoned. While the *Macon* floated above the cruiser's planes, other Fleet units were only beginning to appear on the horizon. Half an hour later the cruiser *Portland* arrived, picked up the pilots, and retrieved their planes.

When ComBatFor reviewed the exercises, he commended the *Macon* and her planes for performing "a valuable service in a highly efficient manner" in locating the *Cincinnati*'s planes.[17] Quite aside from this commendation, the rescue of the cruiser's pilots was a personally satisfying experience to Wiley. Only eight months before, he had been on board the *Cincinnati*, listening to her aviators ridicule airships in general and the *Macon* in particular. On this occasion he was able to give them a personal demonstration of the value of at least one airship.

Regardless of ComBatFor's commendation, when Admiral Reeves assessed her general operations in the exercises, he observed that "the *Macon* again failed to

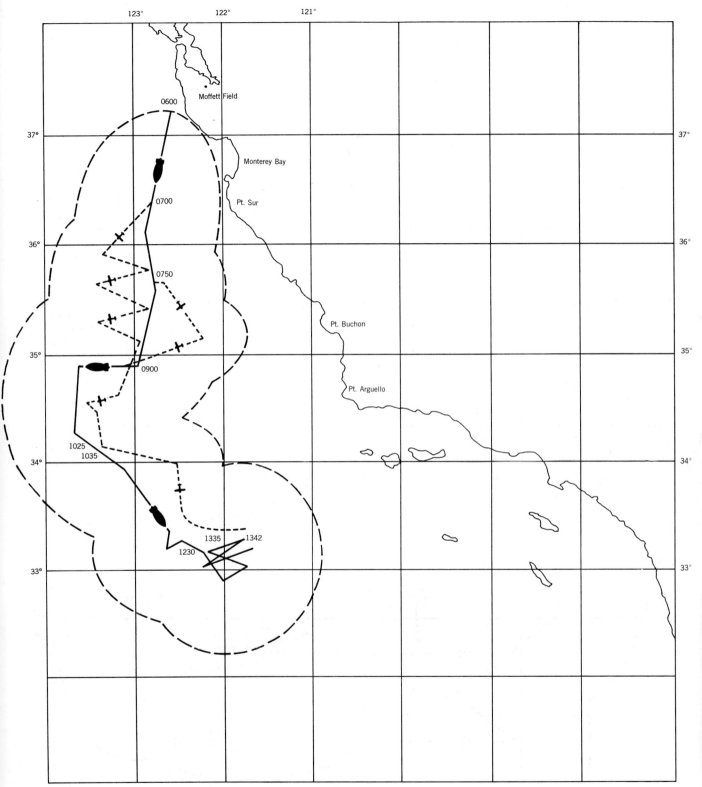

Searches flown by the Macon *and her planes during the Fleet exercise of 6 December 1934. Operations began at 0600.* *At 0700* Miller *and* Huff *were launched on a search to the west. At 0750* Kivette *and* Simpler *began searching to the* *east. The* Macon *sighted a force of enemy battleships and their escorts dead ahead at 0900, and she turned west* *to detour the enemy.* Kivette *and* Simpler *were recalled, while* Miller *and* Huff *went south to develop the contact.* *At 1230 the* Macon *was "damaged," and later resumed participation in the exercise until 1627.*

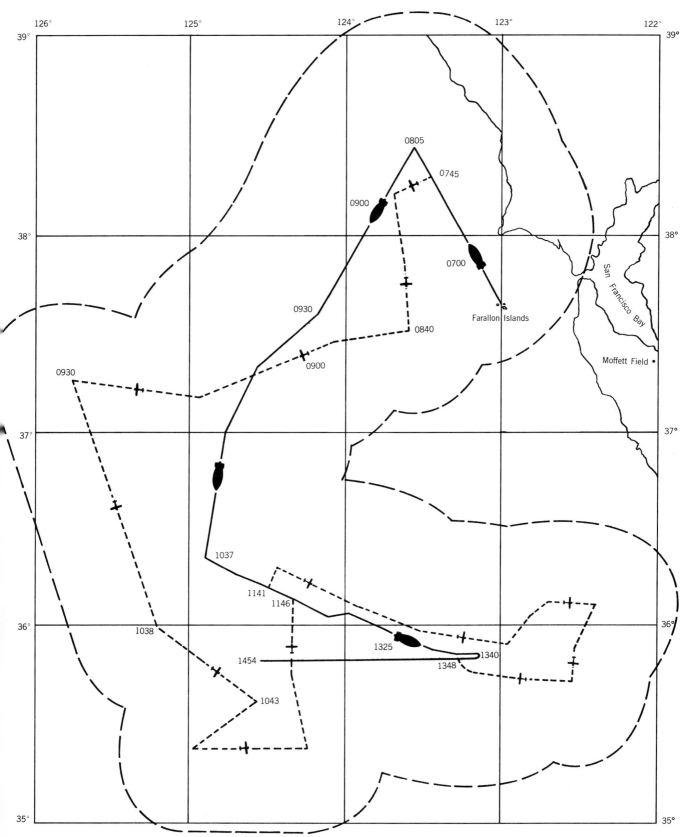

During the Fleet exercise of 7 December 1934, the Macon *began her search north of the Farallons at 0700, launching* Kivette *and* Simpler *on a sortie to the south and west at 0745. At 1325 the exercise was terminated and all forces began searching for two seaplanes from the cruiser* Cincinnati. *By 1542* Miller *and* Huff *were circling the downed seaplanes, which were later rescued by the* Portland. *All planes were recalled by 1620. The charts have been reproduced as accurately as possible from the original plotting sheets, but discrepancies exist between them and the log.*

The Macon *rests with her tail secured to Calvin Bolster's stern beam, preparatory to unmooring from Moffett Field's south circle, 26 October 1933. The stern beam was 184.5 feet long, weighed 133 tons, and was a signal advance in the ground-handling of large airships. Here the beam is being transferred from the 61.5-foot gauge railroad track leading from the hangar to the standard-gauge track of the mooring circle, so the* Macon's *tail can vane around parallel to the wind.*

144   The Airships Akron & Macon

demonstrate fitness for service under conditions where assailment by enemy planes is a probability."[18] But however dark the *Macon*'s predicament seemed on the West Coast, the horizon was brightening in Washington.

Admiral King was always convinced that the airship's effectiveness was in very-long-range patrol work, and by the summer of 1934 he was insisting to the Chief of Naval Operations that the *Macon* be given this employment. By fall, King had obtained the General Board's support on the matter, and the Board recommended that the *Macon* should be used only in strategic problems, with emphasis upon expanding the search function of her planes.

The Chief of Naval Operations could not agree; Admiral Standley actually thought that restricting the *Macon* to very-long-range operations would hinder the effort to determine the airship's wartime utility.[19] He anticipated using her in some bombing experiments which had been in the planning stage since the *Akron*'s days.[20] But it was King's argument which prescribed the *Macon*'s future—as far as it went.

In early December Admiral Standley reluctantly recommended that the *Macon* prepare a schedule of flights between the West Coast and Hawaii. The mooring facilities at Ewa would be put in shape for her service. Admiral Reeves agreed with the remark that "Hawaii is a logical place from which to operate a large dirigible."[21] It finally appeared that the *Macon* was going to be liberated from her onerous status as a highly sophisticated kite balloon. But fate would not have it this way. Since the afternoon of 21 April the *Macon* had been flying with a serious sickness in her tail structure. Before she could fly to Hawaii it would precipitate a series of events which would bring her to her end.

After the *Macon*'s return from Florida, Dresel reported in detail the structural damage received over Texas. He believed that the emergency repairs at Opa-locka "made the damaged portion of the ship as strong or probably stronger than it had been originally," but thought that the entire question of fin strength should be investigated.[22] The Bureau of Aeronautics and Goodyear-Zeppelin took up the matter, and it was decided that a reinforcement of frame 17.5 at its fin junctions was desirable. Wiley was informed of this when he took command. The situation is best described in the words of BuAer:

1. Following reports of the failure of certain girder elements of frame 17.5 during turbulent air conditions on 21 April 1934, and with the collaboration of the Goodyear-Zeppelin Corporation, a very careful check has been made on the basic assumptions and the stress calculations for fins and the adjacent parts of the hull structure. The original assumptions made were very conservative and no flaws could be found in the stress analysis or in the proof testing given the fins and structure. In other words, there is no explanation in past theory or experience which will account for what actually occurred. This leads to the suspicion that local damage to the girder parts in question may have been the fundamental cause of the trouble, but being unwilling to dismiss the matter with this explanation a new stress analysis for these parts has been worked out, using new assumptions, and results of wind tunnel investigations, frankly attempting to find a theory that would explain failures such as did actually occur. In doing this it has been necessary to assume conditions which are very unlikely to occur in practice.

2. On the basis of this new theory, justification can be found for reinforcing certain parts of frame 17.5 and certain parts of the fins themselves. While the Bureau hesitates to prescribe the additions of weight which is perhaps unnecessary, since the present structure is considered to be amply strong for any operations over the sea, it does seem wise to provide the additional strength in order that the *Macon* may be prepared to carry out any mission without risk of even local damage on these parts. Because the work is not urgent, it is considered that it can be accomplished from time to time, as opportunity offers, at the discretion of the Commanding Officer, and, therefore, will not interfere with operating schedules. In fact, the type of all-internal reinforcement has been adopted because it is simple, rather than to employ the more complicated external wire method.

---

5. The relative order of importance for the reinforcements is:

Frame 17.5, in the vicinity of horizontal fins.
Frame 17.5, in the vicinity of vertical fins.
Horizontal fins.
Vertical fins.

and it is recommended that the work be executed in this order.[23]

On 14 September 1934, two boxes containing 598 pounds of reinforcement parts were shipped from the Goodyear-Zeppelin plant in Akron. But when C. P. Burgess visited Moffett Field six weeks later no work had been done on their installation. He reported that "it is felt by the ship's officers that the additional strength is not required for ocean operations."[24] This was not an unreasonable assumption. The air masses over the sea are far more stable than those over land. But too much was being expected in this instance.

Between the *Macon*'s first flight at Akron and the end of 1934 she logged a fraction more than 1,695 hours in the air, 789 of which were flown since 11 July 1934. These latter hours were the ones which had whipped the *Macon* and her personnel into an unexcelled condition of military readiness.

This time was obtained by what appeared to be a compromise; the hours in the air so necessary for training, drilling, and experimentation were obtained by delaying the hours on the ground necessary for installing the tail reinforcements. But this was not a compromise in hours; it was strictly borrowed time.

Time ran out quickly on the *Macon* in 1935 and soon ended the *Akron-Macon* epoch of naval aviation.

CHAPTER TEN

The End of an Era

At the dawn of 1935 the *Macon*'s future, and the future of the rigid airship in the Navy, seemed to be brightening. In only six months of intensive effort the *Macon* had achieved a remarkable improvement in her performance, and it seemed that the next six should see even greater improvements. More importantly, it seemed that future operations should finally allow exploitation of her unique characteristics.

The patrol operations planned between Moffett Field and Hawaii would permit the airship to operate in her own realm—over the trackless area of a great desert sea, where no airplane could possibly compete with her. The congested exercises of 1934 had put the airship at a terrible disadvantage; but Fleet Problem XVI, scheduled for the spring of 1935, outlined a deployment of the Fleet west of Hawaii. Here the *Macon* and her planes would have sufficient space in which to demonstrate their unusual abilities, and possibly turn in an inspiring performance.

There was also a revival of airship interest in Washington. In January 1935 the President's Federal Aviation Commission recommended that the Navy expand its airship operations; that a training airship to replace the *Los Angeles* be built immediately; and that a seventeen-million-dollar program to initiate commercial airship operations be commenced. The latter would include two large Zeppelin-type airliners, a Metalclad airship transport of moderate size, and an airship passenger terminal on the East Coast.[1]

The General Board, too, reviewed the Navy's airship policy and recommended immediate construction of a 2,500,000-cubic-foot, rigid airship for training purposes which would carry two or three airplanes.[2] Admiral Standley strongly disagreed with the spirit of this recommendation. He reluctantly acceded the construction of the training airship, but echoed Hilary Jones's codicil

of 1926, that "in view of the necessity for expenditures of funds on items of greater known naval value, it is recommended that such dirigibles be built only if funds can be obtained for the purpose other than those provided for the Navy in the annual appropriation."[3]

But considered in its broadest scope, the prospects of the rigid airship in the Navy had not been as hopeful since the fall of 1931. There was a difference, however; the high hopes of 1931 were to a certain extent based on wishful thinking, but by 1935 a measure of creditable performance existed on which a realistic appraisal of the airship could be formulated and projected into the future. Unfortunately for the airship, the sole means of this projection were flying in the *Macon*. As 1935 opened, only 43 days remained until everything would end in 250 fathoms off Point Sur, California.

The *Macon*'s 1935 operations got under way on the afternoon of 2 January, for a flight to San Pedro to rendezvous with the *Lexington* for "visibility tests." A sore point of discussion for too many years had been how easily the airship was seen from great distances; these tests were to obtain a measure of this. The results proved what might have been supposed in advance: the sun gauge was the determining factor. The tests nevertheless provided some data for future reference and suggested that there was nothing unusual about the airship's conspicuousness, if she were careful.

There were no other operations until mid-January; in the meantime Wiley and his officers were working on chart and weather problems relative to the Hawaiian flights. On the morning of the tenth, Wiley was alerted by CinCUS to be ready in case of an emergency during Amelia Earhart's flight from Honolulu to the West Coast. For 22 hours during 11–12 January the *Macon* and her crew were standing by, ready to go on two hours' notice, if she were forced down at sea.

The crew of the Macon *pose beneath the huge airship at Moffett Field. Below: The* Macon's *officers in 1935.*
l. to r. front: Lt. Cdr. Scott E. Peck; Lt. Cdr. Jesse L. Kenworthy, Jr.; Lt. Cdr. Edwin F. Cochrane; Lt. Cdr. Herbert
V. Wiley, commanding officer, USS Macon; *Cdr. A. T. Clay, commanding officer, Moffett Field; Lt. Cdr. George H. Mills,*
Lt. Cdr. Donald M. Mackey. Center: Lt. (j.g.) Gerald L. Huff, Lt. (j.g.) Harry W. Richardson, Lt. Howard N. Coulter, Lt. (j.g.)
Earl K. VanSwearingen, Lt. Calvin M. Bolster, Lt. Harold B. Miller, Lt. Anthony L. Danis. Top: Lt. (j.g.) Leroy C. Simpler, Lt.
(j.g.) John D. Reppy, Lt. George W. Campbell, Chief Boatswain William A. Buckley, Lt. Walter E. Zimmerman,
Lt. (j.g.) Frederick N. Kivette, Chief Machinist Emmett C. Thurman.

During 15–16 January the *Macon* rendezvoused with the Fleet off the Channel Islands for the purpose of checking a Fleet darken-ship test. She had four planes on board, but they were operated only briefly. On 31 January, however, she got under way for a 47-hour flight into the Pacific for some intensive drilling. While the F9C's flew attacks on the airship, her lookouts and gun crews were drilled at battle stations. Homing and communications tests with the F9C's were very successful. They were able to take accurate radio bearings on the airship from 185 miles, which was almost at the limit of their radius of operations; communication by radio key was worked with ease at 140 miles, and clear voice transmission was obtained out to 95 miles.

After sundown the F9C's were drilled in night hook-ons, and the next day long-range homing exercises were resumed. These drills anticipated a scheme which Wiley and Miller had worked out for Fleet Problem XVI. It was planned to track the *Lexington* until evening, and under cover of darkness send out the four F9C's in a series of "dive-bombing" attacks on the carrier. The planes would be returned to the airship by their homing sets, and launched on second and third strikes.

Everyone was confident of the success of this clandestine operation. During the 1930's, night operations by a carrier's squadrons were the exception, so it was calculated that the *Lexington* would be a sitting duck for the *Macon*'s "dive bombers." And whereas night operations by carrier aircraft had yet to achieve the efficiency they only began to realize during World War II, the *Macon*'s F9C's had no difficulty in operating from their trapeze, day or night. Unfortunately for the airship's cause, the *Macon* met her end before this startling demonstration could be given.

On 1 February trapeze work continued, as well as the drilling of lookouts and gun crews. On this day, from 1715 to 1745, complete control of the *Macon* was shifted from the bridge in the control car to the auxiliary control station in the leading edge of the lower fin. Wiley remarked that "although this is the first time that complete control has been shifted [thus] in an American airship, the complete success of the operation probably will lead to its frequent practice."[4] When the *Macon* moored at Sunnyvale on the morning of 2 February, everyone on board had good reason to believe she was adequately prepared to turn in good scouting performance for the Fleet during the forthcoming operation of 11–12 February.

The crucial test of 11–12 February, however, would not occur in the *Macon*'s military performance. Quite the contrary; she executed her most imaginative and successful scouting performance. The test would occur with a crisis in the structural malady in the *Macon*'s tail, and the ability of her crew to cope with it. For this the *Macon* was not at all prepared.

During seven overhaul periods between 10 November and 10 February, the reinforcement of the *Macon*'s tail structure had been under way. This consisted of riveting duralumin channels within certain girders of frame 17.5 and in the fins at their junctions with the hull. On the evening of 10 February the reinforcements were completed around the lower and horizontal fins, but no work was done in the upper parts of frame 17.5 where the upper fin was attached.

Aside from the fact that the Bureau's letter of 24 July 1934 seemingly assigned the upper part of frame 17.5 a position of lesser importance, this area posed a special problem. Gas cells II and I pressed in on both sides of the upper part of frame 17.5, and in order for workmen to have access to the area the cells would have to be partially deflated. This promised to be time consuming, so this work was delayed until last, and was scheduled for the *Macon*'s overhaul period in March.

The call to general assembly on the morning of 11 February 1935 sounded at 0600. Already, the interior of Moffett Field's Hangar No. 1 was a blaze of lights, resembling a Christmas tree turned outside-in. When the hangar's doors rolled open at 0620 they revealed a bleak world. At the end of the mooring mast's tracks, the south circle lay soft and glistening under a drizzle from the lead-colored sky which crowded the field. At 0630 the *Macon* was towed into the circle, and at 0710 cast off from the mast. Boosted by four of her engines, she dissolved into the low ceiling, and was put on a course for sea via San Jose and Gilroy.

As the *Macon* moved across Gilroy, 33 minutes after takeoff, Miller and Huff zeroed in on her with their homing gear, and flew in to hook onto the trapeze. Their F9C's were no sooner secured on their trolleys than Chief Cody had his men removing their landing gear, installing their range tanks, and topping off their fuel for the scouting flights.

At 0805 the *Macon* crossed the coast to sea at Moss Landing, and by 0834 was headed south along the coast, with Point Sur's lighthouse on her port beam. While off Point Arguello, between 1010–1023, Miller and Huff were swung out in their F9C's. They had instructions to make a sweep down Santa Barbara Chan-

*Looking down into the inside of the Macon's lower fin. At center: The windows of the auxiliary
control room on the fin's leading edge, and the wheel for controlling the rudders. Foreground, left and right:
Line-handler's stations for mooring, platforms for them to stand on, lines coiled, ready to slide through the ports.
Top, foreground: The sheaves for carrying the control cables to the fins' movable surfaces.*

nel and to reconnoiter the fleet anchorages at Long Beach and San Diego. Five minutes after their departure, Kivette and Simpler homed in from Sunnyvale, hooked on, and were swung into the hands of Cody and his mechanics.

During 11–12 February, the Fleet was moving from San Diego and Long Beach to San Francisco, conducting minor tactical exercises en route. The *Macon* had orders from ComAirBatFor that she would not participate directly in the exercises, but should use the Fleet's movement for training in strategic scouting. ComAirBatFor was finally doing something about Admiral King's request of January 1934.

The *Macon* was directed to search for all fleet units, identify them, and to maintain a plot of their movements and dispositions during the two days. She was to remain unobserved, have her planes avoid detection, and maintain radio silence until 1800, 12 February. Except for the inconvenience of radio silence, this was exactly the type of operation for which the *Macon* and her HTA Unit had been preparing. Their execution of the operation proved to be remarkably successful; but this has been obscured by the sensationalized events of the evening of 12 February.

Upon arrival off Point Arguello, the *Macon* hove to and restricted herself to serving as an airborne hangar for her planes. At 1235, two hours after launching the first sortie, Kivette and Simpler left the trapeze to overlap the first flight. At 1410 Miller and Huff returned. Their four-hour flight had taken them 200 miles south, within view of the fleet anchorage at San Diego, which was almost at the limit of the F9C's extended range. Between 1503 and 1508, Kivette and Simpler returned from the south and hooked on; they had checked the usual fleet rendezvous points off San Clemente, Santa Catalina, and San Nicolas Islands.

The planes had determined the positions, courses, general speeds, and disposition of the fleet units. With this information, Wiley took the *Macon* west and then south, to circle around the advancing surface forces. At 1705, south of San Nicolas Island and on the western flank of most of the Fleet, two planes were launched. Miller and Huff made a sortie to the north, to the vicinity of Anacapa Island, and returned with information which confirmed the character of the enemy's concentration of his forces, and its composition, for his movement north.

During the night the *Macon* circled north of Catalina in a triangular area bounded by Anacapa and the Santa Barbara Islands and Point Vincente on the mainland. Daybreak on the twelfth was as gray as on the eleventh. While she cruised around Anacapa, Kivette and Simpler were swung out into the bleak dawn. The enemy was moving away to the north, and they had instructions to fly a search up Santa Barbara Channel as far as Point Arguello, and to return to the airship by a course west of the Channel Islands, in case a secondary force might be using the more seaward route.

After launching this flight, the *Macon* made a quick run south to Catalina to observe any fleet units which might have detached themselves from the main body and were returning to Long Beach or San Diego. By 0940 she was back at the Anacapa rendezvous to recover her planes.

Between 0945–0952, Kivette and Simpler were swung back on board, and after 1000 the *Macon* struck off to the north, snaking her way among the clouds in the wake of the enemy surface units. At 1230, Wiley launched Miller and Huff on a second search to the north, where he expected the Fleet to be concentrating for its entrance to San Francisco Bay. Forty minutes later the *Macon* received word from CinCUS that she was released from the operation, and was at liberty to return to Sunnyvale. At 1550, off Point Piedras Blancas, Miller and Huff were recovered, and the *Macon* continued north for Point Sur, Monterey, and the mountain gateway to the Santa Clara Valley via Watsonville and Gilroy.

Cruising at 2,500 feet, the *Macon* began to encounter a lowering ceiling and a series of rain squalls. Altitude was changed to 1,700 feet in an effort to duck under the weather. At 1630 a Luckenbach intercoastal freighter was observed below, paralleling the *Macon*'s course; a few minutes later the airship flew into a curtain of rain, and visibility dropped to less than a mile. Because of increasingly high fog off Cape San Martin, altitude was further reduced to 1,400 feet.

At 1656 Point Sur's lighthouse appeared in the gloom, flashing two points off the starboard bow. At this moment a shaft of sunlight suddenly pierced the weather in the west, and the watch in the control car could see seven cruisers on the surface, working against relatively heavy seas. At 1704 Point Sur was almost abeam. Wiley noticed that the *Macon*'s course was slowly bringing her closer to the coast, and preferring to keep her well out to sea and away from the rain-shrouded mountains, he ordered left rudder.

Coxswain William H. Clarke put his wheel over and

Aviation Chief Machinist's Mate C. S. Solar puts in a call from a phone station in the Macon's port keel gangway. Looking on is Edward H. Morris, AMM/1c, and an unidentified man. The keels were the main avenues of communications between the control car and the stern, and engine rooms in between. At right: one of the fixed fuel tanks; top: small fairleads which guide control wires from the engine telegraphs on the bridge to the annunciators in the engine rooms.

was holding about five degrees rudder when what seemed like a sharp gust struck the *Macon*. The airship lurched violently to starboard; the helm was wrenched from Clarke's hands and went spinning wildly.[5] In this same moment, Aviation Metalsmith First Class William M. Conover, who was at the *Macon*'s elevator controls, noticed the airship pass into a veil of haze, which alerted him for turbulent air. He had just recovered the airship from a shallow dive when he felt the gust. The control wheel was torn loose from his hands for a moment, but he quickly regained control.[6]

The time was 1705. This was the beginning of the end. Within 90 minutes the *Macon* would be on the bottom of the Pacific.

Shortly after 1600, Chief Davis felt the *Macon* flying into unsettled air conditions, and began his customary rounds of her structure. By 1700 his inspection of the horizontal fins and the lower areas of frames 17.5 and zero was finished, and he was headed aft along the upper keel's catwalk. The keel's walkway was a nine-inch path along a triangular passageway, bounded on its sides by the walls of the gas cells and roofed over by the *Macon*'s outer cover. Because of a gas hazard it was against regulations for anyone to go into the upper keel alone, and Davis was accompanied by Joseph E. Steele, aviation ordnanceman. Steele was new to the *Macon;* this was only his third flight.

Upon reaching intermediate frame 23.75 in the tail's area, Davis reached above him to check the "breathing" of the upper fin. There was a space of two inches between a transverse girder in the bottom of the fin and matching member in the hull's structure; when the airship was in turbulent air it was Davis' practice to put his hand in here to feel how far the fins were flexing away from the hull. This "breathing" of the *Macon*'s fins was in no way extraordinary; everyone on board had been aware of it for years.

While Davis was examining the space between the girders, the airship lurched to starboard and he heard a crashing sound from aft. From where he stood at frame 23.75, he could see into the structure of the upper fin above him, and as far aft as frame zero. But he could see nothing wrong. Believing the sounds came from frame zero, he started aft to investigate. He had only gone a few feet when he was met by a rush of helium which rapidly began to fill the passageway.

Dizzy from the gas, Davis retreated down the catwalk toward the bow, pushing Steele ahead of him. The *Macon* was now inclined up by her nose, and the lighter-than-air gas was literally chasing them up the narrow passageway as it sought an outlet to the atmosphere. Worried about the airship, himself, and Steele—a greenhorn whom Davis feared might fall off the catwalk and through one of the gas cells—Davis clambered forward to the phone at frame 57. He called the bridge, but the line was busy. Helium continued to fill the corridor, so they hurried on to frame 170, where they finally made their way to the lower part of the airship.[7]

Coxswain Joseph R. Connolly, on watch at frame 35 in the starboard keel, felt the violent lurch and heard something snap in what he took to be frame 17.5. He immediately phoned the bridge and reported a casualty. Then he heard what sounded like bits of metal striking the catwalk. He did not see the metal. When he went aft to investigate, he was startled by the sight of the control cables to the fins' movable surfaces—which branched out to the four fins at frame 17.5—spinning wildly around each other. After reporting this by phone, he returned to frame 17.5 where he noticed gas cells II, I, and zero were deflating. Simultaneously, he received orders from the bridge to cut loose fuel tanks.[8]

Quartermaster First Class Theodore Brandes, also on watch in the tail section, was standing beneath cell I when the *Macon* made her lurch. He, too, heard something snap. Looking up, it appeared to him that cell I was only 60 per cent full, and he thought the area around its top was brighter than usual. He rushed forward to the phone at frame 35 port, to call the bridge; but directly opposite him in the starboard keel he saw Connolly on the phone, and could hear him making his report. It was Connolly's *second* report. Brandes started back to frame 17.5 to see if he could do anything to check the deflation of cell I. He was intercepted by the chief of the watch, who had orders to drop slip tanks; he told Brandes to cut loose all slip tanks between frames 17.5 and 125.[9]

Two others were in the *Macon*'s stern section at the time of casualty. Chief Boatswain's Mate Andrew B. Galatian and Aviation Machinist's Mate Second Class Mathew G. Fraas were off watch and were taking in the sights from the auxiliary control room in the lower fin. They felt the stern take a breath-taking fall, saw the *Macon*'s bow lurch toward shore, and in the same instant heard a crashing noise above them.

Aware that something was wrong, they clambered up the ladders inside the fin to the main part of the airship. As Galatian turned to leave the after-control room, he saw fuel already spewing from the hull outlets of the *Macon*'s dump tanks. Upon reaching the keel, Galatian met Brandes who was about to cut loose slip tanks, and he turned-to to help him. Fraas met Connolly, who was just hanging up his phone after receiving his orders to drop tanks. The two immediately set about it.[10]

At this time, no more than two minutes had passed since the instant of the gust.

Almost everyone in the *Macon*'s control car and stern section knew that there was a bad casualty aft. There was a massive deflation with serious loss of lift in the stern cells; there was evidently a structural failure in frame 17.5, or zero, or both; and the upper rudder's controls had carried away. But no one knew exactly what had happened. No one had seen anything except the slackening of the after cells and the failure of the control cables. Much less would be known with certainty of the *Macon*'s casualty had she not been only three miles off Point Sur, where two experienced observers were watching her through binoculars.

At Point Sur, lighthouse keeper Thomas Henderson and his assistant, Harry Miller, were watching three cruisers when the *Macon* appeared out of the south. As she hurried along beneath the overcast, both men put their glasses on her. Just as the *Macon* came abeam of them, her stern took a sharp dip, and an instant later they were startled to see her upper fin literally disintegrate.

Henderson had his glasses trained on the airship's stern section; he was interested in the motion of her elevators. He saw the upper fin's leading edge lift away slightly from the *Macon*'s hull; then the fin suddenly, but progressively, flew into pieces.

They watched the *Macon* swing sharply away from them and fly off on a circular track to the south. As she made her turn, gray streams of gasoline and ballast trailed from her, and they heard dull explosions as her slip tanks struck the sea. Miller looked at his watch. The time was 1707. As the *Macon* came about on her southerly heading and was again almost broadside to them, Miller noticed that the rudder post and its rudder were still sticking up above the airship's hull. A few seconds later the *Macon* disappeared into the overcast, but they were able to follow her track for awhile by her trail of splashing ballast and slip tanks. Then a curtain of rain cut off their view.[11]

Immediately after the gust hit the *Macon* no one on the bridge knew, or suspected, that a casualty had occurred. As the airship recovered from her shallow dive to starboard, she began to settle by the stern. Scotty Peck was taking drift sights out a window; he became concerned by the sudden swerve toward shore, and told Clarke to correct his rudder. Calvin Bolster went to the assistance of Conover, who it appeared had lost control of the elevators. At this moment the phone rang. It was Connolly at frame 35, with news of a casualty aft.

Wiley immediately ordered all ballast dropped aft of amidships. A few seconds later, after Connolly reported that cells II, I, and zero were deflating, the order was given to drop all slip tanks aft. This was the *Macon*'s critical moment. The orders given in these few seconds created the circumstances which dictated the course of the next 33 minutes and made the *Macon*'s situation irretrievable.

After her casualty the *Macon* lost about 100 feet of altitude. But upon the release of large quantities of fuel and ballast, she shot skyward. In less than two minutes she climbed through the overcast and past 2,800 feet, her pressure height. Regardless of other circumstances, it can be said with certainty that this was her fatal moment. Her casualty caused a serious gas loss in her stern cells; but beyond pressure height, the automatic valves on all her cells opened, blowing her remaining lift to the atmosphere. And she did not simply bob over pressure height; she stayed above it for 16 minutes.

Yet, in spite of her total loss of lift in cells II, I, and zero; in spite of her automatics blowing away helium; and in spite of the bridge manually valving cells VIII and IX in a futile attempt to restore trim; the *Macon* continued climbing. She literally zoomed to 4,850 feet. By that time she had lost so much helium that she had nowhere else to go except down.

Within four minutes of the casualty Wiley ordered an S O S sent out. This was intended as a precautionary measure; but everyone soon realized that the *Macon*'s condition had become hopeless. Above the overcast the sea was obscured; control of the airship was difficult, and Wiley was worried that the *Macon* might drift over the coast. Bringing the airship to a forced landing in the foggy mountains would be dangerous. If she had to come down, he wanted it to be at sea. Not only would the landing be easier and less hazardous, but the Fleet was somewhere below the overcast, and would be standing b to pick up survivors.

During the eight minutes of the *Macon*'s wild ascent to 4,850 feet, it was practically impossible to steer her. Throughout the ascent she flew nose up, her stern heavy from the loss of helium. All hands off watch were ordered to the bow in a futile hope that their weight would bring the nose down and restore a measure of trim. Wiley tried to steer by using his engines, but without much success. It was not only awkward, but after the *Macon* passed the peak of her ascent it intruded on another need for the engines—to brake her fall.

The *Macon*'s initial descent was at an alarming rate of 750 feet per minute. Engine speeds were increased in hopes of pulling her into a more-or-less level attitude and obtaining some flying control. It braked her descent, but gave no control. At 1,700 feet she fell through the ceiling, and as the sea became visible word was passed to stand by to abandon ship. The water ballast and slip tanks which remained forward were jettisoned, slowing her to 150 feet per minute.

By the time the *Macon*'s tail hit the sea at 1739, almost everyone on board had had time to get on a life jacket, and rubber rafts had been inflated. Of the 83 persons on board, two were lost.

The more fortunate survivors sat huddled in the rafts, shivering against the evening air in their wet clothes, watching for the rescuing cruisers, and watching the *Macon* sink. The less fortunate floated in their life jackets and clung to the sides of the rafts. The weather had become quite calm, and the *Macon* settled slowly by the stern. Under the attack of the ocean's long, oily swells, her hull slowly broke up frame by frame, and by 1800 she was awash at the control car with her nose pointed straight up. About a dozen men were still aboard her, standing around the bow hatches at her mooring spindle. As she settled lower, these last survivors slid down over the curves of her bows into the water, and struck off for the rafts.

The USS *Macon* was observed to sink at about 1820.[12]

Within half an hour of the *Macon*'s sinking, the cruisers *Concord* and *Richmond* were in the area, taking aboard survivors. A search of several hours was conducted for the two missing men, but they were not found.

Once again the banners of the nation's press were black with "AIRSHIP DISASTER!" Once again there was a great hysterical outcry against airships and public funds for their construction. Airships were alleged to be "ghastly monuments to a stiff-necked, incredibly stubborn Navy Department."[13] Even the sober elements of the press felt that the loss of the *Macon* was the last straw. After the *Akron* disaster *The New York Times* argued that if airships had a value before her crash, the crash had not altered that value, and to abandon its de-

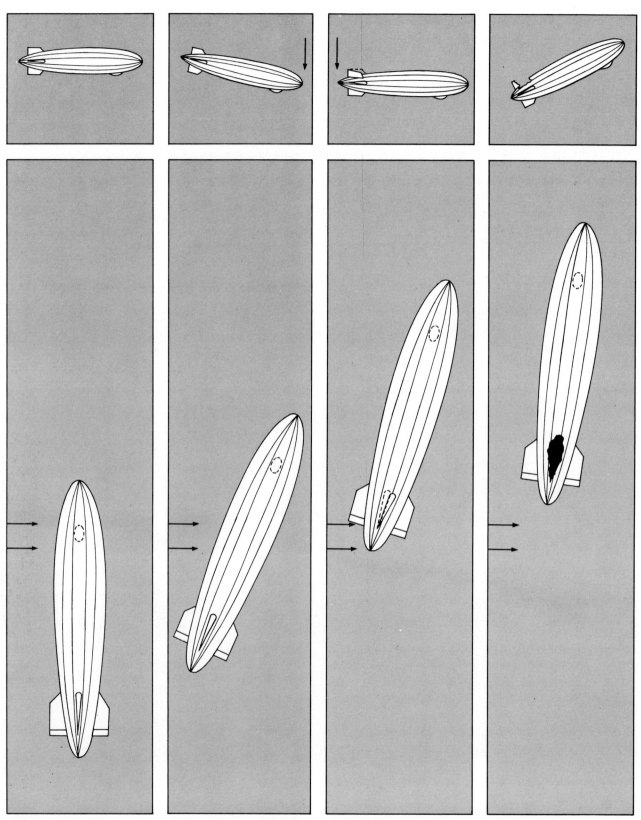

Phase one: Gust strikes bow from port. (Left rudder has been applied.)

Phase two: Bow swings down and to starboard (against left rudder).

Phase three: Fin breaking up, controls slip, and tail is dropping.

Phase four: Cells deflating, swinging slowly to port, down elevator.

velopment would be violating the spirit of scientific enquiry. But after the *Macon*'s loss, *The Times* conceded the "twilight of Zeppelins."

In Washington, President Roosevelt remarked that "there is no thought at the present time of asking Congress for an appropriation for another airship . . . we would like to put that money into long-range patrol planes."[14] And in the Navy Department, Admiral Standley told the press:

This should be a solemn warning to this country with respect to the use of lighter-than-air craft.

I have never approved of the use of lighter-than-air craft for other than commercial purposes, and I am more than ever convinced of their unsuitability for military and naval purposes.[15]

There were two investigations of the *Macon*'s loss. One was the Naval Court of Inquiry which met on board the USS *Tennessee* in San Francisco Bay for six days between the fourteenth and the twenty-first of February. The other was conducted by a special committee of the Science Advisory Board, at the request of Secretary of the Navy Claude A. Swanson.

The naval court was concerned with establishing only the immediate facts of the *Macon*'s loss, thus its opinions were had within a few weeks of the crash. As compared to the court which investigated the *Akron*'s loss, however, the *Macon*'s was not nearly as thorough, although it had much more information from which to work. Its proceedings have a perfunctory quality which suggests that something of longtime unpleasantness was at last disposed of, albeit in an awkward fashion, and it must now be swept under the rug as nicely as possible.

The special committee—the so-called Durand Committee—was asked to study not only the *Macon*'s loss, but airship design and construction in general, and to submit recommendations for future policy. Because of this broad responsibility, its reports were not made until 1936 and 1937.[16] Although the Durand Committee produced some excellent reports and made some farsighted recommendations, with benefit of hindsight it is possible to see the committee as the unwitting instrument of the Secretary of the Navy to sidetrack the airship question. For the next 18 months Admiral King would insist upon beginning a new program of rigid airship development; and Swanson, who despised airships, would beg off with the excuse that he could do nothing until he had received all of the committee's reports.

The testimony at the court, correlated with the Du-

rand Committee's studies, indicates that the immediate causes of the *Macon*'s loss were hurried actions to correct a condition about which no one was certain, an excessive concern for restoring the airship's trim, a breakdown in the poor system of communications that existed, and an inadequate casualty control organization aboard the airship. Finally, there was the tremendous confidence which most persons had in the *Macon*'s structure, which contributed indirectly to the loss.

Relative to these causes are the most remarkable aspects of the *Macon*'s loss. Immediately after the casualty, the *Macon* did not fall out of the sky and "crash"; she went *up*—too far up, and she went up rapidly. During the critical 120 seconds after receipt of information of a casualty aft, the period in which the final decisions were made, no one on the bridge knew exactly what had happened. And there is reason to suspect that some of the information the bridge received was not only exaggerated, but was patently false. Finally, after Davis and Steele were driven from the after end of the upper keel's passageway by the escaping helium, no one—not even by way of curiosity—returned to the area to obtain an estimate of the damage.

The sequence of events to the casualty were (1) an order for a turn to port, the rudder being put over; (2) a strong gust striking the airship, turning and rolling her to starboard;[17] (3) the gust imposing a load on the upper fin which was transmitted to frame 17.5, causing the failure of girders in the frame's upper part; (4) as the girders broke they tore gashes in gas cells II and I; (5) with frame 17.5 thus weakened, the normal loads of the upper fin became extraordinary, and the fin pulled away from the hull, carrying part of frame 17.5 with it; (6) as the fin began to pull away, the air through which the *Macon* was moving at about 70 mph entered the fin's structure and literally blew it apart; and (7) the fin structure at frame zero held firm, but flying debris punctured cell zero, and inflicted further damage on cells II and I, accelerating the loss of helium.

The loss of the *Macon* was triggered by a relatively minor structural failure which instantly developed into a major problem in aerostation.[18]

At the time of the casualty the *Macon* was flying about one degree light. The damage to the three after gas cells resulted in a loss of helium whose value in lift has been estimated at 41,200 pounds, about 20 per cent of the *Macon*'s useful lift. In the instant of the casualty the *Macon* lost about 2,700 pounds in the weight of her upper fin, and within the next five minutes 32,700 pounds

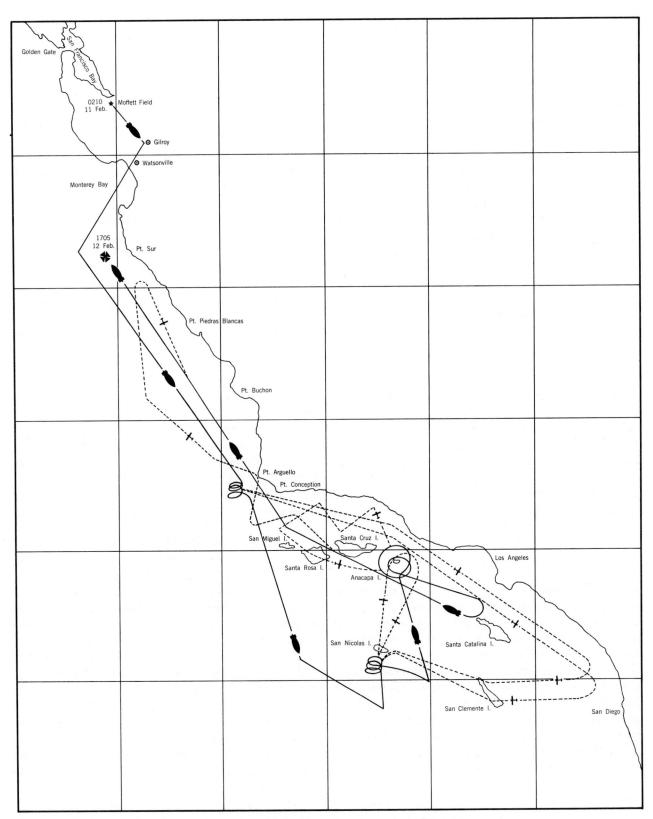

The Macon *had been training in strategic scouting with the Fleet when she crashed off Point Sur.*

of fuel and ballast were jettisoned. Dr. William Hovgaard of the Durand Committee remarked that during these few minutes it appeared that "probably the airship was then in nearly aerostatic equilibrium."[19] And the committee wondered if the *Macon* did not possess a measure of "excess buoyancy."[20]

Relative to the guarantee of disaster which the *Macon* received when she shot way beyond her pressure height, the sudden and massive de-ballasting is important in only one respect. It served to put the airship in a condition approximate to equilibrium, which permitted her engines to drive her over pressure height.

The Durand Committee remarked that, with the information it was able to gather, it was at a loss for an explanation of the *Macon*'s wild ascent to 4,850 feet—in terms of static lift. The rest—in fact most—of the explanation was in dynamic lift. The committee observed that information on the use of the *Macon*'s engines was "neither complete nor clear,"[21] but declined to speculate.

From the time of the casualty to the time she hit the water, the *Macon* retained a nose-up attitude. This angle varied from 6 to 25 degrees, providing angles of attack in which the thrust of her engines would naturally send her climbing. Testimony at the court of inquiry indicated that the engines were slowed to idling after the casualty, and used only intermittently during the ascent. But after studying all available data, Dr. Hovgaard remarked that "actually, it appears that the engines were used more or less all the time."[22]

The *Macon*'s engine control was not the best during the emergency. They should have been stopped immediately, if only to relieve aerodynamic stresses in the airship's structure. It is possible that the engine telegraph system was damaged, and what the bridge ordered on the telegraphs may have been one thing, the signal received in the engine rooms may have been something else. Conversely, there is a possibility that oral orders were given to the engine rooms which confused or even countermanded orders from the bridge.

Of no small significance is the fact that there were 83 men on board the *Macon,* 34 minutes elapsed from casualty to crash, and yet not one person was ordered to inspect the area of the casualty in order to obtain an estimate of the damage—in fact, simply to find out what had happened. There were less than a dozen persons in the *Macon*'s stern during the emergency, but none of them went above the level of the lower keels; they all had orders to cut loose tanks. And except for

those in the control car, and a handful of men who were engaged in a futile effort to jettison the F9C's, everyone else responded to the order "all hands forward."

The only detailed information we have of the *Macon*'s damage was obtained by Lieutenant John Reppy, who went aft on his own initiative after the casualty. He wanted to shift control to the auxiliary station. When he reached the control system's clutches at frame 23.75 he could not find anyone to assist him, so he returned forward. By this time the *Macon* was climbing through pressure height and the situation was passing beyond redemption.

But while Reppy was aft he took time to examine the damage. There was a large gap in the top of frame 17.5 where the upper fin had been attached, and the top of the airship was ripped wide open between frames 23.75 and 8.75. As far as he could see around the flapping gas cells, there was no trace of the upper keel's catwalk, which had terminated at frame 17.5. But aft he could see part of the fin's structure still standing above frame zero, forward of the rudder post.

On both sides of frame 17.5 gas cells II and I hung limply in the centers of their bays, their folds stirring in the wind that was coming through the gash in the top of the hull. Cell II had a large bubble of gas bulging in its forward end; but cell I was practically empty, only a tiny bubble showing at its after end.[23] The positions of the bubbles indicated that the cells were ripped open where each had butted against frame 17.5.

To all practical purposes, an organization for casualty control did not exist aboard the *Macon.* Even after the *Akron*'s disaster there was no general alarm signal. Quick action saved the *Macon* over Texas in 1934; but this was due to Davis' personal initiative, and the spontaneous reaction of those who happened to be at hand. Of course, Davis' "Texas cure" could not have any effectiveness in this emergency; everything happened too fast and in a location too difficult of access. But the presence of a trained repair party on the scene within a minute or two of the casualty would have provided the bridge with considerably more information than was available to it during the first few critical minutes.

There is at least one indication that the bridge may have been acting in response to false information. Immediately after word of the casualty was received, an officer started aft to prepare for shifting control to the lower fin's auxiliary station. In the keel a crewman told him that the stern was "crumbling."[24] He returned to the control car. He evidently believed this false infor-

*On 12 February 1935, the blimp J-4 and Moffett Field's Hangar No. 1 maintain a
futile vigil for the airship that never came home. It was the end of an era in
naval aviation, and the end of an era of aeronautics in the United States.*

160   The Airships Akron & Macon

mation: it made him cancel his trip to the stern. Upon his return to the bridge, to whom did he tell this? What weight was it given? What decisions did it affect or effect? At this date it is probably impossible to know with any degree of certainty, but this factor of misinformation should be given due consideration.

Because the *Macon* proved to be the Navy's last rigid airship, her loss came to have an exaggerated emotional value in certain quarters, and provoked speculations which sought a single cause for the unhappy ending. These tended to focus on the design of the ZRS4&5's tail structure, and were the type of nonsense which eclectic casuistry will produce.

At the *Macon* Court of Inquiry the Judge Advocate raised a question about an "inherent defect in design"[25] in the airship as being a contributory cause to her loss. This referred to the fins' attachments to the hull at only two points—frames zero and 17.5—and their leading edges extending about 34 feet forward of frame 17.5. Considered against the background of the *Akron-Macon* design, this is a sophism. And if it was an "inherent defect" it was one in which everyone, including the airship operators, concurred by means of Change Order No. 2. Interestingly enough, the alteration of the fins on Project I was done to accommodate a peculiar need of the operators: to permit them visual communication with the auxiliary control station in the lower fin —the auxiliary station they used only once during the airships' 41-month existence.

Related to the "inherent defect" was another fallacy; this one focused on the fins being simply bolted to the hull, and not being carried through the hull framing to join in the fashion of a cruciform. The Germans were especially loquacious on this point.

It was suggested that Goodyear-Zeppelin overlooked a sort of "magic ingredient" in the design of rigid airships by omitting a cruciform tail structure in the *Akron* and the *Macon*. This was typical of the nonsense that flourished in the hotbed of German hypernationalism in the 1930's. It has been observed that the ZRS4&5's use of deep rings permitted cantilever fins. But it deserves note that if Goodyear-Zeppelin's engineering staff had elected to multiply the redundancy of the ZRS4&5's tail structure, it had both the background and talent to provide a cruciform. Most of them had worked on the wartime Zeppelin designs, and their chief engineer, Dr. Arnstein, had worked out basic principles for several variations in cruciform design relative to different types of hull structure.[26] What is

more, if BuAer had been unable to appreciate the obvious principles of cantilever construction, it could have had an airship with a cruciform tail structure in Goodyear's Project III of 1928.

A third line of speculation sought to tie together the *Akron* and *Macon* losses in a neat package. In view of what was known of the *Macon*'s fin failure and how little was known of the *Akron*'s loss, it was contended that the *Akron*'s loss was also due to a failure in the tail structure. This was seemingly supported by the coincidence of their operating hours. The *Akron* had made 73 flights and had 1,695.8 flying hours when she was lost; the *Macon*, 54 flights and 1,798.2 hours. But the *Macon*'s tail difficulties first announced themselves over Texas when she had only 719.5 hours on her, and there is nothing comparable in the *Akron*'s experience.

As the rigid airship's prospects degenerated into a tangle of frustrations after 1935, these lines of intuition became peculiarly attractive. They rationalized the airship's failure to revive: it could all be explained away by an "inherent defect."[27] But any comparison of what the *Falcon*'s divers found on the floor of the Atlantic in 1933, with what occurred over the Pacific in 1935, refuses credence to such satisfying paralogisms.

There was only one "defect" in the *Macon* on 12 February 1935, and it was the absence of the duralumin channels which should have been reinforcing frame 17.5 at its junction with the upper fin.

It has been deplored that Wiley did not have the fin reinforcements completed. We are all wiser after the event. Everyone—the Bureau, Goodyear-Zeppelin, and the airship's personnel—was very concerned by the problems which displayed themselves in her tail during the flight over Texas. But no one was worried. Grounding the *Macon* until the reinforcements were made was regarded as unwarranted.

What stands out here is the remarkable faith which the airship men had in the ZRS4&5's structural integrity. Instances of this are seen in Rosendahl's bulling the ice-covered *Akron* around the storm over Virginia in 1932, and especially in Dresel's fighting the unusually heavy *Macon* through the violent air of the Texas canyons in 1934. Calvin Bolster, who was more familiar with the *Macon*'s structure than most of his contemporaries, remarked that "previous to the failure of them [the fins, over Texas and Point Sur] . . . I thought that they were amply strong." And after the Texas experience, he "felt that the airship was perfectly safe to fly in anything but extremely violent air."[28]

Wiley told the court of inquiry that he "had no concern over it [the incomplete reinforcements] and I believe that none of my officers had any concern in this connection." He added that the tail reinforcements would have been accelerated "if we had considered it important enough to give it priority."[29] Wiley's absence of worry is given evidence by his doubling the *Macon*'s hours of operation,[30] and putting the airship through violent turning maneuvers in an effort to work out evasive action tactics against dive bombers.

This is not to say that the airship men's faith in the integrity of the ZRS4&5's structure was ill-founded. Quite the contrary. But faith without works can lead to disaster. It did on 12 February 1935.

In the last analysis, the loss of the *Macon* must be pinpointed to the two-minute interval between 1705–1707 off Point Sur. It has been observed that "while the structural failure precipitated the events which followed, it was the panic of the crew which ultimately lost the airship."[31] The line between panic and confusion can be a thin one. No panic reads from between the lines of the record, but confusion most certainly does. Especially during 1705–1707.

Whether the *Macon* could have been saved is in the realm of speculation. Some airship men believe that it was very possible; they point to the evidence which indicates that she was prepared to float in equilibrium if she were simply let alone. In this condition, a careful shifting of weights could have restored a measure of trim and she could have been nursed home on one rudder. There is much to be said for this; during 1914–1918 the Germans returned to base with battle-damaged Zeppelins in worse shape than the *Macon*. On the other hand, others say that it was out of the question. Whichever the case, the opportunity vanished in the actions of 1705–1707.

One thing seems fairly certain. If the *Macon* had limped back to Sunnyvale, it would have been a great victory for the airship. Some of the edge would have been taken off the wearisome criticism of vulnerability. Her unsupported stern section would have experienced some damage upon landing, but probably no worse than the *Akron*'s did in February 1932. But even the carcass of an airship would have been more with which to begin again than what was available on 13 February

1935—which was nothing. And the rigid airship's experience in the Navy might, just might, have turned out a bit differently.

The loss of the *Macon* has been sometimes regarded as the safe evacuation of an aircraft downed at sea, or as an orderly abandon-ship evolution. This is old casuistry contrived to make the *Macon*'s loss seem more palatable. But its rhetoric is more concerned with tree-counting, than examining the forest. The loss of the *Macon* was a disaster, and *the* disaster of the rigid airship in the Navy.

When the ZR2 was lost, the *Shenandoah* was moving toward construction. When the *Shenandoah* was lost, the *Los Angeles* was available to continue operations, research, and development. When the *Akron* was lost, the *Macon* was almost ready to fly, and the *Los Angeles* could have been recommissioned for limited operations. But when the *Macon* met her end, she had no standby. The *Los Angeles* could still have been restored to a limited flying status, but the Navy Department was opposed to asking Congress for the $75,000 necessary to recondition her. In any case, at this late date her value was questionable.

There was no airship available to continue where the *Macon* left off, and for most persons, her loss was the last straw. There were many influential elements within the airplane industry, among the commercial airline interests planning transatlantic and transpacific services, and in government and Congress; in the Navy Department, the Fleet, and in the Bureau of Aeronautics, which were determined that there should not be another airship. However diverse the roots of their individual motives, they were at one in their conviction of "no more airships." And it was they who dictated the course of the future.

Once again, Carl Vinson made the accurate forecast of the future when he remarked, "the curtain has been rung down on lighter-than-air craft in the Navy."[32] As far as he referred to the rigid type he was correct.

The loss of the *Macon* marks the end of the ZRS4&5 epoch of naval aviation. But her loss signals more than this. The *Macon* was the Navy's last rigid airship, and she was the last rigid airship built in America. Her loss also marks the end of an era in naval aviation, and the end of an era of aeronautics in the United States.

CHAPTER ELEVEN

The Years of Confusion

The curtain had been rung down on the rigid airship in the Navy, but several acts remained to be played out backstage during 1935–1940. These were active years within the Bureau's Lighter-Than-Air Design Section, but the prospects of the rigid airship nevertheless degenerated into a hopeless tangle of frustrations, which Fulton has described as "the years of confusion."

In this period many new ideas were explored, new projects developed, and several constructive proposals made. Airship policy was studied, reviewed, and reviewed again; policies were recommended, seemingly accepted, and paid great lip service. But very little by way of material support for the policies was even promised, and in the end there was nothing.

In the fall of 1935 Moffett Field was turned over to the Army Air Corps[1] and the Navy's airship operations retreated to Lakehurst. Here the operational aircraft consisted of the old blimps J-4 and K-1, the new G-1,[2] and the still unique "tin balloon," ZMC-2. There was also a handful of free balloons, and the *Los Angeles* which was, between her mooring-out experiments, reigning as hangar queen. The Navy's airship materiel did not increase a cubic foot beyond these units until 1937, when it was supplemented by some excellent hand-me-downs from the Air Corps.[3]

Within a few weeks of the *Akron*'s loss, Admiral King had tried to obtain a replacement for her and the *Los Angeles;* he proposed using WPA funds. But Secretary Swanson was not receptive to the proposal;[4] and after the *Macon*'s loss he axed all airship proposals with the excuse that he could do nothing until he had all of the Durand Committee's reports. The Navy's airship policy, as formulated by the General Board and approved by Swanson in the fall of 1934, favored continuing airship development and specifically recommended a rigid airship to replace the *Los Angeles*. This was good enough for King. Always impatient with vacillation, a few days before he left the Bureau to return to sea duty in 1936, King offered a criticism of the airship's moribund condition which concluded with the observation:

> To sum up . . . it seems to me that there is no necessity for any change in the wording of present existing and approved naval airship policy. The Department, through its inaction in carrying out the said approved policy, has placed itself in the unenviable position of not knowing its own mind, or else being unwilling to accept its responsibilities with regard to lighter-than-air. It should be one thing or the other.[5]

In the long run it would be the "other"; in the meantime, however, it continued to be neither.

During this period, the LTA Design Section was continuing its studies of the "next airship." The idea of a true flying aircraft carrier which possessed offensive qualities had become an ideal among those interested in airships. The experience with the *Macon* proved that it was practicable; thus during 1936–1937, C. P. Burgess prepared a series of design studies of very large rigid airships capable of carrying a striking force of dive bombers. This was the ZRCV airship.

The ZRCV studies described an airship of 9,550,000-cubic-foot gas volume, 897.3 feet long, 147.6 feet maximum diameter, with a useful lift of 297,000 pounds. It carried nine dive bombers similar to the Northrup BT-1, prototype of the Douglas SBD series. The gross weight of the nine planes bombed-up was estimated at 54,000 pounds. The ZRCV was powered by eight 750-hp Allison V-1710 engines paired in four outside power cars, each pair geared to drive a four-bladed propeller. The airship's maximum speed was 75 knots; at a cruising speed of 50 knots it had an

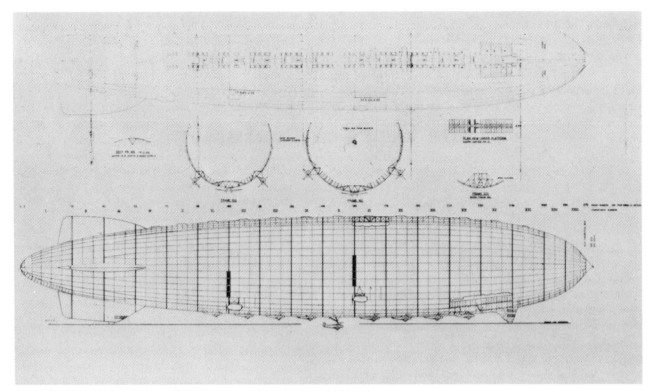

*Of 9,550,000 cubic-foot volume, 897 feet long, with a gross lift of 592,000
pounds, and an endurance of 175 hours at 50 knots, C. P. Burgess' ZRCV design
of 1937 would have carried nine dive bombers similar to the Douglas-Northrup
BT-1. The BT-1 was the prototype of the SBD dive bomber of World War II.
Funds for the ZRCV's development were never forthcoming.*

endurance of 175 hours, an out-and-back range of 4,375 miles.

The ZRCV's nine bombers were stowed in tandem beneath the hull, each plane on its own trapeze; all could be launched within a few seconds. This stowage arrangement dictated a strong keel in the airship, and thus a return to "conventional" airship construction, similar to the principles of Goodyear-Zeppelin's Project III of 1928.

In January 1937, Rear Admiral Arthur B. Cook, the new Chief of the Bureau of Aeronautics, forwarded Burgess' studies to the General Board, remarking that:

It is my opinion that in the ZRCV type herein described lies the most promising future utility of the large rigid airship for naval purposes. . . . The size airship herein described is in a sense an ultimate conception, and probably should be the second or third step in a series; a first, and essential step, being the acquirement of a moderate-sized rigid airship for training . . . whether or not the second step could extend to the 9.5 million-cubic-foot size would depend upon developments in the airship field in the next few months.[6]

The "developments" which Cook referred to were the General Board's studies of the Durand Committee's reports and recommendations, and the Board's review of the Navy's airship policy.

The Durand Committee's[7] report to the Secretary of the Navy on airship policy offered a series of farsighted recommendations. Their report emphasized that "experience with large airships in the United States has not yet been sufficient to give ground for a wholly settled opinion as to the character and extent of their usefulness, either commercial or naval." Therefore, the Navy's airship experiments should be continued.

In conclusion, they recommended a "positive, carefully considered program of airship construction, including blimps and rigid airships of small or moderate size . . . and extending to a ship or ships of large size." And it was urged "most strongly that the first large airship built under such a program should, at least for a time, be considered not an adjunct to the Fleet, but rather a flying laboratory or flying training ship."[8]

The Bureau translated the spirit of the committee's recommendations into a proposed five-year program for 1937–1941. It included six blimps, the training airship to replace the *Los Angeles,* two ZRS-types equivalent in performance to the ZRS4&5, and an experimental Metalclad of 1,500,000 cubic feet. The total cost was estimated at $16,750,000, about 3.3 million per year; the total was less than what the Navy spent on airplanes in the one year of 1929. But as far as the Navy Department was concerned, this was too much money for "flying laboratories."

After conducting hearings on airship policy in early 1937, the General Board concluded its review of the question and submitted its recommendations to the Secretary of the Navy. The Bureau's five-year program was dismissed, and the Durand Committee's outline of a policy was given the narrowest interpretation; nevertheless, the Board's judgment was not unfavorable.

Although it found itself in agreement with the general criticisms of the airship made by the various commanders in chief—Admirals Schofield, Leigh, Sellers, and Reeves—the Board admitted that during 1931–1934 the airship had not been used in its proper sphere. Direct contact scouting in tactical situations was finally officially recognized as a bankrupt proposition. The airship's ability to carry airplanes, however, cast it in a wholly different light, and the Board observed:

If airplanes are carried by an airship the usefulness of both could be enhanced. . . . With two or three times the speed of a surface cruiser, an airship carrying airplanes could advance a scouting line much more rapidly than would be possible by ships carrying aircraft. . . . The conception of utilizing rigid airships as carriers of airplanes has not been thoroughly explored, but it is the field in which a naval airship's greatest possibilities seem to lie.[9]

The pilots of the ZRS4&5's HTA Unit could have told this to the Board as early as 1931; but no hook-on pilot appeared at a General Board hearing until King and Fulton brought Harrigan with them to the hearings held in the fall of 1934. In earlier hearings the airship men who gave testimony had remarked that airships could carry airplanes; but there was no recognition that the military environment of the 1930's made the hook-on planes the *raison d'etre* of the airship's mission. Of course, in 1931 and early 1932 the powers at Lakehurst had no patience with the heretical and challenging view of the "orphans"[10] of the HTA Unit. The vital role of the hook-on planes as the airship's stand-off capability was not emphasized to the Board until Admiral King presented the case in the fall of 1934.[11]

The Board's final conclusions of 1937 noted that a ZRCV type would be necessary in order to obtain full value from an airship, but it did not feel that large airships should be built "at this time." Nor did it hazard a

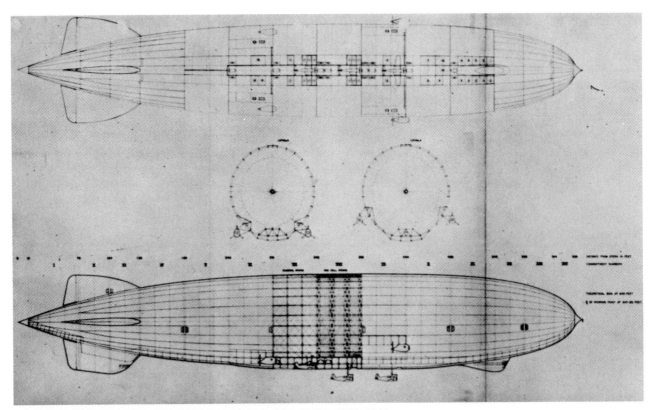

*The ZRN training airship that the Bureau of Aeronautics wanted in 1938–1940
was 3,000,000 cubic feet, as authorized by Congress, with a gross lift of
192,000 pounds and capable of carrying three airplanes. But it was 650 feet
long, which was just twice as long as President Roosevelt would allow.*

guess when such might be built. Instead, it recommended procurement of the long-discussed training airship and specified that it must be of 3,000,000 cubic feet and carry at least two airplanes. This would be the controversial ZRN airship of 1938–1940.[12]

In the spring of 1938 the House Committee on Naval Affairs acted on the General Board's recommendation by authorizing the training airship in the first Vinson Naval Expansion Act. While the Bureau was preparing specifications, President Roosevelt took a sudden interest in the airship's size, and stipulated that it could not be more than 325 feet long.[13]

Cubic volume, not length, is an airship's basic specification. An airship of 3,000,000 cubic feet was authorized; if it were squeezed down to a 325-foot length it would have an impossible aerodynamic configuration. A practicable airship of 325 feet could not have a volume of much more than 1,000,000 cubic feet, which was only a trifle larger than Luftschiffbau Zeppelin's *Bodensee* of 1919 and little more than twice the size of the Navy's largest blimp.[14] The Bureau hoped to resume trapeze experiments with the ZRN, but this 325-foot dwarf could not carry even one airplane. In short, Franklin Roosevelt's dwarf airship was a militarily useless joke. And it was a grim joke on the rigid airship; the ensuing controversy over size would smother the ZRN in its cradle and carry the rigid airship to its political vanishing point in the Navy.

Congress reluctantly appropriated initial funds for the ZRN, and the Bureau revised its specifications to dwarf size. This was BuAer Design No. 186. In the fall of 1938 the Navy called for designs and bids; only Metalclad and Goodyear-Zeppelin competed. After studying the designs, C. P. Burgess remarked, "In view of the superior performance of the Metalclad over the conventional Zeppelin type of equal length, and neglecting considerations of price, the Metalclad seems to be the more desirable ship to fulfill the peculiar specified condition of a rigid airship not over 325 feet in length."[15] But Metalclad's prices were higher than Goodyear's, and a decision was made for the latter.

As in 1927 and 1928, Goodyear offered a package of designs, four in all. Two were alternate dwarf designs, and the third described an airship of 3,000,000 cubic feet, 650 feet long, and capable of carrying three airplanes—as desired by BuAer, specified by the General Board, and authorized by Congress. Their fourth proposal was an anomaly in a design competition for a rigid airship: it was a four-engine blimp of 800,700

cubic feet—extraordinarily large for a nonrigid airship in that day. It was probably included to show that a blimp of this size could provide approximately the same performance as the dwarf rigid, and for about half the cost.[16]

The Bureau, of course, wanted the 3,000,000-cubic-foot design—but it was exactly twice the length of the President's idea of an airship. And the Navy Department did not especially care about an airship of any size. Assistant Secretary of the Navy Charles Edison was an exception; he sought to convince President Roosevelt that the larger airship was the more desirable, but the President felt that his hand was being forced. After observing, "I made it perfectly clear, and have done so for two years, that I do not approve the construction of another large rigid airship for the Navy," the President ordered that all designs and bids on the ZRN be rejected.[17]

In 1939 the long-ailing Secretary of the Navy Swanson died, and Edison was appointed to succeed him. Edison felt that the airship was a victim of its high cost and over-reaction to its crashes, and that the Navy had not built, much less operated, a sufficient number to really determine the airship's value. He requested Admiral King and Captain Garland Fulton to prepare a study of the airship situation and make suggestions for future development.

The King-Fulton Report[18] is a concise summary of the airship situation in the Navy as of 1940. It pointed to the need of a national policy with regard to lighter-than-air aeronautics and observed that the rigid airship's development by the Navy could be regarded as only partially completed. The Navy had accepted custodianship of this development in the United States and its stewardship had become deplorable:

For the past five years the lighter-than-air situation in the Navy has either been static or growing worse due to uncertainties as to the attitude or future policies of the Department with reference to lighter-than-air matters. This indefiniteness in the Navy Department's position has been a handicap not only as relates to the Department's own program, but has served also to retard or discourage the development and establishment of commercial airship service and the availability of such airships as naval auxiliaries.

The total effort expended on lighter-than-air developments in the past 20 years is infinitesimal in comparison with the effort expended in other aeronautical developments. Definite improvements in lighter-than-air equipment are available, ready for application.

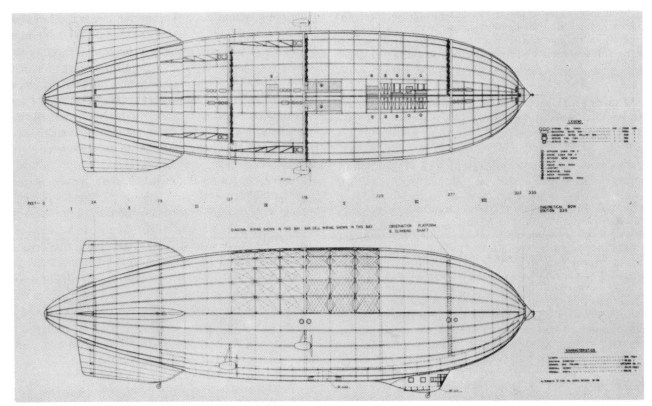

The President insisted that the ZRN could not exceed 325 feet in length.
The result was this "dwarf" design proposed by Goodyear-Zeppelin in 1939.
Its small size made it useless for continuing airplane-carrying operations,
and in the end the project became submerged in controversy and confusion.

From every standpoint, a clarification of the Navy Department's position on lighter-than-air matters is essential. . . . The existing "status quo' or "standing by" awaiting some future action or future decision is getting nowhere, and is, in reality, dissipating the progress already made.

The myopic employment of the *Akron* and the *Macon* was pointed out, and emphasis was placed upon the airplane-carrying mission:

The experiences to date in use of rigid airships do not justify a final verdict against the utility of the rigid airship as a naval tool. Rigid airships, as operated by the Navy, were not utilized so as to demonstrate adequately their value in scouting work. The promising development of operating airplanes from airships was arrested before its full possibilities could be appraised.

The large plane-carrying airship for naval purposes offers decided possibilities for appropriate usefulness in war commensurate with the risks and costs involved. Airships of largest size should be retained in naval plans as the objective toward which naval rigid airship effort is directed, and at an appropriate time construction of two such airships should be undertaken. For the present, the Navy's immediate need is a moderate-sized rigid airship (a replacement for the *Los Angeles*) to give continuity to naval rigid airship work.

The "minimum program" which the report recommended was simply implementation of the General Board's program of 1937, which the Board had reaffirmed in October 1939. Projected over the years 1941–1945 at an estimated cost of $10,000,000, it called for the 3,000,000-cubic-foot ZRN and 15 blimps. The King-Fulton Report was practically ignored. During the exigencies of World War II, the Navy's blimp force was hurriedly expanded to more than 165 airships, operating from bases strung along the East and West Coasts, and as far away as Brazil and Gibraltar. But no rigid airships were built.

Meanwhile, the ZRN authorization was still on the statute books, and Secretary Edison was determined to have the airship in its larger size. In the spring of 1940, when a supplementary defense appropriation was being prepared, he told Rear Admiral John H. Towers that he wanted "to have $300,000 or so included for . . . the rigid airship now authorized." Towers had relieved Cook as Bureau Chief in June 1939. But Edison also told Towers that he was "*assuming* that all deficiency items [in the estimates] will be cleared by the President."[19]

On 5 June, Towers argued the ZRN's case before the House Subcommittee on Appropriations, and asked that funds be made available for the 3,000,000-cubic-foot airship.[20] Two days later the subcommittee was confused by a contradictory note from the President which asked $300,000 for the construction of three airships of about 1,000,000 cubic feet.[21] The President later explained to Edison that he thought "the needs of the Navy can be better met by obtaining three small airships."[22] But Congress was left to wonder what was going on.

When hearings on the same measure were held before the Senate's subcommittee on 17 June, its members were quite hostile toward the airship question. Admiral Harold R. Stark, CNO, told the subcommittee that the President's three dwarf rigids would be something in the nature of an experiment.[23] But when Senator James F. Byrnes took the discussion "off the record" and categorically questioned the Admiral, Stark admitted that the dwarfs would probably be militarily useless.[24] And with that, Senator Byrnes scratched off the rigid airship money. To all practical purposes, this was the political end of the rigid airship.

The ZRN's principal difficulty was that by the end of the 1930's relatively few persons could imagine the rigid airship having any military significance. When the ZRN was becoming a money issue in 1938, Admiral William D. Leahy, retiring CNO and later Franklin Roosevelt's close adviser, had counselled the President that the "possible value of lighter-than-airships for naval purposes [do not] justify . . . the expenditure of $3,000,000 from the naval appropriation and all available funds can be used to better advantage for other purposes."[25] And it appeared to the President that "the principal pressure [for the ZRN] has come from a very few officers and from a very powerful lobby conducted by the rubber company which is seeking to salvage a fairly heavy speculative investment."[26]

By the summer of 1940, World War II was nine months old; there was the crisis of the collapse of France and England's dangerous isolation, and the burning issue of America's "isolationism." The crying need was for thousands of airplanes. Most persons holding a responsible position in the Naval Establishment, or in other organs of the government, could not imagine where a single rigid airship for training purposes fit into this urgent picture.

The year 1940 terminates the rigid airship's denouement. In early 1940, the *Los Angeles* was finally scrapped; her viscera of duralumin girders and steel wiring brought $3,667.80. And on 16 December of that year, the Goodyear-Zeppelin Corporation was formally liquidated.[27] Only 15 years before, the Goodyear-Zeppelin alliance had been hailed as the hope of the rigid airship in America. Now it was gone.

In the fall of 1939, the General Board had undertaken yet another review of the Navy's airship policy, and on 23 July 1940, Secretary of the Navy Frank Knox approved the Board's recommendations:

To build and maintain rigid airships as necessary to explore and develop their usefulness for naval purposes; and to cooperate with other agencies in developing commercial airships.

To build and maintain nonrigid airships for coastal patrol and other naval uses.

This was essentially the policy orginally formulated in 1934 and repeated in 1937; and the Navy Department's willingness to execute the policy in 1940 was no greater than it was in 1934. But the General Board formally scrapped the rigid airship only in the postwar years. In its reformulated airship policy, approved by Secretary of the Navy James C. Forrestal on 23 January 1947, all reference to the rigid airship was omitted. The paragraph on blimps stood alone.

In 1940, too, Captain Garland Fulton voluntarily retired from the Navy, terminating a naval career of 28 years. At least 18 of those years were devoted to lighter-than-air aeronautics in general and to the rigid airship in particular. Relatively few persons associate Fulton's name with the airship. But those persons familiar with the Bureau of Aeronautics during 1924–1940 knew that he was the man to see about all matters pertaining to lighter-than-air aeronautics.

Fulton had been Admiral Moffett's right hand on airship matters and was only a little less so to Admiral King. He had been instrumental in bringing together the elements of the ZRS4&5 program, and one of the key figures in achieving its realization. He had done everything within his limited power to provide at least the material conditions for the ZRS4&5's success; toward this end he and his small staff were largely successful. The operational concepts which guided, or misguided, the ZRS4&5 were quite another thing; they were far beyond the reach of Fulton's cubicle on Constitution Avenue. Indeed, they were beyond even Admiral King's ordinarily iron grasp, until July 1934.

If there was any hope for the rigid airship's military function in 1940, it vanished when Garland Fulton cleared his desk in the Bureau of Aeronautics.

A footnote to the rigid airship's denouement occurred in January 1942 after Admiral King hoisted his flag as Commander in Chief, U. S. Fleet. He sought to revive and implement the ZRCV idea. This created a flurry of excitement in the Navy's airship organization, and prompted some further design studies by C. P. Burgess; but for all practical purposes and the realization of timely results, King's effort was too late.

Admiral Towers explained that the construction of a ZRCV could not begin until after a year's design work, and the first airship's fabrication would require about two years. Goodyear had the only construction hangar in the United States, and it was being used for blimp production. Goodyear's engineering staff was limited; and besides being concerned with blimps, the company was also producing vital subassemblies for TBF torpedo planes and PBM and PB2Y flying boats.

In conclusion, Towers noted that "in view of the diversion of essential materials, the dislocation of industry, the time required to design and build even one such airship, and its undemonstrated value, this Bureau is of the opinion that the proposed experiment should not be undertaken at this critical time."[28] Even C. P. Burgess thought that "the same amount of material and effort put into flying boats of a type already in production would yield much more valuable results, and in far less time."[29] In other words, it was too late.

The airship's proponents will argue that it was never too late. But no decisions are made in a vacuum. What with all the upsetting shifts which occurred in the world balance of power during 1938–1941, the United States simply became too busy with first-things-first to give any serious attention to the rigid airship, an aircraft which had a public record of failure.

But was there ever really a time for the big airship? A great deal of speculation can be spun out of the several interesting might-have-been's which promised to help the airship during the 1930's. John Towers' remark of 1942 about the airship's undemonstrated value, however, initiates the question whether the airship was ever able to do something to help itself.

Here occurs a certain key to an explanation of the rigid airship's failure in the Navy. It is found in the years 1932–1934, in the gap between the ZRS4&5's promise and performance. It was there that time was, and it was there that time was lost.

CHAPTER TWELVE

The Performance

In the limited time available to the rigid airship in the U.S. Navy—which is to say the *Akron* and the *Macon*—it failed to prove its value to naval warfare. The airships' trials were not realistic, they were not exhaustive, nor can they be considered conclusive. But the decision against the rigid airship has been final.

It is easy to dismiss the airship as a technological aberration which was predestined to failure; but this explains nothing. What deserves examination are the political, military, and technological environments in which the airship had to operate.

The only period in which the rigid airship enjoyed a consensus was during 1916–1920 when the General Board and Admirals Benson, Mayo, and Sims, among others, insisted that its services were indispensable to the Fleet. But after the Washington Conference demonstrated that "normalcy" meant niggardly naval appropriations, the "battle for the buck" was joined, and the airship was a subject of controversy until World War II. The airship's opponents did not act out of sheer perversity; it was a very expensive machine in its first costs, and its prototype period promised to be long and expensive even for a few units. There was an honest conviction that it was unreliable, its utility was marginal, and there were always other needs to which funds could be applied with quicker and more certain results.

The airship's proponents were forever insisting that it was not competitive with other naval hardware, it had a mission of its own, was a vital ingredient of the "mix," and it supplemented the missions of surface craft and airplanes. But this was wishful thinking; in the environment of peace and penury the airship was variously in fiscal competition with cruisers, carriers, and airplanes. On 10 March 1924, Marc Mitscher, in reaction to the Truscott memorandum, insisted:

Do not recommend any rigid [airship] construction for Fleet work as long as we are building carriers. When we can compare the scouting abilities of an airplane carrier with the operation of a rigid, then and then only is the time to determine future rigid construction. The visibility from a rigid is no greater than the visibility for a heavier-than-air craft, the speed of the heavier-than-air craft is more than that of a rigid. The vulnerability of the rigid is known to all. Recommend that the time, energy, and money be *not* expended until the capabilities of the rigid versus the aircraft carrier can be compared.[1]

What makes Mitscher's marginalia remarkable is that it was penned when the *Langley* had been in commission as a carrier for less than two years, the *Lexington* and *Saratoga* were more than three years in the future, and many problems were belaboring the launching and retrieving of planes aboard the *Langley*. But coming from one of the most militant exponents of the aircraft carrier, his remarks are exemplary of the heavier-than-air men's confidence in their carriers, and provide insight into their contempt for large airships.

In view of the rigid airship's stunted development and the fact that its funds were always a much debated topic subject to an extraordinary amount of uninformed criticism, the jealousy of the airplane's partisans might seem unwarranted. But an airship represented a substantial sum. The ZRS4&5 cost eight million dollars. During the interwar years this would buy two or three hundred carrier planes or four dozen twin-engine flying boats. So the heavier-than-air men could never resist dividing airships by airplanes—and turning purple over the result.

Compared to the influence of carrier aviation and the flying boat's proponents, which were the major constituents of naval aviation during the interwar years, the voice of lighter-than-air was always a tiny one. The air-

ANOTHER MILESTONE

THE SAN FRANCISCO EXAMINER, 11 MAY 1932.

Unscathed!

THE SAN FRANCISCO CHRONICLE, MAY 1932.

ship had no spokesman on the staffs of CNO, CinCUS, ComBatFor, ComAirBatFor, nor ComScoFor, and its representatives in BuAer tended to be isolated. In early 1925, when the *Los Angeles* was in the inventory and the *Shenandoah* was still flying, it was observed:

Lighter-than-air hardly exists as a branch of naval aeronautics. Except in the Material Division, there is no personnel in the Bureau of Aeronautics devoting time and thought to lighter-than-air matters. Even in the Material Division this work is confined to one small sub-section and outside of this sub-section almost the only individuals who take an interest in lighter-than-air are a few whose interest is carried over from work with the *Shenandoah* and the former nonrigids. The result is that lighter-than-air matters are handled practically as a separate activity, frequently by personnel not qualified to pass on the matters presented. . . . This situation is often reflected on occasions where policies, plans, estimates of personnel and funds are prepared and conferences or discussions held without giving due consideration to, or including, the interests of lighter-than-air. Lighter-than-air, if it is to continue to exist, needs representation in all divisions of the Bureau.

There appears to be a general feeling throughout naval aviation that lighter-than-air is in competition with heavier-than-air. It cannot be too strongly emphasized that this is not the case. A clearly defined separate budget within the Bureau might help this situation. On the other hand, it might accentuate the present isolation. A natural result of isolating and curtailing lighter-than-air is that the remainder of naval aeronautics should come to regard airships as interlopers.[2]

This situation had not experienced any substantial change by 1932, contrary to appearances; and after 1935 it became immeasurably worse.

Within the Navy and the realm of naval aviation, lighter-than-air and the rigid airship were stepchildren. They were well-protected stepchildren during Admiral Moffett's twelve years as Chief of BuAer, and only a little less so during Admiral King's 37 months. But when King left BuAer in 1936, they became orphans and were left to shift for themselves.

Also in the realm of politics are the abortive commercial airship plans of the 1930's; their frustration hurt the naval airship badly. After 1930 a series of merchant airship bills, which would have given airships the same economic advantages in transocean commerce that domestic airlines enjoyed in the United States, came within a hair's breadth of congressional approval. The International Zeppelin Transport Company and the Pacific Zeppelin Transport Company were prepared to place construction orders after the *Macon*'s comple-

tion and to begin operations in 1935. Their airships would have been built to Navy specifications for wartime conversion, and would have been manned by Naval Reserve crews. Their construction would have continued research and development, produced follow-on types and experience for a second generation of naval airships, and their operations would have broadened operating experience.

But the airplane interests which were planning transocean airlines for the late 1930's feared that the passenger market was not big enough for both, and that airmail subsidies for airships would mean none for their flying boats. Their lobbyists fought a successful delaying action against all airship legislation; then the losses of the *Akron* and *Macon* shook public confidence, and in the end there was nothing. Otherwise the state of the art would not only have been kept alive, but improved upon, in the same fashion that civil aviation of the 1930's served the military airplane.

The rigid airship's status experienced considerable change during 1919–1936; but it cannot be understood wholly in terms of politics. The military environment was also changing. From the General Board's initial airship recommendation of 1916 to the loss of the *Macon* nineteen years later, the airship's promise was always articulated in terms of a scouting mission. In 1938, however, King's successor in BuAer, Admiral Arthur B. Cook, told the House Committee on Appropriations: "I can frankly say that from the standpoint of the usefulness of rigid airships for scouting duty, I would not give you two cents for such a ship."[3]

This judgment was based on the *Macon*'s performances of 1934, which Admiral King believed to be the "crucial year." In fact, the crucial year was only six months long; it began in January and ended in June. Here the *Macon* was called upon to operate with the Fleet, to come to grips with naval aviation as it had evolved around the aircraft carrier, and to demonstrate that she was not a 1918 Zeppelin but a "lighter-than-air carrier." But here, too, she did very little training, operated but rarely on her own initiative, and seldom exercised her planes outside of fleet operations. In spite of King's appeal for a more intensive schedule, the *Macon* spent most of her time inside Sunnyvale's hangar; the only times she flew were to make her mandatory appearances in fleet exercises, and occasional local flights to round out the month's flight time.

As far as the Navy Department was concerned, it was in this period that the ZRS4&5 was lost, not on 12

WE COULD USE THE AKRON THIS WEEK-END HOLIDAY

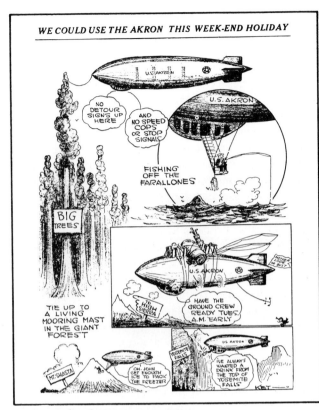

THE OAKLAND (CALIF) TRIBUNE, 29 MAY 1932.

WILL HE LEARN HIS LESSON?

THE CHICAGO DAILY NEWS, 6 APRIL 1933.

THE PENALTY OF SIZE

THE CHICAGO TRIBUNE, 14 FEBRUARY 1935.

WILL WE EVER LEARN?

THE CHICAGO DAILY NEWS, 14 FEBRUARY 1935.

February 1935. The performance the *Macon* achieved after mid–1934 was never tested against a Fleet Problem; she did not survive to be tried in long-range patrols west of Hawaii; and what the airplane-carrying airship's fate would have been if the *Macon* had survived for another five years will always be a debatable question.

There is much to be said by way of extenuation relative to the Fleet's myopic employment of the *Macon*. On this count her trials were wholly artificial. There is no suggestion that anyone on the staffs of CinCUS, ComBatFor, or ComAirBatFor was assigned to work out a place in the Fleet's operations which would exploit the special characteristics of this expensive machine. Nor did CinCUS request a liaison officer from Moffett Field. The *Macon* was simply thrown in to sink or swim with Admiral Sellers' orders to "scout tactically." There is something grotesque, pathetic, and deplorable about this three-million-dollar aircraft with its unique, very-long-range capability being obliged to stooge around in a cramped air space in an effort to execute missions better executed by a $25,000 scout bomber or a $150,000 flying boat.

The lack of criteria by which to judge the *Macon*'s performance was the most significant aspect of the fleet exercises. We are left to wonder with Alger Dresel:

When may the *Macon* be considered to have successfully carried out her assigned tasks? Does success only come when she searches area after area and, after locating the enemy, remain in contact without incurring damage? Can she be considered successful if she searches any area, finds nothing, or locates an enemy unit, reports it, and is destroyed in the encounter?[4]

These questions cried out for answers, but not one was forthcoming. The *Macon* was evidently supposed to be everywhere at once, see everything, and last forever.

It was the airship's technology relative to its technological environment which hurt it most. Essentially tied to the static lift of its helium gas, it was nearing its technological end point by the end of the 1930's.[5] Only marginal improvements in performance stood on the horizon, such as use of artificial superheat to increase the helium's lift; lighter, more powerful, and fewer engine units; lighter and stronger materials; or exploiting dynamic lift to maximum by overloading the airship after takeoff by means of hook-on planes. C. P. Burgess believed that an appreciable increase in performance could be realized through a radical break with the past, by discarding the archaic redundancies of the classic Zeppelin structure for the simplicity of Ralph Upson's stressed-skin Metalclad design, which Burgess speculated would be the "ultimate airship."[6] He also believed that the airship was especially adaptable to exploit boundary layer control, which was the only hope of a quantum advance; but even today the full fruits of boundary layer control remain elusive.

The airship's *raison d'etre* was its extraordinary lift, range, and endurance. But this was nearing its end point; it had no more "growth" except by increasing the airship's volume, and this was limited by the size of its hangars, if no other considerations.

If the Navy opted for an all-out crash program for the ZRCV in the Naval Expansion Act of 1938, it would have cost half a billion dollars in initial outlays alone. Allowing for 20 per cent of the airships being out of service for overhaul or repairs, 50 ZRCV's would have been necessary for a two-ocean striking force. Burgess estimated its cost at $10,000,000 per copy, at 1938 price levels. Each ZRCV required at least nine dive bombers, and the whole force would have required a vast expansion of production, servicing, and training facilities. Planning of this magnitude was necessary in 1938 if the ZRCV was to make any substantial contribution to World War II. It was feasible and practicable; but in 1938 the Navy was reluctant to spend even a mere $3,000,000 on the modest ZRN. This was because in terms of cost-effectiveness the rigid airship was adjudged a "bad buy."

The airplane could not begin to deliver as much by way of range, endurance, and great lift; but it would make good on its limited promise, and quickly, and in more units for the same cost. Admiral Reeves did not need a corps of Ph.D.'s and a battery of computers to figure it out to his satisfaction. As he put it to the General Board in the fall of 1934:

For one dirigible at a cost of $4,000,000 you could have 26 of these patrol planes that you are talking about today [PBY flying boats in prospect], so in that comparison, as Commander in Chief of the Fleet, if you should ask me whether I would have one dirigible or 26 patrol planes, I would answer patrol planes.[7]

The rigid airship's demise marks the first instance of a multimillion dollar weapons system born of twentieth century technology to pass out of existence. It has since been joined by the P6M *Seamaster,* which probably

THE END OF ANOTHER NOBLE EXPERIMENT — By Jerry Doyle.

A Sad Home Coming!

represented the flying boat's last stand; and by the flying-bomb type of guided missile, such as the billion-dollar *Matador, Rascal, Snark,* and *Navaho* systems. And it will soon be joined by the still formidable intercontinental bomber.

The airship weapons system passed through a cycle which transcends lighter-than-air aeronautics. The Germans first exploited their Zeppelins as a reconnaissance vehicle, and later as an over-the-target bomber. Before the end of the first world war, however, the Zeppelin's ability to penetrate targets had become seriously degraded, and there were experiments to carry airplanes as a "built-in" fighter escort, and an effort to develop a remote-controlled glider bomb which would provide a limited stand-off capability.

The U. S. Navy returned the airship to the reconnaissance mission, but to reduce its vulnerability the hook-on planes were introduced for a stand-off capability. Bu-Aer's ZRCV proposals would have made it a bomber again, but with hook-on planes providing the necessary stand-off capability. When the airship experienced a 20-year renaissance in the form of the blimp, its ultimate configuration was the ZPG-3W Airborne Early Warning airship; the reconnaissance mission was revived in terms of radar surveillance, and the airship was brought full circle.[8]

In recent years the world of aeronautics has seen the intercontinental bomber approximate this same cycle. The airplane began its military career circa 1914 as a reconnaissance vehicle, and quickly developed a bombardment capability. But as electronically guided and heat-seeking missiles threatened to degrade its ability to penetrate targets after mid-century, the bomber had to develop stand-off weapons such as the operational *Hound-Dog* and the aborted *Skybolt* air-to-ground missiles. During 1959–1961 the proposed B-70 super-bomber became submerged in a controversy which made that surrounding the ZRN of 1939 seem like an exercise in elocution. It is historically significant that the Mach 3 bomber was not given a production priority in the budget, and that only a token number of experimental articles were procured. Equally significant was its "reorientation" as the RS-70, a "reconnaissance-strike" vehicle, which made it a spotter aircraft for intercontinental missile artillery, returned it to the airplane's original mission of 1914, and nominally closed the cycle.

It is little appreciated that the modern airplane dates only from the first stressed-skin, cantilever-wing designs which began to appear circa 1930; its *raison d'etre* has always been speed, and it reached its end point at Mach 0.7. The jet engine, exotic-wing designs, and novel fuselage configurations carried it to Mach 2, and exotic metals and other innovations took it further to Mach 3. And there the airplane as we have become familiar with it rests today, perhaps at its technological end point—figuratively speaking, a Mach 3 Zeppelin.

Since the airship's demise there has been no end of informal proposals for its revival—as an airliner for the leisurely tourist, a bulk cargo carrier, a transport for extraordinarily large rocket components, as an airborne command and control center of extraordinary endurance, and as a test bed for a nuclear aircraft engine. As long as air weighs 80 pounds per 1,000 cubic feet and helium 11 pounds for the same quantity, the principle of lighter-than-air aeronautics will remain fundamentally sound. But when engines are available with thrust in five and six digits it seems doubtful if the gas-filled aircraft has a renaissance in prospect. On the other hand, a study by the RAND Corporation has suggested that the airship's peculiar characteristics can best perform certain passive missions; but it may be necessary for the present generation to pass away so the airship can be "re-invented."

Naval aviation's rigid airship era lasted only 15 years and its ZRS4&5 epoch only 41 months. When it is considered that the airship men enjoyed only the most infinitesimal percentage of the funds expended upon naval airplane development, had only four aircraft with which to experiment, and managed to fly them for only 8,632 hours,[9] these were remarkably fruitful years by way of technological progress. A comparison of the "Model-T" *Shenandoah* with the ZRS4&5 is adequate evidence of this. And this is aside from the unusual reconnaissance system which the ZRS4&5 represented, by way of promise, to its time.

Considered solely as a research and development project, the ZRS4&5 experiment ranks among the most fascinating in the history of aeronautics. It is certainly unique. The airship men failed to prove their system to the Navy's satisfaction, but they cannot be judged harshly. As Wiley pleaded their case in 1934:

The Commanding Officer [Wiley] has about as much airship experience as any line officer in our Navy, but is constantly confronted with new problems of operation . . . [and] although the Commanding Officer has about 5,000 hours flying experience, this is only about 210 full days.

An average for the other officers attached to the ship is about 2,500 hours. Due account must be taken that the most experienced of us are novices in point of time in our respective elements as compared to surface ship officers, who measure their seagoing experience in years—we, our air-going experience in hours. Most surface ship types have a well-developed system of tactics which represents the thought of many, the experience of years, and the testing of many units. We have no such system, and have only one unit for testing, and a mere handful of officers working on this project.[10]

In the interwar period of aeronautics, it is doubtful if as much was achieved by so very few against so many formidable obstacles.

Because the rigid airship project was terminated does not mean the experiment was a gross waste of effort and resources. Its development was significant in broadening aeronautical knowledge and in intensifying meteorological investigations; it created legacies of no mean value for the airplane and even the realms of nuclear and aerospace research. Little was known about duralumin aircraft alloys in the United States until the Bureau of Standards investigated them for the Navy; and the latter "encouraged" the Aluminum Corporation of America to undertake the industrial manufacture of duralumin for the *Shenandoah*'s structure ten years before airplanes had any widespread use for the alloy.

The airship broke new ground in large aircraft structures, pioneered work on gust theory and gust effects, while Ralph Upson's stressed-skin hull (conceived years before Adolf Rohrbach's memorable 1926 lecture in the United States) was demonstrated well in advance of similar American airplane structures. The same is true of the research and development of impermeable fabrics. The Allison V-1710 airship engine (although a legacy of questionable value), on its test stand when the *Macon* was lost, was subsequently re-engineered and in various modifications provided the original power plants for such Army Air Force fighter planes of World War II as the P-38, P-39, P-40, P-51, and P-63. And the airship alone was responsible for the development of the United States' helium resources. Today, nuclear and aerospace sciences use more helium than the airship ever did.

For more than two decades no rigid airship has flown the world's skies. A generation has grown to adulthood with no immediate familiarity with this type of aircraft, and what acquaintance it has is usually vague and in terms of its most tragic moments. Too little is recalled of its moments of success, of the promise which many men once thought it had, and most specifically the ZRS4&5's novel promise to naval warfare. As flying aircraft carriers they were embryonic; but to this date they remain the only aircraft originally designed to carry and service other aircraft, and no other aircraft of any type has approximated their airplane-carrying performance.[11]

The mooring towers, rail masts, and stern beams have long since been cut up for scrap; the mooring circles' tracks pulled up and their roadbeds leveled to leave curious patterns in evidence yet on the fields at Lakehurst and Sunnyvale. Very little public evidence remains of the ZRS4&5 epoch.

In the National Air Museum of the Smithsonian Institution there is preserved one F9C-2 hook-on plane. There and in other museums are large scale models of the airships. But only at Lakehurst, at Akron, and at Moffett Field is there evidence which adequately testifies to the onetime reality of the USS *Akron* and the USS *Macon*. There—in much the same fashion that the great pyramids at Giza proclaim the onetime existence of their pharaohs—the empty airship hangars still stand, providing mute and massive testimony to the existence of these mammoth aircraft, which were aeronautics' first, and last, flying aircraft carriers.

Appendixes

Significant Chronology
USS Akron and USS Macon

Conceived as a BuAer Project . . . . .10 March 1924
Projected as a BuAer Design . . . . .April 1924
Formulated as a BuAer Proposal . . . . .24 April 1925
Formally proposed to SecNav . . . . .17 November 1925
Authorized by the 69th Congress . . . . .24 June 1926
First Design Competition . . . . .16 May–28 June 1927
Second Design Competition . . . . .26 July–5 September 1928
Contract to Goodyear-Zeppelin Corporation . . . . .6 October 1928

	Akron	*Macon*
Christened	8 August 1931	11 March 1933
First flight	25 September 1931	21 April 1933
Commissioned	27 October 1931	23 June 1933
First planes aboard	3 May 1932	6 July 1933
Lost	4 April 1933	12 February 1935
Formally stricken	30 April 1933	26 February 1935
Total No. of flights	73	54
No. of flight hours	1,695.8	1,798.2

Characteristics and Performance USS Macon

General Dimensions:

Total gas volume, 100% inflation, c.f. 6,850,000
Nominal gas volume, cells 95% full, with helium of standard purity, lifting 0.062 lbs. per c.f. 6,500,000
Total air volume of hull, c.f. 7,401,260
Over-all length, ft. 785
Maximum diameter of hull, ft. 132.9
Over-all width (propellers at vertical), ft. 137.5
Over-all height from ground, ft. 146.5
Aspect ratio of hull (length : diameter) ....5.91 : 1

Hull Structure:

Materials of structure ....Duralumin 17-SRT
Number of main keels 3
Number of main frames 12
Normal spacing of main frames, ft. 74
Number of intermediate frames 33
Normal spacing of intermediate frames, ft. 16.4
Number of sides to polygons of athwartships framing 36
Number of longitudinal girders 36

Fin Structure:

Axial length of fin and movable surface, ft. 119.76
Length of fin, leading edge root to hinges, ft. 104.99
Span of fin at rudder pintles, ft. 41.4
Total span, horizontal fins, across hinges, ft. 144.33
Span of fin balancing surfaces, ft. 14.6
Chord (width) of fin balancing surfaces, ft. 3.6
Area of vertical tail surfaces, sq. ft. 7,200
Area of horizontal tail surfaces, sq. ft. 7,100
Maximum thickness of fin at junction with hull, ft. 11.48
Total weight of each upper three fin structures, lbs. 2,700

Fuel, Oil, and Ballast:

Maximum fuel capacity, lbs. 126,000

Number of fuel tanks 110
Normal fuel load, lbs. 110,000
Maximum oil capacity, lbs. 12,000
Number of oil storage tanks 8
Normal oil carried, lbs. 2,400
Maximum ballast capacity, lbs. 223,000
Normal ballast carried upon unmooring, lbs. 20,000
Number of 4,400-lb. bags for storage ballast 28
Number of 2,200-lb. bags for storage ballast 4
Number of 1,000-lb., quick-release bags for emergency ballast 12

Gas Cells:

Material . . . . .5.3-ounce cotton cloth impregnated with a gelatin-latex compound
Number of gas cells 12
Volume of largest cell, c.f. 900,000
Total cell material, sq. yds. 54,000
Total weight of gas cells, lbs. 22,000
Normal number of gas valves per cell 3
Diameter of all gas valves, inches 32

Outer Cover:

Material . . . . .2.8 ounce, 65-lb. strength, cotton cloth
Treatment . . . . four coats of clear dope, two with aluminum pigment
Weight of material per sq.yd. after treatment, ounces 5.5
Total material, sq. yds. 33,000
Total weight of outer cover after treatment, lbs. 11,300

Powerplant:

Engine . . . . .Maybach VL-II, 12-cylinder, 60° V-type, 560 h.p. at 1,600 r.p.m.
Dryweight of one engine, lbs. 2,600
Ratio: pounds per horsepower 4.5
Number of engines 8
Total horsepower 4,480
Maximum engine r.p.m. 1,600
Maximum propeller r.p.m. 925
Diameter of propeller arc, feet 16.33
Maximum upward thrust (propellers rotated), lbs. 6,000
Maximum downward thrust, lbs. 8,000
Generators (2) . . . . .Westinghouse 8-KW, 110-volt, D.C.
Prime movers (2) . . . . .Universal Lighting Co. 4-cylinder, 30 h.p., gasoline fueled

Complement and Crew:

Complement . . . . .16 officers, 75 enlisted men
Flight crew . . . . .10 officers, 50 enlisted men
Airplane pilots 4
Airplane mechanics 15

Performance:

Total lift, based on nominal gas volume and helium at standard value, lifting 0.062 lbs. per c.f., lbs. . . . 403,000
Deadweight of structure, lbs. 242,356
Useful lift, including crew, fuel, oil, ballast, and military load, lbs. 160,644
Maximum speed, knots 75.6
Standard speed, knots 65.0
Cruising speed, knots 55.0

Endurance and Range with Normal Military Load and 110,000 lbs. of Fuel

Speed in Knots	Hours	Range in Nautical Miles	Radius in Nautical Miles
70	68	4,760	2,380
65	75	4,855	2,427
55	108	5,940	2,970
46	158	7,268	3,268

Characteristics and Performance
Curtiss F9C Airplane

Model	XF9C-1	F9C-2
Wingspan, upper wing, ft.	25′ 5″	25′ 5″
Wingspan, lower wing, ft.	23′ 3″	23′ 3″
Total wing area, sq. ft.	172.8	172.8
Over-all length, ft.	20′ 3″	20′ 7″
Gross weight, lbs.	2,502	2,770
Weight empty, lbs.	1,836	2,089
Useful load, lbs.	666	681
Per cent useful load	26.5	24.6
Engine	Wright R-975-C	Wright R-975-E3
Horsepower (sea level) at 2,200 r.p.m.	421	438
Maximum speed at 4,000 ft., m.p.h.	176.5	176.5
Maximum speed at 4,000 ft., with undercarriage removed, m.p.h.		200.0
Maximum speed at 16,000 ft. m.p.h.	152.0	148.0
Stalling speed, m.p.h.	60.0	63.0
Service ceiling, ft.	22,600	19,200
Initial rate of climb, ft. per minute	2,150	1,700
Climb in 10 minutes, ft.	13,800	11,300
Wing loading, lbs. per sq. ft.	14.5	16.0
Power loading, lbs. per h.p.	5.9	6.4
Internal fuel, gallons	60	60
External fuel, gallons		30
Normal radius at 125 m.p.h. cruising speed, statute miles	190	176
Radius with external fuel, statute miles		255
Armament, .30 calibre machine guns	Two	Two

Left: Typical single-ring type main frame with taut wire bracing and diamond trusses. Right: Typical inherently stiff deep ring with elastic bulkhead of type used in ZRS4&5.

Design and Construction

It has been remarked of the *Akron* and *Macon* that they were not "genuine" Zeppelins because of their "unorthodox" design, among other minutiae. Few have recognized them as a salient step forward in the state of the art; none has tried to view them in their technological environment.

The break-up of the ZR2 (British R38) occasioned intensive investigation of hull strength; one of the most significant results was a study by C. P. Burgess, Jerome C. Hunsaker, and Starr Truscott, "The Strength of Rigid Airships," which won the Royal Aeronautical Society's R38 memorial prize for 1923. The greatest care was given to the *Shenandoah*'s strength calculations, but she was nevertheless torn to pieces by a thunderstorm. At that time the aeronautical world was still relatively ignorant of weather; but this was a forcible demonstration that existing design criteria were inadequate to meet North American storm conditions.

Design No. 60, the basic specification for the ZRS4&5, was in preparation when the *Shenandoah* broke up, and this led to considerable reflection on the state of the art. Special criticism was focused on the "conventional" wire-braced main frame and fresh attention was given to the merits of the inherently stiff type. The conventional ring may be compared to a bicycle wheel which depends on a multiplicity of spokes for rigidity; if too many spokes fail, the wheel collapses. The inherently stiff main frame, variously known as a built-up ring or deep ring, may be compared to a disc wheel in which a local failure will not mean failure of the whole. An example of this is had in the *Macon*'s casualty where the upper part of frame 17.5 failed where the fin was bolted to it, but the remainder of the ring did not collapse.

The advantage of the conventional ring was its lightness; it used only one ring element. The deep ring, however, employed three ring elements: two of equal size and a third of smaller diameter. They were joined by the additional weight of a truss system to form a single unit.

The wire bracing of the conventional ring also provided a bulkhead which separated the gas cells. As long as the inflation of the cells on both sides of the bulkhead was equal, the pressures on the bulkhead were balanced. But if one cell became deflated, the balance was destroyed, and the adjacent cells exerted an undesirable pressure on the bulkheads. The pressure on the bulkhead wiring transmitted high radial tensions to the corners of the rings' framework, which in extreme conditions could create compression loads which might cause the ring structure to fail. This was a serious problem to designers who were studying airships of unusually large hull cross sections in the 1920's.

The deep ring needed no wire bracing, and in the event of deflation in one cell, the adjacent cells were theoretically free to bulge into the empty space. In practice, however, the deep ring was provided with a "slack" or an "elastic" bulkhead which limited the degree of bulge. The result was much lower compression loads transmitted to the ring structure as compared to those in a taut bulkhead, while in normal operations they checked the surging of gas cells in turbulent air conditions, or when the airship was inclined at unusual angles of attack. A further attraction was the triangular space within the deep ring's structure, which provided a crawl space for personnel to have access to the airship's structure, which was impossible with the conventional ring.

The deep ring's structural strength was appreciably greater than that of the conventional type, but so also was its weight. This was a disadvantage; but every aircraft design is a package of compromises, and after the *Shenandoah*'s experience American engineers were will-

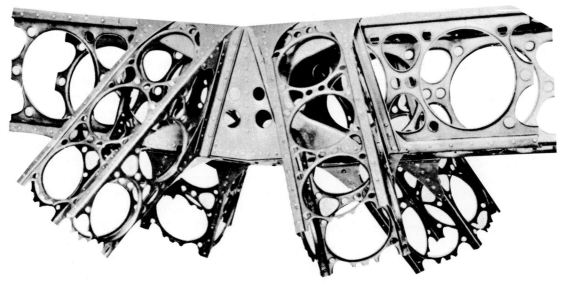

Riveting details at the junction of the Warren truss system with the apex girder of one of the Akron's main frames.

GOODYEAR AEROSPACE CORPORATION

Detail of one of the Akron's intermediate hull rings, showing the channel which carried one of the longitudinal girders.

GOODYEAR AEROSPACE CORPORATION

ing to pay this weight penalty for the concomitant increase in hull strength.

A further incentive toward innovation was that the loss of life aboard the *Shenandoah* was directly due to her suspended control car and two engine cars being wrenched loose, their occupants plunging to certain death. An exposition of the "Technical Aspects of the Loss of the *Shenandoah*," in the August 1926, *Journal of the Society of Naval Engineers,* was emphatic in its recommendations for greater hull strength, an integral control car, and inside engines for future airships. C. P. Burgess worked up alternative inside engine installations and BuAer had the Allison Engineering Company make a study of propeller transmission systems for inside engines. And the "Technical Specifications for a 6,500,000 c.f. Rigid Airship," issued for the design competition by BuAer on 28 March 1928, left no doubt that inside engines were a desirable feature in the new airships.

A Maybach VL-II engine had a dry weight of 2,600 lbs.; with its supporting environment this tripled to about 7,500 lbs., less the weights of the fuel and oil. To support eight such installations inside the hull, the three-keel system used in the ZRS4&5 became an inevitable necessity.

No other rigid airship designs employed inside engines because of the fire hazard relative to their hydrogen lifting gas; only the Americans had helium. So no one else was obliged to reconsider their hull designs on this count. The British found an answer to the problems of large hull cross sections in their R100 by using Barnes Wallis' novel geodetic structure (which he also employed in the Vickers "Wellington" bomber of World War II) and by using deep rings in the R101. The Germans found their answer by using a supplementary axial keel in the *Graf Zeppelin,* the *Hindenburg,* and the *Graf Zeppelin II,* which ran through their hulls' centerline, of itself a radical departure from the so-called "conventional" Zeppelin. Thus were four different answers found to the same problem, and it is doubtful if the alternatives were exhausted.

The innovations in the ZRS4&5 design were not executed out of a desire for novelty for its own sake. The product was a rational answer to a series of very real problems. In any case, a brief examination of Goodyear-Zeppelin Projects I, II, and III will show that BuAer was not without options; if a "conventional" design was desired, it was available in 1928.

Project I

Project I was the ZRS4&5 design, and except for the design of its fins it was exactly like the *Macon* as described in Appendix II. Its main frames were 22.5 meters (74 ft.) apart except at extreme bow and stern. Each frame used Warren truss bracing as joining elements between its two outer rings and inner apex ring. There was no wire bracing in the inherently stiff main rings, but a bulkhead was provided to separate the cells by a web of heavy cord netting attached to the inner circumference of the apex ring, which created an "elastic" bulkhead. Installed with a slight initial tension provided by pneumatic pistons at its anchor points on the apex ring, it could stretch to allow a bulge of about 7.5 feet in order to allow a limited shifting of the gas cells when the airship was in a climbing or diving attitude. The board of judges remarked that this feature combined the advantages of the conventional wire-braced frame's "solid" bulkhead by reducing the surging of gas cells to a minimum, with the excellent static stability of the inherently stiff deep ring.

It was an occasional practice in the short history of rigid airship construction to carry one or more elements of the four fins through the hull structure to meet in the fashion of a cruciform. Wartime Zeppelins used a simple, single element of this type; the LZ-126, *Los Angeles,* was the first one designed with three dimensional "structural" fins of substantial thickness, and was concomitantly the first to employ an elaborate cruciform structure and to use two such elements. This design was necessary with the lightweight "conventional" main frame. But the more rugged deep ring provided a hull strong enough that the fins could be designed on a cantilever principle. Thus Project I's fins were simply bolted to the hull at frames 35, 17.5, and zero.

Project I offered Packard or Maybach engine alternatives. The judges did not like to select an engine of foreign manufacture, but the Maybach's reliability was well known, its fuel consumption was lower, and its time between overhauls considerably greater than the Packard's. Also important in an airship engine, the Maybach was self-reversing, which eliminated the weight and maintenance of reverse gearing.

After studying Project I's aerodynamic calculations and stress analyses, the board of judges reached the conclusion that "structurally, this design appears to be excellent." The price of Project I was $5,450,000 for one airship; $7,995,000 for two.

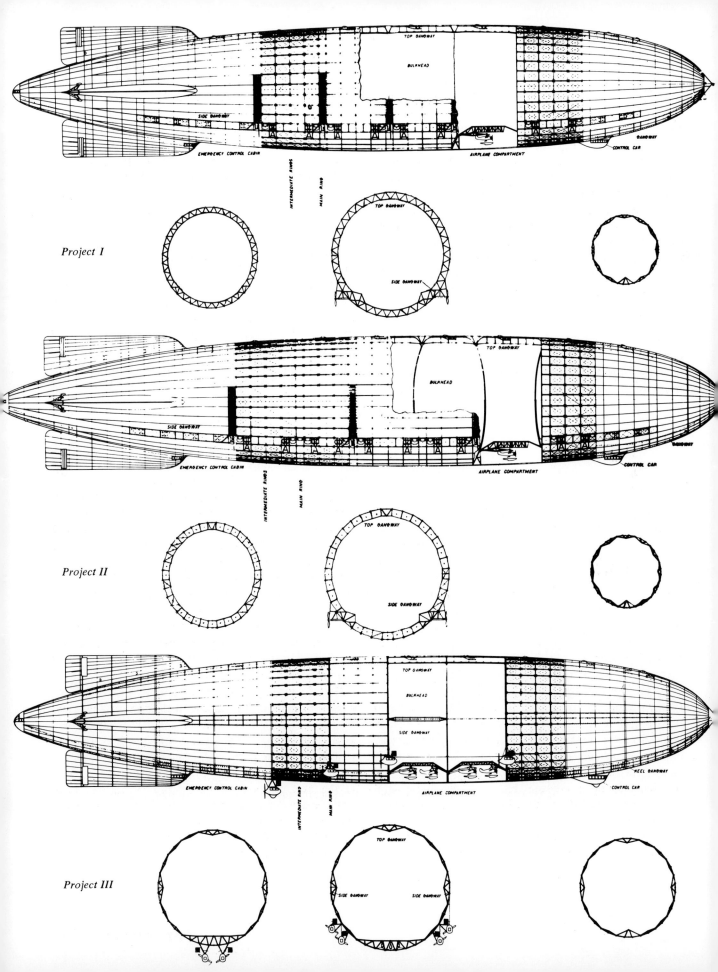

Project I

Project II

Project III

Project II

To outward appearances, Project II was exactly the same as Project I, except that it had only six engines. But its hull structure was essentially different. Its main frames were alternately spaced 22.5 and 17.5 meters, and in order to keep the gas forces of the alternate large and small gas cells in balance, air ballonets were installed under the shorter cells to produce a differential pressure which would make them bulge into the larger cells at all times. Also, instead of using a Warren truss system in its deep rings, Project II used radial struts supported by diagonal wire bracing and the rings employed a "slack" bulkhead. The elastic bulkhead was taut but would expand under pressure. The slack bulkhead was installed with a certain amount of looseness, but would check gas cell surging at a predetermined point.

The judges felt that Project II was an advancement over conventional construction, but was not as satisfactory as Project I. They preferred the latter's Warren truss system and elastic bulkhead, and found Project II's use of ballonets an objectionable complication. The price of Project II was $5,350,000 for one airship; $7,750,000 for two.

Project III

This was a rather conventional design, but contained improvements upon previous practice which were dictated by the large hull diameter and demand for greater hull strength. Of the same volume and linear dimensions as the other designs, it had four keels placed 90 degrees apart from the vertical. A large double keel of M cross section ran along the bottom of the hull, and three smaller single keels of delta cross section along the top and sides. Aft of the control car the lower double keel divided to skirt the airplane hangars, of which there were two in tandem, each with its own trapeze and each housing two planes. Its main frames were of the conventional wire-braced type, employing diamond trusses around their internal circumferences. Alternate gas cell spaces were bridged by an axial girder; in the event of a deflated cell condition these would transmit part of the axial pressures of the cells on both sides of the deflated one to adjacent main frames. These axial girders penetrated their gas cells by means of a sleeve in the cell.

Because of its conventional main frames, the fins of Project III employed two cruciform elements. Its power plant consisted of eight engines suspended in conventional power cars. These had no provision for their propellers to deliver vertical thrust. The judges remarked that Project III was an excellent design, it deserved credit for the minimum of uncertainty involved in its construction, but it did not promise an advance in the state of the art as did Project I. Its price was $5,275,000 for one airship; $7,575,000 for two.

Construction

The ZRS4&5 were built according to airship construction practice as it had evolved in Germany, which numbered framing from aft to forward. All framing was numbered according to their metric distance forward or aft of the rudder post, which was frame zero. Those forward of frame zero had regular numbers; those after were given negative values. The first main frame forward of frame zero was frame 17.5, which meant that it was 17.5 meters forward of zero. The other main frames were 35, 57.5, 80, 102.5, 125, 147.5, 170, 187.5, 198.75, and station 210.75 at the nose. Between each pair of main frames were three intermediate rings, their numbering being interpolated with their respective main frames. There were no main rings aft of frame zero, but the stern cap's frame was numbered −23.75. All ring elements, except those at extreme bow and stern, were joined by the girders of the three keels and the principal longitudinals. The latter were numbered 1 through 18, port and starboard, from the bottom of the airship to its top.

The volume between a pair of main frames (the space occupied by the gas cell) was called a bay. Their numbering, like their respective gas cells, was expressed in Roman numerals, and used frame zero as the point of reference. Thus the bay forward of frame zero was bay I, while the single bay aft of it was bay zero and contained cell zero.

Bay V amidships was erected first. After the framing was fabricated in jigs on the hangar floor, the main frames were hoisted into cradles 22.5 meters apart, and three intermediate rings were positioned at five-meter intervals between them. After being checked for alignment with surveyors' transits, the five rings were joined by the keel girders and longitudinal members. Then each rectangular space between the framing and longitudinals was cross-braced with six lengths of hard steel wire called sheer wiring; literally miles of sheer wiring went into each of the airships.

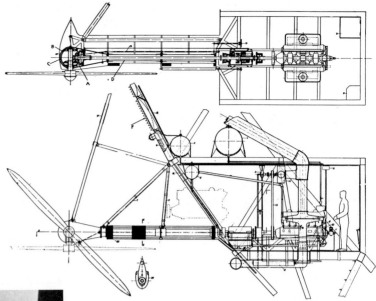

Cross section of an inside engine installation similar to those in the ZRS4&5. The reversibility of the engines permitted the propellers to deliver thrust either forward or astern; by tilting the propellers they could deliver vertical thrust, either up or down.

GOODYEAR AEROSPACE CORPORATION

One of the few differences between the Akron and the Macon was in the installation of their radiators. The Akron's were stuck on the leading edge of the propeller outrigger; the Macon's were in streamlined housings on the hull.

After bay V was subjected to extensive proof testing, work turned to bay VI and bay VII which enclosed the airplane hangar, and continued forward to bay X. With the forward structure complete, work was directed aft. Bay XI, the nose section, and bay zero, the tail cone, were fabricated on the hangar floor and later hoisted into position, as were the structures of the four fins.

With the hull structure complete, the installation of internals was begun. Along the lower keels were the eight engine rooms, their engines and transmissions, and water-recovery apparatus. The latter was a mechanical means of collecting moisture from the engine exhaust in order to maintain the airship's static condition by replacing the weight lost through fuel consumption. This was necessary because as fuel was consumed the airship became lighter, and the only other countermeasure was valving gas to the atmosphere, a luxury the cost of helium did not permit in the ordinary run of operations. Water recovery was devised for the express purpose of conserving helium, and because of the weight and drag of its condensers, it was the most serious compromise met in using the nonflammable gas. It was theoretically possible to recover ten pounds of water for each pound of fuel burned, but in practice this varied according to the hydrogen content of the fuel, the air-fuel ratio, and atmospheric humidity. A better than 1:1 recovery was normal and satisfactory.

The Allison propeller transmissions extended 19.5 feet from engine coupling to its tilting gear at the propeller hub, and possessed a 97 per cent efficiency. With the engine turning from 900 to 1,000 r.p.m., the propeller could be tilted through 90 degrees to face downward in about 40 seconds. The tilting gear, combined with the Maybach's reversibility, allowed thrust in four directions: forward, aft, up, or down. The only direction the ZRS4&5 could not move under its own power was sideways. In an exaggerated sense, the *Akron* and *Macon* remain the world's largest VTOL aircraft.

Along the two lower keels were 110 cylindrical fuel tanks for 126,000 pounds (about 20,700 gallons) of gasoline which were variously clustered near the engine rooms. Thirty were "slip tanks," suspended inside guides from a wire which could be cut to jettison the tank in an emergency. Also in the keels were hung 44 fabric bags for about 72 tons of water ballast. Thirty-two were amidships and held "storage" ballast; six tons of emergency ballast used to correct small changes in fore and aft buoyancy were in the remaining 12 bags, six forward and six aft. Both the fuel and ballast systems were connected by piping which terminated at a filling connection in the nose for mooring mast services, and others in the lower amidships area for hangar service. Both were served by high speed pumps which allowed fuel and ballast to be transferred around the airship, such as is done aboard a seagoing ship. All ballast bags and fuel tanks could be dumped by means of remote-control wire-pulls on the bridge of the control car. The lower keels also enclosed the main electric and telephone wiring, as well as the airship's control cables, which joined the rudder and elevator wheels on the bridge with the moveable surfaces of the fins more than 500 feet aft.

Straddling the airplane hangar were the living quarters, galley, messrooms, and domestic power plant. The crew's quarters were on the port side, consisting of seven bunk rooms with four bunks each, a toilet, and a washroom. The officers were billeted in two bunk rooms on the starboard side near frame 147.5. Immediately aft of them were messrooms for the officers, CPO's, and crew, and finally the propane-fueled galley. Aft of the galley and immediately forward of No. 7 engine room at frame 125 was the generator room with its two Westinghouse 8-kw., 110-volt, d.c. generators, each driven by a 4-cylinder, 30-h.p. internal combustion engine. The generators could be paralleled, and overloaded up to 11 kw.

Forward of the airplane compartment was the control car, which was divided into three compartments. Foremost was the navigating bridge. The center section was the navigator's chart room; the after space was for machine-gun stations, but usually served as a smoking room. By today's standards the bridge was remarkably empty of instrumentation for so large an aircraft. This was principally because the engine controls and their instrumentation were in the engine rooms where men were on watch around the clock while the airship was in flight. Watch routine was four hours on, four off. The only control the bridge watch had over the engines was by means of mechanically operated, visual indicating telegraphs similar to those used aboard ships; there was an annuciator in the bridge with repeaters in the engine rooms.

Another thing which seems strange today is the presence of two control wheels on the bridge, one for the rudders, another for the elevators. The rudder man's wheel was at the forward end of the bridge; the elevator man's was on the port side, and he held his wheel facing outboard, parallel to the airship's longitudinal axis,

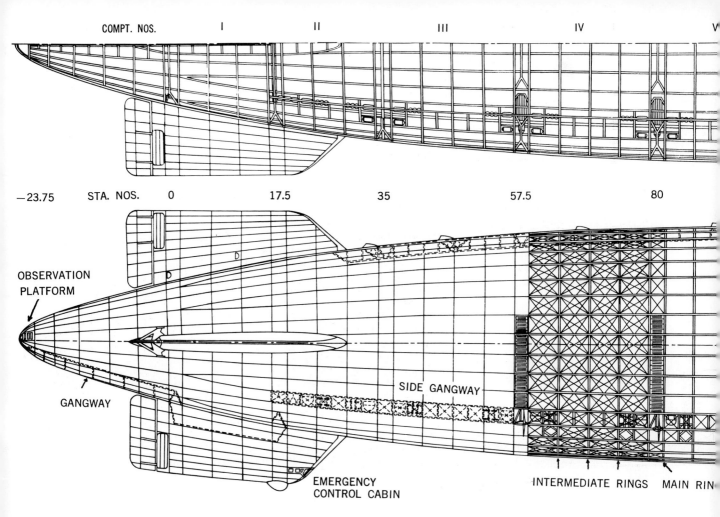

—23.75   STA. NOS.   0   17.5   35   57.5   80

OBSERVATION
PLATFORM

GANGWAY

SIDE GANGWAY

EMERGENCY
CONTROL CABIN

INTERMEDIATE RINGS   MAIN RIN

General Arrangement
USS Akron

Built by the Goodyear Zeppelin Corporation

Length Overall, 785 ft.
Max. Diameter, 132.86 ft.
Max. Width, 144.4 ft.
Max. Height, 155.03 ft.

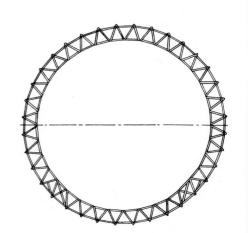

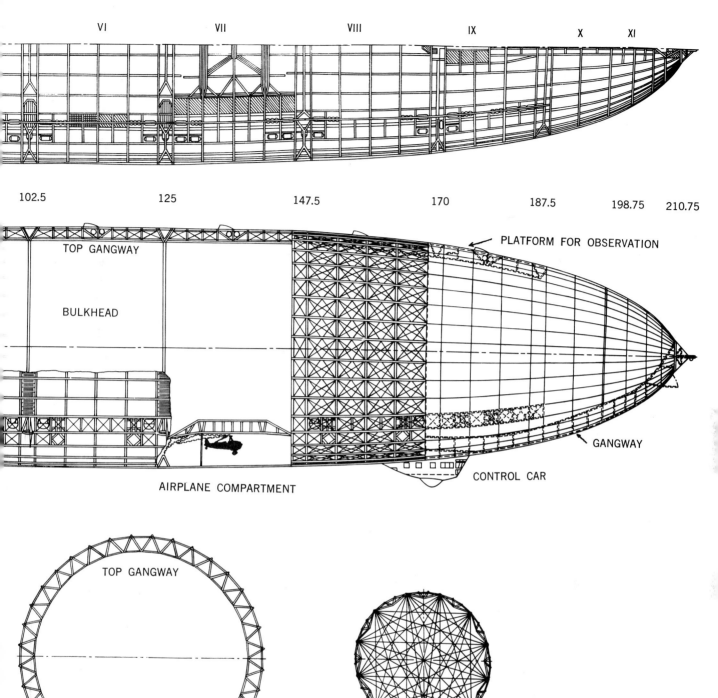

VI   VII   VIII   IX   X   XI

102.5   125   147.5   170   187.5   198.75   210.75

TOP GANGWAY

BULKHEAD

PLATFORM FOR OBSERVATION

GANGWAY

CONTROL CAR

AIRPLANE COMPARTMENT

TOP GANGWAY

SIDE GANGWAY

so he could more readily detect changes in trim and correct them. A rigid airship was not *flown* by any one man; it was *commanded*. And this may well have been the most serious shortcoming of its control.

Directly above the control car was the captain's cabin, the radio room with its two a.c./d.c. motor generator sets, 300–606 and 3000–18,000 kilocycle transmitters, RDF gear, and facsimile receiver. Next door was an office for the aerologist and two bunk rooms. In this area too, beginning at frame 170, the nose-keel gangway ran along the lower centerline up to station 210.75, behind the bow hatches at the mooring spindle.

As work progressed on the internals, the airship's outer cover was also being applied. The workmen who applied the 33,000 square yards of covering to the ZRS4 were schooled at the work for weeks before they were allowed to lay a yard of the cover on her framing. The outer cover was 2.8-ounce cotton cloth sewed into panels 74×12 and 74×24 feet, the length being the distance between a pair of main frames, the width the distances between two and three longitudinals. The panels were edged with eyelets by which they were laced to the structure. After being allowed to set for 24 hours, the lacings were retightened and painting was begun. One coat of clear dope was applied by hand, three more were sprayed on, and then sealing strips of fabric were glued along the seams of the panels in order to provide a smooth flying surface. Finally, two finishing coats of dope with aluminum pigment were applied. The final weight of the outer cover was 5.5 ounces per square yard, and it had approximately the same initial strength as aluminum of the same thickness.

The whole skin of the ZRS4&5 was given this aluminum coating except the port and starboard strakes between frames 17.5 and 187.5, longitudinals 5 and 6. These areas were the walls of the lower keels and were painted without pigmentation so the fabric would be translucent for daylight illumination of the gangways. However striking this "metalizing" of the fabric with aluminum paint appeared to the eye, it was not done for an aesthetic effect. The high reflective quality of the surface dictated its use, in order to minimize the heating effects of the sun upon the airship's lifting gas. But the "metalized" fabric nevertheless remained porous and absorbent. In a humid atmosphere it would go slightly slack, and in very humid weather it played host to the atmosphere at the expense of the airship's static lift. One ounce of moisture absorbed per square yard of fabric

amounted to a total of more than 2,000 pounds, which was almost the weight of one F9C fighter.

When the airship was essentially complete, the gas cell installations were begun. The ZRS4's cells, which employed about 54,000 square yards of material weighing 22,000 pounds, were a departure from past practice by way of an experiment to reduce diffusion and cell weight. Diffusion is a two-way phenomenon of air penetrating the pores of the cell material to contaminate the gas, and of the gas seeping through the cell wall to the atmosphere. Until the 1930's goldbeaters' skin, which was highly impermeable to gases, was widely used to line gas cells. This material came from the large intestine of cattle, and its odd name came from ancient times when goldsmiths found its toughness a useful buffer between the gold they were working and their hammers, in beating out gold leaf. Each animal skin provided about six square feet of material and not all of this was usable. It was a delicate material, its supply was limited, and its processing was expensive, as was the labor of its installation; a substitute was clearly in order.

During the 1920's, the Goodyear Tire & Rubber Company developed a rubberized cotton fabric which, although heavier, was much cheaper and far more durable than goldbeaters' skin. It was used in the *Los Angeles* as her German skin cells wore out, and was to be used in the ZRS4&5. In the meantime a Navy-financed project at the Bureau of Standards developed a cotton-base material impregnated with a gelatin-latex compound. It was a bit more expensive than the rubberized substitute, but lighter than the skin material, and promised to be more gas tight than both. It was decided that the ZRS4 would have half of its cells of rubberized fabric and half of gelatin-latex. The latter proved so satisfactory that the ZRS5 used it throughout.

The installation of the gas cells and their inflation was painstaking work because they were so big and clumsy to handle and their material so relatively delicate. They were drawn through hatches in the bottom of the airship and hoisted to the top of their bay where they hung suspended from the upper keel. At the top of each cell were a number of valves, each 32 inches in diameter; the larger cells in the ZRS4 had four valves, but in the ZRS5 the valves were reduced to three. They were spring-loaded, some fully automatic, set to open when the gas pressure exceeded 1.7 inches of water (about 0.064 p.s.i.); others were of a combined automatic and manual type which could be controlled from the bridge. Once inflation was under way the helium began to support the cell's weight, and as the cell inflated it ballooned out to fill the gas cell netting inside the bay, which transmitted the lift of its gas to the airship's structure. In this work great care had to be taken in straightening out irregular folds in the cell material and against the cell snagging and tearing on parts of the structure, resulting in an expensive loss of helium.

The only significant change in the ZRS4&5's design from 1928's Project I occurred as a result of Change Order No. 2 of 1930, which altered the fin configuration of the original design. In December 1929, the airship operators pointed out that with the control car and fins as they existed on Project I it was impossible to see the lower fin from the control car. In maneuvering to a landing it was desirable for the captain to see the lower fin's position relative to the ground; and it was considered necessary to have visual communication between the control car and the auxiliary control station in the fin's leading edge.

This need was met by moving the control car aft about eight feet, and the slender, dart-like fins of Project I were shortened in length and had their spans ex-tended. And whereas the fins had been attached to three main frames, the points of attachment were reduced to frames 17.5 and zero. The fins' leading edges which extended forward of frame 17.5 did not stand free; they were anchored to the hull at the junctions of their longitudinals with intermediate frame 28.75, and were reinforced by four diagonal cables. Aside from settling visibility problems, the reduction in attachment points reduced redundancy and made strength easier to calculate, and the larger fins provided superior control characteristics at low speeds. This is the alleged "inherent defect" which received much unwarranted publicity at the *Macon* court of inquiry; if it was that, it was one in which all concerned concurred in 1930.

The erection of the ZRS4's structure was begun in March 1930 and was completed 18 months later in August 1931; the ZRS5 was begun in November 1931 and was completed 16 months later in February 1933. It deserves appreciation that these two airships rank among the largest machines ever built by man and remain the second largest to navigate in the air. And it is only in very recent years that airplanes have surpassed the gross lift of the *Akron* and the *Macon*.

Vought UO-1

Curtiss XF9C-1

Curtiss XF9C-2

APPENDIX V

The Skyhook Airplanes

During 1929–1935, seventeen Navy airplanes were modified with skyhooks and operated with the *Los Angeles,* the *Akron,* or the *Macon:* one Vought UO-1, six N2Y-1's, one XF9C-1, one XF9C-2, six F9C-2's, and two XJW-1's. All were expedients; none were designed for the peculiar service. There was also one glider and several might-have-been's.

Vought UO-1

The UO-1 (BuAer serial No. 6615) was the last delivery of thirteen such aircraft procured on contract No. 57207 of 1923 as a standard fleet observation plane. It was modified with a skyhook at the Naval Aircraft Factory (NAF), in the fall of 1928, was used in the initial trapeze experiments with the *Los Angeles,* and was still at Lakehurst in 1931 when it was displaced by the N2Y's. The UO-1 had a gross weight of 2,230 lbs.; wingspan 34'1"; over-all length 22'1"; and was powered by a 180 h.p. Wright E-3 radial engine which gave it a top speed of about 120 mph.

Consolidated N2Y-1

The six N2Y's (Nos. 8600–8605) were originally procured from the Fleet Aircraft Corporation on contract No. 16684 of 17 March 1930. The contract lot was six; delivery was made to NAS Pensacola in mid-1930, after which they were sent to NAF for modification and turned over to Lakehurst for use with the *Los Angeles* and the *Akron.* It was originally anticipated that they would serve the *Akron* and the *Macon* as operational hook-on planes until a special design was developed for the airships. They operated with the *Akron* and *Macon* until the latter flew west in 1933, when Nos. 8600, 8601, and 8602 were detached and sent to NAF for storage. In 1935, No. 8602 turned up

on a pair of floats, its upper wing replaced by a rotor, and redesignated XOZ-1, an experimental autogiro. On 17 July 1934, No. 8604 was wiped out in a crash north of Moffett Field, and the remaining two planes were surveyed shortly after the loss of the *Macon.* The N2Y-1 had a gross weight of 1,637 lbs.; wingspan 28'; over-all length 21'5"; and was powered by a 115 h.p. Kinner K-5 radial engine which provided a top speed of about 108 mph.

Waco XJW-1

The two XJW's (Nos. 9521 and 9522) procured on contract No. 34222 of 9 January 1934, were modifications of the Waco UBF, a 3-place sport plane. They were bought "off the shelf" of the civil airplane market because there was nothing of similar performance in the Navy inventory which would fit through the *Macon*'s hangar door, and a utility plane was necessary to replace the low performance N2Y "running boats." Delivered to Moffett Field in March 1934, they operated with the *Macon* less than a year. After the *Macon*'s loss the XJW's had their skyhooks removed and were put into utility service: No. 9521 at Lakehurst, No. 9522 at Anacostia. In August 1936 there was discussion of having a plane hook onto a trapeze on the German airship *Hindenburg,* to pick up special mail from the Zeppelin airliner by way of demonstrating how hook-on planes could be used with commercial airships. BuAer ordered No. 9521 to NAF to have its skyhook reinstalled. But the wisdom of having a Navy airplane hook onto the swastika-emblazoned airship was opened to question, and there were legalistic problems relative to the possibility of an accident; and a few days later the skyhook reinstallation was canceled. In March 1938, No. 9521 was surveyed at Lake

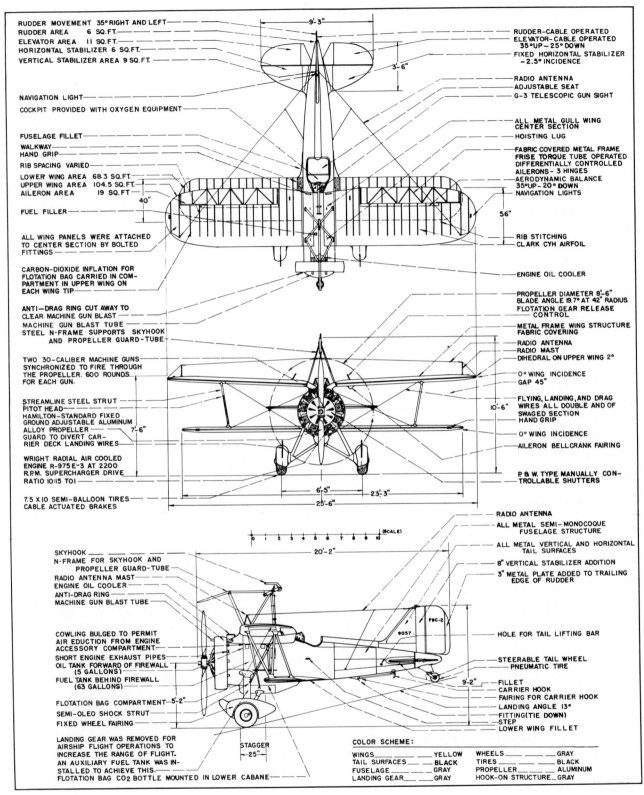

RUDDER MOVEMENT 35° RIGHT AND LEFT
RUDDER AREA   6 SQ.FT.
ELEVATOR AREA   11 SQ.FT.
HORIZONTAL STABILIZER 6 SQ.FT.
VERTICAL STABILIZER AREA 9 SQ.FT.

NAVIGATION LIGHT
COCKPIT PROVIDED WITH OXYGEN EQUIPMENT

FUSELAGE FILLET
WALKWAY
HAND GRIP
RIB SPACING VARIED
LOWER WING AREA 68.3 SQ.FT.
UPPER WING AREA 104.5 SQ.FT.
AILERON AREA   19 SQ.FT.

FUEL FILLER

ALL WING PANELS WERE ATTACHED
TO CENTER SECTION BY BOLTED
FITTINGS

CARBON-DIOXIDE INFLATION FOR
FLOTATION BAG CARRIED IN COM-
PARTMENT IN UPPER WING ON
EACH WING TIP

ANTI-DRAG RING CUT AWAY TO
CLEAR MACHINE GUN BLAST
MACHINE GUN BLAST TUBE
STEEL N-FRAME SUPPORTS SKYHOOK
AND PROPELLER GUARD-TUBE

TWO 30-CALIBER MACHINE GUNS
SYNCHRONIZED TO FIRE THROUGH
THE PROPELLER. 600 ROUNDS
FOR EACH GUN.

STREAMLINE STEEL STRUT
PITOT HEAD
HAMILTON-STANDARD FIXED
GROUND ADJUSTABLE ALUMINUM
ALLOY PROPELLER
GUARD TO DIVERT CAR-
RIER DECK LANDING WIRES

WRIGHT RADIAL AIR COOLED
ENGINE R-975E-3 AT 2200
R.P.M. SUPERCHARGER DRIVE
RATIO 10:15 TO1

7.5 X 10 SEMI-BALLOON TIRES
CABLE ACTUATED BRAKES

RUDDER-CABLE OPERATED
ELEVATOR-CABLE OPERATED
35°UP—25° DOWN
FIXED HORIZONTAL STABILIZER
—2.5° INCIDENCE

RADIO ANTENNA
ADJUSTABLE SEAT
G-3 TELESCOPIC GUN SIGHT

ALL METAL GULL WING
CENTER SECTION
HOISTING LUG
FABRIC COVERED METAL FRAME
FRISE TORQUE TUBE OPERATED
DIFFERENTIALLY CONTROLLED
AILERONS— 3 HINGES
AERODYNAMIC BALANCE
35°UP—20° DOWN
NAVIGATION LIGHTS

RIB STITCHING
CLARK CYH AIRFOIL

ENGINE OIL COOLER

PROPELLER DIAMETER 8'-6"
BLADE ANGLE 19.7° AT 42" RADIUS
FLOTATION GEAR RELEASE
CONTROL
METAL FRAME WING STRUCTURE
FABRIC COVERING
RADIO ANTENNA
RADIO MAST
DIHEDRAL ON UPPER WING 2°

0° WING INCIDENCE
GAP 45"

FLYING, LANDING, AND DRAG
WIRES ALL DOUBLE AND OF
SWAGED SECTION
HAND GRIP

0° WING INCIDENCE

AILERON BELLCRANK FAIRING

P & W. TYPE MANUALLY CON-
TROLLABLE SHUTTERS

RADIO ANTENNA
ALL METAL SEMI-MONOCOQUE
FUSELAGE STRUCTURE
ALL METAL VERTICAL AND HORIZONTAL
TAIL SURFACES
8" VERTICAL STABILIZER ADDITION
3" METAL PLATE ADDED TO TRAILING
EDGE OF RUDDER

SKYHOOK
N-FRAME FOR SKYHOOK AND
PROPELLER GUARD-TUBE
RADIO ANTENNA MAST
ENGINE OIL COOLER
ANTI-DRAG RING
MACHINE GUN BLAST TUBE

COWLING BULGED TO PERMIT
AIR EDUCTION FROM ENGINE
ACCESSORY COMPARTMENT
SHORT ENGINE EXHAUST PIPES
OIL TANK FORWARD OF FIREWALL
(5 GALLONS)
FUEL TANK BEHIND FIREWALL
(63 GALLONS)

FLOTATION BAG COMPARTMENT

SEMI-OLEO SHOCK STRUT

FIXED WHEEL FAIRING

LANDING GEAR WAS REMOVED FOR
AIRSHIP FLIGHT OPERATIONS TO
INCREASE THE RANGE OF FLIGHT.
AN AUXILIARY FUEL TANK WAS IN-
STALLED TO ACHIEVE THIS.
FLOTATION BAG CO2 BOTTLE MOUNTED IN LOWER CABANE

HOLE FOR TAIL LIFTING BAR

STEERABLE TAIL WHEEL
PNEUMATIC TIRE
FILLET
CARRIER HOOK
FAIRING FOR CARRIER HOOK
LANDING ANGLE 13°
FITTING(TIE DOWN)
STEP
LOWER WING FILLET

F9C-2
9057

STAGGER
25"

9'-3"
3'-6"
40"
56"
10'-6"
7'-6"
6'-5"
23'-3"
25'-6"
20'-2"
9'-2"
5'-2"

(SCALE)
0 1 2 3 4 5 6 7 8 9 10

COLOR SCHEME:

WINGS	YELLOW	WHEELS __ GRAY
TAIL SURFACES	BLACK	TIRES __ BLACK
FUSELAGE	GRAY	PROPELLER __ ALUMINUM
LANDING GEAR	GRAY	HOOK-ON STRUCTURE GRAY

Airship Fighter F9C-2

DRAWN BY WILLIS L. NYE, AMERICAN AVIATION HISTORICAL SOCIETY

hurst; its partner survived until June 1942, when it was finally surveyed at Anacostia. The XJW had a gross weight of 2,355 lbs.; wingspan 29′6″, over-all length 20′8″; and was powered by a 210 h.p. Continental R-670-98 radial engine, which provided a top speed of about 128 mph.

Curtis XF9C-1

Built to meet the specification in BuAer Design No. 96 of 10 May 1930 for a very small carrier fighter, the XF9C-1 (No. 8731) was procured on contract No. 17901 of 30 June 1930. Designed and built by Curtiss' plant in Garden City, Long Island, with George A. Page, Jr., as its project engineer, it was delivered to the Navy test center at Anacostia on 27 March 1931 and was put through its test program between 31 March and 30 June. It was judged a good airplane with excellent fighter characteristics, but the shoulder height of the upper wing seriously interfered with visibility in normal flight, more so in landing approaches; and its wing and power loadings were considered too high for carrier landings. In other words, it was a hot plane. Purchased as an experimental type without any plans for putting it in production, it was subsequently turned over to Lakehurst as an expedient for use as a high performance hook-on plane.

It is of historical interest that the contract called for the XF9C-1 to be delivered to Anacostia for testing within 175 days of its date. The total cost was $74,750; the design work $20,000, miscellaneous data $3,000, final and corrected data and drawings $12,000, and $39,750 for the airplane itself. It is to be wondered if this sum would begin to pay for the landing gear on one of today's Convair F-111B (TFX) Mach 3 fighters.

In the summer of 1931, the XF9C was equipped with a skyhook by NAF and delivered to Lakehurst in the fall, and made its first hook-on to the *Los Angeles'* trapeze on 27 October. It was always considered a spare aircraft by the HTA Unit and not one of the regular "squadron" machines. After the loss of the *Akron* and at the time the *Macon* went west in 1933, it was transferred to NAF where its skyhook was removed, and it was used in utility service until surveyed in 1936.

Curtiss XF9C-2

The XF9C-2 (No. 9264) was a creature of the Curtiss Company's initiative, inspired by the hope extended in BuAer Detail Specification No. SD-169-2 of 20 July 1931, which described an improved version of the XF9C-1, and by the possibility of its becoming a production hook-on plane. So the Curtiss engineers scurried back to their drafting rooms, Garden City relinquished the work to the Buffalo plant, and within 90 days the XF9C-2 was produced.

The XF9C-2 and the production models were practically identical aircraft, but were essentially different from the XF9C-1. The prototype's 421 h.p. Wright R-975-C engine was replaced by a 438 h.p. Wright R-975-E3. The heavy fuselage structure necessary to withstand the shocks of carrier landings was, unfortunately, retained. Cockpit visibility was improved slightly by raising the upper wing four inches, giving it a distinct "gull" configuration. This required new strength members, besides those necessary to decrease wing deflection in terminal velocity dive pullouts (8.5 to 10 g's at 289 to 295 mph) and those necessary to carry the novel loads imposed by the skyhook. Cantilever landing gear was replaced by a tripod-type, which was lengthened to allow an increase of propeller diameter from 96 to 102 inches, and a steerable tail wheel was added. The XF9C-1's balanced rudder was eliminated and the vertical stabilizer lengthened by eight inches. All this served to make the XF9C-2 about 250 lbs. heavier than its prototype.

In September 1931, the XF9C-2 turned up on the Department of Commerce's civil register as NX-986-M, and on 12 October 1931 the Navy concluded contract No. 24020 with Curtiss, a one-dollar agreement which called for the aircraft's demonstration. Its performance was satisfactory, and two days later Curtiss received an order for six productions. Only 45 days after the production articles were delivered did the Navy decide to relieve Curtiss of the NX-986-M by its purchase, executed by contract No. 29095 of 9 November 1932. The plane was subsequently designated XF9C-2, given the BuAer serial 9264, sent to NAF for a skyhook, and delivered to Lakehurst on 10 January 1933.

Like its sister prototype, the XF9C-1, it was always considered a spare. After the loss of the *Macon* it was stripped of its skyhook and assigned to Anacostia as a utility plane. In November 1936 someone flopped it into a pea patch near Monaskon, Virginia, an event which led to its survey.

Curtiss F9C-2

The six F9C-2's (Nos. 9056-9061) were procured on contract No. 24021 of 14 October 1931, and were

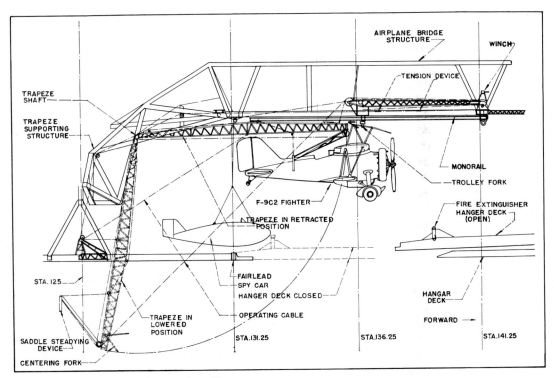

Longitudinal Section—Airship Airplane Hangar

DRAWN BY WILLIS L. NYE, AMERICAN AVIATION HISTORICAL SOCIETY

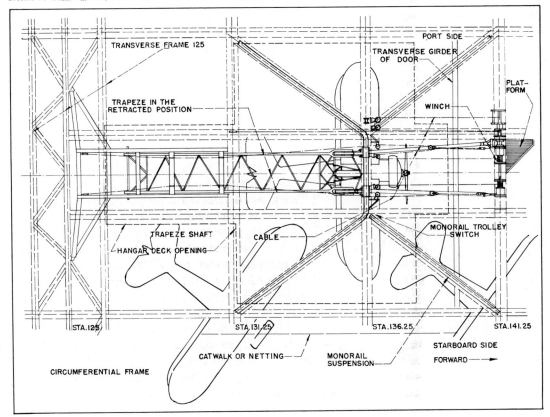

Plan View—Airship Airplane Hangar

direct follow-ons to the two X-types. The first article (No. 9056) was given its first flight at Curtiss' Buffalo plant by test pilot William Crosswell on 14 April 1932, and was delivered to Anacostia on 3 May. It was put through a test program there, and again at the arresting gear facility at Hampton Roads until 20 June, and on the twenty-ninth was first tested on the *Akron*'s trapeze, where it was flown through 22 hook landings. These hook-on trials revealed considerable directional instability created by the skyhook, which was overcome by adding three inches to the rudder.

The first three serials were ferried from Buffalo to Lakehurst on 12 September 1932; the remainder on 21 September. These six were considered "squadron" planes, and accordingly received distinctive, Harrigan-conceived paint jobs which the other aircraft did not. Each machine had its own color code with a 21″ fuselage band, a section leader's chevron on the upper wing, and on the engine cowl and wheel spats. The individualistic trim of each plane was:

9056	Royal Red	9061	Lemon Yellow
9057	White	9059	Black
9058	True Blue	9060	Willow Green

The distinctive paint jobs were allegedly for purposes of "recognition"; but it seems that *esprit* was of at least equal consideration. In any case, it was nonregulation, and there was a teapot tempest when some of the moguls in BuAer's Plans Division discovered that the HTA Unit had their planes all dolled up in gaudy colors. Besides this, the Unit had its distinctive "Men on the Flying Trapeze" insignia; and after the *Macon* joined the Fleet they were color coded as a group by ComAirBatFor by having their empennage painted black.

By way of contrast to the frightful problems in cost and lead time attending aircraft development and procurement since World War II, a breakdown of the F9C-2's contract costs deserves citation:

Design information	$ 9,234
Miscellaneous data	1,765
Six airplanes at $22,965 each	137,790
Ferrying first article to Lakehurst	1,000
Spare parts	34,448
Final corrected data and drawings	7,211
Total cost	$191,448

Relative to present-day costs these figures seem quaint, but such things are relative, and in 1930 funds were so short that BuAer spent weeks haggling with Curtiss over the price of $9.25 per airplane for having "U.S. Navy" painted on the undersides of the lower wings. They finally decided it was too costly and they would have to do without it.

Of greater historical significance is that the production contract was let on 12 October 1931, the first serial flew on 14 April 1932, and was fully tested by the end of July. By September (within 27 months of the XF9C-1 prototype contract; 11 months of the production contract) all of the production models were in the Navy's inventory. Small wonder that the period 1925–1935 has come to be regarded as the "Golden Age" of aviation!

No planes were aboard the *Akron* when she was lost; but when the *Macon* went down she took four F9C's with her. The surviving F9C's, Nos. 9056 and 9057, and the XF9C-2, were turned over to the Battle Force aircraft pool and eventually wound up in utility service. The No. 9057 article was salvaged at North Island, San Diego, during March 1937. In June 1939, No. 9056 was pending survey at NAS Hampton Roads when Commander Alan P. Flagg, the station's CO, suggested to CNO that it should be turned over to the Smithsonian Institution. In late 1940 it was finally transferred to the Smithsonian, where it was restored, and placed among the exhibits of the National Air Museum, where it remains today.

Miscellaneous and Might-Have-Been's

In the category of miscellany there is only the 196-pound Prüfling glider (No. 8546), procured from the American Motorless Aviation Company on contract No. 15507 of 2 January 1930. It has the distinction of being the Navy's first glider. Procured for experiments with the *Los Angeles*, it made only two flights from the airship. It met its end at the Akron Municipal Airport, Labor Day 1931, when its towline failed to release. This was the crash which hospitalized Rodney Dennett.

There were two outstanding might-have-been's. One was the utility and tanker plane for in-flight servicing of the airship, which was discussed in the text. The other was BuAer Design No. 124 of 5 October 1933, a proposed replacement for the F9C.

Design No. 124 was a very small, low-wing monoplane of stressed-skin design, equipped with flaps and retractable landing gear, and having remarkably clean lines. It was a "radical" in its day, even as it stood on paper. Its skyhook was not retractable, but its drag factor was negligible at speeds less than 250 mph. It had a design gross weight of 2,618 lbs.; over-all length 23′9″; and its elliptical wings of 29′ span and 142 sq. ft. area promised fine handling characteristics. Its proposed power plant was a "Ranger" type in-line, air-cooled engine of 500 h.p., in the experimental stage at that date. With 80 gallons of internal fuel its radius was estimated at 180 miles.

In early 1934, Design No. 124 died on the drawing board. Before Trapnell left the *Macon* he prepared a memo for BuAer on the desirable characteristics of an airship-based scout plane. His specification of no armament whatever and a simple stick-type landing gear which could be easily removed conflicted with Design No. 124; but there is nothing to indicate that BuAer was moved to revise the design. By that time the *Macon*'s performances had opened the airship's future to serious question, and the Sellers Report came a few weeks later. In 1936, C. P. Burgess prepared the preliminary design for a ZRCV which carried a dozen airplanes similar to Design No. 124; but shortly thereafter ZRCV proposals were "re-oriented" in terms of an offensive mission carrying dive bombers.

The remaining might-have-been's are the Northrup BT-1, nine of which Burgess contemplated using with his ZRCV of 1937; and a Goodyear-Zeppelin ZRCV design study of 1938 carried seven BT-1's and three fighters similar to the Vought V-143. Nor was the Navy alone with a ZRCV idea. The Army Air Corps had developed the first skyhook, and as late as 1934 its airship men were proposing a 13,000,000-c.f. airship which would carry nine Boeing B-9, twin-engine bombers; but they were fighting a long-lost cause. The end of the line was reached during World War II in Burgess' studies of the Curtiss SC "Seahawk" as a hook-on plane for the 1,500,000-c.f. O-type blimp; both were canceled in the design stage. Hook-on flying was continued after 1945, but not by the Navy, or with lighter-than-air craft as the mother vehicle.

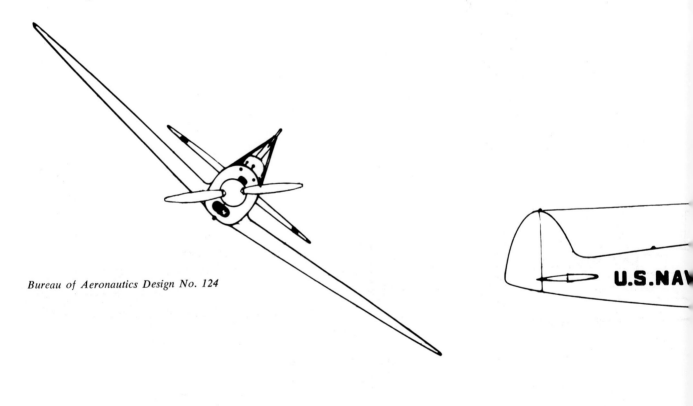

Bureau of Aeronautics Design No. 124

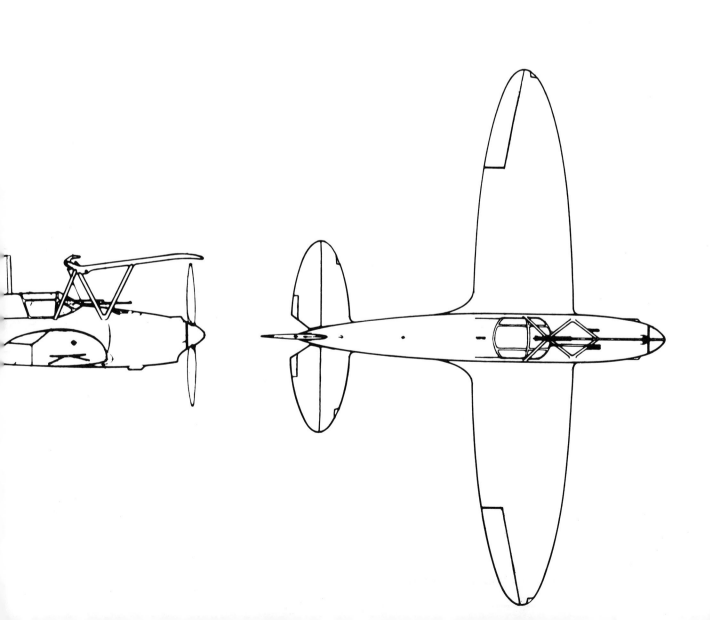

Comparative Generalized Performances: Macon and World War II Flying Boats

Aircraft	Prototype Flown	Normal Gross Lift, lbs.	Disposable Lift lbs.[1]	Cruising Speed mph	Range Statute miles	Radius Statute miles[2]
USS *Macon*	1931	403,000	160,644	63	6,842	3,078
Consolidated PBY-5A "Catalina"	1935	32,415	11,505	117	2,545	1,145
Consolidated PB2Y-3 "Coronado"	1937	68,000	27,065	141	2,370	1,066
Martin PBM-3D "Mariner"	1939	51,330	18,155	127	2,240	1,008
Boeing XPBB-1 "Sea Ranger"	1942	62,006	20,475	127	6,300	2,835
Martin XPB2M-1 "Mars"	1942	144,000	68,427	149	4,945	2,225

[1] Includes fuel and military load.
[2] Radius taken to be 45 per cent of range.

Notes

INTRODUCTION

The Promise (pp. xix–xxii)

1. Strictly speaking, "Zeppelin" is a trade name applicable only to a rigid airship of a specific manufacturer, such as Spiess, Schütte-Lanz, Vickers, Metalclad, *et al.*
2. This called for four 32,600-ton battleships of the *Maryland* class, three of which were completed; six 43,200-ton battleships of the *Indiana* class, none of which were built; and six 43,500-ton battlecruisers of the *Lexington* class, none of which were completed as such. The hulls of the *Lexington* and *Saratoga* were converted to aircraft carriers.
3. The *Indianapolis,* two of the *Pensacola* class, and six of *Northampton* class.
4. The *Portland* and eight *Minneapolis*-class ships.
5. Jerome C. Hunsaker, "The Present Status of Airships in Europe," *Journal of the Franklin Institute,* Vol. CLXXVII, No. 6 (June, 1914), 597–639.
6. Thomas Drayton Parker, "An Air Fleet: Our Pressing Need," *U.S. Naval Institute Proceedings,* Vol. XLI, No. 3 (May–June, 1915), 709–63.
7. Quoted in *Joint Committee to Investigate Dirigible Disasters,* 73 Cong., 1 Sess., *Hearings* (1933), 573. (Hereafter cited as *Dirigible Disasters.*)
8. U.S. Navy, Office of Naval History, General Board, *Hearings,* Vol. II (1919), 654.
9. *Ibid.,* Vol. III, 953–54.
10. William L. Sims, "The Value of Rigid Dirigibles for Naval Operations," *Air Power,* Vol. IV, No. 12 (April, 1919), 451–52. Sims's second paragraph is a slightly revised version of a cablegram sent by Admiral William S. Benson, CNO, in Paris, to the General Board, *Hearings,* Vol. III (1919), 735–37.
11. Quoted in memo, Naval Air Station, Lakehurst, New Jersey, 26 July 1930, from the private papers of Captain Garland Fulton. Hereafter cited as "Fulton Papers."
12. "ZRS4&5" is thus expressed throughout the text because it is a convenient abbreviation for "the *Akron* and the *Macon,*" and because it can be suggestive of more than the *Akron* and the *Macon.* It will be used to represent the two airships, a general type of airship, or a concept of airship operations, the meaning depending upon context. The expression "ZRS4&5" was the filing code used in Navy correspondence which related to both of the airships.
13. This allows for retirement during the night. For want of a device which could "see" in the dark, such as radar, search operations were usually suspended at dusk, and in order to avoid steaming past (or flying over) the enemy during the night, the searching force retired the distance the enemy could be expected to advance between dusk and daylight.

CHAPTER 1

Toward a Farsighted Development (pp. 3–18)

1. *Z* does *not* stand for *Zeppelin;* it is the Navy designation for *all* types of lighter-than-air craft. The *R* designates a rigid type; and in the case of the ZRS4&5, the *S* further designates a scouting type.
2. General Board, *Hearings,* Vol. I (1926), 8–9. Quoted in statement of Rear Admiral Montgomery M. Taylor, U.S. Navy.
3. Logbook of the USS *Los Angeles,* 19 February 1931, 133, Record Group 24, the National Archives.
4. Quoted in memo by Rear Admiral William A. Moffett, USN, n.d., Fulton Papers.
5. Truscott to Chief, Material Division (Emory Land), O-R-25/601, 10 March 1924, Box 5560, Record Group 72, BuAer General Correspondence (1925–1942), Box 5560, the National Archives.
6. The TS-1 was a small, twin-float biplane fighter built by Curtiss and the Naval Aircraft Factory; the UF-1 was a Vought design of the early 1920's that never got off paper and should not be confused with the later FU-1.
7. C. P. Burgess, "History of Design No. 60," 7 May 1927, Record Group 72, LTA Design Branch, General Files (1921–1942), Box 35, the National Archives. The standard lift of hydrogen is .068 lb. per cu.ft., whereas helium is only .062.
8. The word "conventional" is used advisedly, and it should be understood that its value is only relative. It is usually used to describe a rigid airship with a single keel; with single-ring, wire-braced main frames; and engines in suspended cars. Some persons like to believe that only the Germans built "conventional" airships; but any study of German design reveals constant innovation, however conservative.

9. These engineers were Dr. Wolfgang Klemperer, former assistant head of the aeronautics department, University of Aix-la-Chapelle, specializing in aerodynamics; Paul K. Helma and Kurt Bauch, structural analysis; Benjamin Schnitzer and Walter G. E. Mosebach, structural design; Herman Leibert and William Fischer, projects and aerodynamics; Hans Keck, mechanics and control systems; Eugene Brunner, car designs and interiors; Lorens Rieger, power plants; Erich Hilligardt, electrical installations and instrumentation; and Eugene Schoettel, balloon fabrics and gas valves.

10. The Construction Corps was abolished on 25 June 1940, at which time its officers were integrated into the general line with the designation "Engineering Duty Only."

11. It is of interest to note how often Fulton's expressions occur in Moffett's correspondence on the subject, as recorded in the BuAer files, the National Archives. It is common practice for official correspondence in BuAer composed by a subordinate for a superior's signature to show the subordinate's name or initials on the "green" file copy. Other evidence also points up the fact that Moffett depended greatly upon Fulton.

12. E. J. King to Dr. Joseph Ames, chairman, National Advisory Committee for Aeronautics, 20 April 1934, Record Group 72, BuAer General Correspondence (1925–1942), Box 5561, the National Archives.

13. Fulton to Chief, Bureau of Aeronautics, 24 April 1925, Aer-M-50-Wn/ORO, Record Group 72, BuAer General Correspondence (1925–1942), Box 5561, the National Archives.

14. Special Board to Secretary of the Navy, 17 January 1925, Office of Naval History, SC-AV. This 80-page report gives airships only 8 pages of comments, none of them very favorable, and airships receive no mention in the report's "Recommendations."

15. Admiral Eberle was concerned to the extent that he sent this information, in a special communication, to the Senate Committee on Naval Affairs, as recorded in Senate Committee on Naval Affairs, 69 Cong., 1 Sess., *Hearings on an Act to Authorize Aircraft, etc.* (1926), 100.

16. General Board, *Hearings*, Vol. I (1926), 33.

17. *Ibid.*, 77.

18. *Ibid.*, 26, 74–75.

19. Senate Subcommittee of the Committee on Appropriations. 69 Cong., 1 Sess., *Hearings on Navy Department Appropriation Bill, 1927* (1926), 134.

20. The board consisted of Commander Sydney M. Kraus, Lieutenant Commanders Ralph G. Pennoyer and Clinton H. Havill, and Lieutenant Roland G. Mayer, with Admiral Moffett as senior member.

21. William C. Young to Richard K. Smith, personal interview, 21 June 1959; House Committee on Naval Affairs, *Two Airships Instead of One,* 70 Cong., 1 Sess., House Doc. 200 (1928); *The New York Times,* 20 March 1928 (17:3).

22. House Subcommittee of the Committee on Appropriations, *Supplemental Hearing, Navy Department Appropriation Bill, 1929,* 70 Cong., 1 Sess. (1928), 23.

23. The board consisted of Commander Kraus, Lieutenant Commander Havill, Lieutenants T. G. W. Settle and George V. Whittle, with Admiral Moffett as senior member.

24. All the Goodyear-Zeppelin materials are to be found in Record Group 72, LTA Design Branch, General Files (1921–1942), Box 52, the National Archives.

25. The board's enthusiasm over Project I is transparent in its reports. That there was very little doubt about the choice was confirmed by Captain George V. Whittle to Richard K. Smith, conversation, 8 September 1959, and by Vice Admiral T. G. W. Settle in a letter dated 24 November 1959. Both were members of the board.

CHAPTER 2

The Men on the Flying Trapeze (pp. 19–30)

1. General Board, *Hearings,* Vol. I (1937), 46.

2. First Lieutenant R. S. Olmsted to Major Westover, 400.11, 29 September 1921, Record Group 18, Army Air Force, Box 800, the National Archives.

3. Lawrence B. Sperry, *Device for Launching and Landing Aeroplanes from and upon Suspended Positions,* U.S. Patent Office, No. 1,716,670 (June 11, 1929).

4. Engineering Division, McCook Field to Chief, Air Service, 452.1, 6 January 1925, Record Group 18, Army Air Force, Central Decimal Files (1917–1938), Box 998, the National Archives.

5. During the first hook-on experiments there was an imitation of carrier plane-retrieving technique, i.e., bringing the airship into the wind. It was soon realized that because both aircraft were moving in the same medium this was unnecessary.

6. *Los Angeles* Log, 3 July 1929; A. W. Gorton to Richard K. Smith, conversation, 1 July 1959.

7. Due to the nature of the *Los Angeles'* construction, which did not anticipate airplane hook-ons, she could not have an internal airplane hangar; and due to the experimental nature of her trapeze, it did not have an electric hoisting winch.

8. D. W. Harrigan, "A Discussion of the Problems Encountered in the Operation of a Squadron of Fighting Planes from a Lighter-Than-Air Carrier," 15 June 1931, Record Group 72, General Correspondence (1925–1942), Box 5709, the National Archives.

CHAPTER 3

ZRS4: "Our Hearts, Our Hopes . . ." (pp. 31–44)

1. The largest *at this date.* In 1936 and 1938 the ZRS4&5 were exceeded in size by the sister ships *Hindenburg* (LZ–129) and *Graf Zeppelin II* (LZ–130), which were 7,062,150 cu.ft. and 804 ft. long.

2. The *Akron Beacon-Journal,* 28 November 1929.

3. Jahncke to SecNav, ZRS4&5/F-40, 4 December 1929, Record Group 72, General Correspondence (1925–1942), Box 5624, the National Archives.

4. It is worth noting in retrospect the remarkable scope

permitted the Naval Inspectors on the spot during the ZRS4&5's construction. There was relatively little red tape involved, as compared to the bureaucratic mire in which a project of similar magnitude would find itself today.

5. House Committee on Naval Affairs, *Naval Airship Base on the West Coast*, 70 Cong., 2 Sess., House Doc. No. 132 (1929).

6. This is a condition in which a layer of warm air exists a few hundred feet above the cool air near the surface of the earth. When taking off, the airship ascended into this warmer, thinner air, which caused the airship's buoyancy to diminish at the moment it was needed. Conversely, when landing, the airship descended out of the warm layer into the cooler, more dense air near the ground, and its buoyancy increased at a moment when it was undesirable.

7. The *Akron Beacon-Journal,* 5 August 1931 (15:2).

8. The *Akron Beacon-Journal,* 8 August 1931 (3:5). During the speech Karl Schmidt remarked to George Whittle that the acoustics were so bad there were only two persons who knew exactly what was being said—Admiral Moffett and Garland Fulton: Moffett was giving the speech and Fulton had written it. Captain George V. Whittle to Richard K. Smith, personal interview, 8 September 1959.

9. The *Akron Beacon-Journal,* 8 September 1931 (17:3). It should not be assumed that the *Akron*'s "bad press" is being given an exaggerated value. Research revealed inexplicably intense hostility against this machine whereas, by contrast, the German *Graf Zeppelin* was always handled with enthusiasm and the *Macon* was practically ignored. *The New York Sun,* which for years conducted a rabid editorial crusade against airships, is an exemplar. Because of certain items of information revealed in *The Sun*'s criticisms, Admiral Moffett, among others, came to believe that *The Sun* was being fed its information by certain factions within the Navy Department.

10. The board consisted of Rear Admiral George C. Day, president; Captains Horatio G. Gillmor and Harry E. Shoemaker; Commanders Sydney M. Kraus and Kinchen L. Hill; Lieutenant Commander Vincent A. Clarke; and Lieutenants Thomas P. Jeter, G. W. Henderson, Calvin M. Bolster, and Edward E. Roth.

CHAPTER 4

Too Much, Too Soon (pp. 45–62)

1. Aside from low mobile masts at Lakehurst and Akron, there were expeditionary masts at Parris Island, South Carolina, Camp Kearny, and Sunnyvale; high masts at Detroit, Michigan, Scott Field, Illinois, and Fort Lewis, Washington.

2. The gassing facilities were at Lakehurst, Akron, the Army's LTA center at Scott Field, and the helium plant at Forth Worth, Texas.

3. Calvin Bolster, *Handling Apparatus for Airships,* U.S. Patent Office, No. 1,972,863 (11 September 1934).

4. CO *Akron* to ComScoFor, ZRS4/A4–3, 10 December 1931, Record Group 38, CNO Classified Files (1927–1939), Box 212, the National Archives.

5. Logbooks of *Leary* and *Dickerson,* Record Group 24, the National Archives.

6. Dispatch, ComScoFor to CNO 14/2338, 15 January 1932, Record Group 38, CNO Classified Files (1927–1939), Box 212, the National Archives.

7. Quoted in CinCUS Report, A16–3, 23 May 1932, Record Group 38, CNO Fleet Training Division, General Correspondence (1914–1941), Box 343, the National Archives.

8. *Sundry Legislation Affecting the Naval Establishment, 1931–1932* [No. 388] "Akron Investigation," 72 Cong., 1 Sess., *Hearings* (1932), 1249.

9. *Ibid.* [No. 525] "Statement of Findings on Akron Investigation," 72 Cong., 1 Sess. (1932), 1831–36.

10. Dispatch, CinCUS to CNO, 18 March 1932, Record Group 72, BuAer Confidential Correspondence, Box 1732, the National Archives.

11. *Akron* log, 29 April 1933; Rear Admiral C. M. Bolster to Richard K. Smith, personal interview, 17 June 1959.

12. ComScoFor to ScoFor, "Comments and Remarks: Strategic and Tactical Exercises, 30 May–3 June 1932," ComScoFor file A-16-3, 23 June 1932, Record Group 38, CNO Classified Files (1927–1939), Box 110, the National Archives.

13. *Ibid.*

14. In addition to evidence in the records, Rear Admiral Harrigan remarked, "In some of our practices with the *Akron* we found it was much nimbler than one would expect." Letter from Rear Admiral D. W. Harrigan to Richard K. Smith, 18 March 1962.

15. ComScoFor to ScoFor, 23 June 1932, *Op. cit.*

16. *Ibid.*

17. Dispatch, ComScoFor to CNO, 7 June 1932, Record Group 72, BuAer General Correspondence (1925–1942), Box 5591, the National Archives; discussed in *Dirigible Disasters,* 469–70, 477.

18. Dispatch, CO Akron to CinCUS, 5 June 1932, Record Group 72, BuAer General Correspondence (1925–1942), Box 5591, the National Archives. This read: "Replacement of water recovery equipment necessarily hangar repair * Repeat * Hangar repair * As are other major * Repeat * Major repairs beyond capacity existing equipment. Because of various considerations given in my letter forwarded today, believe retention Akron on West Coast beyond about 10 June without hangar facilities jeopardizes * Repeat * Jeopardizes safety of *Akron*."

CHAPTER 5

Training and the Harrigan Report (pp. 63–75)

1. This coincided with a similar move within naval aviation as a whole by which relatively senior officers of varied experience with the Fleet were moved into flight training and aviation billets. Aside from preparing for expansion, this was a political move to "freshen up" naval aviation which, through the 1920's, was largely

controlled by men who had to be more concerned with flying than with the machine and its closer integration with the Fleet. Here, too, these officers were somewhat resented as Johnnies-come-lately, cashing in on a good thing after the dirty work was seemingly finished.

2. CO, *Akron,* to CNO, ZRS4/A4–3, 1 August 1932, Record Group 72, BuAer General Correspondence (1925–1942), Box 5591, the National Archives; also R. S. Booth, "Airship Development Abroad," *Journal of the Royal Aeronautical Society,* Vol. XXXVII (December, 1933), 366–80.

3. CO, *Akron,* to CNO, ZRS4/A4–3, 1 December 1932, Record Group 72, BuAer General Correspondence (1925–1942), Box 5592, the National Archives.

4. Senior Aviator, HTA Unit, to CO, *Akron,* ZRS4/P16–1, 21 November 1932, in the private papers of Rear Admiral D. W. Harrigan.

5. H. V. Wiley, quoted in Edward Arpee, *From Frigates to Flat-Tops* (Lake Forest, Ill.: by the author, 1953), 256.

6. Senior Aviator, HTA Unit, to CO, *Akron,* ZRS4/A4–3, 15 December 1932, Record Group 72, BuAer General Correspondence (1925–1942), Box 5592, the National Archives. (Hereafter cited as "Harrigan Report.")

7. Daniel W. Harrigan, *Parachute Life Raft Pack,* U.S. Patent Office, No. 2,144,301 (19 April 1938).

8. CO, *Los Angeles,* to Chief, BuAer, 31 December 1929, File ZR3/F1–F15–14, the National Archives.

9. CO, *Akron,* to Chief, BuAer, ZRS4&5/F–15, 24 March 1932, Record Group 72, BuAer General Correspondence (1925–1942), Box 5709, the National Archives. Bureau comments on the routing sheet indicate a consensus among Fulton, Weyerbacher, Webster, and Nicholson that this was a good idea, but should wait for more experience with existing trapeze. Mitscher commented, "Take under consideration for (dim) [*sic*] future developments."

10. Harrigan Report, routing sheet comment.

11. *Ibid.*

12. *Akron* log, 25–26 January 1933; CO, *Akron,* to CNO, ZRS4/A4–3, 31 January 1933, Record Group 72, BuAer Correspondence (1925–1942), Box 5592, the National Archives.

13. *Ibid.,* Fulton's marginalia; CO, *Akron,* to CNO, ZRS4/A4–3, 8 February 1933. Record Group 72, BuAer General Correspondence (1925–1942), Box 5592, the National Archives.

14. CO, *Akron,* to CNO, ZRS4/A4–3, 30 March 1933, Record Group 72, BuAer General Correspondence (1925–1942), Box 5592, the National Archives.

CHAPTER 6

The Beginning of the End (pp. 77–92)

1. *Akron* Court of Inquiry, H. V. Wiley, 1–30. A copy of the court's record is in Box 5598, Record Group 72, BuAer General Correspondence (1925–1942), the National Archives. Except as noted, all events relating to the *Akron*'s crash are taken from Wiley's testimony.

2. *Akron* Court of Inquiry, Dartsch, 150–153.

3. All courses cited are true headings.

4. It should be kept in mind that because the elevators were at the after end of the airship, the tail had to be brought down in order to point the nose up.

5. Statement of Captain Karl Dalldorf to United States Consul, Tampico, Mexico, 12 April 1933, State Department letter 811.348–Akron/161, Record Group 72, BuAer Confidential Correspondence, Box 1732, the National Archives. An article by J. A. Moffett, "The Akron Rescue," *U.S. Naval Institute Proceedings,* Vol. LIX, No. 12 (December 1933), 1717–1719, was obviously prepared from information in Dalldorf's statement, which was supposed to be "confidential." The author was an employee of the company which operated the *Phoebu*s and probably came by his information there.

6. The court consisted of Rear Admiral Henry V. Butler, Captain Harry E. Shoemaker, and Commander Sydney M. Kraus, members; Lieutenant Commander Ralph C. Pennoyer, judge advocate; and Lieutenant Charles J. Maguire, counsel to judge advocate.

7. The chart with Wiley's reconstruction was Exhibit No. 1, *Akron* Court of Inquiry, and is held by the Office of the Judge Advocate General, Department of the Navy, Washington, D.C.

8. *The New York Times,* 7 April 1933 (4:2), quoted in full.

9. *The New York Times,* 5 April 1933 (14:3).

10. *Akron* Court of Inquiry, Wiley, 48–50.

11. *Akron* Court of Inquiry, Lieutenant Commander James L. Fisher, 427–40; Maneuvering Board from USS *Falcon* plotting *Akron* wreckage, Exhibit No. 56, *Akron* Court of Inquiry, Office of Judge Advocate General.

12. *Akron* Court of Inquiry, "Facts and Opinions"; quoted in full *Dirigible Disasters,* 4–8. It deserves note that a reviewing authority quietly expunged the "error in judgment" portion, and as evidence of the Navy's final estimate of McCord, a destroyer (DD-534) was later given his name.

13. John Toland, *Ships in the Sky, The Story of the Great Dirigibles* (New York: Henry Holt and Co., 1957), 257.

14. *Akron* Court of Inquiry, Gordon E. Dunn, 302–305.

15. *Dirigible Disasters,* Charles L. Mitchell, 204, 219, 222.

16. This may have been her course, but the location of her wreckage indicates that her track was 140 degreees true.

17. *Joint Committee to Investigate Dirigible Disasters,* 73 Cong., 1 Sess., *Hearings* (1933).

18. The committee consisted of Senators King, David I. Walsh, F. Ryan Duffy, Hiram W. Johnson, and Hamilton F. Kean; Representatives John J. Delaney (vice chairman), John J. McSwain, Dow W. Harter, A. Piatt Andrew, and Clifford R. Hope. Johnson, however, did not attend the hearings.

19. *Dirigible Disasters,* Harrigan, 164, 168–69, 171, 175.

20. *Ibid.,* Rosendahl, 510–11, 801–806.

21. *Ibid.,* Settle, 292.
22. *Ibid.,* Rodgers, 156.
23. *Ibid.,* Weyerbacher, 363–65.
24. *Ibid.,* Trapnell, 194.
25. *Ibid.,* Lindbergh, 663–64.
26. *Ibid.,* Dresel, 132–33, 144.
27. *Ibid.,* Wiley, 101–102.
28. *Report of Joint Committee to Investigate Dirigible Disasters,* 73 Cong., 1 Sess., Senate Doc. No. 75, House Report No. 266 (1933).
29. Captain Garland Fulton to Richard K. Smith, conversations, 31 July and 17 September 1959; Rear Admiral Thomas Robbins to Richard K. Smith, conversation, 12 July 1959. Robbins was Admiral Moffett's aide.
30. Admiral Moffett to Captain H. E. Shoemaker, 17 October 1931, in Arpee, *Frigates to Flat-Tops,* 235–37.
31. Committees on Commerce, *Merchant Airship Bill,* 72 Cong., 1 Sess., Senate Report No. 874, House Report No. 1308 (1932).
32. *Newsweek,* Vol. I, No. 9 (April 15, 1933), 25.

CHAPTER 7

ZRS5: Off to the Wars (pp. 93–106)

1. Chief, BuAer, memo for files, ZRS4&5/FH, 30 March 1931; Chief, BuAer, to SecNav, ZRS4&5/FI–1, 14 January 1932; CNO to SecNav, ZR5/FI–2 (320114), 5 February 1932; G. Fulton, memo for files, ZRS4&5/FI–1, 23 November 1931, Record Group 72, BuAer General Correspondence (1925–1942), Box 5599, the National Archives.
2. Chief, BuAer, to Alfred B. Sloan, Jr., president, General Motors Corporation, ZRS4&5/F21, QM (1935), 5 November 1931; Fulton memo, 23 November 1931; Chief, BuAer, to Naval Attache, Berlin, 5 November 1931, Record Group 72, BuAer General Correspondence (1925–1942), Box 5613, the National Archives.
3. Vinson's remarks after the *Akron*'s crash probably reflected his feelings of the moment, but should not (except with hindsight) be taken literally. By late 1934 he was prepared to support a limited expansion of rigid airship materiel; the *Macon*'s loss quashed this until 1938.
4. *Macon Telegraph,* 5 July 1932 (1:2); 10 July 1932 (4:2).
5. *Ibid.,* 8 February 1933 (2:2); 9 February 1933 (3:2).
6. *Ibid.,* 16 February 1933 (8:6); *Macon Telegraph and News,* 19 February 1933 (7:5); 26 February 1933 (5:1).
7. *The Akron Beacon-Journal,* 11 March 1933, 1 ff.
8. At this time Settle was in Chicago making arrangements for his abortive ascension in the stratosphere balloon *Century of Progress;* on 21 November 1933, he and Major Chester Fordney, USMC, used the same balloon in a successful ascent from Akron to 61,237 ft., a world record at that date. For an account of this flight, see J. Gordon Vaeth, "When the Space Race Began," *U.S. Naval Institute Proceedings,* Vol. LXXXIX, No. 726 (August 1963), 68–78.
9. *The New York Times,* 4 February 1934, Sect. 4 (8:2); Eventually, Captain Ford O. Rogers, USMC, ferried Harrigan's plane west.
10. Lieutenant Commander H. E. MacClellan, "Report on Prospects of Using Miami, Florida, for a Terminal for Flights to California," ZRS4&5/A4, 23 January 1933, Record Group 72, BuAer General Correspondence 1925–1942), Box 5592, the National Archives.
11. Superheat is the temperature differential between the airship's gas and the atmosphere. As the expression was used aboard airships, it had positive and negative values, the former when the gas was the warmer, the latter when the gas was the cooler. This is most easily understood by the example of getting into an automobile in a parking lot on a hot day. The air outside is 85°, but the air inside the car is 95°, and thus has 10° of superheat and is lighter in density than the air outside. If the 95° air could be preserved and the car driven into Death Valley where the atmosphere is 105°, the air inside the car would be "supercooled," or said to have 10° of "negative superheat," although it is still 95°.
12. *Macon Evening News,* 13 October 1933 (4:6), 14 October 1933 (4:1); *Macon Telegraph,* 13 October 1933 (1:4), 14 October 1933 (1:4).
13. All data on the *Macon*'s flight west were taken from the *Macon* log, 12–15 October 1933.
14. These situations are set out in detail in CinCUS to Fleet, CinC file A16–3 (2976), 24 October 1933, Record Group 38, CNO Fleet Training Division, General Correspondence (1914–1941), Box 145, the National Archives.
15. *Macon* log, 14–17 November 1933; CinCUS to Fleet, CinC file A16–3 (3463), 28 November 1933, Box 145, Record Group 38, the National Archives.
16. *Macon* Umpire to Chief Umpire (CinCUS), CinCUS file A16–3(5), 24 November 1933, Record Group 38, CNO Fleet Training Division, General Correspondence (1914–1941), Box 145, the National Archives.
17. *Ibid.* In BuAer some rather cynical marginal remarks were made on Mackey's report after King routed it down the line. Someone noted, "Even if she reports *nothing* the information is not reliable." To Mackey's suggestion that the airship remain out of sight and use her planes was noted, "How? She can't see then," and, "Some trick." These remarks were not initialed and therefore the commentators could not be identified.
18. CinCUS to Fleet, A16–3 (3463), 28 November 1933, Record Group 38, CNO Fleet Training Division, General Correspondence (1914–1941), Box 145, the National Archives.
19. Chief, BuAer's second endorsement, 1 February 1934, *Macon* Umpire to Chief Umpire, *Op. cit.*

CHAPTER 8

The Crucial Year (pp. 107–26)

1. King to Dresel, 11 January 1934, Fulton Papers.
2. Holloway H. Frost, *The Battle of Jutland* (Annapolis: U.S. Naval Institute, 1936), 514–18, 521.

3. King to Halligan, 11 January 1934, Fulton Papers.
4. "All" the carriers were the *Langley* and *Lexington.* After Exercises D and E the *Saratoga* went to Bremerton, Washington, for overhaul, and did not resume operations until Exercise J.
5. *Macon* Umpire to Chief Umpire, ZRS5/A16–3, 10 January 1934, Record Group 38, CNO Fleet Training Division, General Correspondence (1914–1941), Box 145, the National Archives.
6. Derek Wood and Derek Dempster, *The Narrow Margin, The Battle of Britain and the Rise of Air Power 1930–1940* (New York: McGraw-Hill, 1961), 166–67. This volume includes an outstanding account of the development of the R.A.F.'s interception and radar techniques.
7. *Macon* Umpire to Chief Umpire, 10 January 1934, *Op. cit.*
8. CinCUS to Fleet, A16–3/872, 5 March 1934, Record Group 38, CNO Fleet Training Division, General Correspondence (1914–1941), Box 145, the National Archives.
9. *Ibid.*
10. CinCUS to Fleet, A16–3/872, 17 January 1934, *Op. cit.*
11. *Akron* Court of Inquiry, *Op. cit.* On p. 352 Dresel remarks: "My ideas of the operation of rigid airships are probably very conservative and . . . I do not concur in statements which I have often heard, that these ships can stand any kind of weather." Here Dresel was rightly leveling an indirect criticism at the exaggerations of airship "sales talk."
12. CinCUS to Fleet, A16–3/872, 5 March 1934, *Op. cit.*
13. CinCUS to Fleet, A16–3(1612), 23 April 1934, Record Group 38, CNO Fleet Training Division, General Correspondence (1914–1941), Box 145, the National Archives.
14. CO, *Macon*, to Chief, BuAer, ZRS5/F14(288), 25 May 1934, Record Group 72, BuAer General Correspondence (1925–1942), Box 5607, the National Archives. The *Macon* principals with whom the author has spoken or corresponded are unequivocal in their statements that Davis saved the airship.
15. *Macon* log, 5–6–7 May 1934; *Macon* Umpire to CinCUS, 28 May 1934; and CinCUS, to CNO, A4–3/7 (2719), 15 June 1934, Record Group 38, CNO Classified Files (1927–1939), Box 212, the National Archives.
16. She moored at 1740, after a flight of 46 hours, 40 minutes, covering 2,903 nautical miles; she took off with 81,050 lbs. of fuel, returned with 33,510 lbs. on board.
17. During the early 1930's carriers usually operated apart from the main body because of their disorderly operations; they had to leave formation to launch and retrieve planes, which upset the battle line, and so were put off by themselves with a cruiser escort.
18. *Macon* Umpire to CinCUS, 28 May 1934, Record Group 38, CNO Fleet Training Division, General Correspondence (1914–1941), Box 337, the National Archives.

19. Trapnell went to the *San Francisco,* Young to the *Tuscaloosa,* Larson to the *Milwaukee.* Larson was killed on 11 June 1936, near Guantanamo Bay, when the wing collapsed on the plane he was flying.
20. CinCUS to CNO A4–3/7(2719), 15 June 1934, Record Group 38, CNO Classified Files (1927–1939), Box 212, the National Archives.
21. King to Rear Admiral F. H. Clark, ZRS4&5/AF–4, 23 July 1934, Record Group 72, BuAer General Correspondence (1925–1942), Box 5592, the National Archives.

CHAPTER 9

Wiley Takes Command (pp. 127–146)

1. There are enough references in the record to suggest that Admiral King sent Wiley to Sunnyvale with explicit instructions to make the *Macon* get up and go. King became well known for this stratagem in the late 1930's when, as ComAirBaseFor, he shook out the flying boat squadrons.
2. H. V. Wiley, "The Value of Airships," *U.S. Naval Institute Proceedings,* Vol. LX, No. 5 (May, 1934), 665–71.
3. Miller to Harrigan, 5 March 1934, Harrigan Papers.
4. CO, *Macon,* to ComAirBaseFor, ZRS5/A4–3(408), 31 July 1934, Record Group 72, BuAer General Correspondence (1925–1942), Box 5591, the National Archives.
5. Miller to Harrigan, 6 August 1934, Harrigan Papers. In this same letter, Miller remarked of Wiley: "He's done more already than has been done in the past two years."
6. Wiley to E. J. King, ZRS5/A4–3, 28 August 1934, Record Group 72, BuAer General Correspondence (1925–1942), Box 5591, the National Archives.
7. CinCUS to CNO, A4–3/FF2–3 (3805), 23 August 1934, Record Group 72, BuAer General Correspondence (1925–1942), Box 5592, the National Archives. A few weeks later, Admiral Standley remarked of this operation: "We considered it a publicity stunt and that he had no business doing it." General Board, *Hearings* (1934), 211. Four years later, 12 May 1938, three Army Air Corps B–17's made a carefully pre-arranged noontime "interception" of the Italian luxury liner *Rex* in the Atlantic steamer lane, a mere 375 miles east of Cape Cod, and it was hailed as a great demonstration of "air power." The Navy Department was similarly disturbed by this "protracted flight to sea," but for quite different reasons.
8. Wiley to King, 28 August 1934, *Op. cit.* The fact that Wiley would write a personal letter of this type, and King would see that it was appended to the official files, is one of the items which suggests an "understanding" as to what Wiley was supposed to work out of the *Macon.*
9. Howard N. Coulter and Gerhard R. Fisher, *Visual Indicating Radio Direction Finder,* U.S. Patent Office, No. 2,124,544 (26 July 1938).
10. Harold B. Miller and Gerhard R. Fisher, *Radio Re-*

ceiver and Direction Finder, U.S. Patent Office, No. 2,207,750 (16 July 1940).

11. His "Bob Wakefield" stories, published under the pseudonym of "Blaine Miller," first appeared in the magazine *Boy's Life* during 1935, and later in book form: *Bob Wakefield, Naval Aviator* (1936); *Bob Wakefield, Naval Inspector* (1937); and *Bob Wakefield's Flight Log* (1940). His history of naval aviation was *Navy Wings* (1937), with a revised edition in 1942. All were published by Dodd, Mead & Co. The "Wakefield" books are obviously drawn from his experiences, the first one detailing hook-on flying from the airship "USS *Miami*," and how Bob Wakefield devised a radio homing device for the hook-on planes. However "dated," they still make exciting reading.

12. CO, Lakehurst, to Chief, BuAer, NA/ZR3/F1/A4–1, 31 August 1934; E. J. King's marginalia on Plans to Material Division, ZRS4&5/VV, 8 October 1934; Fulton memo to Material Division, 13 December 1934; and E. J. King's marginalia on J. E. Ostrander to Plans, 4 February 1934, Record Group 72, BuAer General Correspondence (1925–1942), Box 5631, the National Archives. The civil types studied for a tanker plane were the Bellanca "Airbus," Lockheed "Altair," and unspecified models by Kinner, Spartan, and Stinson.

13. Heinen was an airship pilot for Luftschiffbau Zeppelin during World War I who was brought to the United States at the instance of Commander Ralph D. Weyerbacher and was employed in instructing the *Shenandoah*'s original complement. He became a lieutenant commander in the Naval Reserve. After 1925 he moved in and out of the airship scene until World War II.

14. CO, *Macon* to ComAirBatFor, ZRS5/A9–6(593), 14 October 1934, Record Group 72, BuAer General Correspondence (1925–1942), Box 5592, the National Archives; Rear Admiral H. B. Miller to Richard K. Smith, 23 May 1960; Rear Admiral L. C. Simpler to Richard K. Smith, 9 January 1961.

15. Quoted to CO, *Macon*, to ComAirBatFor, ZRS5/A9–6(642), 11 November 1934, Record Group 80, CNO Classified Files (1927–1939), Box 212, the National Archives.

16. ComBatFor to Battle Force, 7 December 1934, Record Group 38, CNO Classified Files (1927–1939), Box 159, the National Archives.

17. *Ibid.*

18. *Ibid.*

19. General Board No. 449 (Serial 1663), 23 October 1934, Record Group 72, BuAer General Correspondence (1925–1942), Box 5631, the National Archives. This was a result of General Board *Hearings*, 1934, 169–218, at which Standley, King, Fulton, Rosendahl, and Harrigan appeared.

20. Fulton memo to Plans, ZRS4&5/F41, 19 February 1932, Record Group 72, BuAer General Correspondence (1925–1942), Box 5624, the National Archives. This was prepared at the request of Plans. It will be recalled that Marc Mitscher preferred the *Akron* and *Macon* as "bomb carriers"; he recommended the installation of racks for

eight 1,000-lb. or sixteen 500-lb. bombs. Their design was begun by the Bureau of Ordnance, the installation never made.

21. CinCUS to Chief, BuAer, A4–3/FF2–3(5475), 24 December 1934, Record Group 72, BuAer General Correspondence (1925–1942), Box 5592, the National Archives.

22. CO, *Macon*, to Chief, BuAer, ZRS5/F14(288), 25 May 1934, Record Group 72, BuAer General Correspondence (1925–1942), Box 5607, the National Archives.

23. Chief, BuAer, to CO, *Macon*, ZRS4&5/F14/L9, 24 July 1934, Record Group 72, BuAer General Correspondence (1925–1942), Box 5607, the National Archives. The wind tunnel data referred to is Report No. 432, in *18th Annual Report, NACA* (1932); and Report No. 443, *19th Annual Report, NACA* (1933). If consulted, they should be compared with the much later Report No. 604, *23rd Annual Report, NACA* (1937).

24. Burgess to Fulton, 1 November 1934, Fulton Papers.

CHAPTER 10

The End of an Era (pp. 147–162)

1. *Report of Federal Aviation Commission,* 74 Cong., 1 Sess., Sen. Doc. No. 15 (1935), 197–209.

2. General Board, No. 449 (Serial 1663), 23 October 1934, Record Group 72, BuAer General Correspondence (1925–1942), Box 5631, the National Archives.

3. *Ibid.,* CNO's fourth endorsement.

4. CO, *Macon,* to ComAirBatFor, 4 February 1935, Record Group 72, BuAer General Correspondence (1925–1942), Box 5591, the National Archives.

5. W. H. Clarke, *Macon* Court of Inquiry, 77–78, Record Group 72, BuAer, LTA Design Branch General Files (1921–1942), Box 61, the National Archives. Hereafter cited as MCI.

6. MCI, W. M. Conover, 75–76.

7. MCI, R. J. Davis, 25–33.

8. MCI, J. R. Connolly, 51–52.

9. MCI, T. Brandes, 48–50.

10. MCI, A. B. Galatian and M. G. Fraas, 72–74, 110–111.

11. MCI, T. Henderson and H. Miller, 63–66, 67–69.

12. The *Macon*'s position upon sinking was approximately 13 miles from Point Sur Light on a bearing of 142 degrees true.

13. *New York Post,* 14 February 1935 (16:2). The *Macon*'s loss practically concluded *The New York Sun*'s peculiarly zealous crusade against airships; and by way of an "I-told-you-so" directed at the Navy, *The Sun* took the extraordinary step of buying a full-page ad in *The Washington Post,* 15 February 1935, p. 10, in which it ran a selection of its anti-airship editorials of the previous ten years.

14. Franklin D. Roosevelt's Press Conferences, No. 183, 13 February 1935, Franklin D. Roosevelt Library, Hyde Park, NA-240 (microfilm), July 1952.

15. *San Francisco Examiner,* 13 February 1935 (1:5).
16. There were five reports, all of which are cited in full in this work's bibliography. Here they will be cited by number, and "Special Committee on Airships" will be abbreviated "SCA."
17. Some persons in the control car testified that they felt the gust blow through the car's windows, others said they felt nothing and doubted if there was a gust. This led to speculation that it was actually the fin letting go which caused the lurch. But Davis was standing directly beneath the fin at the moment of the lurch, and he saw nothing wrong.
18. If this sounds far-fetched, the reader has only to imagine the *Macon*'s condition if the fin had carried away without tearing up any gas cells.
19. Dr. W. Hovgaard to Dr. W. F. Durand, "Memorandum on the Loss of the *Macon*," August 1935, Fulton Papers.
20. SCA, Report No. 3, 8.
21. *Ibid.,* 7, 8, 22. They had access to transcripts of the *Macon* Court of Inquiry, as well as to an interesting set of documents entitled "Statements Made to the Commanding Officer," quasi-depositions made by officers and crew shortly after the crash; copies in Box 61, Record Group 72, LTA Design Branch General Files (1921–1942), the National Archives. Dr. Durand and Dr. Hovgaard visited Moffett Field to interview the survivors.
22. Hovgaard memo, *Op. cit.*
23. MCI, J. D. Reppy, 35–41.
24. MCI, J. L. Kenworthy, 15.
25. MCI, T. L. Gatch, 79; also his summary to the court, 122. This item was played up in most newspaper reports of the court's proceedings.
26. Karl Arnstein, *Stern Construction of Rigid Airships,* U.S. Patent Office, No. 1,517,885 (5 December 1924).
27. There has been more mumbling about this than words written. Wiley himself came to believe it; in his review of Rosendahl's book, *What About the Airship?* in the *U.S. Naval Institute Proceedings,* Vol. LXIV, No. 7 (July, 1938), 1043–1044, he took exception to Rosendahl's judgment that the *Akron* flew into the sea, and suggested she had a structural failure similar to the *Macon*'s. It is implied in Ernest A. Lehmann and Leonard Adelt, *Zeppelin, The Story of Lighter-Than-Air Craft* (1937), 314; and in J. Gordon Vaeth, *Graf Zeppelin* (1958), 223. It is directly postulated in Harold B. Miller, *Navy Wings* (1942), 314–15; and in Edward Arpee, *From Frigates to Flat-Tops* (1953), 244, n. 5. And it has been a point of argument among those associated with airships for the past 30 years.
28. MCI, C. M. Bolster, 46, 82.
29. MCI, H. V. Wiley, 117.
30. When Wiley took command he planned to triple the *Macon*'s operating hours, but the price of aviation fuel went up in the summer of 1934 from 10 to 15 cents per gallon, operating funds remained the same, and there were "political" difficulties in getting the airship's money transferred from the station's funds. Moffett Field was

allowed $30,000 per month to support the *Macon;* of this the *Macon* was directly allotted $3,500 (per month), and $2,700 of this was expended on fuel, a sum which brought about 125 hours in the air.
31. Captain Ronald W. Hoel, USN, "The Airship as a Multipurpose Platform, Including Impact on Military Logistics," Thesis No. 65, (1 March 1961), Industrial War College of the Armed Forces, 8. This interesting 33-page study is reprinted in full in House Subcommittee on Appropriations, 87 Cong., 1 Sess., *Hearings, Department of Defense Appropriation for 1962* (1961), Part 6, 393–430.
32. *Chicago Tribune,* 13 February 1935 (13:2).

CHAPTER 11

The Years of Confusion (pp. 163–170)

1. Executive Order No. 7217, 26 October 1935. The base was returned to the Navy early in World War II; it was recommissioned on 16 April 1942 by Commander Donald M. Mackey, its new commanding officer.
2. The G-1 was purchased from Goodyear's fleet of advertising blimps in September 1935; it was formerly known as the *Defender.*
3. On 30 June 1937, the Air Corps terminated its airship operations and turned over its gear to the Navy. This included the blimps TC-13 and TC-14, which were superior to any the Navy had at that time.
4. Chief, BuAer, to SecNav, 17 June 1933; SecNav to the President, 21 July 1933, Record Group 72, BuAer General Correspondence (1925–1942), Box 5563, the National Archives.
5. Chief, BuAer, to General Board, 9 June 1936, Record Group 72, BuAer General Corrospondence (1925–1942), Box 5561, the National Archives.
6. Chief, BuAer, to General Board, Aer-la-NW, QB/EN15, 15 January 1937 (copy), Fulton Papers.
7. Selected by Dr. Karl Compton of M.I.T., the committee consisted of Dr. William F. Durand of Stanford University, chairman; Dr. Theodor von Karman, director of the Guggenheim Aeronautical Laboratory at CalTech; Dr. Robert A. Millikan, also of CalTech; Dr. William Hovgaard, professor of naval design, and Dr. Alfred V. de Forest, associate professor of mechanical engineering, both of M.I.T.; Dr. Stephen Timoshenko, professor of mechanical engineering at the University of Michigan; Frank B. Jewett, president of Bell Telephone Laboratories; and Charles F. Kettering, president of General Motors Research Corporation.
8. SCA, Report No. 1, 5, 12.
9. General Board, *Hearings,* 1937, Vol. I, 1–72; General Board, No. 449 (Serial 1732), 17 February 1937, Record Group 72, BuAer Confidential Correspondence, Box 1732, the National Archives.
10. Expression used to describe the HTA Unit's status in Miller to Harrigan, 5 March 1934, Harrigan Papers.
11. General Board, *Hearings,* 1934, 169–218.
12. The *N* designates an aircraft for training purposes. At this date the use of *N* was somewhat confusing because

the Navy also used it to designate nonrigid airships (blimps), which were ZN's.

13. How did the President arrive at this 325-foot figure? It was probably inspired by Representative John D. Dingell (Democrat, Michigan), influential member of the Ways and Means Committee, who was trying to do something nice for the Metalclad Corporation of Detroit. There was considerable correspondence between Dingell and the White House on the subject. The Durand Committee said a "next step" in a Metalclad should be "about" twice the ZMC–2's length (149′5″); in a memo to Roosevelt, 8 September 1938, Edison remarked, "Your early instructions to me were of a general nature, indicating your desire to build a metalclad ship 300 feet long." This also provided Roosevelt with an oblique means of disposing of the large rigid airship, which he did not believe in anyway.

14. This was the K–2, 400,000 cu. ft., delivered to Lakehurst on 16 December 1938.

15. C. P. Burgess, *Design Memo No. 312*, "Discussion of Specification for Metalclad Airship Submitted by the Metalclad Airship Corporation."

16. The price of the dwarf was $1,997,482, about $1.87 per cu.ft.; the blimp was $760,916, about $1.00 per cu.ft. This blimp design is strikingly similar to the *M*-type developed only during the latter part of World War II.

17. President to SecNav, 3 May 1939, Record Group 80, SecNav General Correspondence (1926–1940), Box 4217, the National Archives.

18. House Committee on Naval Affairs, *Hearings on Sundry Legislation Affecting the Naval Establishment, 1940* [No. 283], "Special Report on Lighter-Than-Air Craft," 76 Cong., 3 Sess. (1940), 2267–78.

19. SecNav memo, 29 May 1940, Record Group 72, BuAer General Correspondence (1925–1942), Box 5611, the National Archives. (Italics mine.)

20. House Subcommittee on Appropriations, *Hearings on First Supplemental National Defense Appropriation Bill for 1941*, 76 Cong., 3 Sess. (1940), 164.

21. House Committee on Appropriations, *A Communication from the President*, House Doc. No. 814, 76 Cong., 3 Sess. (1940).

22. The President to SecNav, 11 June 1940, Record Group 72, BuAer General Correspondence (1925–1942), Box 5611, the National Archives.

23. Senate Subcommittee of Committee on Appropriations, *Hearings on First Supplemental National Defense Appropriation Bill for 1941*, 76 Cong., 3 Sess. (1940), 19.

24. The Unpublished Diaries of Admiral John H. Towers, 17 June 1940, courtesy of Mrs. John H. Towers. After Starks's remarks, Towers could not possibly defend the airship. Later, when Fulton suggested trying again for the ZRN in 1941, Towers remarked "hopeless in my opinion"; marginalia on Fulton to Chief, BuAer, 18 June 1940, Record Group 72, BuAer General Correspondence (1925–1942), Box 5611, the National Archives.

25. CNO to the President, 16 September 1938, "Corre-

spondence from the Papers of Franklin D. Roosevelt Pertaining to Lighter-Than-Air Craft," File 18-I (Bureau of Aeronautics, 1933–45), Franklin D. Roosevelt Library, Hyde Park.

26. President to Assistant SecNav, 10 September 1938, *Ibid.*

27. Contrary to misconception, the Goodyear Aircraft Corporation is not a direct "successor" to Goodyear-Zeppelin. The organization of Goodyear Aircraft was first discussed in November 1939, executed 8 January 1940, after which Goodyear-Zeppelin was finally liquidated because of the "awkward" German affiliation.

28. COMinCH to CNO, 7 January 1942, ZRCV/F1 (420107); Chief; BuAer's second endorsement, 20 January 1942, Record Group 72, BuAer Confidential Correspondence, Box 1732, the National Archives. It deserves remark that if King was not convinced of the ZRCV's impracticability in these circumstances, he probably could have forced the issue; a few months later he also became CNO and wore both hats for the rest of the war.

29. Burgess to Commander Scott E. Peck, 29 December 1941, Aer–P1–92–MW, from the private papers of Rear Admiral Scott E. Peck.

CHAPTER 12

The Performance (pp. 171–178)

1. Routing sheet comment on Truscott memo, file O–R–25, n.d., Bureau of Construction and Repair correspondence. (Emphasis mine.)

2. Unsigned, undated memo for Chief, BuAer, Fulton Papers. The "small sub-section" referred to was Fulton's LTA Design Section. Of note is the expression "former nonrigids"; at this date the Navy had no blimps in operation. The memo went on to say that the Army was getting the idea that it had exclusive responsibility for blimp development, and suggested BuAer put some blimps back in commission to dispel such an idea.

3. House Subcommittee of Committee on Appropriations, *Hearings on Second Deficiency Bill, 1938*, 76 Cong., 3 Sess. (1938), 605.

4. CO, *Macon*, to CinCUS, ZRS4&5/A4–3 (267), 21 May 1934, Record Group 72, BuAer General Correspondence (1925–1942), Box 5592, the National Archives.

5. Helium's loss of relative lift in terms of its airplane-carrying mission is illustrated by the increase in airplane weights between 1930 and 1942. The F9C–2's gross weight was 2,770 lbs.; the Grumman F4F–3, the standard fighter around 1941, was 7,002 lbs. The BT–1 dive bomber for the proposed ZRCV was 6,978 lbs., 2.5 times an F9C's; and when it's design was finalized as the SBD–3, it had grown to 9,407 lbs. The standard lift of helium remained 62 lbs. per thousand cu.ft. It deserves emphasis, however, that Burgess hoped for a special airplane design, stripped down for airship service.

6. C. P. Burgess, "The Ultimate Airship," Design Memorandum No. 274 (August 1937), BuNavWeps Library.

7. General Board, *Hearings* (1934), 137.

8. Blimp operations were formally terminated 30 June 1961, although various flight operations were continued until 31 August 1962. The widespread ignorance of the blimp's existence is remarkable. Bernard Brodie, the RAND Corporation strategist, has remarked that the airship could not survive in an age of radar; yet the ZPG–2W and ZPG–3W airships carried the largest search radar installations ever airborne, and for three years provided all-weather, offshore Early Warning service for the North American Defense Command.

9. The *Shenandoah*—57 flights, 740 hours; the *Los Angeles*—331 flights, 4,398 hours; the *Akron*—73 flights, 1,695.8 hours; the *Macon*—54 flights, 1,798.2 hours.

10. CO, *Macon,* to ComAirBatFor, ZRS5/A4–3 (453), 15 August 1934, Record Group 72, BuAer General Correspondence (1925–1942), Box 5592, the National Archives.

11. A survey of parasite aircraft developments up to 1957 can be found in Richard K. Smith, "Forty Years of Skyhooks," *Air Progress* (Fall, 1962), 20–30.

Bibliography

For its greatest part this book has relied upon the old Navy records in the National Archives. The most helpful were the *ZR* files of Record Group 72, "Bureau of Aeronautics General Correspondence, 1925–1942," which held a day-to-day correspondence relating to the airships' design, construction, and operations. The *VF* files of the same Group were equally informative on the hook-on airplanes. Also in Group 72 were two other series of materials, "Lighter-Than-Air Design Branch, General Files, 1921–1942," and "Bureau of Aeronautics Lighter-Than-Air Correspondence, 1930–1935"; but they are of a technical rather than an operational nature.

The details of the airships' military operations were in four series of materials within three Groups: Record Group 72, "Bureau of Aeronautics Confidential Correspondence"; Record Group 38, "Chief of Naval Operations, Classified Files, 1927–1939," and "Chief of Naval Operations, Fleet Training Division, General Correspondence, 1914–1941"; and Record Group 80, "Chief of Naval Operations, Classified Files, 1927–1939," and "Office of the Secretary of the Navy, General Correspondence, 1926–1940." The airships' operating logs are in Record Group 24.

Equally useful were the *Hearings* on naval policy held by the General Board, which are in the custody of the Office of Naval History. Congressional documents were invaluable sources. In addition to the key items cited in this bibliography, there are other data scattered among hearings and reports of the Senate and House committees and subcommittees on appropriations.

The books and articles by primary sources are usually of a technical nature, and for such data they are invariably excellent. In addition to these published items there are C. P. Burgess' *Design Memoranda,* 401 in number, which are held by the library of the Bureau of Naval Weapons.

Most secondary sources on the subject have rehashed the same threadbare information, misinformation, myths, and hearsay of the past thirty years. The majority have been more concerned with exploiting the entertainment value of the airships' inherent sensationalism than with trying to understand the subject. As a result, the secondary works cited here are rather few.

PRIMARY SOURCES

Public Documents (Listed Chronologically)

U.S. Congress. Select Committee. *Hearings on Matters Relating to the Operations of the U.S. Air Services.* 68 Cong., 2 Sess., 1925. 6 Vols. And House Report No. 1653, 68 Cong., 2 Sess., 1925. This is the so-called Lampert Committee.

U.S. President, 1923–1929 (Coolidge). *The President's Aircraft Board, Hearings.* Washington: U.S. Government Printing Office, 1925. 4 Vols. And U.S. Congress, *Aircraft in National Defense,* Senate Doc. No. 18, 69 Cong., 1 Sess., 1925. This is the so-called Morrow Board.

U.S. House of Representatives. Committee on Naval Affairs. *Hearings on Sundry Legislation Affecting the Naval Establishment, 1925–1926.* [No. 64] "Findings of *Shenandoah* Court of Inquiry," 217–24; [No. 103] "Statement of RAdm. William A. Moffett," 455–64; [No. 122] "Replacement of the USS *Shenandoah,*" 539–1176. 69 Cong., 1 Sess., 1925–26.

U.S. Senate. Committee on Naval Affairs. *Hearings on an Act to Authorize the Construction and Procurement of Aircraft and Aircraft Equipment in the Navy and Ma-*

rine Corps, and to Adjust and Define the Status of the Operating Personnel Therewith. 100 pp. Senate Report No. 848; House Report No. 389, 69 Cong., 1 Sess., 1926; and *U.S. Statutes at Large*, Vol. XLIV, Public No. 422 [H.R. 9690] 24 June 1926, 764–68. This is the Five-Year Aircraft Program, one of the most significant legislative packages in the history of the Navy.

U.S. House of Representatives. Committee on Naval Affairs. *Hearings on Sundry Legislation Affecting the Naval Establishment, 1926–1927*. [No. 53] "Statement of Edward P. Warner, Asst. SecNav," 307–10; [No. 61] "The Helium Situation," 327–42; [No. 43] "Comparative Air Strength of the Five Great Powers," 179–88. 69 Cong., 2 Sess., 1927.

U.S. Congress. *To Provide for Investigations for the Establishment of a Naval Airship Base*. Senate Report No. 2025; House Report No. 2434, 70 Cong., 2 Sess., 1929.

———. *Naval Airship Base on the West Coast*. House Doc. No. 132. 71 Cong., 2 Sess., 1929. 59 pp. Report of the so-called Moffett Board on the Sunnyvale air station.

U.S. House of Representatives. Committee on Naval Affairs. *Hearings on Sundry Legislation Affecting the Naval Establishment, 1930–1931*. [No. 583] 3241–3301; [No. 584] 3303–14; [No. 739] 4131; [No. 748] 4153–54; [No. 784] 4285–4300. 71 Cong., 3 Sess., 1931. All relate to the creation of the Sunnyvale air station.

U.S. Congress. *Authorizing the Secretary of the Navy to Accept a Site for a Lighter-Than-Air Base, and to Construct Necessary Improvements Thereon*. Senate Report No. 1492; House Report No. 2114. 71 Cong., 3 Sess., 1930.

U.S. House of Representatives. Committee on Mines and Mining. *Hearings, Amarillo Helium Plant*. 71 Cong., 2 Sess., 1930. 231 pp.

———. Committee on Naval Affairs. *Hearings on Sundry Legislation Affecting the Naval Establishment, 1931–1932*. [No. 388]. "Akron Investigation," 1235–1423; [No. 525] "Report, Akron Investigation," 1831–36. 72 Cong., 1 Sess., 1932.

U.S. Congress. Joint Committee. *Hearings, Investigation of Dirigible Disasters*, 944 pp. And Senate Doc. No. 75; House Report No. 266. 73 Cong., 1 Sess., 1933.

———. *Report of Colonel Henry Breckinridge*. 73 Cong., 1 Sess., 1933. 177 pp., illus., maps, diagrs. Analytical summaries of testimony at airship disaster *Hearings*.

U.S. House of Representatives. Committee on Naval Affairs. *Hearings on Sundry Legislation Affecting the Naval Establishment, 1937–1938* [No. 620] "Naval Expansion Program," 1937–2889. 75 Cong., 3 Sess., 1938.

———. *1939–1940*. [No. 283] "Report on Lighter-Than-Air Craft," 2267–78. This is the King-Fulton Report.

Books

Blakemore, Thomas L., and W. Watters Pagon. *Pressure Airships*. New York: Ronald Press Company, 1927. 311 pp. A textbook on blimp design and fabrication.

Burgess, Charles P. *Airship Design*. New York: Ronald Press Company, 1927. 300 pp. A textbook on rigid airship design.

Chandler, Charles deForrest, and Walter S. Diehl. *Balloon and Airship Gases*. New York: Ronald Press Company, 1926. 226 pp. A textbook reference.

King, Ernest J., and Walter Muir Whitehall. *Fleet Admiral King, a Naval Record*. New York: W. W. Norton & Company, 1952. 674 pp. With respect to King's actual views toward the airship, this volume is more biography than autobiography.

Knight, Richard H., and Ira E. Hobbs. *Tactical Graphics For Aircraft Operations*. Washington: U.S. Hydrographic Office, 1935. 112 pp.

Rosendahl, Charles E. *Up Ship!* New York: Dodd, Mead and Company, 1931. 311 pp., illus. Mostly the *Shenandoah*, the *Los Angeles*, and the *Graf Zeppelin*.

———. *What About The Airship?* New York: Charles Scribner's Sons, 1938. 437 pp., illus. Essentially polemical, but it contains several references to his command of the *Akron* and much useful data.

Upson, Ralph H., and Charles deForrest Chandler. *Free And Captive Balloons*. New York: Ronald Press Company, 1926. 311 pp., illus., diagrs., tables. A textbook reference.

Warner, Edward P. *Aerostatics*. New York: Ronald Press Company, 1926. 112 pp., illus., diagrs., tables. A textbook reference.

Periodicals

Arnstein, Karl. "The Development of Large Commercial Airships," *Transactions*, American Society of Mechanical Engineers, Vol. L (1928), AER-50–4, 1–6.

———. "Developments in Lighter-Than-Air Craft," *Society of Automotive Engineers Journal*, Vol. XXIV, No. 5 (May, 1929), 465–73.

———. "The Field of the Large Commercial Airship," *Journal of the Aeronautical Sciences*, Vol. III, No. 10 (August, 1936), 358–63.

———. "The Logical Development of Airships for Fast Ocean Transportation," *Metal Progress*, Vol. XXII, No. 12 (December, 1932), 38–42.

———. "Research and Development Problems Arising in Airship Design," Guggenheim Airship Institute, Akron, Ohio. *Publication No. 1* (1933), 23–35.

———. "Some Design Aspects of the Rigid Airship," *Transactions*, American Society of Mechanical Engineers, Vol. LVI (1934), 385–92.

———. "Why Airships?" *U.S. Air Services*, Vol. XVII, No. 12 (December, 1932), 25–31.

Bartlet, H. T. "Mission of Aircraft with the Fleet," *Air Power*, Vol. V, No. 1 (May, 1919), 15–17.

Betancourt, Gilbert. "The Status of the Airship in America," *Transactions*, American Society of Mechanical Engineers, Vol. LV (1933), AER-55–8, 61–64.

Bottoms, R. R. "The Production and Uses of Helium," *Transactions*, American Society of Mechanical Engineers, Vol. LI (1929), AER-51–20, 107–17.

Bolster, Calvin M. "Mechanical Equipment for Handling Large Rigid Airships," *Transactions*, American Society of Mechanical Engineers, Vol. LV (1933), AER-55–15, 113–19.

Burgess, Charles P., Jerome C. Hunsaker, and Starr Truscott. "The Strength of Rigid Airships," *Journal of the Royal Aeronautical Society,* Vol. XXVIII, No. 162 (June, 1924), 327–448. Illus., drgs., diagrs., bibl.

———. "A Method of Determining the Dimensions and Horsepower of an Airship for Any Given Performance," NACA Technical Note No. 194 (1924), 14 pp.

———. "Mooring the U.S. Airship *Shenandoah* to USS *Patoka,*" *U.S. Air Services,* Vol. IX, No. 9 (September, 1924), 418–19.

———. "The Rigid Airship *ZR-3,*" *Journal of the American Society of Naval Engineers,* Vol. XXXVI, No. 4 (November, 1924), 553–72.

———. "New 6,000,000 Cubic Foot Airship for Our Navy," *Scientific American,* Vol. CXL, No. 12 (December, 1926), 418–19.

———. "The Application of Least Work to the Primary Stress Calculations of Space Framework," *Transactions,* American Society of Mechanical Engineers, Vol. LI (1929), 131–39.

———. "Progress in Aeronautics," *Mechanical Engineering,* Vol. LII, No. 1 (January, 1930), 11–12.

———. "Airship Design, Progress in from USS *Shenandoah* to USS *Akron,*" *Journal of the American Society of Naval Engineers,* Vol. XLIII, No. 3 (August, 1933), 419–25.

———. "Water Recovery Apparatus for Airships," *Transactions,* American Society of Mechanical Engineers, Vol. LIV (1932), AER-54–11, 83–92.

———. "Some Airship Problems," Guggenheim Airship Institute, Akron, Ohio, *Publication No. 1* (1935), 54–63.

———. "Airships as Cruisers," *U.S. Air Services,* Vol. XX, No. 10 (October, 1935), 19–21.

———. "Aeronautics in Naval Architecture," *Society of Automotive Engineers Journal,* Vol. XL, No. 1 (January, 1937), 13–18.

Chandler, C. deF. "Airships for Military Purposes," *U.S. Air Services,* Vol. X, No. 7 (July, 1925), 20–25.

Fritsche, Carl B. "A Comparative Examination of the Airplane and the Airship," *Transactions,* American Society of Mechanical Engineers, Vol. L (1928), AER-50–20, 9–20.

———. "The Metalclad Airship," *Transactions,* American Society of Mechanical Engineers, Vol. LI (1929), AER-51–36, 245–66.

Fulton, Garland. "Rigid Airships," *U.S. Naval Institute Proceedings,* Part 1, Vol. XLVII, No. 10 (October, 1921), 1565–91; Part 2, Vol. XLVII, No. 11 (November, 1921), 1697–1723.

———. "Some Matters Relating to Large Airships," *Transactions,* Society of Naval Architects and Marine Engineers, Vol. XXXIII (1925), 187–207.

———. "Airship Progress and Airship Problems," *Journal of the American Society of Naval Engineers,* Vol. XLI, No. 1 (February, 1929), 30–63.

———. "Some Features of a Modern Airship—USS *Akron,*" *Transactions,* Society of Naval Architects and Marine Engineers, Vol. XXXIX (1931), 135–57. The

best description of the *Akron-Macon* design in the public record.

———. "Improving Airship Performance," *Transactions,* American Society of Mechanical Engineers, Vol. LVI (1934), AER-56–8, 301–303.

Hunsaker, Jerome C. "The Present Status of Airships in Europe," *Journal of the Franklin Institute,* Vol. CLXXVII, No. 6 (June, 1914), 597–639. Excellent.

———. "Naval Airships," *Transactions,* Society of Automotive Engineers, Vol. XIV, Part 1 (1919), 578–89.

———. "Uses of Airships With the Fleet," *U.S. Air Services,* Vol. I, No. 3 (April, 1919), 6–9.

———. "The Navy's First Airships," *U.S. Naval Institute Proceedings,* Vol. 45, No. VIII (August, 1919), 1347–68.

———. "Airship Engineering Progress in the United States," *Aviation,* Vol. VII, No. 2 (August 15, 1919), 72–76; and No. 3 (September 1, 1919), 123–28.

———. "Naval Architecture in Aeronautics," *Journal of the Royal Aeronautical Society,* Vol. 24 (July, 1920), 321–405.

———. "The Day of the Dirgible," *North American Review,* Vol. 229, No. 4 (April, 1930), 432–436.

———. "Transoceanic Airship Service," *Society of Automotive Engineers Journal,* Vol. 29, No. 3 (September 1931), 198–99, 222.

Lansdowne, Zachary. "The Story of the *R34* Flight," *Flying,* Vol. 8, No. 7 (August, 1919), 608–609. He was U.S. Navy observer on board for the east-to-west flight, and thus the first American to fly the Atlantic nonstop!

———. "Helium: An Important National Asset," *U.S. Air Services,* Vol. 7, No. 1 (February, 1922), 13–16.

———. "The Birth of an Industry," *Aero Digest,* Vol. 4, No. 5 (May, 1924), 200–201.

———. "With the *Shenandoah,*" *Saturday Evening Post,* Vol. 198, No. 17 (October, 1925), 7, 214, 217–18.

Litchfield, Paul W. "The Goodyear Tire and Rubber Company has Entered into an Agreement to Control the Zeppelin Rights for the United States," *Aero Digest,* Vol., III, No. 6 (December, 1923), 399–401.

———. "The Case for the Super-Dirigible," *World's Work,* Vol. LI, No. 1 (January, 1926), 248–62.

———. "Establishing an Airship Building Industry," *U.S. Air Services,* Vol. XVII, No. 4 (April, 1932), 24–26.

Mackey, Donald McA. "The Control of Airship Planes," *American Aviation Historical Society Journal,* Vol. VIII, No. 1 (Spring, 1963), 13–22.

Moffett, William A. "All honor to the Germans! They Lead the World in Lighter-Than-Air; Is America Boasting Instead of Doing?" *Aeronautic Review,* Vol. VII, No. 11 (November, 1920), 13, 45.

———. "The Aeronautical Engine; Some Differences Between the Airship and the Airplane Power Plant." *U.S. Air Services,* Vol. VIII, No. 3 (March, 1923), 13–15.

———. "Rigid Airship Building and Operations in this Country Originated with the U.S. Navy," *Aero Digest,* Vol., III, No. 6 (December, 1923), 402–404.

———. "The U.S. Airship *Shenandoah,*" *Aero Digest,* Vol. IV, No. 1 (January, 1924), 25–26.

————. "The Stub Mast for Airships," *Slipstream,* Vol. IX, No. 6 (June, 1928), 14–15.

————. "Five Progressive Years of Naval Aviation," *Aero Digest,* Vol. XVIII, No. 3 (March, 1931), 34–37.

————. "Rigid Airship Development and the USS *Akron,*" *National Aeronautical Magazine,* Vol. X, No. 1 (January, 1932), 6–12.

Moore, Richard B. "Helium: Its History, Properties, and Commerical Development," *Journal of the Franklin Institute,* Vol. CXCI, No. 2 (February, 1921), 145–97.

Norfleet, Joseph P. "One Rigid Airship has the Military Value of Two Battlecruisers," *U.S. Air Services,* Vol. IV, No. 1 (August, 1920), 15–17. He was on Admiral Sims's staff during the war, a noted balloonist in the early 1920's, but had left LTA by the end of the decade.

Peck, Scott E. "Navigation of Rigid Airships," *U.S. Naval Institute Proceedings,* Vol. LIX, No. 8 (August, 1933), 1150–53.

Reichelderfer, F. W. "Some Aerological Principles Applying to Airship Design and Operation," *Transactions,* American Society of Mechanical Engineers, Vol. LI (1929), AER-51–29, 171–75.

Rogers, G. Sherburne. "Helium, The New Balloon Gas," *National Geographic,* Vol. XXXV, No. 5 (May, 1919), 441–56.

Rosendahl, Charles E. "Reflections on the Airship Situation," *U.S. Naval Institute Proceedings,* Vol. LIII, No. 7 (July, 1927) 745–48.

————. "Airship Personnel," *U.S. Naval Institute Proceedings,* Vol. LV, No. 4 (April, 1929), 305–310.

————. USS *Los Angeles,*" *U.S. Naval Institute Proceedings,* Vol. LVII, No. 6 (June, 1931), 751–56.

————. "The Mooring and Ground Handling of a Rigid Airship," *Transactions,* American Society of Mechanical Engineers, Vol. LV (1933), AER-55–6, 45–52.

————. "What Really Happened to the *Akron,*" *Liberty Magazine,* Vol. X, No. L (December 16, 1933), 4–8; reprinted as "The Loss of the *Akron,*" *U.S. Naval Institute Proceedings,* Vol. LX, No. 7 (July, 1934), 921–33.

————. "Airship Costs and Casualties," *U.S. Air Services,* Vol. XXI, No. 1 (January, 1936), 21–26.

Scott, G. Herbert. "Development of Airship Mooring," *Journal of the Royal Aeronautical Society,* Vol. XXX (August, 1926), 459–81. Scott was the mooring mast's original inventor.

Settle, T. G. W. "Winning a Balloon Race," *U.S. Naval Institute Proceedings,* Vol. LV, No. 8 (August, 1929), 677–84.

————. "Some Recent Aspects of Rigid Airships," *Mechanical Engineering,* Vol. LIII, No. 8 (August, 1931) 567–74.

————. "The Gordon Bennett Race, 1932," *U.S. Naval Institute Proceedings,*" Vol. LIX, No. 4 (April, 1933), 521–25. Here Settle and Bushnell set a world's record which remains unbroken.

————. "Merchant Airships—a Few Predictions and One Strong Hope," *U.S. Air Services,* Vol. XXI, No. 5 (May, 1936), 15–17.

————. "Why No Blimps?" *U.S. Naval Institute Proceed-*ings, Vol. LXV, No. 2 (February, 1939), 238–40.

Sims, William L. "The Value of Rigid Dirigibles for Naval Operations," *Air Power,* Vol. IV, No. 12 (April, 1919), 451–52.

Squier, George O. "The Present Status of Military Aeronautics," *Transactions,* American Society of Mechanical Engineers, Vol. XXX (1908), Paper No. 1210, 639–721.

————. "Aeronautics in the United States," *Society of Automotive Engineers Journal,* Vol. V, No. 6 (December, 1919), 402–14.

"Technical Aspects of the Loss of the USS *Shenandoah,*" *Journal of the American Society of Naval Engineers,* Vol. XXXVIII, No. 3 (August, 1926), 487–694.

Upson, Ralph H. "Metalclad Rigid Airship Development," *Society of Automotive Engineers Journal,* Vol. XVIII, No. 2 (February, 1926), 94–96, 117–31; and Vol. XIX, No. 4 (October, 1926), 391–98.

————. "Past Adventures and Future Prospects of Metalclad Airships," *Society of Automotive Engineers Journal,* Vol. XXVI, No. 5 (May, 1930), 567–75.

Wicks, Zeno W. "Helium and its Relation to Airships," *Aero Digest,* Vol. III, No. 6 (December, 1923), 404–405.

————. "Six Years with the Navy in Helium Production," *Journal of the American Society of Naval Engineers,* Vol. XXXVII, No. 4 (November, 1925), 698–718.

Wiley, Herbert V. "A Celestial Cruise," *U.S. Naval Institute Proceedings,* Vol. LI, No. 4 (April, 1925), 604–609. Aboard the *Los Angeles.*

————. "PVT Prime Takes a Hop," *U.S. Naval Institute Proceedings,* Vol. LV, No. 1 (January, 1929), 33–37. Lucid discussion of an airship's static problems in changing atmospheric conditions.

————. "The Value of Naval Airships," *U.S. Naval Institue Proceedings,* Vol. LX, No. 5 (May, 1934), 665–71. Probably the best discussion of the subject in the public record.

Technical Publications

Freeman, Hugh B. "Measurements of Flow in the Boundary Layer of a 1/40-Scale Model of the U.S. Airship *Akron,*" Report No. 430. *18th Annual Report, National Advisory Committee for Aeronautics* (1932), 567–79.

————. "Pressure-Distribution Measurements on the Hull and Fins of a 1/40-Scale Model of the U.S. Airship *Akron,*" Report No. 443. *19th Annual Report, National Advisory Committee for Aeronautics* (1933), 67–79.

————. "Force Measurements on a 1/40-Scale Model of the U.S. Airship *Akron,*" Report No. 432. *18th Annual Report, National Advisory Committee for Aeronautics* (1932), 567–79.

McHugh, James G. "Pressure-Distribution Measurements at Large Angles of Pitch on Fins of Different Span-Chord on a 1/40-Scale Model of the U.S. Airship *Akron,*" Report No. 604. *23rd Annual Report, National Advisory Committee for Aeronautics* (1937), 585–604.

Special Committee on Airships [Durand Committee]. Report No. 1. *General Review of Conditions Affecting Airship Design and Construction with Recommendations as to Future Policy.* Stanford University Press, 1936. 12 pp.

———. Report No. 2. *Review and Analysis of Airship Design and Construction Past and Present.* Stanford University Press, 1937. 127 pp.

———. Report No. 3. *Technical Aspects of the Loss of the Macon.* Stanford University Press, 1937. 32 pp.

———. Report No. 4. *The Metalclad Type of Airship Construction with Recommendations.* Stanford University Press, 1937. 4 pp.

———. Report No. 5. *The Respess Type of Airship Construction with Recommendations.* Stanford University Press, 1937. 4 pp.

Silverstein, Abe, and B. G. Gulick. "Ground Handling Forces on a 1/40-Scale Model of the U.S. Airship *Akron.*" Report No. 566. *22nd Annual Report, National Advisory Committee for Aeronautics* (1936), 405–18.

U.S., Department of the Navy. *Rigid Airship Manual, 1927.* Washington: Government Printing Office, 1928. No continuous pagination; roughly 300 pp.

U.S. Naval Air Station, Anacostia. Report No. 91. "Report on XF9C-1 Curtiss Single Seater Fighter" (1 July 1931), 69 pp.

———. Report No. 122. "Report on F9C-2 Curtiss Airship and Carrier Fighter" (28 July 1932), 66 pp.

SECONDARY SOURCES

Books

The Aircraft Yearbook. New York: Aeronautical Chamber of Commerce of America; annually since 1920. Very informative up to 1932, when its editing was subverted by public relations experts and information was sacrificed to extravagant rhetoric.

Higham, Robin. *The British Rigid Airship, 1908–1931, A Study In Weapons Policy.* London: G. T. Foulis & Company, 1961. 426 pp. Excellent; an exhaustive account.

Kirschener, Edwin J. *The Zeppelin in the Atomic Age.* Urbana: University of Illinois Press, 1957. 80 pp. Speculative; has useful bibliography.

Larkins, William T. *U.S. Navy Aircraft 1921–1941.* Concord, California: Aviation History Publications, 1961. 391 pp. Profusely illustrated. An outstanding source of data, although it fails to recognize airships as "aircraft."

Robinson, Douglas H. *The Zeppelin in Combat, A History of the German Naval Airship Division, 1912–1918.* London: G. T. Foulis & Company, 1962. 417 pp. Excellent; a definitive work.

———. *The LZ-129, Hindenburg.* Dallas, Texas: Morgan Aviation Books, 1964. 54 pp. Definitive description of the aircraft, extensively illustrated.

Turnbull, Archibald, and Clifford L. Lord. *A History of United States Naval Aviation.* New Haven: Yale University Press, 1949. 345 pp. A pioneer work with many flaws; tends to be unconcerned with Navy lighter-than-air efforts, but is useful for policy.

Van Wyen, Adrian O., and Lee M. Pearson, editors. *United States Naval Aviation, 1910–1960:* Washington: U.S. Government Printing Office, 1961. 239 pp. A detailed chronology and excellent reference to the subject.

Periodicals

Miller, Harold B. "Navy Skyhooks," *U.S. Naval Institute Proceedings,* Vol. LXI, No. 2 (February, 1935), 234–40. Historical survey of hook-on flying to that date.

Mitchell, John C. "A Chronological History of the F9C-2 and its Use on the *Akron* and *Macon,*" *American Aviation Historical Society Journal,* Vol. III, No. 2 (April–June, 1958), 100–109.

Nye, Willis L. "The Genealogy of the Curtiss Sparrowhawk Dirigible Fighters," *American Aviation Historical Society Journal,* Vol. III, No. 2 (April–June, 1958), 70–99.

Robinson, Douglas H. "The Airplane-Carrying Airship; The First Experiment," *American Aviation Historical Society Journal,* Vol. IV, No. 4 (Winter, 1959), 265–68.

———. "The Zeppelin Bomber, High Policy Guided By Wishful Thinking," *The Airpower Historian,* Vol. VII, No. 3 (July, 1961), 130–47.

Smith, Richard K. "A Bibliography of Articles Pertaining to Lighter-Than-Air Aeronautics in the *U.S. Naval Institute Proceedings,* 1912 to 1960," *American Aviation Historical Society Journal,* Vol. VI, No. 1 (Spring, 1961), 59–61. An annotated bibliography of 57 items.

Topping, A. D. "The Etymology of 'Blimp,'" *American Aviation Historical Society Journal,* Vol. VIII, No. 4 (Winter, 1963), 253–55.

Index

mony, 90, 99; on design boards, 210 (n.23), (n.25); stratosphere ascent, 213 (n.8)

Sewall, Arthur, 40

Shenandoah, USS, 3, 7, 9, 13, 15, 37, 45, 56, 127, 162, 177, 218 (n.9)

Shoemaker, Capt. Harry E., 44, 211 (n.10)

Simpler, Lt.(j.g.) Leroy C.: 125, 128, 135; with damaged skyhook, 139, 140, 141; on *Macon*'s last flight, 151

Sims, Adm. William S., xxi, 171

60–60 degree navigation system, 110–112, 128, 131; *see also* Flight Control Officer and Radio Communications

Sperry, Lawrence B., 19, 210 (n.3)

Spy basket: with *Akron,* 55; with *Macon,* 131, 133–35, 137

Standley, Capt. William H.: 13; Admiral and CNO, 58–59; 103, 123; opposes change of mission for *Macon,* 145; opposes replacement of *Los Angeles,* 147; comments on *Macon*'s loss, 157; criticizes *Houston* contact, 214 (n.7)

Stark, Adm. Harold R., CNO, 169

State, William C., 33

Steele, Joseph E., AOM3c, 153, 157

Stern beam: 47, 53, 66; *see also* Calvin M. Bolster

Stevens, Lt.Cdr. Leslie C., 23

Superheat, explanation of, 213 (n.11)

Swanson, Claude A., Secretary of Navy, 157, 163, 167

Swidersky, Tony F., Coxswain, 84

Temperature Inversion, explanation of, 211 (n.6)

Tennessee, USS, 127, 157

Texas, USS, 3, 113

Thurman, Emmett C., CWO, 121

Tizard, Sir Henry T., 110

Towers, R.Adm. John H., Chief Bu-Aer, 169, 170, 217 (n.24)

Trapeze, Sperry: 19; U.S. Army, 19–21; Los Angeles, 21–23, 29–30, 47; *Akron-Macon,* 47, 66–67

Trapnell, Lt. Frederick M.: with *Akron,* 65–66, 73, 77, 78; congressional testimony, 90; with *Macon,* 99, 101, 103, 105, 106, 109, 121, 123, 125; to cruiser *San Francisco,* 214 (n.19)

Truscott, Starr, 5

Upson, Ralph, 15, 175, 178

Vinson, Rep. Carl, 92, 95, 97, 101, 162, 213 (n.3)

Vought planes: UO-1, 21, 23, 25, 119; 02U-1, 25; 02U-2, 25, 58; UF-1, 5

Waco XJW-1, 113–15, 199–201

Walsh, Senator David I., 91

War Plan ORANGE, xxi, 103

Warner, Edward P., Asst. Secretary of Navy, 90

Water recovery apparatus, 43, 65, 135, 193

Watson, Lt. George F., 21

Weems, P. V. H., 7

Wescoat, Lt. Herbert M., 77, 78, 82

West Coast Airship Base, *see* Moffett Field

Weyerbacher, Cdr. Ralph D., 35, 41, 90

Whittle, Lt. George V., 33, 99, 211 (n.8)

Wilbur, Curtiss D., Secretary of Navy, 9, 13

Wilder, Lawrence, 17

Wiley, Adm. Henry A., 13

Wiley, Lt.Cdr. Herbert V.: as C.O. *Los Angeles,* 21; as X.O. *Akron,* 40–41, 53, 69, 77–80; at *Akron* Court of Inquiry, 84–85, 87; congressional testimony, 90–91; early career, 127; as C.O. *Macon,* 128; *Houston* contact, 129–31, 133, 137, 139–40, 141, 145, 147; on *Macon*'s last flight, 149–54; at court of inquiry, 162; states case for airship, 177–78

Willard, Adm. Arthur Lee, 49, 51, 59, 61

Young, Lt. Howard L.: with *Los Angeles,* 29–30; with *Akron,* 56–57, 61, 65, 73; with *Macon,* 103, 105, 122, 125; to cruiser *Milwaukee,* 214 (n.19)

Young, William C., 15, 17

Zacharias, Ellis M., 7

Zimkus, Joseph J., BM2c, 84

Zimmerman, Lt. Walter E., 117

ZMC-2, 15, 77, 163, 217 (n.6), 217 (n.13); *see also* Metalclad airship; Ralph Upson

ZR-1, *see Shenandoah*

ZR-2, 3

ZR-3, *see Los Angeles*

ZRCV, 163, 165, 170, 175, 177, 217 (n.28), 217 (n.5), 204

ZRN, 167, 169, 175, 177, 217 (n.13), (n.16), (n.24)

ZRS4&5 Design: explanation of term, 209 (n.1), (n.12); Design No. 60, 5, 7, 209 (n.7); Project I, 17, 18, 161, 189; Project II, 17, 191; Project III, 17, 161, 191; Change Order No. 2, 35, 161, 197; general discussion, 187–97

Richard K. Smith holds a bachelor of science and master's degree from the University of Illinois at Urbana and a Ph.D. in history from the University of Chicago. He has taught at the University of Illinois Urbana and Chicago Circle campuses and the University of Maryland, served as historian at the National Air & Space Museum of the Smithsonian Institute, was on the staff of the Milton S. Eisenhower Library of The Johns Hopkins University, and has worked as a naval and aviation analyst for various consulting firms.

Since 1967 he has been the American literary editor for the British monthlies *Flying Review International* and *Air International*. He has collected, ordered, and catalogued the papers of Dr. Hugh L. Dryden (1898–1965), the last director of the National Advisory Committee for Aeronautics and the first deputy administrator of the National Aeronautics & Space Administration. His book, *First Across! The U.S. Navy's Transatlantic Flight of 1919,* published by Naval Institute Press in 1973, won the history prize of the American Institute of Aeronautics and Astronautics.

A native of Joliet, Illinois, Dr. Smith first went to sea at the age of sixteen, shipping out on coastal tankers. Later, as a civilian marine engineer and a Naval Reserve officer, he spent several years at sea. He is married to the Reichsgräfin Maria Theresa v. Tursky. They live variously in Washington, D.C., Wilmington, N.C., and Vienna, Austria.

Dr. Smith's interest in lighter-than-air aeronautics came about when he chanced to buy a book on airships, expecting to learn why the *Akron* and the *Macon* failed to gain acceptance. The book he bought, however, told him little, and was typical of existing airship literature, which focused on the ephemeral and sensational. Unable to find a definitive book on the subject, he set out to write one himself.